Women of Jordan

Gender, Culture, and Politics in the Middle East
Leila Ahmed, miriam cooke, Simona Sharoni, *and* Suad Joseph, *Series Editors*

Other titles in Gender, Culture, and Politics in the Middle East

Women of Jordan

ISLAM, LABOR, & THE LAW

Amira El-Azhary Sonbol

Syracuse University Press

First Edition 2003
03 04 05 06 07 08   6 5 4 3 2 1

The paper used in this publication meets the minimum
requirements of American National Standard for
Information Sciences—Permanence of Paper for Printed
Library Materials, ANSI Z39.48–1984.∞™

Library of Congress Cataloging-in-Publication Data
Sonbol, Amira El Azhary.
Women of Jordan : Islam, labor, and the law / Amira El-Azhary
Sonbol.— 1st ed.
p. cm.—(Gender, culture, and politics in the Middle East)
Includes bibliographical references and index.
ISBN 0–8156–2964–8 (cloth : alk. paper)—ISBN 0–8156–2985–0 (pbk. :
alk. paper)
1. Women—Jordan—Social conditions. 2. Women—Jordan—Economic
conditions. 3. Women—Legal status, laws, etc.—Jordan. I. Title. II.
Series.
HQ1729 .S66 2002
305.42'095695—dc21
2002012942

Manufactured in the United States of America

To Abla—sweet daughter and dear friend

Amira El-Azhary Sonbol is associate professor of Islamic history, society, and law at the Center for Muslim-Christian Understanding at Georgetown University. She is the author of *Women, the Family, and Divorce Laws in Islamic History* (1998) and *The New Mamluks: Egyptian Society and Modern Feudalism* (2000), both published by Syracuse University Press, and the editor and translator of *The Last Khedive of Egypt: Memoirs of Abbas Hilmi II* (1998).

Contents

Acknowledgments

This book would not have been possible without the assistance of a large number of persons in Jordan who extended their support, ideas, and advice. I begin by thanking Reem Abu-Hassan, colleague and now dear friend, who opened her home and gave me her time and very wise advice. Without Ramadan al-Khouli, my research in Jordan's archives would not have been as thorough and as helpful for reconstructing the history of women that is an essential part of this book. Hind Abdel-Jaber opened the doors of the Business and Professional Women's Club of Amman, an excellent institution under her leadership. Her discussion of the life of women in Jordan and their future business and work potential were enlightening. Sobhiyya al-Ma'ni guided me through the intricacies of the life of a business woman with sharp abilities and a competitive edge, a true example to those aspiring to enter the business world and succeed.

I met many lawyers and women activists in Jordan; each in her own way led me to understand certain aspects of women's lives and the legal entanglements with which they have to deal on a daily basis. Two lawyers in particular were a key to the various issues facing Jordanian women; without them it would have been very hard to become involved in the complexities of the legal and living issues that are integral to Jordanian families. Manal Shamut and Hanan al-Qinna volunteer their time and services to help Jordanian women who have little knowledge and access to legal recourse by providing them with legal consultation, representing them in court, and handling the various intricate details of their business problems and family disputes. With them I visited schools where they gave lectures advising students and their mothers about their legal rights, perhaps the only means available to them to discuss the various legal complications they face, or could face. I watched and learned, and I could see the impact of the excellent work of these two young lawyers and their deep commitment to improving the lives of their sisters. I met many other lawyers who gave their help unstintingly, realizing the important need to change the lives of women and to push for greater legal equality. Jordan is a country rich with women activists, from princesses to local community leaders. I want to thank in particular Rihab al-Qaddumi, whose impact seems to be evident in the many activities and laws that have been promulgated or attempted by women's groups. Here I will also include Nur al-Imam, who gave me her time and patiently went through lists of names of people whom I should meet, important laws, and the history of women activism in Jordan. Sahar Naseer illustrated the important role that international organizations can play in promoting change in women's lives.

Male lawyers were just as important for this project, some having been as active in promoting the rights of women as many of their women colleagues. Here I point out in particular Ahmad 'Ubaidat, once head of Jordan's government, a man of great knowledge, deserving of the deepest respect for his efforts in working toward greater rights for women through the Royal Committee on Human Rights established by King Abdullah for the express purpose of changing Jordan's gender laws. Ratib al-Zahir, a lawyer and previously a judge in Jordan's *shari'a* courts, was invaluable for this study. His responses to the questions I asked him about Islamic law and the handling of various issues by the *shari'a* courts provided important areas of discussion and raised possibilities about opening such questions to greater scrutiny by Jordan's learned authorities and by the general public. I am deeply grateful to him. Hamza Haddad spoke of his efforts as minister of justice to change the laws regarding honor crimes and the reasons these efforts failed. It was important to discuss possibilities with him to try and formulate an agenda for the future. Muhammad Abu Hassan graciously discussed the view from the bench, the logic of Jordan's legal system, and even the inconsistency of its laws. His inherent sense of justice and his view of the Jordanian family are admirable, as is his uncanny knowledge of history and the long-term relations between Islam and the West, about which he has written illustrating the intellectual and legal debt that Western culture and law owe to Islam. I would like to extend my appreciation to these male leaders and to others, such as Nabil al-Kilani, Sa'ed Karajah, 'Asir Mada'in, and Salah al-Bashir and his legal staff, namely Firas al-Mu'nis, Mahir Hamdan, Rana Junbalat, Rawan 'Antabawi, and Nisrin al-Bashir. Thank you for the long, controversial discussions on Islamic law and gender. We may not have agreed, but you helped focus and direct my ideas.

Microfinance is gaining ground in Jordan, as it is in other places around the globe. The success of such projects depends to a large degree on those who run them—to their honest dedication and their unequaled patience. 'Arub al-Khayyat not only explained what microfinance in Jordan is all about, but took me out to meet with women participating in these projects. Through her I met the various owners of businesses discussed in this book, Umm Muhammad, Umm Khalid, Umm 'Umar, and many others. I am grateful for the time they took and the trust they extended in opening their minds and experiences to me. Thank you 'Arub al-Khayyat for showing me how similar women's problems are, whether in the world of Islam, the Arab world, or the world of women wherever they are. Professional women involved in microfinance working from the Business and Professional Women's Club were a fountain of information. We had very stimulating and, I should add, pleasant discussions about various subjects that we all felt strongly about: children and marriage, jobs and harassment, dreams and the difficulties of fulfilling them. Here my special thanks and good wishes for success in their business pursuits go to Randa Qibti, Maha al-Misri, Mona Mundhir Malhas, and Mona Haddad. Mentioning professionals, I would like to include Dr. Sireen Musmar, director of Jam'iyyat al-Umma wa Tufulaba of the Ministry of Health, for showing me the dedication of Arab woman doctors. Through her I got a glimpse of the important dedication of women working in the service of their people as well as the essential need to pay greater attention to the health, physical, and emotional well-being of our children. An'am al-'Asha is a unique woman, a lawyer and television personality. Our meeting lasted much longer than anticipated and we could have gone on talking about women's issues, women's experiences, and the depiction of women in the media for hours longer.

Jordan has many women's organizations. I was lucky to be well received and helped by a number of the very important ones. My thanks to the Business and Professional Women's Club for extending their assistance, contacting and arranging meetings, allowing me to use their library and join with their lawyers in the lectures they gave regularly to the Jordanian public, and most particularly for allowing me to look at their exemplary hotline, to which women in need of legal assistance have open and fast access. I also thank the Federation of Jordanian Women, and particularly Hilda Ayoub, for meeting with me and discussing their activities. My appreciation goes to Bothaina Garana, who headed al-Amal Foundation; Amal Sabbagh of the Jordanian National Committee for Women; Hind al-Nasser of the Jordan River Foundation; Judy Salem of Al-Kutba; and Lamis Nasser at UNIFEM.

I am grateful to the University of Jordan. Mustafa Hamarnah, friend and colleague from Georgetown University, was generous as usual, giving me space and helping me maneuver my way at the University of Jordan. Ahmad Furaysat, head of the archival section at the University of Jordan library, assisted me and Ramadan al-Khouli by facilitating the research for this book. My thanks also go to Intissar al-Qihwi and Towfic Shomar for explaining the various problems with children's education in Jordan.

A special thank-you goes to Sally Khalaf of the Royal Press and the staff of that office, particularly Musa.

Women of Jordan

1

Introduction
Women in Jordan Today

THE village of Samma, made up of fifty-five houses and a population of three hundred people, located near Irbid, is typical of the other nine hundred-plus villages in Jordan. Samma's first school was opened in 1952 by the United Nations Relief Organization to accommodate Palestinian refugees who moved to Samma. Since then, education has continued to grow in importance to Samma's residents with the state's national educational project. In 1997 Samma had six schools, three for girls and three for boys, covering the various levels of education from primary to high school.[1] A study of the town written by one of its residents, Sheikh Samih al-'Azm, lists the names of all school graduates who went on to a university education and the various professions they entered, which included engineering, teaching, law, journalism, accounting, and public service. Names of those who remained in Samma to become merchants, craftsmen, and local administrators are also included, as are the names of graduates who left Jordan and migrated to different countries of the world, including the United States, Europe, Australia, and Arab countries. The problem with this picture of success for a village like Samma is the fact that not a single woman was listed among the school graduates who went on to receive university degrees or pursued careers either inside or outside of the village, despite the fact that Samma had a girls school at every level of education: primary, secondary, and high school.

Perhaps the results of Sheikh al-'Azm's study would not have been so surprising if not for the universally accepted belief that extending educational opportunities is the most important step toward achieving greater gender equality and a greater economic role for women. As societies move from the more traditional to the more modern, women are expected to gain greater freedoms as their expectations change. This change, however, does not seem to have been the case in Samma. What makes it even more serious is that boys who graduated from

1

Samma's schools went on to receive university and higher degrees in numbers and specializations that show Samma to be an upwardly mobile community. Over the years, Samma seemed to modernize its infrastructure, implemented modern health for its people, and enjoyed greater wealth through its graduates.[2] Yet, women do not seem to have participated or contributed to this picture of growth and development. The reasons for the noninclusion of women among Samma's professional and working graduates may be due to the fact that girls dropped out of school early to help in housework or to get married. It could also be that they married and moved away and were therefore no longer considered Samma residents. But the author does include the names of men who moved outside the town, and he also presents a long list of "firsts," that is, men who were the first from the village to advance in particular professions. There are also the names of all who took up government positions in the town, who were elected for various administrative positions, and so on, and none were women. The only employed women mentioned in the book are two female nurses who were part of an otherwise all-male staff at the local health center. There is no mention of a woman doctor, even though the center had a program for "motherhood" and pre- and postnatal care that seemed to be a great pride to the community.[3] This picture, however, could not be totally accurate: the three girls schools must have been staffed by women, and women must have helped in running family businesses, in agriculture, and other activities. Still, the basic impression of educated men going to work and girl graduates not pursuing further education or taking jobs seems to be accurate.

Given the efforts spent on education in Jordan and the significant results in female literacy that place Jordan at the top of all Arab states, it is rather disappointing to see the difference in expectations and results based on gender among school graduates. A 1980 study of Arab women and education summarized three conditions for Arab women to have greater access to higher education without which effective participation in economic development and achievements of greater rights were considered by the study to be practically impossible. In the first place, primary and secondary education had to have made sufficient progress. Second, attitudes toward the role of Arab women in society had to have changed. The third condition was the materialization of the need for educated women in the professions and other occupations.[4]

Even though the study concluded that these conditions were actually met "at different periods in the various countries of the Arab world," the three conditions continue to be valid today. Whereas Jordan has taken great strides in regards to the first condition, much more still needs to be accomplished. Jordan's primary and secondary schools for women are without doubt better equipped and staffed than most other Arab countries, and the literacy rate among Jordanian women is the highest in the Arab world. Still, the number of women school graduates who pursue higher degrees and careers continues to fall short of expectations, particularly given Jordan's efforts in that direction. This book tries to find answers to this dilemma. Having started quite early and at an impressive rate in building an educational infrastructure for women, Jordan should have also witnessed at minimum an equivalent growth in women's participation in the economy. That development has not happened, however. One important reason is that even though Jordan, like other Arab and Islamic countries, has planned equal educational facilities and opportunities for boys and girls, the school curricula and expectations upon graduation continue to be gendered. The same goes for the third condition: the market for women's labor may have become larger, but large sectors of the economy remain closed to women, and other sectors that are normal areas of employment for women, such as tourism, remain poorly developed. It is in the second condition, regarding attitudes toward the role of women in society, that Jordan continues to face its greatest challenge. Without a change in social attitudes and reciprocal changes in Jordan's gendered laws that these attitudes extend and continue to strengthen, the results from women's education or other forms of investments in women's development will have but little impact on generating greater gender equality, human rights, or participation of women in economic, political, and intellectual life. The life experiences of three women who represent different levels of Jordan's business classes will help illustrate the contradictions under which women live in Jordan and the necessity of tackling legal and social issues if change is to be achieved.

Sitt Sobhiyya al-Ma'ni is one of Jordan's most recognizable businesspersons. She is chief executive and part owner of various industries and enterprises. Having started her life as a teacher, she entered the world of business with her husband very early in their marriage and continued to work with him to build what has become one of the most respected businesses in Jordan. With two sons, several houses, businesses, and factories behind them, Sitt Sobhiyya continued to work beside her husband; as he traveled to create greater business opportunities and clinch deals, she was the actual force behind the success of their enterprises at home. Yet, the day came when she stood to lose all she had worked for, the day when her husband suddenly died and to the pain of losing her lifetime companion and spouse was added the worry about the power that Islamic laws of inheritance would have over her life. According to these laws, she could inherit only one-eighth of her husband's estate because they had children (in a childless marriage, she would have gotten one-quarter). Because the husband was survived by his parents, they stood to inherit one-third of all he owned, which was in turn inheritable by their other sons and daughters once the parents died. Like most Arab women, the businesses, homes, and all assets were in the husband's name.

Ending up with one-eighth of what would be considered "communal property" in other parts of the world is the fate of all wives who do not do something about the situation while their husbands are alive. Luckily, Sitt Sobhiyya had become increasingly worried about the future some years earlier as her husband traveled all over the world, and so she had asked him to write a half share in her name instead of a 20 percent share in some of the businesses. He was reluctant and agreed only after she threatened to walk out and leave him to run the businesses alone. Even then, he did not write anything outright in her name; rather, he chose a house and one business and sold them in the form of a mortgage to her. Had he not done so, she would have come out with very little. As it was, she had to deal with his parents' share by buying them out to be able to go on administering the companies she had cobuilt but from most of which she inherited a mere one-eighth share.

The second story takes us to a Palestinian refugee camp. Like her neighbors, Umm 'Umar lives in a modest brick and mortar home made up of several rooms to accommodate her large family. When we met, she had recently suffered a stroke that left a slight effect on her left hand and side of her face. Yet, her primary concern in the meeting was to discuss the loan she was receiving from a microfinance nongovernmental organization (NGO) whose capable representative, 'Arub al-Khayyat, was my very appreciated guide. Negotiating a new loan, Umm 'Umar explained the problems with the old loan, her needs to expand her trade and grocery business, and the loan her daughter needed to expand the grocery that Umm 'Umar had opened for her. As the main breadwinner of her family, Umm 'Umar seems to be a law unto herself. She travels to buy her goods and to negotiate sales agreements, and finds no problems in moving and dealing outside her home, although she is not particularly enthusiastic at having to do so. Her husband of thirty years actually works in her grocery shop, which she considers a family enterprise, although it is registered in her name and the loans are in her name. The NGO will not give a loan to a woman unless the business is registered in her name. Married before reaching the age of fifteen, Umm 'Umar gave birth to eighteen children—boys and girls—who have all married and left home except for the youngest. It is in regards to this daughter, aged twenty, that the contradictions of women's lives become most obvious. Umm 'Umar is absolutely unwilling to let her out of the house. She did finish school and trained in baby care and handicrafts, but not for the purpose of taking a job—that idea was not one even contemplated by the family. Rather, the daughter has taken out her own loan, guaranteed by the mother, and is now doing piecework, embroidering costumes that are distributed in a cottage-industry scheme that allows her to earn about three dollars per week. When I asked Umm 'Umar why she does not allow her daughter to leave the house except accompanied by father or brother, she indicated that the father and brothers forbid her from doing so and that today's society is a failed society and does not protect the innocent to begin with. "The family could do without her income even if it meant her earning a hundred dinars a month," Umm 'Umar added. In other words, Umm 'Umar's sharp entrepreneurial mind is not confused when it comes to the old image of home industry where women worked and earned money for the family finances as long as this work was done within the home. Umm 'Umar is not aware that she is living a life of social contradictions as viewed by outsiders. Her priorities are clear, and protecting her family name and her children from the uncertainties of life today is on the top of her list, even while earning a living and improving the living standard of her family are as high priorities.

The third example is a mother of four, two girls and two boys. She is married to her cousin who has two other wives and is about to take the fourth. When I asked her why she agreed to marry someone already married to another, her answer was that "he's my cousin and I had greater right to him" (*ibn 'ami wana awla bih*). But she did admit that the marriage was a mistake. A hard worker with a sharp entrepreneurial mind, she buys used imported clothes by the bundle and sells them by the piece to her local customers. She nets about a hundred dinars per month that she uses to support her family almost alone, as her husband gives them barely two to three dinars a day for all expenses, including the children's pocket money. At present, she is focused on getting her husband married to a fourth wife so she can get rid of him since she seems to be his favorite, and although she does love him and has a fulfilling, intimate life with him, he beats her and the children for the least cause and the beatings are continuous and severe and she has little recourse to stop him.

The above cases may not present the great diversity of circumstances in Jordan, but they are representative of some of the more serious problems that women in Jordan face in regards to becoming involved in the country's economy and productive activity. Inheritance laws do not favor women, and at the same time property accumulated during the marriage is almost always registered under the husband's name. Umm Muhammad, who owns a grocery shop, wanted to borrow money to pay off a debt caused by her brother-in-law's mismanagement of the store when he was left to run it but could not do so because the grocery was in her husband's name. She was not willing to ask her husband to change title to her name because he had already lost his teaching job in Saudi Arabia after the 1990 Gulf War and has been jobless since. Now she is the primary breadwinner, except for a few hours a day when she rests and the husband stands in the shop; it is she who does the wholesale buying, the retail selling, and the accounting. It is interesting that the husband does not voluntarily move to include his wife's name as co-owner, especially given the fact that he has already faced the adverse effects of inheritance laws once before. As a schoolteacher in Saudi Arabia for more than twenty years he earned good money and was sending it home to his father to support the family and for the father to build him a house to which he could return with his wife and children once his work in Saudi Arabia was terminated. The father built the house but registered it under his own name for expediency. Unfortunately, the father died before Umm Muhammad's husband was able to switch the ownership of the house to his name, which meant that he had to share the house built using his life savings with his mother and siblings. Having learned the lesson, one would imagine that he would give primary consideration to his wife in case something happened to him, particularly since he is fifteen years her senior, but it has not happened. Family affiliation is based on tribalism and relationship by blood rather than on loyalty to the nuclear family. In other words, there are social constraints in regards to opening and owning businesses that may deny a woman her life labor and could leave her destitute in the case of a husband's death. There is awareness of what could happen, but reluctance to challenge traditions, particularly in regards to the power of a husband or father, and hence tribal patriarchy, underscores the whole system.

The same attitude is at the heart of the protection of women and girls. Most of the women of poorer classes who have started their own small businesses are either older married women with children who use their incomes to supplement their families' finances and save for a rainy day or they are the daughters of such families following in their mothers' footsteps from within the family structure.

Widows and single women constitute another important sector of women with small enterprises. However, participation in public enterprises, office jobs, or any position that would mean interaction with men is not acceptable, even to those mothers who would allow their daughters to work outside the home. Facing a husband's anger and possible domestic abuse is a reality in the Arab home, as it is all over the world, a fact that has been taken into consideration by the United Nations and its agencies. The recourse of a wife or children against spousal or child abuse is very limited where tribalism recognizes the father's absolute right over them. The power of a father over his daughter continues after marriage, and it is often the father who refuses to allow the married daughter to take a job, even when her husband agrees and encourages her. The constraints faced by women who want to extend their years of study, who have the ambition to go to college, who want to take jobs, and who want to open their own businesses are severely imposed by the legal system that reflects and enforces social traditions limiting the right of a girl's movement and placing her within the custody of her male relatives regardless of whether said male relatives are the actual financial supporters.

A central point made in this book is that legal change and building an educational infrastructure are vital for transforming the situation of Jordanian women today. Equally important is encouraging them to go on to higher education and to open their own businesses and become more active in public life. But as long as *'urf* (traditional law) discourse is gendered and Jordan's laws support contradictions between expectations and realities, real change will be very slow. Not that traditions have not been changing in Jordan—far from it: Jordan has experienced revolutionary and structural changes that have seen a near end of a way of life among Jordan's tribes, witnessed urban growth in the form of cities and towns active in trade, and moved increasingly toward modernity. But change itself has been gendered by holding on to traditional patriarchal relations and a state-controlled legal system that continues to reflect tribal patriarchy. As this book details, Jordanian laws, though they encourage women to go to work, have at the same time encouraged women—if indirectly—to take early retirement and to consider their work transitory. Simultaneously, personal status laws make women into adjuncts of fathers and husbands with limited legal representation under the control of male "guardians." As the lawyer-activist Rihab al-Qaddumi impressed on me, the main problem inhibiting women's participation in Jordan's economy and political life today is its tribal makeup (*haykal 'asha'iri*), which not only guides the country's laws but also molds the character of its people and the relations among them.

Gendered attitudes typical of an ethnic tribal state encompass women's lives almost completely, setting up the basis for women's expectations from their society and the rules guiding their marriage and family lives. They provide a security cocoon on the one hand and on the other a form of insecurity through cultural fears that keep women under patriarchal control, even when laws are intended to liberate them from such controls.

Areas in which the law has helped support and consolidate women's passivity and helplessness include in particular the handling of honor crimes. Notwithstanding how dishonorable men may act vis-à-vis their community, family, and nation, it is only women who suffer from "honor crimes," and Jordan's laws do little to prevent such crimes and in fact can be said to encourage them. Hence the contradictions in Jordan's legal system and surprising differences between Jordanian laws and the actual application of these laws by Jordan's courts and police. Jordan's laws do not to a large extent discriminate against women; the Jordanian Constitution declares the equality of all citizens, and labor laws basically enforce the general principles laid out by the Constitution. The above is the general understanding of most women lawyers I spoke to who stress the basic equality of the laws, particularly in regards to work and business. A close analysis of the laws and of legal procedures, however, shows deep discrepancies and contradictions between declarations and declared intentions, the fine lines putting the laws into effect, the philosophy of the legal system, and judicial interpretation of laws concerning women whether in the workplace or the home, and illustrates the continued adherence to tribal and traditional laws, even when the code itself is presented as modern and civil.

What is even more critical is the fact that gender relations codified through personal status laws are said to be, or justified as being, dictated by the Islamic *shari'a*. As Islamic *shari'a*, law gains "holy" authority and becomes unquestionable to those people who enforce it as well as to the people to whom it is applied. The power of such a discourse makes it extremely hard to even touch these laws, let alone change them. Yet, a close reading of Jordan's personal status laws and labor laws dealing with gender shows that the *shari'a* referred to in these laws is really a patchwork of *fiqh* (Islamic theological) interpretations from various Muslim schools of law, particularly the Hanafi and Maliki, molded together with a dose of imported pre-World War I Western gender philosophy to form a strict patriarchal attitude enforcing tribal gender laws and attitudes, even though tribal courts have been abolished in Jordan. The inability of a doctor to bring effective action against a father when there is evidence of child abuse, the necessity of the holder of a right to victim's compensation to bring complaint against a relative's killer before the state will prosecute, and the right of a victim's family to exonerate a person who hurt or killed its dependent in return for *diyya* (blood price) are examples of tribalism recognized by Jordanian laws. So, on the one hand, Jordan honors "rule of law"; on the other, "rule of law" means laws acceptable to civil society and reflective of its traditions, even while presenting modern codes universally applicable when it comes to business, commerce, and property rights.

This book focuses on women in Jordan: their history, communities, and participation in the country's economy; the role they play as wives, daughters, and mothers; and the contradictions they face in their everyday lives, given the realities and discourses that are intimately intertwined with their existence. Jordanian women today enjoy social and economic conditions well above women of many other Muslim and Arab countries. Although in most Arab countries the literacy rate among women falls far short of male literacy, the same is not true in Jordan where overall literacy was estimated at 86.6 percent in 1998, male literacy being 93.4 percent and female 79.4 percent, in a population of 4.5 million. Compare these figures to Egypt's 1995 literacy rates among its population of 60 million: overall, 52.4 percent could read and write, 63.6 percent of whom were males and 38.8 percent females. Or Syria in 1997: with nearly 17 million people, 70.8 percent of the total population was literate, of which males constituted 85.7 percent and females only 55.8 percent. The figures for Saudi Arabia, with a population of about 21 million, are close to Syria's: an overall literacy rate of 70.8 percent, with male literacy estimated at 85.7 percent and female literacy at 55.8 percent.[5] Furthermore, Jordanian laws today guarantee equal rights to women, and jobs are open to women in almost all spheres except for night work or jobs that are deemed dangerous, such as mining. Yet, although Islamic law guarantees the right of women to own property and administer their own businesses, when compared to other developing nations, Jordanian women constitute a very low percentage of Jordan's labor force today. Jordan's government may be implementing programs for economic growth and stimulating investments, but women's participation in the economy continues to be resistant to these efforts. At the same time, whereas the laws guarantee women rights and freedoms, including the right to a decent life protected by law, the rate of gender violence and honor crimes is on the increase, and perpetrators of such crimes seem to go without punishment.

Because one goal of this book is to investigate women's poor participation in the economy by raising questions and researching the reasons that the situation remains inflexible given the efforts being exerted, the book will be concerned specifically with legal questions and constraints facing women in Jordan today. The book will place this interest within its historical context with the purpose of showing the roots of the legal system and the construction of patriarchy that underlie the legal and social systems. To begin, the sources of Jordan's contemporary legal codes will be discussed, in particular *shari'a*, tribal, and modern laws. The life of women before the modernization of law will be presented at various points in the book so as to show the impact of new legal codes on women and to point out where we can find answers to problems facing women today from within Jordanian and Islamic traditions. A woman's life within her family and her community, what is expected of her, and the responsibilities of society toward her will take up an important part of this book. Finally, the accomplishments of Jordanian women in private and public life will be of particular interest because of the successes and failures of efforts to improve the lives of women.

The breakdown of the chapters is meant to focus on each aspect of women's lives and pertinent Jordanian laws. Chapter 2, "Background: *Qadis, 'Asha'ir,* and Modern Law," covers the legal background. It presents the most important aspects of modern legal changes. The modern period witnessed reform of law worldwide; the Napoleonic Code seemed to have set a model for legal reforms globally, including the Arab world, which came under the colonial rule of European powers. Jordan, like Palestine, Egypt, and Iraq, came under British rule. A large dose of British laws became integrated in the formulation of modern laws and legal procedures in these colonies. At the same time, like in Syria, Lebanon, and North Africa, French civil law applied throughout Europe became an important model for legal reforms. The result of the reforms was the construction of a multiple legal system of various courts of law and legal codes. The basic model divided courts into (1) national courts to supervise property, commercial, and criminal disputes; (2) family and personal status courts to deal with family disputes, marriage, divorce, inheritance, child custody, and religious endowments for different religious groups; and (3) emergency, military, or government executive courts to deal with issues of national security. Tribal courts were allowed to exist for some time in countries such as Jordan with important Bedouin populations, but they were eliminated over time, and their jurisdiction and laws were integrated into the wider legal system. Still, tribal councils are still held throughout the Arab world to deal with important legal issues.

Given the changes experienced by the legal system, the multiple origins of Jordanian laws will be examined in this chapter to deconstruct the origins of the legal constraints against women. Defining the origins of these laws is the first step toward proposing and enacting changes. As explained above, because reformers define personal status laws as being religious laws, it is almost impossible to budge them. In reality, multiple legal systems and philosophies have entered Jordan's contemporary legal codes. This chapter will discuss the genesis of personal status laws. Here the focus will be on *shari'a* as interpreted by personal status laws and in comparison to original sources of Islamic law such as the Holy Qur'an, hadith, and *fiqh*. Local *'urf* constitutes an important source of law, as do tribal laws that give a particular patriarchal twist to personal status laws. Modern European codes are another source of personal and family laws in Jordan. The latter is unrecognized as a source, even though important laws dealing with crimes of rape and honor are in fact based on French executive laws rather than the *shari'a*. The very concept of "family law" is itself based on European codes and a conceptualization of social relations that are not reflected in *shari'a* laws.

To be able to discuss the genesis of these laws, it becomes necessary to study the legal system before its modernization. Here the intent is not only to look into *fiqh* interpretations of the law before the modern period, but also to study the application of laws particularly as it pertains to women's work, owning and controlling personal property, investments by women in income-producing activity, and the legal maneuverability of women. Records of premodern *shari'a* courts, microfilm copies of which are housed at the University of Jordan Library in Amman, form the core of this research. There are recorded daily transactions of buying, selling, partnerships, commercial disputes, market disputes, quarrels of a personal nature, death and property or inheritance records, and so on. It is through these extensive records constituting seven centuries (the fourteenth through the twentieth) of history that the life of men and women can be studied. So far this life has been studied through religious treatises and exegetics that are more concerned with morality and therefore are only an indirect source for understanding social life, sources that are slanted through the eyes of critics who presented moral discourses they considered better suited to Islamic society.

By learning how people lived, what laws were applied, and how they were applied in court, we begin to see a changing *shari'a*, one that is subject to time and place. We also see a knowledgeable clerical class that is able to interpret the *shari'a* to fit these changes, a dynamic *shari'a* rather than the passive, backward one that seems to comfort those people who do not want to allow Muslim women to advance in the twenty-first century. Unlike *shari'a* court judges today who are given government-selected codes to apply, premodern court judges resorted to precedence of what can be called common law or *'urf* because it constituted *shari'a* in cumulative practice. To them, the *shari'a* was a process for reaching legal decisions rather than a collection of laws to be applied. It is important to show this fact so as to illustrate the role *shari'a* court judges play in Jordanian courts today. As keepers of an unchanging *shari'a*, they practice *jumud* (rigidity) and resist change that would question their function or their powers. Deconstructing the legal system is important to illustrate the connections among law, courts, gender, the state, and power.

Having established the nature of the legal process in Jordan and discussed the actual realities of women's lives before the modernization of law, this book will then focus on the issue of women and work. Chapter 3, "Women's History and Work," begins with the presumption that nothing in Islam forbids women from working or from owning property. Islamic principles laid down by the Qur'an will be important here. For example, the Qur'an admonishes that women have a right to a share of what they have earned as much as men do. Furthermore, the Islamic *shari'a* encourages women to be educated and to serve their communities. Rewards after death would be based on these accomplishments and how worthy a person's life has been. Toward this end, Islam guarantees a woman's right to own her own property, to invest it, and to earn a living from it. She inherits the same as men even though the interpretation of inheritance laws allows her half what men inherit at the same degree of relationship with the deceased. The early formative period of Islam, considered by Muslims as a model for Muslim communities, presents extensive evidence of the role Islam intended for women. Khadija, the prophet Muhammad's first wife, was a wealthy merchant in Mecca, whereas his youngest wife, 'Aisha, was renowned for her knowledge of prophetic traditions and was sought for her opinion on religious matters. Court records tell us that women were often chosen as *waqf* (religious endowment) executors by court judges and were resorted to as creditable and expert witnesses in court, notwithstanding the accepted *fiqh* paradigm that the witness of one woman was not acceptable and the testimony of two women had to be corroborated by a man.

Using court records from the Ottoman period, it will be made clear that women's work was not something questionable, but, to the contrary, was taken for granted. The disputes brought to court illustrate the multiplicity of roles played by women in crafts, lending, selling, and manufacturing. Women were also and continue to be vital in agricultural and animal farming. The peripheralization and control of women's work became established in the modern period with the creation of new industries and a job market different from what existed before. The new nation-state needed employees of a different kind who would be suited to a modern, centralized state and economy. New educational structures were built to form this new white-collar or blue-collar worker. Like elsewhere, and because men were the usual employees of governments in the Islamic world, men became the preferred employees. New jobs and businesses were identified as male jobs, and while traditional crafts began to die and were replaced by modern "male" professions, women were increasingly peripheralized from the job market. Midwives represent one good example. At one time they provided the only available gynecological and obstetrical services to women; the modern period saw them completely replaced by male physicians who made obstetrics and gynecology into "male" sciences. Today, women have to struggle to be admitted into these very lucrative professions; gender competition for jobs, especially when women account for 50 percent of the available market for these professions, has to be seen as an important part of the struggle for women's rights. The right of women to work and the control by a husband of his wife's right to work or by a guardian of his ward's right to manage her own property, both of which are sanctioned by law, cannot be taken out of the wider picture of gender struggle. While we are focused on class struggle, we have undermined gender struggle over jobs, wealth, market share, education, and position. Although we look at Islamic revivalism as necessarily veiling and obstructing the progress of women, by delineating jobs that only women could extend to other women by forbidding gender mixing, Muslim fundamentalist women are very much engaged in a struggle for jobs that have all but been taken over by men.

By discussing the connections among law, gender, and society from both a historical and a contemporary perspective, the causes of gender tensions will be made clear. Similar tensions existed in gender relations in other parts of the world, and it is only with greater economic and political changes that other societies were able to resolve these tensions. The same can be said to be happening in Jordan today; as the economy grows, jobs become more widely available and opportunities show a need for both male and female expertise and experience, which can lead to only greater openness and gender-conflict resolution. The social disparities dividing Jordanian society are what form the biggest obstacles in that direction.

In chapter 4, "Women and Work in Jordan Today," I discuss Jordan's laws that require a husband's permission before a woman can work. Jordan's laws also require that a woman's male guardian approve her marriage, and even though she can appeal to a judge to marry her in case the guardian refuses, the judge has to determine the suitability of the groom and usually defers to the guardian's wishes. In other words, Jordanian laws make it very hard for a woman to act independently of her male relations' approval. Even after reaching majority and legal competence, women are still bound by the authority of male guardians. The philosophy behind guardianship is that women are in need of protection, and therefore family and state must provide this protection. Jordan's laws therefore define work possibilities available to women on the basis of how safe the jobs are and the physical ability of women to perform a particular job. The result of this approach is that women are denied access to many jobs that they could perform and that could increase their income. They provide no competition for men in these areas. Yet, the laws allow businesses to employ women in these jobs and at hours designated as nonwork for women when particular business conditions require it. What the Jordanian Constitution proclaims as equal rights to jobs and opportunities and equal treatment of all Jordanians is contradicted by specific laws—particularly executive and ministerial actions—and by the whole concept of guardianship, which is applied at marital, family, and state levels.

Within her home and family, a woman is expected to be "queen" answerable only to her husband. That expectation is what society tells her, what religious leaders tell her, and what even the law makes clear. As a good Muslim or good Christian she expects to receive good treatment at the hands of father, brother, and husband. In fact, as she is told, as long as she is obedient, she should expect to be treated according to scriptural guarantees that demand that a husband be a good provider, a source of comfort, a protector, and a gentle lover. As chapter 5, "Laws of Guardianship and the Construction of Gender," details, a little girl is told that her future is defined by marriage, that she will be a wife and a mother and should expect to be protected and cherished. No wonder that when asked, schoolgirls see marriage as the primary and even the only future option for them. Working or not working is secondary, if even a viable or welcome option.

The life of most Jordanian women can be said to fit more or less within these parameters, and, like women elsewhere, realities of life never catch up with expectations. Yet, the divorce rate in Jordan is roughly 50 percent. The nonending stream of cases brought to Jordanian courts reflects a much different picture from what the laws say women have the right to expect or society indicates they are experiencing. Rather than living in her own home as the law and Islam require, she finds that it is her mother-in-law who is "queen" in her son's home. The bride finds herself the target of family abuse and victim of her weak husband's inability to protect her from interfemale disputes over territoriality. The law stands by his side in these disputes, and she often finds herself thrown out with little money, work experience, or family to take her in. This chapter traces the contradictions in women's lives at various levels of family, school, workplace, society, marital relations, and personal happiness and expectations.

As chapter 5 also illustrates, laws of guardianship applied in Jordan's courts today are based on *shari'a* law as interpreted and applied through tribal law. In other words, the interpretation and selection of the codes applied today reflect the historical process that saw the genesis of modern law in Jordan. Although the law is officially based on the Hanafi *madhhab* (school of law) as applied earlier through the 1917 Ottoman Family Code, in fact the philosophy and particular interpretation of the law have roots in Maliki and tribal laws that consider the guardianship of females to continue throughout her life because of clan ties and tribal honor. Guardianship also has roots in modern legal codes; for example, the age of majority determined at eighteen or twenty-one has no place in *shari'a* law but is directly imported from European laws. This chapter will discuss the origins of these laws of guardianship and detail them with the purpose of showing how they have a direct bearing on the lives of women in Jordan today.

In chapter 6, "Marriage, Obedience, and Work," the discussion will become more focused on issues of marriage and divorce. The Islamic marriage contract defines the relationship and mutual obligations of husband and wife. The contract as applied in Jordan allows husband and wife to include conditions that they consider of particular importance for the success of their marriage and their willingness to remain in it. As long as these conditions are within the bounds of what is acceptable to the *shari'a*, courts find them legitimate, and either party can sue for divorce if the other breaks the condition and is therefore in a situation of breach of contract. In regards to marriage contracts, Jordan's laws are more woman friendly than similar contracts in other Islamic countries that do not recognize the right of parties to a marriage to include any conditions in marriage contracts. Because including conditions is more beneficial to wives, who could include conditions allowing them to get out of unwanted marriages without losing financial rights, not allowing the inclusion of conditions closes the door to the wife's ability to control her marriage and life. Men and not women have an absolute right to abrogate a marriage at will. Interestingly, even though inclusion of conditions in marriage contracts is of vital importance to wives, this fact is little known among Jordanian women who take little advantage of it.

At the heart of marriage are a number of assumptions that are not written out in the contract but are socially accepted and legally recognized by the law and courts. Most important is the responsibility of a husband to support his wife financially. Schools of law and legists have differed on exactly what constitutes support; for example, does it include medical expenses? Notwithstanding differences, though, all agree that by getting married, a wife expects to be supported by a husband and the support should be according to the social level that she was used to while still in her father's home. As for a woman's own money that she received from inheritance, investment of her dowry, or any other means, this money is considered hers and not the household's or family's. In actual practice today, however, particularly given socioeconomic conditions, a wife's income becomes an important attraction in the marriage market, and she is expected to carry her own weight in supporting her family. Although Christians have a different form of marriage and marriage contract, the same expectations regarding the husband's responsibility for the financial support of his wife apply.

What does the wife owe in return for the husband's support? Here the law is interpreted differently, but it is generally accepted that the wife's obedience to her husband is expected in return for his financial support. When she is disobedient, then he has the right to withdraw his financial support or to divorce her without compensation or payment of the agreed upon financial rights defined by their marriage contract. What constitutes disobedience is problematic and, according to contemporary court records, very often contradicts Jordanian laws. One of the disputes brought often to court involves the wife's right to work against her husband's wishes. Courts have upheld a husband's right to forbid his wife from working, even though he had given prior agreement to her working according to legal requirements. Furthermore, husbands whose wives work question their responsibility for supporting the wife, and others claim the wife's income is family income to be spent by the husband as the financial supporter of the family. Women have left jobs because of these reasons. Others are discouraged from opening their own businesses because ultimately they have no control over their own income or ability to continue in the venture if the husband changes his mind.

This chapter will detail these problems and draw upon actual court cases and "hot line" records of the Business and Professional Women's Club (BPWC) of Amman, Jordan, to show the dilemmas faced today by young men and women whose needs no longer conform with what personal status laws require. Rather, greater numbers are moving to a joint-decision type of marriage in which both work, bring income home, and spend it together for mutual needs. Although this move is positive, the laws do not protect the woman once the marriage begins to fall apart. A woman who works is regarded as not fulfilling her full marital obligations defined within the parameters of the conjugal home. A wife who wants out of a marriage has a very hard time getting divorced and almost always loses all financial rights—often including property she and her husband bought together—in return for being free.

The existence of honor crimes in Jordan has been a matter of particular concern to Jordan's government, which began to take legal steps to control it. However, as I discuss in chapter 7, "Honor Crimes," these crimes in Jordan, like elsewhere in the Arab world, continue to be on the rise, and more is needed to stop them. Honor crimes constitute one of the most important reasons for women's resistance to entering the labor force or to leaving home. The increase in honor crimes—which today are as often perpetrated by teenage brothers as they are by fathers or older brothers and uncles—is a reflection of the growth in social frustrations experienced by youth with few prospects. Not only are family ties becoming less of an assurance of a secure future where young men could be supported in finding jobs or getting married, but because of the leniency of laws toward juveniles, families also actually recruit younger males to punish "disobedient" sisters.

This chapter discusses honor crimes and the laws that continue to make it possible for the courts to deal leniently with their perpetrators. It also draws connections between family relationships and contrasts gender and class in regards to family. Most important, as chapter 5 also shows, this chapter suggests that the upbringing and education the individual receives, rather than Jordanian law or *shari'a* law, constitute an important basis for social and family relations, including questions of honor. Education at the school and university levels continues patterns begun within the family, and with today's rise of fundamentalism, the trends seem to be reinforced.

Chapter 8, "Regarding Work and the Modern Jordanian Woman," focuses on continuing efforts undertaken by Jordan to change the lives of its women and children. It begins by discussing dominant discourses on women and work in Jordan and other Arab countries. The purpose is to show that only a minority of thinkers today really view women as having no role to play in their communities' development and public life. Even conservative elements view women's work as essential and inevitable. It is really in areas involving morals, politics, and power that there is the greatest resistance. Whereas discourses of morality emphasize the "Islamic" requirement that men and women be segregated, there is a close connection between the moral discourse and the wish to keep women out of areas of power. Conversations with women in various professions lead to the conclusion that as long as women are not empowered within the family, then there is little hope of their playing a role outside of the sphere determined and dominated by male authority. Without leverage, women will be effectively kept peripheralized and subservient to a patriarchal society and state.

There is a deep contradiction here, because Jordan's recent history shows the dynamic capability of women who have been playing important leadership roles as individuals and from within organizations in trying to improve their society and developing their country. Although the existence of "hidden" contributions by women covering large sectors of the economy is discussed in the book, the wide-ranging and well-publicized activities of modern Jordanian women cry out against the laws and traditions that constrain them. Even though gender constraints are described as dictated by Islam and the *shari'a*, it is really a continued acceptance of discrimination by the state and its laws that strengthens and emphasizes such ideas. As earlier chapters of the book demonstrate, it is not Islam that discriminates any more than any other religion; what discriminates are the laws enforced by the state and the traditions that have been made into law, thereby becoming recognized legal *'urf*. This chapter discusses individuals and organizations that are active in areas pertaining to the advancement of women, as well as their hopes and achievements. It is important to do so because not only does Jordan present a serious model for other Islamic countries to follow, but also what Jordan has already achieved is rather remarkable yet very little known. I hope this chapter will remedy the latter and help push toward greater action on the part of Jordanian women and government.

The conclusion draws together the various issues and ideas presented in the book. It also provides an agenda of work for the future. The agenda makes suggestions for Jordanian women active in women's issues in Jordan as well as for the Islamic and Arab world as a whole.

About the format and organization of the book: although the book is designed to stand as a study of women, work, and law in Jordan, the various chapters are also intended to stand as separate comprehensive studies of the particular issues with which they deal. This point is important because the book is also designed as an effort to stimulate discussions on changing laws and, one hopes, pushing for other changes in attitudes toward gender, particularly in relation to efforts in schools and by the media and government. Various Jordanian organizations may be interested in particular issues of concern to them, and the format is meant to help them.

2

Background
Qadis, 'Asha'ir, and Modern Law

JORDAN'S legal system takes many issues about women for granted. The necessity of a male guardian to stand by a woman in her marriage is but one aspect of a philosophy underlying the legal system that denies women full legal competence and limits the law's ability to protect her, even though Jordan's Constitution guarantees equality and the rule of law for all citizens. It is in the genesis of Jordan's modern legal system that the roots of legal contradictions facing women today are to be found. Representing an amalgam of *shari'a* codes, tribal laws, and modern Western codes, Jordan's laws and the philosophy molding them have contributed to seeing women as lesser individuals and peripheralized dependents of male relatives with custodial power over women. By deconstructing the origins of Jordanian laws that deal with gender—including personal status, labor, property, and criminal codes—it may be possible to challenge presumptions that lend credibility to these laws by giving them religious authenticity and thereby raise questions in the minds of both legislators and the public as to their validity to Jordanian society today. As long as gender relations are conceived as being part of an unchanging *shari'a*, it will be very difficult to question, let alone change, them.

To begin, the diffusion of law referred to above did not take place with the express intent of creating a modern patriarchal order but took place as part of the normal evolution of Jordan's legal history and transformations experienced by the Arab world as a whole during two centuries that witnessed reform of law worldwide and touched directly upon areas that were part of the Ottoman Empire. It is therefore no wonder that there are great similarities between legal transformations experienced by Jordan and its Arab neighbors who went through similar historical changes. Whether we are talking about Syria, Egypt, Lebanon, Iraq, or North African countries such as Tunisia, Algeria, and Mo-

19

rocco, similar if not identical legal changes took place. In fact, with minor adjustments, the Jordanian civil code was originally copied from Egypt's, as were the Syrian, Palestinian, and Iraqi civil codes. It should also be pointed out that the world as a whole experienced legal transformations related to basic and continual infrastructural adjustments given the modern revolutions in industrialization, commerce, communication, and technology. The diffusion of law from one area of the globe to the other was inevitable with greater exchange and the need to regulate law to facilitate trade and other forms of exchange while at the same time ensuring the power of nation-states over their people and territories. International laws, movements of population, and nationality and citizenship regulations all grew and diffused as centralized nation-states became established as basic political entities of the modern period.

Today's Kingdom of Jordan was until 1918 part of the Ottoman Empire. Like other provinces of the empire, the legal system was formed of *shari'a* Courts, which applied various *madhahib* (schools of law) and whose interpretation of the law was greatly influenced by local traditions. Because of the importance of the tribes inhabiting the area known then as East Jordan, tribal law was also recognized, and tribes relied on their own legal traditions. *Shari'a* courts were sensitive to tribal laws and made allowances for tribal *'urf,* as they did elsewhere in the Ottoman Empire. When the Ottoman Empire began to introduce its Tanzimat reforms during the nineteenth century, its provinces were expected to follow suit. This action took place at differing degrees in different provinces. In the case of East Jordan, which was basically administered as part of Syria until 1920, it meant the introduction of the Ottoman *Mejelle* containing the first separate civil law in the empire. The *Mejelle* was the result of the work of a committee of Ottoman legists known as Jam'iyat al-Majalla, which collected laws in effect in the empire, organized and rationalized them according to updated modern categories, and placed them in one volume "Containing *shari'a* laws and *'adliyya* laws corresponding (*mutabiqa*) to books of *fiqh,*" according to the *madhhab* of Abu Hanifa al-Nu'man. Once completed, the Ottoman Porte recognized the *Mejelle* as a constitution to be applied in its empire.[1] The 1917 Ottoman Family Code was also applied in Jordan and later became the basis of modern Jordanian personal status laws.

After its separation from Syria, East Jordan was ruled by various decentralized local powers until its unification as the Emirate of Transjordan under King Abdullah in 1921. As a centralized nation-state was being built, the legal system was molded to fit its needs, and, similar to what occurred elsewhere, standardization and homogenization of law became the basic approach to structuring legal codes and legal systems. As the world order changed, so did the shape of national hegemonies. Thus, Jordan was faced not only with increasing centralization needs but also with legal requirements for self-definition, international relations, and the imperative of protecting its territory and citizens, issues common to other modern nations in formation. Tribal and *shari'a* courts continued to function as basic elements of the legal system in Jordan. At the same time, in other areas of the Ottoman Empire with large communities of foreigners and foreign businesses, the older privileges enjoyed by foreigners under Ottoman capitulations were integrated into new types of courts allowing for mixed international jurisdiction and national courts that applied European legal codes to handle crimes, trade, and property. These new legal jurisdictions implemented interests of new wealthy elite and bourgeois classes who saw in European law an administratively more rational and efficient way of doing business in a world in which international commerce and dependency were becoming essential.

British presence as mandatory power had a direct impact on the legal situation in Transjordan. The French mandate in Syria and Lebanon had a similar impact on their laws. The British protectorate over Egypt also had a similar effect, as did the mandate over Jordan, although socioeconomic conditions and the political natures of the two countries brought about different results. Whereas Egypt had a relatively culturally homogenous population to deal with, the people living in the northern parts of the Emirate of Transjordan were traditionally attached to greater Syria, which included Northern Palestine, a good example being the close affinity and trade relations between Nablus, Irbid, and Aleppo. Jordan's southern population was more tribal and oriented toward tribal life in Palestine, Sinai, and the Arabian peninsula with whom they were interrelated. After 1948 and the creation of Israel, the area of the West Bank, inhabited by close to a half-million Palestinian refugees, was added to the population of Jordan, plus another half-million Arabs inhabiting the West Bank all came under the rule of Jordan. The cultural and legal traditions of these areas of which Jordan was formed all brought their own sociolegal traditions into Jordan's legal system and social mores. Because of the diversity in cultural background of Jordan's population, its government followed a policy of standardizing laws and narrowing differences in the legal system. At the same time, as mentioned earlier, tribal law was at first recognized in the form of a separate tribal court system where tribal *'urf* was applied, and later after these courts were abolished, Jordan's laws integrated certain tribal laws so as to allow for state hegemony without disturbances from one of its most important elements.

By 1946, the mandate over Jordan came to an end, and Jordan was declared the Hashemite Kingdom of Jordan in April 1949 with a constitution that concentrated a high degree of executive and legislative powers in the hands of the king. A prime minister heading a cabinet was to be chosen by the king and primarily answerable to him. A national assembly formed of a thirty-member upper senate appointed by the king, and an eighty-member lower chamber of deputies elected for four-year terms completed the political picture. Since being founded, Jordan has depended largely on members of East Bank families with strong loyalties to the royal family for political and administrative leadership, whereas Jordan's army has continued to be dependent on tribal elements. The international orientation of Jordan has been toward the West with close relations with its Arab neighbors.

Like other countries of the Middle East, during the past decade, Jordan has witnessed a growth in urbanization as peasants and tribesmen became attracted by towns offering employment in the military, industry, the service sector, and trade. The loss of agricultural land through capitalist production and introduction of new property laws and other methods provided an important push factor toward urbanization. A rough estimate puts Jordan's urban population at 70 percent of the total today, almost 40 percent of whom are residents of Amman. Because of Jordan's advanced education system, university graduates have constituted an important labor export, particularly to Gulf countries where many Jordanians traveled or migrated to live and work. Intermarriage between Jordanians and non-Jordanians, particularly Palestinians, whether in or outside of Jordan, meant constant pressure in regards to laws concerning immigration and nationality. Similarly, the growth in Jordan's labor force in various sectors—including the government, which employs about 40 percent of today's workers— has meant the elaboration of legal codes to guide labor employment, social security, retirement, benefits, and other laws that are the prerogative of welfare nation-states.

This chapter discusses the major sources of Jordanian laws, namely, Islamic law, tribal law, *'urf,* European laws, and to a lesser extent international law. Specific legal codes will be discussed at the appropriate points in other chapters of the book. The approach here will be to detail the basic nature of each type of law and the evolution of the laws given changes in the historical process. Because laws diffuse from one type to another, overlapping and repetition will be essential to the discussion. The goal here is to understand the genesis of laws pertaining to women and work in Jordan today.

Women's access to work, that is, their freedom to leave the home and work outside, is of immediate importance. Although Jordan's laws today promise women equal work opportunities, personal status laws make it impossible for them to do so without the approval of husband, father, or *waliy* (guardian), as the case may be. Economic push factors have played a dramatic role in bringing women into the workforce, but when a woman works it is still under the eye and with the approval of husband and family. These laws also mean that male members of the family have ultimate control over the woman's salary or income, notwithstanding the *shari'a*'s admonition that her money is hers and the husband is the actual provider for his wife and children. Control over a wife's income acts, in many cases, as a deterrent for the willingness of wives to enter employment or be involved in business. Furthermore, the continued prioritizing given to principles of honor that leave the door for honor crimes open also inhibits women from leaving their homes, going to work, or opening their own businesses. In all of the above it is not labor laws that are in question but rather personal status laws and criminal laws in the case of honor crimes. Because the moral and legal discourse, based on government decrees and clerical support, is that personal status laws are in fact dictated by God in his *shari'a*, it will be important to study the genesis of the laws on the books today to determine their actual origins and to deconstruct the discourse so as to make suggestions regarding how these laws could be changed. *Shari'a*, legal practice in *shari'a* courts in the Ottoman Empire, and the changes experienced by both laws and courts as a result of state centralization and nation-building will be discussed.

Islamic Law (*shari'a*)

"Water quenches thirst and purifies, and *shari'a* is running water; it is also the road leading to the watering-place."[2] This quote is how Arab linguists define *shari'a* law, considering it as important to society as water is to living beings. Not only does the *shari'a* answer legal questions, but it also provides the road or method by which to reach these answers. That belief has been the approach to law, courts, and justice in the Islamic world since the founding of Islam in seventh-century Arabia and even earlier in Middle Eastern civilizations of ancient Egypt, Babylonia, and elsewhere.

That justice was an important service expected of Muslim rulers is a well-studied subject. *Qadis* (judges in Islamic courts), independent of theologians, served in courts of law to render decisions regarding disputes brought before them. For consultation, they went back to the learned *fuqaha'* (legists, Islamic thinkers; plural form of *"faqih"*), and quite often *faqih* (theologian) and *qadi* were one and the same. Because the caliph was expected to be a fountain of Islamic knowledge, the earlier caliphs having been companions of the prophet Muhammad, they were often consulted by *qadis* when difficult questions were brought to court. But, at least theoretically, there was no direct control by the state or its *muftis* (Muslim scholars, jurisconsults) over court decisions of judges.[3] The same basic principles remained essential to the Islamic legal system all through the medieval and early modern periods of Islamic history, even though caliphs or sultans were no longer the great fountains of knowledge that their earlier counterparts had been and more elaborate *fiqh* and *madhahib* were formulated.

"*Shari'a*" is taken by scholars to mean Islamic law that is studied as a body of laws formulated by *fuqaha'* during the early centuries of Islam until the closing of the door of *ijtihad* (speculative thinking, rational thought). This event is supposed to have taken place in the tenth century when *fuqaha'* became satisfied that all questions had been answered and that their formulas were good for all time and all situations. As a rule, then, the unchanging nature of the Islamic *shari'a* is accepted by almost all and in particular by today's Islamic theologians who hold on to that principle, give it a holy nature, and are inflexible in regards to changing it. Yet, reading *fiqh* from different periods in Islamic history shows that interpretations and legal formulations have been constantly debated among *'ulama'* (Islamic clergy) up to the present time. Usually, *shari'a* laws are divided among *'ibadat* (creed or rituals guiding man's relationship with God) and *mu'amalat* (relations of man to man, or laws pertaining to human relations). If we were to look at *'aqa'id* (central beliefs, faith) separately from the rest of *'ibadat,* and see how *fuqha'* dealt with these different areas of law, we would find that the closed door of *ijtihad* was really about *'aqa'id,* the central Islamic principles of faith that are more specifically based on the Qur'an than any other area of Islam. *'Aqa'id* were the subject of speculative debates during the Abbasid period, particularly by the Mu'tazila under the sponsorship of the Abbasid caliph al-Ma'mun. Closing the door on these debates was a necessary part of establishing Islamic orthodoxy, which was considered formulated by the tenth century and about which no further discussion was to be allowed. The Imam Ahmad b. Hanbal's *mihna* (crisis, revolt) was about issues regarding the oneness of God (*tawhid*), the nature of the Qur'an, prophethood (*nubuwwa*), and the Day of Judgment (*mi'ad*) and was not about marriage and divorce or which hand to wash first while performing ablutions. If anything, his *fatawi* (theological opinions) show an effort to deal with day-to-day problems brought by questioners to his attention. His answers were in the best spirit of Islam but from within the particular conditions of his age.[4] The existence of several legal schools and large numbers of *fiqh* collections dating from various periods of Islamic history and from all over the Islamic world shows that matters pertaining to human relations have been the subject of constant discussion and debate among theologians and exegetes. None, however, dispute the basics of the Islamic faith; the Shi'a may add to them, but the basics remain the same.

When it comes to gender relations, there are certain principles based primarily on the Qur'an and Sunnah that are consistent in the debates among *fuqaha'*. But these debates are dealt with as *mu'amalat* and not as questions of faith or creed. Here we can include the unquestioned principle that a woman cannot have more than one husband at any one time and must wait an *'idda* (three-month period before taking another husband)—sometimes defined as three menstrual cycles—to ensure she is not pregnant and to allow a period of possible reconciliation with her husband. Only after the three-month period is concluded following divorce or widowhood can a wife take another husband. Legal availability and limits on who could marry whom, which are based on degrees of consanguinity, are dictated by the Qur'an. Most rules regarding gender that are considered today to be "Islamic" are actually based on *fiqh* and are practiced differently over time and place. For example, reaching the age of majority for girls differs widely from one *madhhab* to the other; the Shaf'is and Malikis do not consider a woman as having reached majority unless she has become experienced through marriage, whereas the Hanafis do not see this experience as a requirement for a girl to reach adulthood.[5] The payment of the dowry by the bridegroom to his bride or her family is considered an "Islamic" obligation, and the "Islamic" way of paying the dowry is said to be in the form of an advanced dowry paid at the time of marriage and a delayed dowry to be paid to the wife if she is divorced or becomes a widow. Yet, *shari'a* court records show that very often no dowry was paid, the wife sometimes declared that she had already received it, or it was often paid in installments over many years depending on social conditions; more often than not, the wife lost these installments, her delayed dowry, or even the dowry as a whole in divorce settlements. Besides, *qadis* recording marriages did not object when no dowry was exchanged. In many cases the *qadi* simply referred to a dowry as "named between them" (*sadaq musama baynahum*). In short, legal practices differed according to legal interpretation, and there was a great diversity in interpretations of the *shari'a* among legal schools and from one country or town to another.

Many scholars today are moving to understand the *shari'a* in different ways, not as an unchanging, backward-looking structure that continues to be the normative view accepted by Western Orientalists and conservative Islamic theologians. Taking issue with the normative view that looks at *shari'a* as a collection of laws that has been emulated through a system of *taqlid* (imitation), Haifaa Khalafallah has shown how learned *fuqaha'* conceptualized *shari'a* as a "method" and used its principles and resources to think through the problems of particular periods—political, social, or religious—to formulate responses to them.[6] Using the collective works of the important twentieth-century figure Sheikh Muhammad al-Ghazali (1917–1996), Khalafallah shows the *shari'a*'s "commotion and dynamism in the present . . . debate over Islamic legal principles and their applications [and how] . . . Sheikh Muhammad al-Ghazali argued for and applied the 'Islamic legal method' to argue for radical changes in both the law and norms governing society." Whereas a young al-Ghazali originally described women's role as primarily in the home and believed in the necessity of veiling, an older and wiser al-Ghazali, using *shari'a* and its sources as an "Islamic legal method" rather than a finalized collection of decisions and interpretations, accepted that women were capable of being political leaders and court judges.[7]

It seems that definitions of such legal terms as *shari'a*, like other issues tied with human society, are highly dependent on the particular sources privileged in interpreting meaning. In the case of Islamic law, high dependence on *fiqh* by modern states for interpreting law and the almost total disregard of legal practice in premodern courts as precedent have strengthened the impression of the *shari'a* as a collection of laws formulated long ago that has survived unchanged and applied throughout Islamic history. Different approaches and using different and more diverse sources of knowledge produce different conclusions. Ideally, all possible sources should be used to try to understand social institutions. However, doing so has proved difficult for practical reasons such as linguistic abilities of researchers and the difficulty of getting to particular sources. When it comes to language, it is not only the ability to know or master Arabic, the language of the Qur'an, hadith, and Arab *fiqh*. The matter is more complicated because language itself changes from age to age and the meanings of words differ from place to place and over time in the same location. There are early Qur'anic Arabic and modern theological Arabic, and the two differ, notwithstanding the refusal of theologians or society to conceptualize this fact. Medieval Arabic is very different from modern Arabic; each is directly connected with its cultural and socioeconomic context.

Another problem with sources—which is at the heart of the normative picture of women in Islamic societies past and present—has to do with overprivileging the religious literature produced by exegetes and theologians, all of whom were and continue to be men. There has been too much dependence on the writings of theologians who are seen as representing the actual condition of women and gender relations during the premodern period when they were really painting a picture of what they considered an ideal "moral order" that conservatives wish to establish today. Denise Spellberg explains the impact of this approach on Islamic societies and law:

> Sources for the study of gender in Islamic society, whether found in the Qur'an, sacred commentaries, *hadith,* biographical dictionaries (*tabaqat,*) or chronicles (*ta'warikh*) represent a central repository of medieval male definitions about the differences between the sexes, differences that underscore relationships of power in the preservation and creation of a presumably shared Muslim past. . . . These ostensibly religious sources are thus central to the development of a medieval male interpretive discourse about women and their meaning. They are at the heart of Islamic gender definitions and the emergence of a unique historiography. This medieval male conversation about women, often brilliantly argued, utilizes the Qur'an and its interpretation, along with the prophetic utterances and actions found in *hadith,* but often takes these precedents into new venues and refines them with distinct authorial intent and intertextual results.[8]

That method is the same one used by Muslim intellectuals and *'ulama'* today in their effort to control change within their societies by emphasizing their power over the moral discourse through legitimating selections of medieval theses that were originally intended to create moral discourses addressing their authors' dissatisfaction—personal or otherwise—with the specific period in which they lived. It is this formula that is today being used to deny women the freedom to act independently, to choose to go to college, to work, or even to decide on a future husband. Gender is confined within a medieval discourse that is repeated and perpetrated not only by conservative religious elements today, but also by those espousing patriarchal control over women. It is rather curious that patriarchal elements do not refer to medieval *fiqh* to question society's application of new laws of obvious foreign origin such as banking, insurance, crimes, and nationality, but question only any efforts that touch on patriarchal controls over women and children. As Bernard Botiveau concludes, "in their application of Islamic laws to family law, *fiqh* was conceptualized as being synonymous to Islamic law and yet *fiqh* was not applied to other types of law but rather foreign European sources were preferred even though *fiqh* is as involved in these other types of laws—criminal, contracts, property, etc.—as it is in regards to family law."[9]

Even within Jordanian legal codes modeled after Western ones, a tribal patriarchal outlook continues to be present. For example, Jordan's criminal laws and procedures are largely imported from Europe with exceptions. Modern criminal laws regarding rape have introduced the principle of "intent," which could work against the victim, especially if she is an adult woman and could be said to have enticed the rapist. Proving that rape has taken place is no longer enough in Jordanian courts as it was in *shari'a* courts before the modernization of courts and law. Yet, at the same time that rape laws have made it more difficult to prosecute rapists, Jordan's laws have bent over backward to give men the right to kill a daughter, sister, or wife whom they suspect of illicit sexual conduct by allowing reduced sentencing based on European "crimes of passion" laws without the strict application of rules of evidence that crimes of passion require. In both cases, the male gets away with a minor prison sentence, and the woman victim seems to have little significance except for the amount of *diyya* that a rapist's family may have to pay to hers.

Part of the reason *fiqh* is today accepted as being what Islam dictated is that whereas medieval *fiqh* has been studied and researched to formulate codes of honor, theologians and legists have paid little attention to investigating the realities of human and social relations and the nature of the legal order that preceded the modern period. One can take this point a step further by noting that there is a general lack of acceptance that premodern Jordan was guided by the rule of law. Although archival sources, particularly legal records of *shari'a* courts and records of *awqaf* (religious endowments), provide extensive knowledge of actual legal practices and social relations in premodern society, little attention has been given to them. Rather, the attention of scholars and legists has been directed toward what a particular *'alim* (clergyman) or *mufti* had to say about a specific point, and they have conceptualized what were in reality no more than legal opinions as being actual legal and social practices. At the same time, scholars who did make use of *shari'a* court records may have contributed toward our understanding of Islamic society; unfortunately, such studies have not made enough use of exegetic and legal interpretations from various periods in Islamic history. This book tries to combine the two sources in an effort to understand gender relations and legal practices before the modern period. Without this background, challenging modern gender laws would be difficult because of the Islamic discourse that defines existing gendered laws in Jordan as God's unchanging word through his *shari'a*. Therefore, exegetic and juridical literary production constitutes an important background to this type of research.

Muhammad Fadel's article "Two Women, One Man: Knowledge, Power, and Gender in Medieval Sunni Legal Thought" presents a good opportunity to illustrate the importance of rereading *fiqh* from a different perspective. *Fiqh's* approach to the witness of women is often used as evidence of Islam's view that women are meant to be adjuncts to men, that they are "more prone to error" and are less equipped intellectually and religiously (*al-nisa' naqisun 'aqlan wa dinan*). This image is accepted by conservative Muslims and Western thinkers who believe in the essential misogynistic nature of Islam. According to this popular image, evidence given in court by two women is considered equal to the testimony of one man, and women's legal testimony is not acceptable in Islamic courts without the corroborative witness of a male. This image is based on the Qur'an (al-Baqara 282): "Get two witnesses out of your own men, and if there are not two men, then a man and two women, such as ye choose, for witnesses, so that if one of them errs, the other can remind her." Here the Qur'an was discussing a specific situation dealing with finances in which women would not likely have been present or would have had little involvement in the proceedings. Unfortunately, this specific situation with which the Qur'an dealt was generalized into an absolute Islamic requirement by *fiqh* and hence became a popular belief and developed further into the generalization that women need to be reminded because their memory is faulty, and that they are unreliable and less competent than men.

Principles and procedures regarding giving witness in *shari'a* courts dating from the Ottoman period raise serious questions about these types of presumptions. The procedures followed in these courts were quite sophisticated and based on strict rules of evidence and not on discourses detailed by *fiqh*. In fact, Fadel shows that *fuqaha'* actually present a more complicated analysis of the question of women's witness than is generally accepted. He does so by noting that certain *fuqaha'* came quite close to admitting the equal validity of a woman's witness to a man's. Included among them are the important figures of Ibn Qiyyam al-Jawziyya and Ahmad Ibn Taymiyya, two widely quoted *fuqaha'* today.[10] So, through a close reading of exegetic literature Fadel was able to show that not all *fuqaha'* agreed with the idea that a woman's witness must be corroborated by another witness and that there must be a man corroborating the witness of both. Another important point here is that in discussing matters of witnessing, the *fuqaha'* were really concerned with issues of morality and were trying to establish public and private divides defining the parameters of women's domain as separate from the public domain. To ascertain public morality women had to be secluded at home and not go out; their seclusion therefore lessened their ability to function as witnesses. According to these *fuqaha'*, then, because a woman is expected to stay home to "avoid social corruption and disorder," she should not be expected to go to court to render witness, and could not really render witness except in matters limited to the household that is within her experience. Therefore, women's witness regarding public matters could not be reliable because they could not have been present in public situations. Their witness could also not be reliable in regards to marriage, divorce, and other issues pertaining to the human body because their seclusion prohibits them from having knowledge about these matters. The Aristotelian logic, an absolute truth leading to another then back to the original absolute truth, is clear in this method. Unfortunately, this basic formula has been applied in regards to gender philosophies calling for confinement of women and using such confinement as reason to keep her peripheralized as well as dependent on and controlled by male relatives. Today, even though the law speaks about equality and individual competence, it is this discourse of confinement and incompetence that continues to predominate, and because it is reinforced by certain aspects of the civil code and by personal status laws, it remains the most important hindrance facing a public role for women in Jordan and other Islamic countries.

But how realistic is this discourse when faced with actual legal practices? In other words, what light do actual legal practices throw on the gender equation? Did *qadis* presiding over *shari'a* courts before the modern period take the findings of *fuqaha'* and apply them as law in their courts? Did *qadis* rule according to what *fiqh* or *muftis* of their period told them was Islamic or not Islamic, or was the purpose of courts to settle disputes and render justice? Although chapters 3 and 4 will focus on the life of women and work during the premodern and modern periods, respectively, the following court case from sixteenth-century Jerusalem will help illustrate what I mean. A man came to court to inform that the night before, while he and his wife were sleeping, the roof caved in and the debris had fallen on his wife. He removed her from under the debris but found her dead. Four women had examined the body and gave their witness in court that they had found her head and face swollen from the falling debris and had seen no signs of foul play on the part of the husband.[11] Here confirmation by a man was not required, and the witness of the women sufficed, even though the matter involved financial compensation because the parents of the deceased woman were in court to see if any payment was due to them from the husband for the daughter's death. On the basis of the witnesses, the court found the husband bore no responsibility in his wife's death.

It is important to point out here the discrepancies between what *fiqh* discourses tell us about public and private divides and actual legal practice in courts of law. By doing so, we will see that *shari'a* law changes with time and place and that it is not synonymous with *fiqh*. What I am suggesting is a deconstruction of the dominant picture presented by *fiqh* discourse that underlies the social and legal outlook in Jordan today. Because *fiqh* has become almost synonymous with *shari'a* in people's understanding and the application of law in Jordan's *shari'a* courts, it is important to show that *fiqh* presents a moral discourse rather than a holy, unchanging *shari'a* designed by God that all Muslims are expected to follow. One way of doing so is presented by Fadel, which is to show that not all *fuqaha'* agreed on the same thing and that the same *faqih* changed his stand on issues with fluctuations in the social conditions of his age, as Khalafallah has shown. Still another way is to look into legal practice to show that legal practice and *fiqh* were regarded as separate matters, one as a moral discourse and the other as legal practice based on cumulative laws that changed given the time and place. So the question to ask here in an effort to see *shari'a* in theory and practice, and following up on the issue of women's witness as an example, is how valid are *fiqh* arguments pertaining to public and private divides and the legal witness of women before the modern reform of courts and law? Is it true that a woman's single witness was not acceptable and that the corroboration of a man was necessary? After spending some time reading records of Ottoman courts of law it becomes obvious that the existence of a private-public divide in Islamic communities is fiction at best. That women spent more time at home and were responsible for running the home is not synonymous with distinct private-public divides. Such patterns exist the world over and do not lead to similar characterization. Bedouin society, in which men and women are responsible for the various economic activities, can have no such divides, nor can peasant societies where women join husbands in working the fields. It is probably more accurate to talk about a divide between women and men in the sense of each group spending time or working together. But as court records illustrate, women were very much part of the live public tableau of the premodern period. If coming to court was a possible cause of immorality, as some *fuqaha'* wrote, then Islamic society must have been corrupt indeed. Women appeared in court all the time, sometimes bringing someone to represent them or vouch for who they were. The latter was particularly necessary with regards to a completely covered woman, as is evident from the record, and was usually a case involving a Bedouin woman who would appear unveiled in her own tribe but not in an urban center. For the most part, however, women came in person, presented their cases to the *qadis,* and disputed cases brought against them. The diversity of cases brought by or against women tells us how women lived. Women came to declare *waqfs* (religious endowments), buy and sell goods and property, transact marriages for themselves and their children for whom they acted as guardians, sue their husbands for divorce or ask for their delayed financial support or dowries, ask for custody of their children, report violence, demand compensation, bring business disputes against those people they were in partnership with or who had tried to usurp their spot in the marketplace, register and get a license to run a business or open a shop, or form a group business with other women, which seems to have been more prevalent among Palestinian women than women in other areas of the Ottoman Empire.

But there is more, and the question of women's work is essential if we are to understand gender relations. *Did women work?* If so, what jobs did they perform? The picture regarding women and work is very interesting. Suraiya Faruqi has shown that women were involved and constituted an important part of silk manufacturing, weaving, and the like in the Ottoman Empire. But here she was mainly discussing secluded practices, that is, women not in a working place but rather involved in a take-out system by which they produced their product at home. What do Ottoman archives reveal? They show us women doing work at home and having access to the market in various forms to sell their products. We are also given detailed evidence of the retail part of women's activities in the form of various types of references, perhaps the most important being disputes between women or between women and men. After all, courts were places to lodge and resolve disputes.

Although "women and work" will be central to chapter 3 of this book, one should mention here that *dayas* (midwives) were considered professional experts recognized as such by the community. It was also normal for women to bring goods and sell them in the marketplace, a fact corroborated by travelers to the Levant who described the kinds of foods sold by vendors, many of whom were women. Certainly, women were very involved in what we can call "petty capitalism" at that time, working as washerwomen, cooking at home for vendors, and acting as *mashatas* (beauticians) or as *dalalas* (saleswomen who went from house to house). Furthermore, women owned shops and were involved in their day-to-day management. Women also administered *waqfs* and were very often assigned as executors by *qadis*. As executors they were responsible for collecting income, and even when this job was delegated, it involved contact with strangers, including men.

To conclude, Jordan's personal status laws, like in other Muslim countries today, are said to be based on the *shari'a*. Because *shari'a* is viewed as an unchanging body of laws representing the Qur'an and prophetic hadiths, it is very hard to change laws dealing with gender. As the above discussion has shown, *shari'a* has been studied differently by scholars who see it as a method by which *fuqaha'* of different periods found answers to problems of their age. Much of what is considered *shari'a* is in fact the *ijtihad* of theologians during the medieval period, which was presented more as a moral discourse and theological opinion than as a representation of the actual application of law in *shari'a* courts. It is in comparing the actual life of women to what *fiqh* dictates their life should be that the dialectic between thought and practice becomes obvious as a process in which the *ijtihad* of theologians becomes more of a mental and intellectual exercise than a representation of the reality of women's lives. In other words, what is described today as being *shari'a* according to which gender relations are molded is an intellectual product rather than the unchanging word of God.

Put differently, even though Islamic law was followed by *qadis,* legal procedures did not follow *fiqh* or classical Islamic law as we understand it. Perhaps we make a serious error when reading sources of Islam, Islamic history, or Islamic law from a position that looks at Islam as a system that frames, confines, and sets limits to what is possible according to very clear lines of what is acceptable or unacceptable, *halal* or *haram,* and what is preferred for society and community, *istihsan* and *istihbab.* Gender has always been studied that way, through limits set for it by the Qur'an as interpreted by *fuqaha'.* Modern interpretations have implicitly accepted this discourse of confinement or restriction, and Islam itself is seen from within such parameters. Archival records show a very different picture: what the *fuqaha'* say is more a commentary on legal procedures than the other way around; their commentary is intended to restrict what they believe to be more Islamic or moral. In contradistinction, court cases do not speak of the good of the community; rather, it is the right of the individual that they are concerned with. The individual could be male or female. For example, a victim of rape is usually given the choice of how to deal with her rapist: she could marry him and be paid the dowry of her equal, she could have him pay her *diyya,* or she could have him punished. There may be other choices, but I did not come across them. In short, we are not looking at a legal system built on the confining discourses of *fuqaha'.* How *fiqh* defined the role of women and how women actually lived in Islamic society are not necessarily the same. That discrepancy is to be expected because *fiqh* is an intellectual product representing particular opinions about how society should be, portraying the concerns of the thinker with the world in which he or she lived.

Having pointed out discrepancies between theory and application in regards to premodern laws, I will move on to discuss the modernization of courts and law that began in the nineteenth century. First, the court system as it moved from premodern structures to modern structures will be discussed, and then the changes experienced by the laws dealing with gender will follow. The intent will be to illustrate the genesis of the laws on Jordanian books today.

Modern Law and Modern Courts: A New *shari'a*

The Islamic *shari'a* is a recognized part of Jordanian laws. It is applied in particular to personal status laws that handle marriage, divorce, child custody, inheritance, and *awqaf.* Before the nineteenth century, *shari'a* courts were the main courts handling legal disputes between members of the public. People took all sorts of personal disputes in front of the *qadi* who rendered his judgment according to the specifics of the case guided by the particular *madhhab* to which he belonged. There were four such schools recognized in the Ottoman Empire, namely, the Maliki, Hanafi, Shaf'i, and Hanbali. Whereas the Ottomans deferred to the Hanafi code, populations from Syria to Egypt preferred the Maliki and Shaf'i, with large percentages of Syrians adhering to the Hanafi and North Africans to the Maliki. Without going into too much detail, it should be pointed out that although the Maliki was preferred in areas where tribal and kinship ties predominated, the Shaf'i was preferred in settled urban and agricultural areas. As for the Hanafi, it was preferred among the richer capitalist and merchant classes and people related to or in service of the Ottoman government.

In that system, it was up to the individual to choose the *qadi* of the particular *madhhab,* and courthouses usually had *muftis* and *qadis* if not of the four schools, then of the schools to which most of the residents of the town or area belonged. The *qadi* in turn applied Islamic law from his particular school as well as the *'urf* acceptable to the population of the particular district. More often than not, the judge himself originated or was of long residence in that area. So there was a certain extent of maneuverability among the population, and it was in the hands of the judges to pick and choose the laws to be applied. *Shari'a* courts did not serve Muslims alone, but also served non-Muslims who came to court to register land, document inheritance, solve property and business disputes, and even marry and divorce against their churches' orders. Ottoman archives illustrate that Christians and Jews often came to court to divorce husbands or wives, to take a second wife, or to buy slave women.[12]

> In majlis al-Shar'i . . . in front of *mawlana* (honorable sheikh) . . . the Christian woman named Maryam bint 'Abdel-Ahhad al-Siryani, vouched for by her father, asked her husband 'Ibriyan wild Habiyan the Copt who is present with her in court, to divorce her (*an yakhla'ha*) from his *'isma* and marriage knot (*'uqdat nikah*) in return for her relinquishing her *mu'akhkhar sadaq* (delayed dowry) amounting to ten qurush and from her *nafaqat al-'idda* (alimony for period of *'idda*) and housing expenses [during the *'idda*] and from fifteen qurush leftover

from her previous *nafaqa* according to this earlier document. . . . He accepted and *khala'ha* (removed/divorced) her so she is divorced from him and cannot go back to him except with a new marriage contract and new dowry.[13]

This sixteenth-century document ended with the signatures of the judges and members of the *majlis* (council), all of whom were Muslim sheikhs. The wording and expectations from this divorce document show that Muslims and non-Muslims lived very similar social lives, their marriages and divorces being transacted in very similar ways.

Modern reforms divided the court system into various types, and each was provided with a legal code that judges were required by the state to apply in reaching their decisions. It happened by stages with the Jordanian Constitution of 1928 that recognized the existing Ottoman codes as applicable in Jordan until such time as they were changed. In the 1952 constitution, the legal system was reconstructed and the court system divided between *mahakim nizamiyya* (national courts), *mahakim diniyya* (religious courts), and *mahakim khassa* (special courts held for specific reasons). The first were given the responsibility of looking into all civil and criminal cases, disputes involving trade, exchange, property, and crimes, including cases brought by or against the government. The second, religious courts, were to serve Muslims and non-Muslims; *shari'a* courts were to look into the personal affairs of Muslims, whereas Milla councils of different non-Muslim sects would each determine the personal affairs of its constituency. As in national courts, *shari'a* court judges were given a code compiled by state committees and lawyers that they were asked to enforce in all marital, inheritance, and child custody disputes. So even though the personal status laws applied in Jordan today are based on the Islamic *shari'a* as represented by the massive collection of books of *fiqh,* they are really a selective reading of these sources, specific laws preferred whereas others are discarded. The philosophy applied in this selection took state interest into consideration and brought a modern conceptualization of gender (of the late nineteenth and early twentieth centuries) as a binding discourse for these laws. In other words, one can call the laws *shari'a,* but the particular laws themselves, the application of the laws, the philosophy behind the laws, and the execution of the laws were in many ways different from what was applied earlier. Finally, religious endowments of the various communities were also made the domain of these religious courts.

In 1951 the first Jordanian law organizing *shari'a* courts was passed. It stayed in effect until 1972 when several amendments were introduced to it during 1973, 1978, 1979, and 1983. Decree 41 for 1951 defines: "First degree *shari'a* courts are to be formed in the Hashemite Kingdom of Jordan: first degree primarily, then one or more second degree courts (*isti'naf*) according to needs and what the chief judge (*qadi al-qudat*) decided from time to time, according to an organization accepted by His Majesty the King." [14] The functions of these courts were described as follows:

> *Shari'a* courts assume responsibility for adjudicating personal status among Muslims and to look into disputes involving the establishment and internal administration of *waqfs* in the benefit of Muslims . . . and what [problems] may entail from a marriage contract registered at the *shari'a* court or any of its *ma'd-huns* [official licensed to contract marriages and divorces] and that in accordance to what is most widely accepted from the *madhhab* of Abu Hanifa with the exceptions of any of its special laws. [15]

"Personal status" meant not only marriage and divorce, but also child custody and guardianship (*wisaya, wilaya*), appointment and removal of the *wasi* (guardian with power over property of minor orphan) and *waliy* (legal guardian), inheritance, payment of blood price, and family disputes over such matters as dowry or spousal support (*nafaqa*), in fact "anything that takes place between husband and wife as result of a marriage contract."

All other matters that were earlier the domain of *shari'a* courts were placed under the jurisdiction of various forms of national courts of different degrees. This move was in itself a continuation of the split that had taken place during the nineteenth century under the auspices of Ottoman reforms with the introduction of the *Mejelle*, which took its final form by 1877. The *Mejelle* was based on the Hanafi *madhhab*, which was the dominant *madhhab* in Ottoman Turkey if not in other parts of the empire. It allowed for great government authoritarianism and was much more friendly toward capitalism. For example, when it came to loans, the Hanafi *madhhab* required that a loan be paid in a similar value in bullion allowing for market fluctuations, whereas the other *madhahib* allowed its payment in the exact same monetary value notwithstanding devaluation. Another example concerns rentals. Whereas the Hanbali *madhhab* recognized the inheritance of a deed of rent for *waqf* land and kept the value of rent as determined at the time the original contract was signed, the Hanafi *madhhab* did not allow the inheritance of rental deeds to *waqf* property and allowed for raising rent according to market forces. Also, the Hanafi *madhhab* was quite elitist. For example, Hanafis allowed a father to have the courts annul his adult daughter's marriage if she was married to a man whom the father considered less than her equal and therefore not befitting the family.

Jordanian laws declared that *shari'a* law applied in Jordan would be based on the Hanafi *madhhab,* yet when it came to laws of guardianship, they mixed between the Hanafi and Maliki *madhahib.* Hanafi law required rationality (*'aql*) and puberty (*bulugh*) as a basis for reaching majority, whereas Maliki law added experience gained through marriage as a requirement for a girl to reach majority. Until then she was under the power of her *waliy.* Modern law established the minimum age for the marriage of girls to be fifteen and determined that age to be according to the Hanafi code because at fifteen a girl would have reached both rationality and puberty. At the same time, however, unlike Hanafi requirements, a Jordanian girl who reaches majority is not allowed to contract her own marriage but has to receive her father or guardian's approval before a marriage of her choice can take place. This requirement is true even if she has passed the age of legal competence recognized by Jordanian laws: eighteen for partial competence and twenty-one for full individual competence. It is the Malikis rather than Hanafis who demand the approval of a *waliy* (who could be the judge replacing the guardian for an adult woman) for a previously unmarried girl, notwithstanding how old she is because she had yet to gain experience. Furthermore, Jordanian laws use the Hanafi interpretation of *kafa'a* (social parity), which gives the father the right to ask the judge to annul a marriage entered into by his adult daughter when he considers her bridegroom not her social equal. In other words, Jordan's guardianship laws are a patchwork of Hanafi and Maliki laws by which the more patriarchal aspects of the two were put together to form a modernized code allowing for greater control of women than was practiced before the introduction of these laws. These details are important because they explain the genesis of personal status laws. A system of *talfiq* (patching), quite orthodox to the Islamic legal method, was applied by which laws from different sources and legal philosophies emphasizing more "controlling" attitudes toward gender were amalgamated together to establish what became known as personal status laws.

The point I am making here is that the *shari'a* applied in modern Jordanian courts may be described as Muslim jurisprudence, but a jurisprudence that is in fact the result of a methodology in which laws were compiled, picked, and chosen by state-assigned committees under the auspices of jurists selected by the government. The *qadi*'s discretion to choose the particular law or *'urf* to apply in a particular case and the individual's choice to go in front of the *qadi* of the *madhhab* of his choice practiced in Ottoman courts were replaced by a government code that was selectively extracted from the Hanafi code and to a lesser extent the Maliki code. There was only one law, selected and compiled by the state, to be uniformly applied to all citizens, and this code became the instrument for constructing gender, family, and all other personal relations. Furthermore, notwithstanding the belief that the *shari'a* continued to be the basis for personal and family laws, laws applied in reformed *shari'a* courts were in the form of new statutes rather than a continuation of previous practices. Ironically, even though *shari'a* court records dating from the premodern period presented an important source of legal precedent, a common law with consistency of application, this precedent was not taken into consideration in the construction of the new *shari'a* courts and provides no basis for court decisions today. Rather, new statutes were handed to the *qadis* of *shari'a* courts who sat in court and applied them, finding justifications for them in the *fiqh* of various schools, but accepting them as the way things have always been. It is in these new statutes that we find the legal basis for the subjection of women in the modern state.

European Codes

European laws made their way into the court and legal systems of Jordan and other Arab countries in different ways, but first as part of Ottoman nineteenth-century reforms that adopted European systems sometimes willingly and other times under duress. Given world transformations, the Ottoman Empire was forced to introduce changes to its legal system. Although the system already allowed for different types of courts (for example, non-Muslims had their own sectarian courts, and foreigners were judged in their own embassies according to the capitulations), there were brand-new issues that had to be handled. Perhaps the most important had to do with citizenship and nationality. The Ottoman Civil Code of 1867–1877 modeled after European codes—French and Belgian—formed the basis of the Egyptian Civil Code that was later adopted by Syria and Jordan as the prototype for their own codes. The legal system departed from what had been practiced in Ottoman courts before. Where there were no reciprocal laws, European codes were applied directly. Furthermore, precedents from European courts, particularly French courts, were used for legal decisions in new Arab courts.

European laws were also introduced indirectly to personal status matters. For example, the Ottoman Family Code became the first step toward modern personal status laws that continue in power in Jordan today. The Ottoman Family Code brought in a new outlook toward gender with grids of conceptualization reflecting Europe's new industrial society and its legal needs. The idea of family became the central construct of the new society, rather than the individual, clan, or tribe, as was previously the case. Although "family" plays little role in Islamic legal thought, modern laws conceptualized society as a construct of family units in which various individuals play clearly defined roles. The Hanafi code may have been the basis for new personal status laws, but a new form of patriarchy based on the concept of the "family" became the basis of the law, and the state became an effective participant in enforcing personal matters that were not its business before.

Another set of important laws the Ottomans finally accepted, under duress, were nationality laws that continue to be the basis of citizenship discrimination in Jordan today. According to the 1869 Firman Ottoman imperial laws, and following legal practices in Europe at that time, a woman's nationality was defined as "following that of her husband." Children from a mixed-nationality marriage were defined accordingly, that is, following the nationality of the father. In other words, faced with new questions such as nationality, moot issues to the Ottoman world as they were to Europe before the nineteenth century, gender became the focus for defining nationality rather than domicile, allegiance, interest, birth, or any other factor that could be used to allow children to take their mother's nationality. For example, Ottoman *shari'a* court records refer to an individual by his name and address. If he was from out of town, then his town was included in the record. He would not be referred to as a Syrian but as a Salti, Qudsi, Himsi, Halabi, Maghribi, and so on in reference to the location he originated from or where his permanent residence was to be found. Other ways of referring to an individual in Ottoman court records was through his craft or profession: for example, as *'attar* (herbalist), *tabib* (doctor), and so on. The same is to be found in European court records dating into the nineteenth century. An individual was referred to by his address or the particular town he originated from and his particular profession. So we are talking about international transformations that were diffusing from nineteenth-century Europe to other parts of the world with the growth in trade and population movements. The Ottoman Empire had no choice but to follow given international pressures.

Nationality laws confronting Jordanian women today by which a wife can take her Jordanian husband's nationality though a Jordanian woman's husband and children are forbidden it have their roots in these nineteenth-century legal shifts. This situation is not unique to Jordanian women, as it is applicable to other countries that were colonies of the Ottoman Empire. A Jordanian woman married to a foreigner may wish to return home to her family for various reasons, including loss of job by her or her husband, divorce, or widowhood. Even if her Jordanian family could provide her and her children with the only support open to her, she cannot acquire a residency for her children or her husband. The same situation exists in Egypt, Syria, Iraq, and elsewhere. Ironically, the justification used for these laws is the idea that the child belongs to the father according to Islamic *fiqh,* which states that "the child belongs to the marital bed" (*al-wild lil-*

firash), meaning that he belongs to those who conceived him. There is no masculine attribute to the statement, yet it is taken to mean the child belongs to the father without dispute.

In other words, Islam is used as an excuse to justify a situation that had no bearing on Muslims before the creation of the present nation-state system. Although states have existed in the Middle East since early history, the nation-state as a centralized geographical entity with definite borders and citizenship requirements is quite new to the Islamic world and is in fact organically linked to European historical developments and experiences. Roots of the system are usually traced back to Europe's seventeenth-century religious wars and the 1646 Peace of Westphalia, culminating with the end of the Napoleonic Wars and the Peace of Vienna in 1815 when Europe was divided into sovereign nation-states, usually kingdoms. But after World War I, even though one European country after another recognized the nationality rights of women in regards to spouses and children, remnants of European laws had yet to be changed in the Arab world. Needless to say, today nationality laws are closely connected to the basic outlook toward women as having incomplete legal competence. Today, nationality and residency problems have become critical and are expected to grow in importance given the greater movement of populations and intermarriage between groups. For Jordan, marriages between Jordanians and Palestinians and the unwillingness to change nationality laws continue to constitute real hardships when the wife and not the husband is Jordanian.

Another interesting case of the application of modern law has to do with crimes. Here again the intermixing of law among the modern, traditional, and Islamic worlds puts women at a disadvantage. For example, Islamic law divides crimes into three types. First, *hudud* are considered crimes against God whose punishments are clearly defined in the Qur'an. They include adultery (*zina*), defamation, drinking alcohol, forced robbery, immorality or perversion, and apostasy. *Qisas* are crimes involving murder and other forms of physical harm that are due compensation through the payment of *diyya* to the victim or his family. *Ta'zir* involves all other crimes, whose punishment is determined by the judge (for example, cheating and usury). Perpetrators of *ta'zir* and *hudud* crimes usually received corporal punishment. Criminal laws in contemporary Jordan do not apply these categories. Rather, modern Western procedures are applied in Jordan's courts, which came about because of the rationalization and organization of the legal and court systems following European patterns. Crimes and criminal justice were placed under the jurisdiction of national courts, to be investigated by the police and considered prosecutable only if the state's district attorneys bring them to the attention of judges. Here the idea was to introduce a system with greater probity and not leave crimes to be handled by individuals. Because the state was responsible for individual safety, then it was up to the state to ensure security, control crimes, and punish offenders. It would be a system built on correcting the offender rather than punishing him; it would be civilized and not include corporal punishment. The ideals of the Enlightenment with its enthusiasm for reform so as to allow progress are at the heart of the nation-state with its welfare system of controls. And who could doubt that it is better to put a person in prison for a particular period rather than have his hand cut off making him into a state and social dependent unable to feed himself or his family? What is curious, however, is that Jordanian laws kept the payment of *diyya* on its books, a system by which the family of a murder victim is compensated by the killer in the form of a cash payment. Furthermore, in capital crimes, crimes where a victim sustains often serious bodily injury, and crimes involving questions of honor—such as rape—it is the victim's family that determines whether the perpetrator is to be punished. The courts may pass judgment on the offender, but the family could choose to drop their rights in lieu of payment of *diyya* and the legal system has no more recourse against him.

The combination of Western criminal law and procedures together with remnants of tribal law such as *diyya* explains the genesis of Jordan's laws, which mixes the foreign with the traditional, transferring the rights of the victim into rights for his family or guardian. But it is in regards to honor crimes pertaining to women that criminal laws applied in Jordan today, representing a combination of the old and the new, mostly fall short. If the state's primary function is to protect its citizens, why is it that even when a perpetrator of an honor crime is caught and prosecuted, he is able to get away with a very short prison sentence, often a mere two or three months? There are two separate issues here that allow for the continuation of such practices. Here there is a philosophy regarding honor that at heart considers women dispensable once the question touches on clan or tribal honor, whether she was the participant or victim. This philosophy is behind the laws and judges' decisions in honor crimes; it is not the letter of the law that is applied, and therefore deterrence measures or at least principles of reforming the perpetrator, but the diffusion of tribal ideals into national laws. As a judge in Jordan's high court of appeals (*mahkama 'ulya*) explained to me, "We can't simply let the women run free to do what they want," a theme repeated by the people who defeated governmental efforts to abolish Law 340 allowing for reduced sentencing for perpetrators of honor crimes.

The second point has to do with the nature of the modern criminal system that actually enables the judges to act patriarchally rather than requires them to observe strict principles regarding the rule of law. Here we can mention contradictions in the laws and applications of such issues as "intent" and "crimes of passion." If a person kills another under the influence of irrational anger but without previous *intent* to kill, he or she receives a reduced sentence. Therefore, even if honor crimes are treated with force by Jordan's courts and laws allowing for reduced sentencing are changed, the very existence of the principle of crime of passion in Jordanian laws would make it possible for judges to hand down reduced sentences to perpetrators of honor crimes. Moreover, these laws directly discriminate against women, whereas French criminal laws of "intent" and "passion" do not differentiate between a wife who discovers her husband committing adultery or a man discovering his wife doing so; the way the borrowed laws are applied in Jordan means the law privileges men alone. A woman who commits an "honor crime" is not even eligible for reduced sentencing as the males are. Given the seriousness of these crimes and the lack of real action against their perpetrators, it is no wonder that Jordanian girls are afraid to leave their homes or go against a father or younger brother—most killers in honor crimes are juvenile males. How can such a situation help in promoting the participation of Jordanian women in the country's economy?

This discussion on "honor laws," which will be covered in greater detail in chapter 7, illustrates that the combination of laws from different sources categorized in different legal codes (personal status, civil, or criminal) has been an important method followed in legislating modern legal codes in Jordan and other Arab countries. An example of a different nature is presented by banking. Whereas Islam frowns on interest taking, banks in Jordan pay out interest to depositors, which is quite acceptable to the population. It is therefore curious why Jordanian courts continue to accept legal practices such as reduced sentences for honor crimes in which a father or brother kills a daughter or sister because they suspected her of immoral actions, yet Islamic laws regarding interest taking are simply bypassed! The answer lies in the fact that the right of the male to "punish" or prevent the female member of his clan from any act touching on the clan's name is based on tribal common law (*'urf*). Here lies one contradiction in Jordan's laws: modern methods are used liberally in the case of commerce, whereas conservatism is the preferred philosophy in the case of social relations. Consistency in the application of law would be a good start in allowing for gender equality based on principles of human rights.

Tribal Law (*Qada' 'Asha'iri*)

The predominant social structure in premodern Jordan was the tribe formed of numerous related clans. In such societies, the protection of the tribe's animal and agricultural wealth was paramount. Battles against attackers, or attacks against other tribes for defensive or raiding purposes, were part of daily existence. Hence, it is not surprising to find that certain characteristics were expected from members of a tribe, particularly chivalry, courage, generosity, strength of character, physical strength, endurance, agility, loyalty, and functionality. Tribal societies were quite patriarchal to a large extent because of man's primary function as protector. Yet, there was also a sense of equality among members of the tribe whose fate was dependent on one another, and this equality was translated into gender relations. Thus, most of the work was divided by the two sexes who contributed their share by herding the tribe's camels, sheep, and goats; through the upkeep of dwellings made of tents or other materials; or in agriculture, if this work was part of the activity of the particular tribe. Recreation included storytelling and poetry recitation recounting the great days of the tribe and its famous individual members in the past and present.[16] Living closely together and being highly dependent on each other meant greater tribal unity cemented by possessive pride in tribal honor, the tribal name, and an intertribal clan hierarchy built on loyalty and respect. At the same time, because of this great dependency on one another and the close proximity in which tribesmen lived, it was clearly impossible to separate the sexes, even though chastity and purity of blood were critical for tribal loyalty, without which people could not survive in a desert environment. Moral discourses that made any sort of tribal misconduct punishable by extreme measures, death in the case of adultery, allowed for "legal" mixing. They also allowed for a tribal justice system that handled offenses against the tribe's honor whose approach was to make such crimes ultimately the responsibility of the perpetrator's clansmen—father, brothers, male cousins—referred to as the *akhmas* (fifths) in reference to the degree of consanguinity between the perpetrator and the ones who would be ultimately held responsible for the crime committed.

Tribal honor today has been placed almost exclusively on the shoulders of women. At one time, stealing, discourtesy, or even gossip about another clan or clan member was considered an offense against the tribe requiring immediate and usually violent action to alleviate the dishonor. With the changes faced by tribes during the modern period, their sedentary nature and integration within nation-states, issues of honor became more narrowly family oriented and pinned on the actions or potential actions of its female membership rather than its males. A male's dishonorable act—for example, rape or murder—can be negotiated with the victim's clan and a *diyya* paid. Here we see both the remnants of tribalism and at the same time tribal structures in retreat. The inordinate impact of tribalism when compared to the reduced numbers of Jordanians who continue to live within tribal structures is because of the important role that tribes have played in the Jordanian army and in supporting the hegemonic order, making tribalism a powerful element in the fabric of Jordanian sociopolitical alliances.

Lingering tribal traditions constitute a formidable part of *'urf,* which molds the whole legal system and philosophy behind decision making in court. Here we can point to practices that go all the way back to the early Islamic period and even pre-Islamic discourses and behavior. Whereas some scholars have emphasized the idea that pre-Islamic society was less patriarchal and allowed for greater empowerment of women and for sexual mixing, in fact sexual "purity" and fidelity were required and expected of women. Ensuring descent was essential for clan solidarity, hence the requirement that women be chaste before and after marriage. *'Uthri* (platonic) love relationships are a perfect example of the expected pure nature of love among pre-Islamic Arabs. In poetry, a man addresses his words of love to a woman whom he places on a pedestal and whose praises invariably revolve around her unavailability to him as a sexual partner. In fact, that very unavailability becomes the reason for his unrequited love and admiration. A famous poem sung by Hakam al-Wadi about his neighbor on her wedding night tells of his *'uthri* love for her, a love mingled with pride for the long night she spent with her new husband, a night from which she came out having proved that she was the "noblest of her race." [17] Besides, open mingling between the sexes was witnessed by the whole tribe, and the woman's father or husband was aware of what was taking place. The story of Buthaynah's association with Jamil is representative. Not only were her husband and brother worried that there was more to their friendship than what was morally acceptable, Jamil himself began to have his doubts, so he put her to the test. "'Would you like to do as men and women do for the quenching of love's thirst and the extinguishing of passion's fire?' 'No,' said she. 'Why?' he asked. 'Because,' she replied, 'true love is spoiled when one has sexual intercourse.' Then Jamil produced a sword which he had hidden under his garment, saying, 'Had you granted the favor I asked, I would have plunged this into you.' " [18] Thus, a woman was admired for her strength of character and physical beauty, but was even more desirable for being untouched, chaste (*'afifa*), and hard to get (*"muhasana, sa'bat al-manal"*).[19]

Women taken into captivity by raiding tribes exemplified the importance of loyalty among tribesmen who were often raiding or going to war. Captured men were usually ransomed or put to death, but the women, if not ransomed, were usually made into the slaves of their captors, who often married them. Yet, no matter how long the woman stayed with her captor, her loyalty remained with her tribe, and if the situation presented itself for her return to her tribe, she was expected to take it, however unwillingly. Loyalty to the tribe was equated with the tribe's honor and the honor of each of its members. A woman was often glorified for committing suicide rather than succumbing to her captor, no matter how notable the latter may have been.[20] A famous story involves a woman named Um Salama from the Kinana tribe who married her captor, 'Urwa b. al-Warda, and lived with him for eleven happy years during which she bore him many children. When the chance presented itself, she tricked him into returning her to her own tribe, even though leaving him and their children broke her heart.[21] The first case of girl infanticide (*wa'd al-banat*) is said to have been undertaken by a leader of the Kinda tribe whose daughter refused to leave her captor husband and return to her former husband. Her father was enraged; he fought, defeated, and killed her captor, then killed her. Later, he committed female infanticide by burying the ten female children subsequently born to him.[22]

Because loyalty to tribe was paramount to both men and women, marriage was contracted in accordance to the larger needs of the tribe, which could entail marrying a cousin or discouraging cousin marriage, depending on the need to form alliances with other tribes. Interestingly, the tradition of cousin marriage was quite widespread, even though there was awareness of the possible ill-effects from inbreeding: "I did not marry my paternal cousin who is my beloved, for fear of being disgraced by my progeny," sung a poet.[23] One reason for cousin marriage is that tribal honor necessitated that members marry only their equals. Intertribal power relations based on tribal alliances made it a necessity. Therefore, marriage could not be left to the feelings of either the man or the woman, although such marriages did take place. Arab marriages, before and after Islam, were based on parity in religion, ethnicity, nobility, and freedom. 'Antar b. Shadad's love for his cousin 'Abla of the tribe of 'Abs exemplifies this *kafa'a* in the Arab cumulative mythology. 'Antar is always seen as the ideal knight, taking on whole armies and defeating them single-handedly. His loyalty, pride, and valor are legendary. But because he was a slave born of an African mother, his uncle refused him the hand of his daughter *'Abla*.[24] *'Abla* herself saw nothing wrong with *'Antar*, but her father's objection added to the disapproval of 'Antar's father— leader of the tribe—because of the lack of social equity between them was a formidable obstruction to the marriage. It did not mean that a girl's opinion regarding her marriage was not taken into consideration by Arab tribes—far from it.[25] When the girl was an adult (*rashida*), her opinion was crucial in marriage decisions. For example, given al-Khansa's attributes as a wise intellectual and healer, her refusal of a suitor was honored, even though he was considered eminently suitable by her father.[26] Majority and personal ability continued to form the basis of traditions in regards to gender relations; at the same time, *kafa'a,* based on tribal requirements of giving daughters only to men who were their equals, was integrated into Islamic laws and is the basis today of the Jordanian law allowing a father to annul his daughter's marriage if she marries a man the father does not consider to be her social equal.

Tribal laws are a recognized part of Jordanian laws. But just as in the case of *shari'a* law, tribal law is applied selectively and according to modern *'urf* much more than according to actual tribal practices. It should be noted that tribal laws constitute a major part of laws in the Arab world, even though this fact is not readily recognized. The laws are sometimes overt, but most of the time they are integrated in the selectivity of actual laws included in personal status laws. Selectivity of laws has worked toward greater patriarchy perhaps because moral concerns in a tribal context where a woman is between her people and clan, and hence under their direct protection and support, are very different from an urban context where women could be in daily contact with strangers. Furthermore, in the rural context certain freedoms and functions that women enjoyed were curtailed under more male-dominated systems. Here, important examples illustrate how integrated a woman was within her clan or tribe and how her individual actions enhanced or hurt the clan. For example, according to a tradition that at one time existed among Bedouin tribes in *diyya* settlements involving killing—intentional or accidental—a killer's sister or daughter, or another woman closely associated to the clan, would be sent to a close male relative of the victim to marry him and serve him until she bore him a son to replace the member of the clan who was killed. She then left her son and returned to her tribe, having fulfilled her duty. She could remain with him if she wanted. In other words, a woman was expected to be part of fulfilling the obligation of her tribe toward a victim of one of its members.

It is perhaps in the philosophy and traditions behind tribal law that we see the hegemonic power of tribalism even with the changes in the legal and court systems. "[I]n Bedouin society the supreme authority is represented by the tribal chiefs and judges, and that compulsion derives from the consent of individual members of this society to abide by the penalties imposed by customary law in the case of deviation from these laws or from the principles of fairness." [27] This statement means that members of a clan are bound by the decisions of the clan's elders, regardless of whether it is legally sanctioned by the government. In other words, the power of tribal law continues within social and cultural hegemony, and unless the state takes very effective action to enforce its laws, the power of tribal law, beyond the state's laws, will remain a living fact in Jordan. This consequence is problematic because of the nature of the hegemonic order in Jordan and the historical alliance between the state and its tribal population. As Laurie Brand points out:

> The role of the military in the evolution of the Jordanian state takes on additional importance if one considers the patterns of armed forces' recruitment. The basis for the earliest forces established by the British were the powerful Bedouin tribes of the southern part of the country. Such recruitment filled the ranks of the military and security apparatus and provided a key means by which these tribes were incorporated into the state. This cooptation, or establishment of patron-client ties between the tribes and the leadership, was a central element in building a legitimacy formula for [King] 'Abdullah [I].[28]

Tribal laws and courts were a reality in Jordan until May 1976. Even after their termination, certain aspects of these laws were codified into law for Jordan as a whole. For example, *diyya* traditions were codified into law in 1989. These laws itemized the crimes—assumed to be unintentional crimes—that could be compensated by the payment of *diyya* by the perpetrator to the victim or his or her family. The amount to be paid for each specific crime was also stated. For example, the *diyya* for unintentional death was established at ten thousand Jordanian dinars in 1989. The law also took into consideration other forms of homicide not itemized and added an extra one-third of the *diyya* for death. Here, the method in establishing the *diyya* for various crimes closely followed *shari'a* practices, determining estimates for each crime at a certain percentage of the full *diyya* for death. For example, the *diyya* for violence leading to miscarrying a fetus was one-tenth of the *diyya* for loss of life.[29]

More important, the tribal outlook toward gender continued to form the basic philosophy toward gender in Jordanian society and is therefore a basic part of *'urf* practices. Tribal laws therefore constitute an important basis for the way judges rule in Jordanian courts. That there is a constant need for a *waliyy* to directly or indirectly approve the marriage of his adult daughter is based on the assumption that a daughter belongs to her people and carries family honor with her. The same logic underlies reduced sentences for honor crimes allowed by court judges, even though most of the victims are quite innocent of the "crimes" for which they were killed. Allowing reduced sentencing only encourages others to commit honor crimes, and judges give credibility to the act by legitimating it. The same logic applies to a husband's absolute power over his wife, her movements, and her work. Without doubt, the continued influence of tribal laws on Jordanian society and its legal system is at the heart of discrimination against women. As with *shari'a* law, tribal law seems to be focused today on the control of women and family issues, and it is in this form that it has become an integral part of the legal system in Jordan. Whereas tribal law originally applied to all aspects of a tribe's life, including handling brigandage, theft, kidnapping, control of tribal land, and so on, today national laws and courts have taken over authority of these diverse issues, and it is in regards to issues pertaining in particular to women and to committing murder that tribal laws have in fact become the basis of the law in Jordan. As long as the legal system and its judges continue to view the individual as belonging to his larger clan and give the clan the right to "handle" its women, we cannot talk about the rule of law because law is ultimately intended to protect the weak and not to ensure that the weak is a victim of the system handed over to those people who intend him or her harm while the perpetrator of a crime is exonerated through the payment of compensation.

'Urf or Traditional Law

The Jordanian Civil Code is explicit about the importance of traditional law and traditional usage in Jordan's legal system. For example, Article 173ii, dealing with contractual consent, states: "Silence means granting permission if it [said silence] is considered consent according to *'urf.*" This article is particularly important for women because their vocal consent can be bypassed in important transactions such as contracting a marriage or selling property. *'Urf* can also bind the actions of a court judge, as he is expected to apply tradition as part of his decision making. Article 177 of the civil code details: "In contracts which are open to *faskh* [annulment] . . . if [the parties to the contract] do not agree on a specific period, the judge is permitted to decide it according to *'urf.*" The civil code adds another level to traditional law based on the "nature of the *tasaruf* [right to administer or to dispose of]." Article 202ii states: "[T]he contract does not limit the contractor's responsibility to what it states, but it also entails what is determined according to the law, *'urf* and the nature of the transaction [*tabi'at al-tasarruf*]."

Although *'urf* is considered to be local traditions appearing mostly in practice and not in a written form, social practices and norms are only one type of *'urf.* Therefore, we really should be talking about *a'raf* (plural form of *"'urf"*; traditional laws) rather than *'urf.* For example, there are certain expectations of the government that are not written in law but are considered "Islamic" because they have always been expected of rulers. Here we can include the building and upkeep of mosques. It is not written in the law that doing so is a government's duty, but it is one of the most important expectations of the public. It is also expected that rich people should somehow benefit the communities in which they live. This assistance used to take place in the shape of *awqaf khayriyya* through which schools, water fountains (*sabils*), *sufi* hospices (*zawiya*), hospitals (*maristans*), and mosques were built and supported. At one time, it was also assumed that villages, towns, and town quarters would be responsible for their own cleanliness, payment of taxes, and running their internal affairs. With the introduction of government centralization, *'urf* changed, and it is the central or municipal government that is now considered to have the responsibility for all these tasks. Because *awqaf* property, donations to mosques and *zakat* (charity), is collected by the Ministry of *Awqaf* today to be spent on its projects throughout the country as well as to pay the salaries of its employees, one result has been the relatively unclean environment in many Muslim cities today whose inhabitants no longer feel responsible for undertaking the cleaning as before. Another important form of *'urf* is *fiqh*. Even though *fiqh* is a part of Islamic law, because of the role played by *fuqaha'* and *muftis* and the implications that the writings of theologians and *fatawi* have over the general public, I am including *fiqh* and *fatawi* under the rubric of traditional law. One reason is to differentiate among what theologians say and what *qadis* practice in courts. A cautionary point is perhaps necessary about *fatawi*. Scholars have tended to equate *fatawis* with actual social practices, which is not the case. They have also tended to consider *fatawi* as paralleling settlement of disputes by *qadis* in court. *Qadis* do take findings of *muftis* into consideration and often refer to a particular *fatwa* to support their decision, but a *qadi* is not bound by what the *mufti* determines.

One of the ways by which *fiqh* is perpetuated and renewed as *'urf* is through republication. Yearly, large numbers of books of *fiqh* are published throughout the Islamic world. The growth of Islamic revivalism brought about a virtual avalanche in *fiqh*-collection republication. Some are subsidized by governments with particular Islamic hegemonic intentions in mind, others by Islamic groups of various types, and still others are for profit purposes by publishing houses that can see the demand and move to fulfill it. Books of *fiqh* are sold at all sorts of prices depending on the subsidies involved and on the quality of the publication. Some are abbreviated and present only the ideological parts of interest to the subsidizer or publisher. Others are published in complete form and are usually hardback and may be gilded. In fact, the actual selections of *fuqaha'* can tell us much about the press, group, or country responsible. The appearance of particular subjects or titles is itself an indication of the particular movement behind the publication. For example, the appearance of a profusion of books about the prophet Muhammad's family and in particular his cousin 'Ali b. Abi-Talib; Ali's sons and wife, Fatima; as well as Shi'i *fuqaha'* with Persian names of little significance to Sunni theology is an indication of Iranian Shiʻi influences. The same can be said about the appearance of books by Ibn al-Taymiyya and other Salafi writers, an indication of active Salafism. When it comes to anti-gender-equality conservative elements, we find a profusion of literature on Islamic veiling rules, the right of a husband to marry four wives, or emphasis on the Prophet as a polygamist.[30] Other titles emphasize the role of women in the family and home, the evils of the workplace, and the duties of a wife toward her husband, which includes everything from feeding him, obeying him unquestioningly, and sexual rights of the husband. Other books offer advice to couples who want to live the Islamic life and so on. The point is that they all offer some form of *fiqh* and *fatwa* and support their arguments from old *fiqh* works by famous medieval *fuqaha'*. The significance here is that people take what is published under the banner or symbol of what is Islamic to be what God requires, as the moral way of life by which they can enter paradise. In other words, new ideas of confinement are spread through gender discourses using religious arguments.

One of the reasons for the success of such discourses is the fact that people look at *muftis* for answers to their daily questions, that is, for guidance regarding matters pertaining to their everyday lives. It is therefore part of the traditions in Islamic societies to refer questions to an *imam* (religious leader) or a *faqih*. It is similar to people asking their local priest what to do in regards to personal problems and decisions about family in Christian communities. The difference is that a Muslim cleric does not have any power to absolve sin, as is the belief in Catholicism. The fact that the state recognizes the Muslim clerics as the "keepers" of Islamic laws pertaining to gender and family through the division of courts into what is "religious" and what is "civic" or national has emphasized further the power of the moral discourse and the prestige of the *fatawi* delivered daily in answer to questions from the general public. It was the tradition in Islam; in fact, one of the most important ways of learning about the moral discourse in earlier Islamic centuries is to read the questions addressed to *muftis* and *fuqaha'* and their responses. Today, book collections with these *fatawi* are published all over the Islamic world and are helping propagate and universalize ideas that in many cases are pseudo-Islam at best.

Given the power of the religious discourse, it is surprising that the state has not introduced moral discourses to counteract the conservative elements that refuse to budge on gender issues. Although governments in the Islamic world use mosques and the pulpit to voice their opinions regarding political and economic matters, there is a clear reluctance to touch on cultural matters that are left to conservative elements, perhaps as a measure of balance and hegemony building. With the power in the state's hands in the form of an army of *ʻulama'* who are employees of the state working directly under the auspices of the Ministry of Awqaf, and who have a virtual captive and believing audience at the minimum every Friday during communal prayers, it is rather strange that their media power is not used to introduce a different outlook toward such matters as gender equality, honor crimes, or women's work. If knowledge is power, then the best medium to get ideas across must be utilized to disseminate this knowledge. Why is the state reluctant to use the most important method to disseminate ideas and correct presumptions that is readily available to it if in fact the state is interested in seeing a greater role for women in the economy and politics of Jordan? As old *a'raf* were set up, so could new ones be, and what better way than through a religious discourse that is still the most acceptable to Jordanian society?

International Laws

Jordan is signatory to various agreements at the international level with direct relevance to women. Here the most important is the "Convention for the Elimination of Discrimination Against Women," ratified with reservations by Jordan at the beginning of July 1992. This agreement involves basic human rights and demands that such rights be equally enjoyed by both men and women. The agreement stresses in particular fundamental economic, political, and social equality, and demands that women be given equal opportunity in all these areas. To ensure that such equal rights became fact, the convention called upon its signatories to create the legal and executive instruments by which equal rights would become a reality and not mere rhetoric.

The reservations that Jordan made as part of its signing tell us a great deal about the outlook toward women and legal rights in Jordan. Although there was total acceptance of equal job opportunity and other declarations regarding women and work, the reservations made by Jordan emphasize the patriarchal character of Jordanian laws and illustrate how women, their work, and their freedom of choice are controlled by other aspects of the law. Interestingly, the *shari'a* is used as the reason for the reservations. The main one involves Article 9ii concerning nationality rights, which demand that children of mothers receive the nationality of the mother as they do the nationality of the father. Article 9 of the convention was meant to address the severe global problems experienced by women and children who face dislocation and homelessness because of nationality laws. Jordan's laws do not grant a woman's children Jordanian nationality or even residency unless the father is also a Jordanian. I was told by one feminist leader in Jordan that she was granted residency for her Philippine domestic servant but was denied a residence permit for her unmarried daughter whose deceased father was a Palestinian American. Jordan also had reservations about the wording in Article 16i (subsections c, d, and g) that called for equality between men and women regarding contracting marriage, rights during marriage, and rights and responsibilities in divorce. Equal rights would have impeached the prerogative of the husband to divorce at will and the control of a wife's ability to get out of a marriage she no longer wished to remain in. It would also mean that men could no longer call their wives to obedience (*ta'a*), and forbid them from taking a job as a condition of being married. Jordan did commit itself to changing its laws to fit with the requirements of the convention, but it has yet to happen, and given the reservations made, it probably will not be fully implemented. Still, the newly formed Royal Committee on Human Rights headed by the highly respected lawyer Ahmad 'Ubaidat, a previous prime minister of Jordan, has been studying the issues and has put forth serious considerations, particularly directed toward changing laws pertaining to women, work, and the family. These considerations—presented to Jordan's government as this book goes to press—if applied in Jordan, would have important repercussions throughout the Islamic world and would place Jordan in the lead in regards to women's human rights.

Even though personal status laws are said to be based on the Islamic *shari'a*, which makes it almost impossible to question these laws or ask for their amendment, the realities are different, as can be seen from the above discussion on the sources of law in Jordan. The basics of gender laws are *shari'a* laws, but *shari'a* was applied selectively and subjected to a historical process during which different types of laws and the philosophy behind them diffused to create the laws practiced in Jordan and applied in Jordanian courts today. If there is any hope of changing these laws, the legal codes in practice today need to be deconstructed before alternatives can be suggested.

By alternatives I mean, first of all, legal consistency. One philosophy and one approach to law should underlie all Jordan's codes and courts. When it comes to personal status laws, there is a strong need to turn to Jordan's own legal traditions as represented in premodern *shari'a* courts. Two points need to be emphasized: (1) *shari'a* legal practices were different then from *shari'a* practices today, and (2) *shari'a* is flexible, fitting with different times. Once these facts are established, then it will be made clear that the *shari'a* codes in practice today are based more on the Ottoman Family Code and should therefore not be seen as a permanent and unquestionable *shari'a* in the sense of being God's words that cannot be questioned. This point should give women's groups fighting for this issue an edge in several ways. First, the job of studying the past is a big one and needs great efforts. Deconstructing laws is not a simple matter but a necessary one if they are to be challenged. This job is something that Jordanian women, highly intellectual and aggressive lawyers, are more than capable of performing given guidance, assistance, and financial help. This study tries to show them some of the ways it can be done, but it is by no means comprehensive. It will be up to women's groups or individual women. The method is complicated and time consuming but should be productive. Second, the process of studying the question of changing law from this different perspective should outline new lines of action for activists and women's groups. Although lobbying would be extremely important here, there has to be a media campaign to inform people of the realities of the laws and the past. It is unfortunate that the archives remain so inaccessible, because choosing particular court cases and presenting them to the public would be the best way to influence society as a whole and actually change *'urf.* The reading material available today to the public is mostly in the form of Islamic moral literature that readers take to be the actual truth of life under Islam, at least the idealized picture of that life. References to history in the media are also based on this moral discourse, a discourse that was written by men in a different context and as a form of moral preaching. Third, contradictions between one legal code and another need to become a focus of women activists— and not only the codes themselves but also the philosophies behind them. For example, although personal status laws emphasize the good of society and the family, the civil and criminal codes take the rights of the individual into consideration. Yet, honor crimes deny individual rights. This fact works against women because their human rights, which are the philosophical basis of "individualism," are not taken into consideration in personal status laws. This dual philosophy is at the heart of situations in which a woman could aspire to be a prime minister or a court judge yet could face being declared *nashaz* (disobedient) if she refuses to accept her husband's demands that she stop working. Civil laws encourage property, work, and economic independence, whereas personal status laws encourage a woman's dependence on a male relative and economic peripheralization.

3

Women's History and Work

THIS chapter begins with the presumption that nothing in Islam forbids women from working or from owning property, from investing in income-producing undertakings, or from administering a business. Islamic principles laid down by the Qur'an support this contention. For example, the Qur'an admonishes that women have a right to a share of what they earn as much as men have a right to a share of what they earn. Furthermore, the Qur'an calls upon the Prophet to "let-go" of wives who want to live a life of idleness (Qur'an 33:28), and guarantees a woman's inheritance and her right to own property. The purpose of this chapter is to put "women and work" within a historical perspective. It begins with women in early Islamic history and discusses issues pertaining to seclusion, "going out" of the marital home, gender mixing, and women's participation in their communities' activities. Because the early Islamic period is considered by Muslims to be a founding and idyllic period of Islamic history, it is important to understand its gender practices. The chapter will then present empirical data from *shari'a* court records dating from before the modernization of courts and law in the areas of Transjordan and Palestine, as well as other areas of the territories that once constituted the Ottoman Empire, dating from the medieval period into the twentieth century. Records from al-Salt, Irbid, Amman, Nablus, and Jerusalem will be used together with archival records of important centers from other parts of the Ottoman Empire to give a picture of how women actually lived and the types of work they performed before the modernization of law. Because the nineteenth and twentieth centuries were a period of deep structural change for Jordan, it will be important to show conditions before the introduction of modern capitalism, nation-state systems, colonialism, and new class structures.

The purpose of the chapter is to demonstrate that the work of women is nothing new for Islamic societies, that in fact their participation was taken for granted, and to appreciate the role and contribution that women played in the economy. Reading early books of *fiqh* supports this contention; *fuqaha'* did not debate women's participation in the economy—rather, the questions they discussed involved what obedience to a husband meant, how far that obedience extended, and what were a husband's responsibilities toward his wife when she did not obey him. Did she lose her *nafaqa*? *Nafaqa* was of primary concern to the *fuqaha'* who looked at the husband's financial support as being in return for the wife's fulfillment of her duties. What these duties were, however, was another matter. Early Islamic marriage contracts illustrate the negotiability of marriage between husband and wife and how marital relations following the contract were decided at the time of the marriage; it included what she expected of him and what he expected of her (Islamic marriage contracts will be discussed in chapter 6). *Fuqaha'* were mainly concerned with what constituted a good wife. "A woman is a shepherd in her husband's home" (*"al-mar'a ra'iyya fi bayt zawjiha"*) and "your husband has a right over you" (*"li-zawjig 'alayki haqq"*) are widely accepted metaphors among *fuqaha'* regarding marital relations. They are reciprocated by similar words defining the husband's responsibilities toward his wife.[1] But disobedience leading to denial of *nafaqa* was mostly defined as a wife's refusal to live with her husband or have sex with him, or in regard to other home issues. There did not seem to be any particular concern regarding her pursuit of a craft or investing her wealth in some business venture, nor was there a concept that her place was in the home first. These issues become quite important in modern debates on women, the role of women, and how Islam would interpret women's work, which makes sense as it was bound to be an issue with the mobilization of women into government and business employment, a fact that did not exist before the modern period.

It is true that *fiqh* discusses *ihtibas* on a wife's part in return for her husband's *nafaqa*, but the word *"ihtibas"* had a different meaning than it does today: a husband's right to "lock up" his wife. Rather, the legal *'urf* of the word *"ihtibas"* as used by *fuqaha'* concerned a husband's exclusive sexual rights to his wife. In other words, she kept herself sexually for him and him alone. Obedience was in return for *nafaqa,* and the nature of the marital relationship was set in the marriage contract. This subject will be discussed in chapter 6, but it is important to make clear at this point that neither the *shari'a* nor *shari'a* courts found anything wrong with women working. Neither did *fiqh,* for that matter; the concerns of *fuqaha'* focused on the importance of protecting women and harmony between husband and wife.

Women in Islamic *Turath*

Islamic history tells us that the prophet Muhammad's first wife, Khadija bint Khuwaylid, was at one time his employer, "known for her exceptional morals, characterized by decisiveness, wisdom, and chastity; her people nicknamed her 'the Pure' (*al-tahira*). She was a woman of means who hired men to undertake trade for her, and her business was active and lucrative." 'Aisha, daughter of Abu Bakr, was a known Islamic scholar whose abilities as a narrator of hadith were recognized, and acceptance of her *fatawi* surpassed most of the Prophet's male companions. The caliphs Abu Bakr and 'Umar often asked her opinion about important issues.[2] Zaynab b. Jahsh was skilled with handicrafts and fashioned leather items and sold them. In his interpretation of Qur'an *aya* (verse) 33:28, Yusuf 'Ali highlighted the role of the prophet Muhammad's wives as ideal examples for Muslim women to emulate. That example was one not of idleness but of service to their community.

> 'A'isha, daughter of Abu Bakr, was clever and learned, and in hadith she was an important authority on the life of the Prophet. Zaynab, daughter of Khusayman, was especially devoted to the poor; she was called the "Mother of the Poor." The other Zaynab, daughter of Jahsh, also worked for the poor, for whom she provided from the proceeds of her manual work. . . . All the [Prophet's] Consorts . . . had to work and assist as Mothers of the Ummah. Theirs were not idle lives, like those of Odalisques, either for their own pleasure or the pleasure of their husband. . . . [Qur'an Surah] 33:28 tells that they had no place in the sacred Household if they merely wished for ease or worldly glitter. If such were the case, they could be divorced and amply provided for.[3]

Islamic history paints a vivid picture of the contributions of early generations of Muslim women who fought beside Muslim troops, nursed and treated the wounded during the Islamic wars of expansion, and took over the reigns of power when necessary, and whose oaths of allegiance were a normal part of the community's hegemonic structure. Islamic *turath* (traditions, heritage, myths) is full of its heroes and heroines; however, only a few heroines are known by name today. Perhaps because of ignorance of the facts, the media in the Islamic world do not emphasize the stories of these women. When women are featured in story, film, television, or schoolbooks, it is the chastity, sacrifices, or religiousness of these women that is emphasized rather than their significant intellectual, economic, and political contributions. Here the examples are many. Al-Khansa' has been made famous for her recitation of poetry and her religious stand on Islamic principles. But al-Khansa' was well known to her community for her veterinary skills and was sought as a healer of horses and camels. It is said that a potential suitor was attracted to al-Khansa' after seeing her treat a camel for dermatitis and noted her skills as a healer.[4] In other words, not only were women skilled and active, but their abilities were also recognized and admired. The historical discourse that presents a one-dimensional picture of women's roles and contributions in the past and present badly needs correction.

Stories of heroism in war and generosity in early Islam are today reserved for the male companions of the Prophet. Although Jordanian schools teach pre- and early-Islamic Arabic poetry, the accomplishments of tribes and clans as represented by their men are selected for reading and recitation. Yet women went to war during the *Jahiliyya* and early Islam, which is depicted in the poetry of the period as illustrated by the ideals of feminine beauty about which pre-Islamic and early Muslim Arab poets sang. Interestingly, such ideals reflected the same tribal standards expected of the ideal tribal "man." The "looks" of the woman described seemed to be less important than her personal traits, which were judged on ideals of morality, physical strength, courage, and generosity. 'Amru b. Kulthum's description of his beloved is representative: "There she is tilting with the knights, her face glowing with determination, riding her horse, taming the [men] with her charismatic presence, and intoxicating their souls with her beauty and [their] love."[5]

Another example is that of Al-Sulayk b. al-Sulka who tells of a day when his enemies attacked him, intending to kill him. He asked refuge from his neighbor Fukayka who brandished her sword and fought to protect him.[6] Here we see beauty admired in a strong woman of courage who provides help and support. She is strong, chivalrous (*muruwa*), and practical yet feminine.

Whereas women in early Islam generally stood back during battle and acted as adjuncts and assistants, bringing water to warriors and helping remove the wounded from the battlefields and then nursing them—traditions shared by nomadic women all over the world—Muslim women also took up arms when forced to do so. An early example is that of Safiyya bint 'Abd al-Muttalib who witnessed the Battle of Badr (624) and was wounded at Uhud (625) where she shielded the prophet Muhammad by placing herself between him and the attacking Meccans and intercepted a blow meant for him. She is also known to have attacked and killed a male spy who had infiltrated a stronghold in which the wives of the Prophet and his companions were shielded during the Battle of al-Khandaq.[7] Another example is that of Nusayba bint Ka'b al-Ansariyya, a famous companion of the Prophet who acted as a missionary for Islam and who followed the Muslim troops since the very early *ghazwas* (raids) launched by the

Muhajirun (early converts to Islam who went on Hijra from Mecca to Medina with the Prophet) when they were still fighting for their very existence against the power of the Meccan Quraysh (enemies of early Islam). As a recognized leader of her community, she gave her *bay'a* (oath of allegiance) to the Prophet at 'Aqaba, and saw battle at Badr and during the Ridda Wars.[8] Rendering the *bay'a* by women was an expected tradition in Arabia and exemplified the political power they enjoyed in early Islam.

Fighting to protect one's community was not confined to early Islam as an extension of early Islamic traditions stemming from pre-Islamic tribal Arabian traditions; the same phenomenon repeated itself in urban communities under siege by invaders. A good example is the 1798 scene recorded by 'Abd al-Rahman al-Jabarti of the French invasion of Alexandria against a brave but futile effort of its population armed with rifles against Napoléon's cannons and troops. After the battle was over, the bodies of women and men were found on the town's rooftops still clutching rifles with which they had shot at the French troops. The modern examples of Jamila Buhrid, Jamila Bubasha, and the other women *fi-da'iyyin* (freedom fighters) who fought for Algerian independence against French occupation make one pause to reflect on women's participation in Arab history. The same must be said about Palestinian women of the Intifadah and the sacrifices they continue to make in their refusal to surrender to Israeli occupation, and their will to make the world take note of their struggle for human dignity and national rights.

Fatma Mernissi's work *The Forgotten Queens of Islam* reminds us of women who ruled in their actual right, minted their own coins, and were recognized as leaders of their people. Her study is a history of the important political role played by women, particularly at times when there was a vacuum in leadership that left their societies vulnerable to outside invasion and internal chaos. The great Muslim medieval traveler Ibn Battuta witnessed the power of women in various parts of the Islamic world. "Among the Turks and the Tatars," wrote Ibn Battuta, "their wives enjoy a very high position; indeed, when they issue an order they say in it 'By command of the Sultan and the Khātūns.' Each *khatun* possesses several towns and districts and vast revenues, and when she travels with the sultan she has her own separate camp."[9] The power of women in the harems of sultans has been studied extensively, but the usual approach has been to repeat the myth of Oriental despotism, this time in the form of a power-hungry woman standing behind the throne.[10] Leslie Peirce has redrawn this picture of life in court, dismissed the Oriental despot model, and shown that in actuality power was diffused rather than centralized in the Ottoman court. Whereas Peirce's significant work on the Ottoman imperial harem called for a rereading of the harem as an institution, it also showed the actual political power played by women not "behind the throne influence" as presented by the normative picture, but as direct holders of power and participants in decision making. Another important study is Farhad Daftary's article on Sayyida Ilurra who ruled over Yemen as representative of the Fatimid Caliphate in Egypt during the eleventh and twelfth centuries.[11] There was also Sultana Radiyya who ruled the Sultanate of Delhi in place of her father during the thirteenth century and was finally overthrown by princes who resented her power.[12] The same fate was met by Shajar al-Durr who hid news of her Ayyubid husband's death to allow his son to return and lead Egypt's mamluk troops against the Crusaders. Marrying Aybak, the leader of the mamluks, allowed Shajar to rule until a plot did away with her. Mamluk houses became the power in Egypt and greater Syria afterward and were from then on consolidated through the marriage of the widow of the deceased chief mamluk to his military heir who could succeed only if his predecessor's widow chose him and married him. The power held by women heads of mamluk households was therefore quite impressive, which is evidenced by the wealth they controlled, much of which they bequeathed as *waqfs* benefiting people from Damascus to Jerusalem to Cairo.[13]

The best-studied contributions by elite women concern the wives of sultans, mamluks, and *amirs* (princes). Here the activities were directed mainly toward providing services and institutions of importance to Islamic societies. Using their wealth, elite women spent outright on projects benefiting their communities, the contribution often being in the form of a *waqf.* The early Islamic period saw women contributing their money to help the poor, to arm Islamic warriors in their fight against Quraysh, and to buy and free slaves. Over time, they were called upon by the *umma* (Islamic nation) to donate their wealth and jewelry whenever there was a need, such as during times of war, national causes, earthquakes, or other disasters. The first such recorded case happened at the time of the Prophet when women attending Friday prayers in the mosque in Medina were asked to donate their jewelry and Bilal, the first man to call to prayers in Islamic history, was said to have gone around and collected these donations.[14] Modern elite women continue to carry on their share of responsibility in providing services, institutional assistance, and feminist activism.

Islamic architectural *turath* owes much to the building activity and endowments left by the Muslim elite. Structures such as mosques, schools, *sabils,* water fountains, hospitals, and beautiful tombs and mausoleums commemorating beloved ones and important rulers all figure in this rich Islamic heritage that extends from central Asia all the way to Morocco and the Atlantic Ocean. Women contributed their share of these endowments and building activity, and their accomplishments in these areas are rather stunning if relatively unknown and therefore continue to be unrecognized, even though scholars have written about them. The extent of this building activity, according to Gavin Hambly, "contradict[s] the notion of the invisibility of women with indubitable evidence that women were lavish patrons of architecture, and therefore agents in the spatial organization of urban centers." Hambly's edited volume, *Women in the Medieval Islamic World,* presents a number of important articles challenging the persistent view of women's "invisibility" in the history of the Islamic world. Covering various areas of the Muslim world—from India, Syria, and Anatolia to Afghanistan and Egypt—the volume details the many activities in which women were involved, particularly in "building construction," which included palaces, gardens, mosques, and mausoleums. Building patterns of mausoleums are especially interesting, for as Hambly points out, mausoleums were built by women to entomb and commemorate members of their families. At the same time, mausoleums were built in "commemoration of individual women . . . [who] were sufficiently esteemed to warrant commemoration after their deaths." Some of the examples he uses include a mausoleum built by Shah Janan for her niece in Agra and a tomb tower built for Muhammad Jahan Pahlavan by his mother, wife of the Seljukid sultan Tughril b. Muhammad in Narchivan. Describing the extent of women's building contributions in the Safavid and Mughal Empires, Stephen P. Blake makes the following comment that speaks to the role played by elite women builders in various parts of the Islamic world: "The kind, size, and location of the buildings the women constructed reveals a great deal about their freedom, the resources they controlled, and their impact on the larger world." [15] His words speak for the contributions made by women in Islamic history, a role that seemed to be natural and expected by the community.

Education and Theology

From the above we learn that women had an important role in building what today is cherished as the Islamic heritage in the form of palaces, tombs, hospitals, and schools. Yet little is known about this activity among Muslims today. As for women's professional and business pursuits, they are not given due attention, which is surprising because of the availability of the information and the national pride to be gained from showing women's active role in Islamic civilization, putting it on a par with other civilizations that have claimed their women and consequently improved their global image.

A more complicated picture has to do with the theological role played by women. It is commonplace to accept that Islamic law has been the exclusive product of males with very little input by women. This belief is accepted tacitly by Muslim communities today that delegate religious issues almost exclusively to men, a fact that has kept feminists from shunning the Islamic discourse as a route for changing the situation of women today and of introducing a different outlook toward Islamic culture. Shunning or keeping out of theological debates pertaining to gender has hurt the cause of women's rights because Islamic discourses continue to be the most familiar among the very people feminists want to influence. It is also the dominant legitimating instrument used by conservative elements to confine women's empowerment and participation.

Women's role in formulating theology can be seen in two different ways. First, notwithstanding who renders the formal opinion, society is made up of men and women, and therefore women are an important part of *'urf* formation. Their opinions are heard, they are consulted, and their actions are central to social norms. In other words, women figure strongly in determining the laws of their societies despite whether they are actively involved in the formal formulation of the words. This fact becomes evident at times of change when new gender laws are discussed and activists are surprised that women seem to be as unwilling to accept change as are men, even when it concerns giving them greater freedoms. What is forgotten is that women are integral to civil society, which is where legal *'urf* is formed, conserved, or changed. It is therefore imperative that discourses followed by civil societies be challenged and from within the very references that are used if there is a chance to change attitudes toward gender issues.

Second, historical research tells us that women were in fact active in formulating laws, particularly through transmission and interpretation of hadith. But to be able to make this point one has to first challenge the normative view of Muslim women's essential seclusion, for how can she be a participant in the intellectual and theological life of her community if she is secluded in harems and largely uneducated? Here again a return to the formative "ideal" period of Islam will help dismiss this type of stereotypical image. It may be true that the Prophet's *sira* (history and traditions) informs us that Muslim men were told to address the Prophet's wives from behind a *hijab* (veil), yet, as shown earlier in this chapter, women were quite active in public life. Without debating what the Qur'an *ayas* regarding the *hijab* meant—already successfully confronted by Fatma Mernissi [16]—or discussing how universal this admonition of the *hijab* was intended, a separation should be made between women's actual everyday lives and the matter of clothing. Wearing a veil does not reduce a woman's capabilities as a professional any more than not wearing a veil reduces her abilities as a mother and respected member of her community. Symbols of oppression used by women's movements today are of little use in understanding a past where such clothing was the norm, depending on time and place. Here the *sira* helps us. Numerous stories are related about meetings between the Prophet and women companions (*sahabiyyat*) and wives of male companions (*sahabi*). Examples include hadiths recorded by Bukhari and Muslim about the Prophet going into a woman's house to ask about her health: "I feel compassion for her since her brother was killed while he was with me." Or the story related by a companion: "[T]he Prophet, God's Peace be upon him, visited us and asked my mother, my aunt Umm Haram, and I to rise to pray with him." There is also the story of the Prophet's offer to Asma' bint Abi Bakr to ride behind him out of compassion because she was carrying dates from a long distance and Asma's refusal because her husband was too jealous.[17] There are also many stories about the Prophet's wives meeting with other men, such as when they were asked to quote a hadith. There are also stories about the Prophet's first women companions and the wives of his male companions meeting together openly at particular locations and events without being segregated. Besides, women attended Friday prayers, sat with the Prophet to receive his wisdom, as well as listened to his companions at well-known times such as during their *bay'a* rendering.[18] It seems natural in these stories that women be present, and no explanation seems necessary for why they were outside their homes.

The historical evidence from hadith and *sira* refutes the particular interpretations or generalization of selected Qur'an *ayas* that are used misogynistically and applied to all women at all times and all places. One Islamic thinker correctly asks, "[I]f the meeting [between men and women] was forbidden what are the proofs?" The Qur'an words *"waqarin fi buyutakun"* seem to be the usual evidence used to generalize Islam's requirement of women's seclusion. Yet neither the Prophet's wives nor the wives of his companions stayed secluded at home. The answer then is that such admonition depends on time and place; particular conditions may require such seclusion, and particular Qur'an words should not be generalized. One logical conclusion would be that "it was *khuluwwa* and not meetings that were forbidden"; *"khuluwwa"* means the secluded meeting between a man and a woman that could result in sexual misconduct.[19] Therefore, it is not surprising that archival records dating from the premodern Ottoman period paint a picture of a very active and complex Arab society. People were quite litigious, and women came to court with their problems and personal quarrels,[20] with property and money disputes,[21] to contract marriage, to sue for divorce, to ask a husband for financial support, with fights about particular advantageous spots in marketplaces, to ask for payment of fees for jobs done, to receive certificates as *waqf* administrators, to make declarations of the property they owned and that they owed no one any debts, and so on. It was a complex society, very noisy and active, with people who debated and quarreled, who knew what was theirs and went about getting it. Far from being secluded to the "private" sphere, women found it very natural to come to court, sell produce and goods in the marketplace, act as heads of guilds, and accept assignment by the court as *waqf* executors and as *wasis*. Furthermore, court procedures and legal decisions did not differentiate between men and women; both genders had to appear in person in court or deputize someone, and each had to present evidence and witnesses of corroboration.

Once the idea of women's seclusion is put into question, it becomes easier to conceptualize the important role women played in the formulation of law and legal *'urf;* after all, laws are rules agreed upon and enforced in a particular community. At the same time, recent scholarship is contributing to our knowledge of the actual theological contributions of Muslim women in this process of interpretation, particularly during the founding period of Islam. Here *tabaqat* literature have proved most valuable. *Tabaqat* literature follows a chronological division of important Muslims relative to the time between the period in which they lived and the life of the prophet Muhammad. The first level consists of the companions who were part of the founding generation of Islam, who lived, fought, and went on Hijra with the Prophet. Within the generation of companions a division is made between those closest to the Prophet, particularly early converts and the fighters in the early Islamic *maghazi* (campaigns) at Badr and Uhud. The Prophet's wives, wives of his companions, and women companions who were early converts to Islam who went on Hijra, gave their *bay'a,* and fought during the early battles are also included in this early generation of companions. This early generation is followed in importance by that which follows it chronologically, the time of the *tabi'un* (followers); the further away from the time of the Prophet, the lesser the rank given to its members because the information they relayed could have been only secondhand and not from direct witness, as was the case with the *sahaba*.

As authorities on hadith, the earliest women companions of the Prophet, the *sahabiyyat,* constituted a significant proportion of the ones reported in bibliographical dictionaries. Figures change from one source to the other. According to Ibn Sa'd, the Prophet had 529 *sahabiyyat,* among whom 94 were transmitters of hadith. Ibn Hibban estimates that 16.5 percent of early "trustworthy transmitters" were women. With the passage of time, however, the number of women transmitters mentioned in biographical literature shrank. Ruth Roded, who wrote an important work about the subject, concludes that this shrinking was to a large extent because of state structuralism, particularly during the Ottoman period "when formal institutions of learning were established, women were not appointed to teaching positions but continued to study and teach in informal frameworks . . . [women] scholars . . . did not hold endowed teaching positions in the *madrasa* colleges; nor did they hold official posts."[22] In other words, as the scholarly establishment became bureaucratized, women scholars began to lose recognition in biographical collections. As early modern empires, like the Ottoman, depended on bureaucracies to ensure their hold over their provinces, standardization became a requirement, and the legal system as a whole, including the religious hierarchy, became more state controlled and streamlined to suit state needs. Just as the Ottoman state made it a legal requirement that all marriages be registered in courts and fees paid to the officiating *qadi,* so were Muslim scholars, *muftis* of the law, court judges, and recognized authorities in theology also streamlined. Because women had never been involved with formal institutions as holders of professorships and did most of their teaching privately,[23] their role as theologians and educators was bound to lose recognition and significance with greater state structuralism. In such a situation where an active civil society was giving way to state structuralism, women whose power lay within their communities began to lose the positions they had held in various aspects of public life in which they had enjoyed a degree of power. The process of structuralism and women's loss of agency would grow and become institutionalized with the modern nation-state and its dependence on traditionally male-dominated institutions such as the military, *'ulama'* hierarchy, and bureaucracy. Women had not been involved in any of the jobs pertaining to these professions, even though the names of a few women *qadis* are mentioned.

The above does not mean that women ceased to be interested in theology or to be active in intellectual life with the growth of state structuralism. Their activity became less visible, whereas activity on the official level involving only men became visible and all-important and hence became the focus of scholars who later studied the history of Islamic law and theology. One has to look for women's participation at the local and informal level and in sources that are unusual for the study of theology and theologians. Leslie Peirce's work on 'Antab using Ottoman court records illustrates this point by showing the existence of circles of *faqihat* (women theologians) who met together regularly to discuss theological issues and who also invited male theologians to come and discuss these issues with them. Such circles were organized and led by women *fuqaha'.* Most of these *shaikhas,* as they were known, continued a long-standing tradition of apprenticeship at the hands of a father or uncle who was himself a theologian. Training female members of a family in learning and theology seemed to be traditional to *'ulama'* families. Not only did women study with famous *'ulama',* but some very famous Islamic scholars are also known to have studied with women teachers and received *ijazas* (certificates of competence) from them. A good example is Umm 'Umar al-Thaqafiyya with whom Ahmad Ibn Hanbal, the founder of the Hanbali school of jurisprudence, studied.

> Around 405 of the 1075 women (38 percent) in al-Sakhawi's biographical collection for the ninth/fifteenth century studied, received licenses attesting to their learning, and taught others. Among these women are 46 of the 68 women from whom the author received an *ijaza* certifying that he had studied with them, 43 who had taught his teacher and at least 9 with whom his friends had studied. Eleven women were his pupils, and 2 received *ijazas* from his teacher. In other words, the large number of learned women in this dictionary results partly from the author's personal contacts with them and with their students and their teachers.[24]

How widely were women educated before the appearance of centralized modern states? The answer is still open for further research, but already the picture of an ignorant, oppressed female is changing rapidly. As mentioned above, al-Sakhawi's bibliographical dictionary mentions 1,075 biographies of women who received religious education during the medieval period. They are said to have "memorized the Quran, studied with a particular scholar, or received an *ijaza.*"[25]

Studying with a particular scholar was traditional for the medieval period and continued through the early modern period. In the case of women, the student-teacher relationship was usually based on kinship, and in most of the cases in which women later taught, they came from middle-class clerical families where learning was an acknowledged part of life. Women were also directly involved in teaching other female members of their families. A good example is Zaynab al-Tukhiyya (d. 1388) from the village of Mahallat Rih in Lower Egypt who was taught by various members of her family as a child and memorized the Qur'an at the hands of her father, with whom she studied important works on Shaf'i jurisprudence such as Qazwini's and Isfahani's works. Fathers were not the only ones who instructed daughters; mothers did too, especially when the father was not available. "The mother of Umm al-Husayn bint 'Abd al-Rahman b. 'Abd Allah (d. 1422) herself instructed her daughter in certain basics—writing, learning particular chapters of the Quran, and al-Nawawis's popular collection of forty hadith, the *'Arba'in.*"[26]

A husband instructed his wife once she had left the family home and moved in with him. Because clerical families intermarried, education of its female members continued after marriage through direct and indirect instruction, given that it was the vocation involving most members of the family. The medieval Bulqini family of theologians is known for its many learned women members whose biographies are to be found in al-Sakhawi's collection. As Jonathan Berkey notes, quoting al-Sakhawi's reference to women scholars, "Indeed, so accepted was the education of women among families of learning that al-Sakhawi was able to comment regarding one woman that, although he had no direct knowledge of her education, 'I do not doubt that she had obtained *ijazas,* as her family was well known [for its learning].' "[27]

Husbands and fathers were also known to take their wives or daughters to attend lectures given in local *madrasas* (mosque schools) and mosques. Some women followed regular courses given in these institutions, though not on an official basis. Zaynab b. 'Abdal-Halim ibn al-Hasan al-Iraqi al-Qahiri (d. 1461) is said to have begun to attend with her brother in classes taught by her father while no more than five years of age. Another, Zaynab bint Abd Allah (d. 1452), is said to have begun even earlier, at the age of two. The daughter of Ibn Hajar al-'Asqalini is said to have accompanied him to classes when she was only three years old, and the daughter of the famous judge Taqi al-Din al-Subki (d. 1403) is noted for having been a scholar and transmitter of hadith who received licenses "from some of the leading traditionalists of Cairo and Damascus before her fourth birthday."[28] In other words, women studied theology, acted as transmitters of hadith, and were granted *ijazas* certifying their abilities by the teachers with whom they studied, a number of whom are recognized as important authorities on Islamic jurisprudence even today.

Endowing and Administering *Waqfs*

Religious endowments were an important way of providing services to Islamic communities. Hospitals, schools, marketplaces, hostels, housing, and water fountains were all built by charitable persons and endowed with property whose income would be spent on the institution endowed. *Waqfs* were also set up to benefit already existing structures, to renovate them or help with their upkeep. Some *waqfs* provided scholarships to students of theology or medicine, and a *waqf* from nineteenth-century Nablus illustrates that book collections, which were highly prized, were also set up in libraries for use by scholars.[29]

Philanthropic endowments were called *waqf khayri* and were directly intended to benefit the Islamic community. They were therefore often in the form of large structures and usually established by members of elite and upper classes. But the middle classes were also active in setting up charitable endowments, although most of the *waqfs* set up by middle and lower classes were in the form of *waqf dhurri,* established to benefit the endower while he or she was still alive, his direct family, later his descendants, and ultimately a particular institution or service when the line of heirs had run out. The official deed establishing a *waqf* was normally registered with the *qadi* in *shari'a* court, and today Jordanian archives contain a wealth of information about this unique system for handling and preserving—even entailing—property for future generations or of designating property to benefit certain individuals or institutions that donors believed were needy. It is therefore no surprise that even though the majority of *waqf dhurri* benefited sons and brothers or all members of the family equally or were allotted according to Islamic inheritance laws, a substantial percentage were set up for the exclusive benefit of daughters or slave women of the household. Here, it is usually the mother who set up the *waqf* to benefit the women of her family and ensure their welfare after her death when her protection and support would cease.

Substantial information about society and social relations is made available from reading *waqf* documents. The numbers of endowments, the value of property involved, the type of property, the gender of the benefactor, and the names of the beneficiaries tell us about power relations and the power that was held by women of wealth within Islamic societies. The question of empowerment was raised by a number of women activists whom I met in Jordan who considered the lack of financial power to be the main cause for women's weakness and submissiveness today. As Salwa Naseer, the dynamic NGO coordinator of the Jordanian National Committee for Women, explained to me, women need to be empowered within their families before we can have any hope of seeing them play any effective public role within Jordan. *Awqaf* records tell us of the financial power enjoyed by women during earlier periods of Islamic history and of their ability to direct their wealth however they wished. The financial power clearly gave them an important status within the family, and the extent of property held, inherited, and endowed by women was quite substantial and informative of family life and the position enjoyed by women within the family.

Whereas income from endowments was divided according to the instructions left by benefactors, the next generation of descendants usually received benefits according to Islamic inheritance laws unless otherwise indicated—for instance, if the *waqf* was specifically left to only the men or only the women of the family in perpetuity—which, however, was not usually the case. Because benefactors of *waqfs* were sometimes slaves, the document may indicate that they would receive income while alive, but it would not be inherited by their descendants. The same could happen with anyone named in the document, so that although a girl could be privileged in the share she received, after her death the income could be divided in any form that the benefactor decided upon and included in the document. In other words, *waqf dhurri* was a way by which a person could ensure that his or her property would be spent in the way they wished at the time they set it up. If there were no instructions or the instructions ran out with time, then Islamic inheritance laws were invoked and applied. If there were no more persons to benefit from the *waqf*, as was the case when there were no descendants or heirs, then the *waqf* reverted to the state or to any charity that may have been chosen by the benefactor in anticipation of such a situation.

Waqf documents could be a few lines long or large elaborate documents, depending on the assets and property involved. Whereas documents setting up *waqfs* by princes were often beautiful, elaborate, and sometimes gold-leafed booklets, smaller *waqfs* were simple documents in court. Not only were the names of the beneficiaries of the *waqf* detailed in the original document, but so were the names of those people who would administer it. Administrators of *waqfs* were chosen by the *qadi* when the position was vacant. The administrator of the *waqf* could assign deputies answerable to him or her, but he or she in turn was responsible to a *nazir* who was something of a guardian over the *waqf*. Although it is believed that women were allowed to administer but never to be the *naziras* of *waqfs*, court records prove otherwise; women were often assigned as *naziras* by the court with full authority over the *waqfs*. For example, Saliha bint Hussain al-Jorbaji was assigned by the *qadi* to act as *nazira* of her father's *waqf* after his death.[30] In short, women figured strongly in all aspects of *waqfs*: they endowed them, were named as administrators or recipients of income from them, and were assigned by *qadis* to supervise them.

> Al-Hakim al-Shar'i al-Hanafi . . . whose signature and seal are here fixed . . . appointed the holder of this legal document . . . the woman Zahira daughter of . . . as partner with her aunt, the woman Hajir daughter of . . . to oversee her grandfather's *waqf* located inside and outside the town so that she would participate with her aunt in the administration of the *waqf* regarding building, upkeep, with the good of the *waqf* in mind, and to collect its income and distribute it to its recipients. They should do this by conferring and acting together.[31]

Because establishing *waqfs* was normal for Islamic societies and women were beneficiaries of them,[32] either through inheritance or wages for administering them, *waqfs* were a very important source of income for women that allowed them to support themselves and their families, and to later set up endowments of their own. Given the extent of *awqaf* set up and later taken over by the modern state to administer through a ministry of *awqaf*, the financial power held by women before the state took over the *awqaf* system cannot be overemphasized. More important, these activities were not exclusive to upper-class women, who were particularly important in setting up and administering *waqfs*, but was shared by women of the middle classes and even small property owners. Margaret Meriwether gives the following estimates regarding endowments set up in early-eighteenth-century Aleppo, which was experiencing an upswing period in its economy:

> A wide spectrum of property owners were now involved in setting up these endowments. Sixty-two percent of them were set up by individuals who were not from upper-class families, most of whom were probably smaller property owners. Endowment activity therefore was not confined to one class, nor was it gender specific. Women were quite active as founders of endowments. Two hundred fifteen endowments were founded by men, 241 by women and 11 jointly. . . . One hundred sixty-five endowments (35 percent of the total) were established by [upper-class] families, 86 by men, 77 by women, and 2 jointly.[33]

One interesting reason for setting up a *waqf dhurri* was as a means of protecting the rights of women and minors from the greed of cousins who may have placed demands on the property. *Waqfs* in such cases were then simple agreements between members of the family to ensure the relative rights they had to a particular home, usually the one they lived in. Joint properties were therefore common. Al-Ya'qubi concludes his study of the *waqfs* of Jerusalem: "[A]s for women, they most often willed their *waqfs* to their daughters alone even when the daughters were married especially when the donor of the *waqf* is a widow and has no male sons and the intention from the *waqf* was to provide the daughters with income especially daughters who are not able to work and make a living."[34] Meriwether recorded two Aleppine *waqfs* set up by a mother and daughter to protect each other's rights in case one of them died and inheritance laws would allow other family members who did not live with them to dispute their rights to the use of the property. "Zalikha Hamawi and her daughter, Layla Hamawi (Zalikha had married her cousin Muhammad), each owned shares in a house in Frafira. . . . Zalikha owned sixteen shares of the harem part of the house; Layla owned eight shares of the harem as well as all of the *dar al-uta*, inherited from her father and brothers. They each set up an endowment, naming each other as primary beneficiaries. After their deaths, the house went to Layla's husband and their children and descendants." The second case Meriwether presents from Aleppo shows how property was controlled by women and passed through them to their children by means of *waqfs:* "The wife and four daughters of Hashim Muqayyid had inherited nineteen shares of their residence in Frafira from him. With this property they set up an endowment to benefit themselves, stating very clearly that no one else would share in it or dispute their arrangements."[35]

Property and Extending Credit

In his groundbreaking study of the *shari'a* courts of Ottoman Kayseri in Cyprus, Ronald C. Jennings points our attention to the frequency with which women appeared in these records as debtors and creditors, "the latter little more than the former." *Shari'a* court records for Jordan and Palestine show the same patterns, with women often appearing in court to repay a debt they owed or to clear a debt owed them that had been repaid, to demand the payment of a debt owed them, or to transact a brand-new contract in which they were loaning money to another, often a member of her family, but most of the loans made by women were made on a commercial basis and were not exclusive to family members.[36] Examples of such loans from nineteenth-century Jerusalem archives include a loan of 500 *qirsh* from a woman called Sarah to a man called Yusuf Zain, a loan of 1800 *qirsh* from Amna al-Ja'uni to Anduni al-Shama', and Amuna's loan of 21,520 to Ibrahim Rizq.[37] Many such loans were made in return for the payment of interest. To get around Islamic laws against the taking of interest, methods resorted to included *bay' wafa'i,* which "entailed that the debtor would sell a piece of property to the lender equal in value to the amount borrowed, for an agreed period of time after which the loan was discharged." One such case from Haifa reads, "Because I owe the woman . . . the sum of 800 qurush . . . I have given her for one year as security against the loan a room in a house I own . . . she may live in it or let it out for the *fayiz* [interest]."[38]

Women also loaned money, goods, or property to family members, such as brothers, fathers,[39] or husbands, and, as court records illustrate, husbands often owed their wives for various types of loans. Matruka bint Sulaiman al-Mu'awwid of Amman was owed by her husband eighteen-plus riyals, fourteen goats, and four sheep, which he had borrowed from her as registered in court.[40] Borrowing from a wife did not seem to be a problem with men, as the records show that it was quite normal, and very often one comes across cases in which a husband was repaying a debt to a wife and a wife was indicating that she in fact had been repaid. Sometimes such cases look artificial and are more in the form of ensuring that her property would remain with her husband and children and not be disputed by any of her family members, but most transactions appear to be genuine, especially as much of the repayment took place at the time of divorce when all financial matters between the couple had to be settled. A loan recorded in the *shari'a* court of al-Salt is perhaps more explicit in its wording in regards to the exchange of money: "Wadha bint Mar'i al-Yasmin pointing to her adversary, her brother Tafish . . . who is present with her in court, both of whom are . . . residents of al-Salt, claimed that her brother Tafish here present with her, owed her the amount of 11 majidi riyals representing a loan she extended to him according to this matured *sanad* [credit bill]." [41]

As to the source of their money, women inherited it, received it as dowry in cash or in kind, or earned it through work, trade, profit from investments, or as income from an inherited *waqf*. Court records do not tell us directly the source of the money that women were lending, but the records give a good indication of the amounts of money women controlled, and death records give lists of the property women left behind for their heirs. Inheritance, marriage, divorce, and other records dealing with personal matters show them to be important sources of money and property for women. Disputes over transactions in the marketplace or over goods illustrate the trade activities of women and that buying and selling were important areas of occupation for women. Sometimes women inherited debts due to a husband or another member of her family, or she was the recipient of a portion of a *diyya* resulting from a murder of a member of her family. Findings from Jordanian and Palestinian courts regarding women lending or borrowing money fit with Jennings's description of Kayseri.

When contested disputes arose concerning problems of credit, the ones involving women were considered at court by exactly the same procedures as similar cases involving men. Women could make formal claims against any man, including their fathers, grown sons, and husbands. Although sometimes they named *wakils* (agents, proxies, or persons with power of attorney) to handle their cases, most often they managed their own affairs at court. Women's place may have been in the home in seventeenth-century Kayseri, but there was a fair chance that she had a little nest egg tucked away and owned some animals, a field, or even her own home. Such a situation is very much in accord with the strictures of Islamic law, even though it differs considerably from the stereotype of Muslim or Ottoman women. The successful participation of women in the business of credit in the city probably depended upon the existence of well-organized credit and business procedures and a vigorous court system. [42]

Declarations of death and property of the deceased were normal for Islamic societies. When a person died, his or her property was assessed and registered in court so that heirs could receive their legitimate shares. Sometimes a person came to court to declare all they owned and to indicate that they owed no debts to anyone and declared who their heirs were so there would be no doubt after the person's death. Therefore, "death" records are an important way of learning about society, property, and details of how people lived, including their material wealth. Death records of women show the same patterns as the records of men: some were quite poor,[43] leaving hardly anything behind; others belonged to the middle classes and had relative wealth;[44] whereas others were quite wealthy and lived very well. The death record of the daughter of a fifteenth-century Jerusalem goldsmith shows a woman of relative wealth with an extensive wardrobe that included silks and furs, various types of jewelry, and a significant amount of silver and furnishings.[45]

Much of the property that women held came from inheritance. Like boys, when still minors, control of the property was held by the *wasi* who was expected to guard this property and invest it in safe and profitable ventures. A *wasi* was answerable to the court regarding the property of minors. Once the girl reached majority, the *wasi* was expected to turn over to her whatever property he was holding in her name and usually accounted for it in court. A typical declaration would read: "On this day the adult virgin . . . daughter of . . . received from the hands of her paternal uncle . . . the amount of five hundred qurush due her from her father's estate after her declaration that she has now reached majority and can be trusted to care for her property."[46]

Court records detailing the debates of neighbors regarding property lines or building rights provide another way of learning about women and property. Such records are very interesting because they tell us about urban laws regarding building, neighbors' rights, as well as the rights of property owners.[47] In one such case from nineteenth-century Nablus, a woman took her neighbor to court because she had stopped her from building on a piece of land that stood between their two properties. Because the woman bringing the complaint owned most of the surrounding area, she asked the court to clear the matter and allow her to build. The defendant, represented by a *wakil* who did not seem to be related to her, disputed her neighbor's right to build because said building would encroach on her property. In Islamic law, *maslaha* (preference) is taken into consideration in matters of building so that if a building blocks the sun or fresh air from another, the greater harm is taken as a basis in the court's decision. Here, however, the court's experts reported that the intended building would stand far away from the neighbor's house, so the court found against the defendant and ordered her to stop bothering the neighbor. In the details presented by this case we learn of the extent of property owned by women, their understanding of the legal system, and their systematic use of the court system to defend their rights. On the other hand, lack of knowledge of the legal system or of documentation went against women, as would be expected. For example, a woman came to court to sue a man indebted to her deceased husband, which sum she claimed as an inheritance for her and her children. "The woman Fatima bint 'Awwad from the village of Bayt Fur Yakka, claimed that 'Abdal-Karim Khidr from the same village who was present with her in the Majlis al-Shar'i . . . that the said defendant mortgaged a piece of land located in the mentioned village . . . for an amount of six hundred qirsh which the defendant received . . . in return for one third of its product. He then planted it (*hanta[?]*) worth five hundred and thirty qirshs. She demands one third of that amount. . . . [T]he defendant concurs that he planted the land but denies the said mortgage."[48] In this case, the court went against the woman because she did not have the right documentation with her.

How did the courts and society feel about women in the capacity of property holders and creditors? *Qadis* and courts treated women the same way as they treated men when it came to all types of transactions. A woman's word in court did not need corroboration any more than a man's, and in financial disputes she needed to present witnesses the same way men had to. The greatest number of court records about the economic activities of women involve real estate transactions. They bought, sold, and registered property; rented houses; and even invested in constructing rental units, sometimes within their own homes so as to raise funds. "Many women had their houses reconstructed so as to make rooms available for rent, such a profitable way of earning money it had become. One woman spent the quite considerable sum of 1200 qurush to alter the interior of her house so as to be able to rent out three of the five rooms it contained. We learn from the lease that within twenty months she had recouped the investment from the rent she collected."[49] Sometimes a woman sold a share of a house that she may have bought or inherited and was not living in. When merchants bequeathed their shops or businesses to their daughters, they could manage the shop or appoint someone to do the job and receive the income. The same went with agricultural land, although here we see women investing money to increase the size of their holdings, often investing in plots for growing vegetables close to town and therefore with a ready market or in vineyards, a popular investment among women.[50] Women also invested in houses and businesses, sometimes directly[51] and sometimes through a *wakil* of their choice who would collect income due from the investment, from a deceased husband's partnership,[52] or from rent.[53]

The question of who actually controlled property owned by women is not directly answerable through court records. Sometimes the woman was represented by her husband in court, which gives the impression that it was he who was in control and that she followed his wishes. But the evidence points to the opposite. For one thing, women were quite often represented by their brothers or by men not related to them in any way, even though they may have been married. Also, as indicated earlier, it was quite often a husband who owed the wife money or was buying property from her or selling to her. Besides, even though the husband acted as *wakil* for his wife in court, she was usually present with him, following the procedures and presenting her wishes.[54] But women more often represented themselves in court. When registering a sale by a woman, the record more often indicates her presence in court without reference to the presence of a husband, a brother, or a *wakil.* In a transaction where a woman was buying from her brother his share of a house they had both inherited, she would come to court with him and a document of the transaction would be signed in front of the judge.[55] It should be noted that women were themselves chosen as *wakils* to represent others in court.[56]

Crafts and Markets

Court records from the Ottoman period show women active in business and crafts. As discussed earlier, women owned property, loaned and borrowed money, and controlled *awqaf.* They also acted as *multazims* (tax farmers), as 'Abdal-Rahman al-Jabarti described in his famous chronicles of eighteenth-century Egypt. They were also chosen as heads of guilds in crafts where women worked in large numbers. Because we have citations of women having been heads of guilds of physicians, weavers, *dalalas,* beauticians, and entertainers,[57] we know that these areas employed large numbers of women. Here *waqf* documents show their importance as a source of social history. A good example is the *waqf* set up by the Mamluk prince Sayf al-Din Tunkuz (who ruled over Syria three times between A.D. 1298 and 1340 [A.H. 698 and 740]) in Jerusalem. A known builder with extensive contributions to Jerusalem, he set up diverse properties to endow the Tankaziyya School and to provide it with future income for its upkeep and support of its teachers and students. In the five-page document setting up these properties and detailed instructions for spending the income from them, we learn that an income was to be paid to the *shaikha* of the women in the school (*ribat al-nisa'*), the women who lived in that *ribat,* as well as guests visiting the school, such as *sufis* and women.[58]

As Muhammad 'Isa Salahiyya informs us in his impressive study of landholdings in Ottoman Palestine—housed in the ministerial archives in Istanbul and written in old Ottoman Turkish—tax documents contain detailed information vital for the history of people in the Ottoman Empire. Not only do they give details of various types of properties and businesses, but they also give names of property owners and the income derived.[59] According to these records, we know, for example, that Saniyya bint Sayf owned a mill for grinding grain in the village of Ra's al-'Ayn near Saffad (A.H. 978), Hamda bint Yusuf from the village of Qariyat Maghar al-Haruz in Tabariyya owned a share of a mill,[60] and Fatma bint Muhammad owned $5/_{24}$ of a share of a mill in the village of Milaha in Jira (A.H. 918). There were also mills owned jointly between husband and wife in nineteenth-century Amman court records.[61] This evidence seems to indicate that grain-grinding mills were a business in which women invested. Shares in mills could have been inherited, but being a family business, women continued to supervise them and receive income from them rather than sell them. Olive oil production was another popular business among women. Women inherited orchards of olive trees and fruit, but they also invested their wealth in buying them. Together with real estate, olive trees and food-bearing trees constitute the most important business in which women invested their money. In a death declaration of a Nablus woman are included mulberry trees located in an orchard outside of the town.[62] Maryam Ya'qub of Bethlehem invested in an orchard in 1822,[63] as did Qaimiyya bint Radwan of Silwan[64] and 'Adiyya al-Liftawi who bought one and one-half *qirat* of olive trees.[65] Asma' al-Khalidi, whose name appears several times in the archival record for buying, selling, and receiving income, bought an orchard from Hijaz al-Salawini containing olive trees, grapevines, and apricot trees in 1831.[66] Sometimes women joined together in buying olive tree groves and sometimes went into partnerships with men. "Fatma . . . who is known in Nablus, owned together with another three women . . . and one man . . . trees in four different locations."[67]

Women were also involved in crafts, most of which are thought of as being purely male professions. Making soap in soap factories was one such craft for which Nablus, Jerusalem, and other towns were famous. Atika bint Khalil abu Rakhiyya set up a *waqf duhrri* that she endowed with a workshop for producing soap in Bab Dawud, Jerusalem.[68] She must have owned it and received an income from it to wish to protect her right to this income throughout her life and for her children after her death, as the *waqf dhurri* entails. Other properties included in *waqf duhrris*—some dating from before the Ottoman period—were village real estate, orchards, rental houses, shops, olive oil juicers (*ma'sara*), baths (*hamams*), bakeries, sale spots (*masatib*) in marketplaces, and the income produced by these properties.[69] Women were also owners of pottery workshops like the one owned by Safiyya, located in Mahallat al-Sa'idiyya.[70] Although goldsmiths were almost always men, there was a nineteenth-century Jewish woman identified as Yasmine who was a goldsmith jeweler by craft and worked in her own shop.[71] The same can be said about bakeries where bread of various types was baked and sold to the public: archival records indicate that women were very much involved in milling and in bakeries. According to Muhammad al-Ya'qub, who gives a documented survey of Jerusalem's markets in the sixteenth century, Jerusalem had about twenty-five bakers at midcentury, "some of whom were women like Anna bint Ya'qub who baked *al-kimaj,* a type of bread among the many known then."[72]

Perhaps unexpectedly, women are also recorded as having owned coffeehouses. The *waqf dhurri* of Salha bint Khalil in Ban Hatta, Jerusalem, included a coffeehouse and the income from a store.[73] An interesting *wasiyya* by an *Od-abashi* (head of an Ottoman army unit) indicated that all his property should go to his sole legal heir—his wife, Khadija—and to his previous master who manumitted him. As part of his property detailed in the document, he included a coffeehouse in al-Hussayniyya in Cairo that he co-owned with his mother-in-law who was the actual administrator of it.[74]

Women also did manual labor, although the information is harder to find. They worked as house help beside the large number of slave women who worked mainly as domestic help whose labor is not taken into consideration in studies of women and work. Palestinian peasant women "often worked in fields and quarries, of course, sometimes even outside the village," according to Ze'evi Dror. Women, therefore, were mobile, leaving their villages to go to work and holding jobs that the modern state has decided are dangerous for women. Women also worked as *saqqas* (water carriers), an essential service for cities of the Middle East. Huda Lutfi tells us that out of ten water carriers in medieval Jerusalem, two were women.[75] Public baths could be found all over Islamic cities. Because of strict sexual segregation, baths catered to either sex or were divided into two parts, one for males and another for females. Women served in baths as attendants, masseuses, and beauticians, and in other capacities. Hairdresser, beautician, and similar jobs were all areas of employment for women. A sixteenth-century Jerusalem female *kahala* (pseudo-oculist who used *kuhl* [antimony] as a cure) also ran a pawn business.[76] Again, sexual segregation helped here: men had their own hairdressers, as did women; in other words, women almost had a monopoly over particular services to women.[77] Women were also involved in the business of entertainment. They worked at weddings by dancing and singing. The head of the guild of women entertainers was always a woman, as was the case with other guilds in which women predominated.[78]

Women also hired themselves out as day laborers to do transitory work. In one case, a husband and wife hired themselves out to do field labor and had to go to court to sue for nonpayment of wages. The nineteenth-century document from Nablus reads: "The complaint was submitted by Mas'ud . . . from Dar Shinwi against Muhammad Sa'id al-'Aqqad and Salih 'Anbara and Hassan Abi

Radwan from Dar Shinwi. [He is] suing for his pay and his wife's pay for one hundred and twenty days labor." The defendants in this case disputed the claim on the basis that they were all partners in *daman al-zaitun* (trade in olive oil), but it had been a losing project. The matter was settled peacefully with each receiving what was owed to them.[79] Even though the details of how everything was settled are not exactly clear in this case, we learn from it that women hired out their labor on a daily basis.

As they are today, women then were quite skilled in sewing and embroidery. In fact, women were involved in many areas of textile and clothing production and sales. Primary products for this craft were widely available: tribesmen and villagers bred camels, sheep, and goats whose wool and hair went into the production of these goods, as did the cotton imported or grown by villagers. A family could already own stock from which wool could be taken and used for production, but women were also keen on buying sheep and goats for wool production as well as dairy products.[80] Traditionally, it was the women who washed the wool, spun it, and wove it. In medieval Muslim societies spinning was primarily a female profession, the spindle being part of household furniture. Unlike male craftsmen, female spinners worked at home rather than in workshops, although they began to do so in other areas of the Ottoman Empire during the nineteenth century. Although weaving was a predominantly male occupation, there are recorded instances of women weavers, and Lutfi confirms that one fourteenth-century Jerusalem woman owned three weaving shuttles and that seven women sold ginned cotton or clothing in medieval Jerusalem. She also mentions a twelfth-century document informing that a woman fell dead in a dye house in Jerusalem, an indication that she must have worked there, even though dyeing was usually considered a purely male occupation.[81]

Sewing and embroidery were a normal part of women's lives, supplying their families and making items for sale in the market. They also sewed and embroidered tablecloths, sheets, and even the *khurgs* (covering placed under saddles of horses and donkeys), as well as sacks for storing food and clothing.[82] Women also owned workshops for sewing clothes and shops for selling them, although most of the textile retail businesses were owned and run by men. Qastiyya al-Rumiyya, for example, owned a textile shop in early-nineteenth-century Jerusalem.[83] A *waqf dhurri* set up by Janat and Khadija, two *Maghribis* (North Africans) living in A.H. 118 (A.D. 1765) Jerusalem, included a house with its kitchen and water tank. The house was described as containing two apartments on top and three on the bottom besides an old stable that had been converted into a *dukan hiyaka* (a shop for sewing clothes).[84] Safa bint 'Abdal-'Aziz in nineteenth-century al-Salt had her *wakil* sue three partners for 50 *ratls* (approximately 2$^1/_2$ kilos of ghee for which she had paid them 50 riyals. The amount of ghee bought tells us tht she intended either to resell the ghee retail, probably to customers in her neighborhood or in the marketplace, or to use the ghee to make food to sell. One could also assume that the ghee was for personal use, but both the amount and the 50 riyals paid point us to a different conclusion.[85] Another area of sales in which women were and continue to be very active is that of *dalala* or *baya'a* (seller), sometimes referred to as a *simsara* (agent who earns a commission on sales). *Dalalas* sold goods for other merchants or for individuals and in return received an agreed percentage of the price, usually 1 percent. The goods they sold could be new or secondhand and included a large variety of items, including clothes and textiles, footwear, headgear, kerchiefs, household goods, sheets and tablecloths, perfumes, cosmetics, *thawbs* (long shirts worn by men), and so on. Most *dalalas* worked in their hometowns, but others came from Egypt or North Africa, as was usual for the Ottoman Empire where there was no limitation on the movement of people.

Because the job of *dalala* entailed the handling of money and interaction with the public, the rules of the state required that *dalal* and *dalalas* receive certification before employment. This certification was achieved through letters of guarantee vouching for their honesty by persons who were already well established in the trade or another trade, and who were willing to act as a *kafil* (sponsor) and take on the responsibility of repayment of any losses incurred by the new *dalala*. This sponsor had to appear in court in person and present his sponsorship in front of the *qadi*, which was recorded in the court's records. Thus, sponsorship records in *shari'a* court archives are an important source for learning about the work of women in the premodern period. For the year A.H. 1040 (A.D. 1631), for example, two women received licenses to practice as *dalalas* after being sponsored by their sons.[86] Several women who wished to practice the same craft could sponsor one another and take responsibility for each other's actions. If one broke the rules, tried to cheat, or lost the goods assigned to her, then the other women would have to cover for her. Such a document certifying a group sponsorship among three *dalalas* reads: "Appearing in the presence of the guildmaster of the *dalalin* were the following Jewish *dalalas*: Lursiy b. Salem Maghrabi, Saniyya b. Yahya, and Saniyya b. Ishaq, the *dalalas*, who sponsored one another in the craft of *dalala*, so that if one of them was defeated [meaning ruined], they would cover one another."[87] Records also show that women came to court to sue for lack of payment for goods they had delivered.[88] "The Christian woman named Maryam bint Musa the Armenian from Aleppo, stated that she owes the woman 'Aisha bint Mustafa al-Sufa, here present with her in court

. . . seven qurush [which is] the price of a length of linen cloth which she had bought from her . . . and asked for three days in which to pay them." [89]

Sometimes *dalalas* were forbidden from practicing by the *qadi* because of malpractice, as happened to a group in 1701 Jerusalem because "they take things and buy them from their owners with one price then sell them for a higher price." [90] This accusation probably means that they sold on commission and took for themselves a higher commission than had been agreed upon with the owners and buyers of the goods. It is important to point out that the *dalala* system that existed during the Ottoman period is very similar to the system that is today applied by microfinancial lenders in Jordan. Most of their customers are in fact *dalalas* working for themselves rather than on commission, although some do and are required to form partnerships guaranteeing one another. If one fails, the rest have to cover for her, and they all lose the right to take loans if one of them falls through and the rest are unable to cover the loss, notwithstanding how observant of the loan terms they may be. This point will be discussed later in chapter 8.

The Arab world was once famous for its medicine and hospitals. Almost all large towns had at least one *maristan* supported through extensive *awqaf* by rulers and princes. Providing medical help was one of the things people expected from their rulers in the premodern Arab world. Among the famous *maristans* are the Bimaristan al-Salihi in Jerusalem—which also had a Jewish Bimaristan—Maristan Qalawun built in Cairo in 1284, and the one built by Salah al-Din al-Ayyubi in Damascus. Nablus also had a *maristan* west of the Salahi bank, as did other important towns of the Arab world. Descriptions of *maristans* when first built speak of the greatness of their structures and the excellence of their doctors and medical students. Facilities accommodated both in- and out-patient care and included separate quarters for male and female patients. Male doctors and attendants served in the male section, and women doctors and attendants served the women. When the service of a male specialist was required, it was actually a woman doctor or the midwife (*daya* or *qabila*) who undertook the actual examination of the female patient and described the condition for the male doctor to make a diagnosis. Unfortunately, court records do not help us with statistical information, but according to one study there were five *qabilat* in Jerusalem in 1555. [91] Medical education was also widely available for both men and women and to "all segments of society" [92] through private medical schools run by physicians, private apprenticeship, or, most important, hospitals that were usually endowed with libraries and lecture halls. Because medical education and facilities were also open to women and *maristans* were divided according to gender, women doctors trained much the same as did male doctors. Court records frequently mention *dayas* in various capacities. Most usually it was in regards to cases brought to court by women who claimed they had been raped or had suffered forced miscarriages. The witness of *dayas* was vital in such cases, and courts used to have their own *dayas* who were sent out to investigate cases and return to court to act as expert witnesses.[93] *Dayas* were and continue to be a very important element in Arab society, although their prestige took a trouncing in the modern period with the introduction of modern Western medicine within a capitalist structure.

Conclusions on Women, Work, and the State

As this chapter has illustrated, studying sources dating from before the modern period shows a different picture from what is generally assumed of the life of Muslim women. Whether we are talking about the Islamic *turath* in the form of architecture, *awqaf* records, or *shari'a* court archives, they all corroborate the important economic involvement of women and the significance of this involvement to the societies in which they lived. Not that all women worked, but the extent of property they owned and commercial activities in which they participated, as well as their role in agriculture and animal and dairy production, gives an idea of what women accomplished and how their societies benefited. As entrepreneurs, they invested in real estate, loaned money, invested in trade and workshops, and accumulated significant amounts of property. Furthermore, even though they often acted through male relatives, they nevertheless undertook their own businesses, contracted their own transactions, and came to court to protect their rights. Neither their families nor the courts seemed to consider women as having less than full legal competence with equal rights in business as men. It is intriguing that today women are fighting an uphill battle to achieve what their sisters already had a hundred years ago. With modernity one would imagine that there would be greater openness for women and greater participation by them in their countries' economy. The latter is particularly true because Arab governments such as Jordan's have seriously pushed for greater freedoms and participation by women in public life. The question, then, is what could have happened to cause the deterioration of the active economic role enjoyed by women before the modern period?

The answer offered here points to the economic transformations experienced by the countries of the Middle East as they moved from being part of an empire to nation-state hegemony. We do not see premodern *fiqh* debating whether women should work, as does the gender discourse in Jordan and elsewhere today. Rather, "should women work?" seems to be a modern problem that presented itself with the appearance and subsequent mammoth growth in white- and blue-collar jobs that are the result of economic factors related to an industrialized world dominated by nation-states run by bureaucracies. Centralization invariably brings about a growth in bureaucracy and specialization. Modern states turned first to men for employment in its bureaucracies, armies, and industries; only with time and need did they also turn toward women. Employing men in these jobs was simply a continuation of earlier traditions regarding government employment. Thus, in all areas that we might call "civil service" in the premodern period, men held the jobs, not only in the Islamic world but globally as well. Throughout Islamic history we hardly see any women officials in such jobs as judges, ministers, court clerks, *muhtasibs* (marketplace supervisors), *muftis,* and so on. With few exceptions, all were men. So what existed was the modern extension of government service to fill its growing needs, and it was natural that the extension be to men.

The private sector, as it grew, also became dependent on men, particularly for white-collar jobs. It was to be expected because earlier clerks were men. But with time and growing poverty that acted as a push factor for women to enter the workforce, more women began to compete for these jobs. Furthermore, social planning taken up by modernizing governments such as Jordan's and Lebanon's, or in socialist states such as Egypt, Syria, and Iraq in the fifties, sixties, and seventies, moved to actively extend equal educational and job opportunities to women. The socioeconomic situation differed from one country to the other, and results differed in regards to the extent of success in opening up the workforce to women. Laurie Brand makes a good point about Jordan by pointing out the important relationship between security and military needs of a country that privileges men who are expected to carry the burden of active security. Brand explains that doing so has, on the one hand, retarded other areas of the Jordanian economy, and, on the other, hurt women who were not included in governmental plans. "This focus on the state sector had additional import for women, for the lack of attention to developing the private sector has been one factor that has retarded the development of industry. In other regions, such as Latin America, the emergence of industries has been an important step in drawing women into the workforce outside the home." [94]

The same results were experienced in other countries of the world. For example, in Egypt, modernization efforts were begun by Muhammad 'Ali Pasha at the beginning of the nineteenth century. His reforms included in large part the military, administration, agriculture, industry, health, and education. He turned to men for most of his personnel to staff all government agencies and services, and as the army gained importance, other areas paled in comparison; the male nature of the modern nation-state seemed to grow with its powers of control and centralization. As Brand argues, "the state has pursued policies of inclusion and exclusion of various types which, whether consciously so constructed or not, have nonetheless served to maintain various forms of patriarchal control." Afaf Lutfi al-Sayyid Marsot takes this one step further by pointing out that the process of nation-state building, with its accompanying structural changes, also created new forms of patriarchy that cut women out of areas in which they had been active earlier. Focusing on the eighteenth century, Marsot draws the connections between gender relations and the historical context. "Gender relations are determined by politics, religion, culture, changes in the modes of production, and changes in the environment." Because of the decentralized conditions in the Ottoman Empire during the eighteenth century, "women played an active role in the marketplace, corroborating the assumption that they played a more active role in other sectors of society and during other periods. . . . For example, 30 to 40 percent of deeds registered [in court records of Cairo] in the last half of the eighteenth century were made out by women."[95] A large part of the capital and business undertaken by women during the eighteenth century was related to commerce, according to Marsot; this situation was to change drastically under nation-state control.

> The second source of income [for women] was trade and commerce, which were monopolized by the ruler [meaning Muhammad 'Ali Pasha] so that no one else could become involved. Women therefore found themselves in consequence of a new patriarchal, centralized system, devoid of participation in any wealth-generating activities. They could eventually inherit land according to Muslim laws, especially after 1858, when the Ottomans passed the land law that simply ratified what had already existed for decades, but then they turned the land over to their male relatives. Which begs the question. The new centralized system also introduced new institutions derived from Europe that militated against women. Banks, stock exchanges, insurance companies, etcetera, in Europe did not recognize the legal existence of women; and so they followed the same strategies in Egypt. Women were not allowed to open bank accounts in their names or to play the stock market or to indulge in other activities in their own right. Once the male relative became the active partner, even though it may be the woman directing him, he nonetheless became the wielder of power and the retainer of income.[96]

There is a definite gender division in regards to the type of work performed by men and women. One possible pattern that can be discerned involves the power of the state and the nature of the connection between the particular job or function and the state's hegemony during various historical epochs. The stronger the connection and the more state-oriented the job, the greater the male orientation of the job. At the same time, the more socially oriented and loosely controlled the particular business or job, the greater the participation of women. If this hypothesis is correct, it would explain the greater participation of women as hadith transmitters and interpreters during the early period of Islam and the gradual reduction of their importance as the state became more centralized under male hegemonic power. Since the Abbasid period, the state became directly involved in religious discourses, first through speculative thinking sponsored by Mu'tazilism during a period of rapid change and diffusion of cultural input from various parts of the empire. Then, as the Abbasid state became more settled and administration grew, orthodoxy through Murji'a theology replaced the speculation of the Mu'tazila, and the religious discourse became intimately interconnected with state hegemony. Hence the importance of al-Ghazali and his amalgamation of Sunni, that is, orthodox, Islam with Sufism, which had grown in great popularity and had at one point become a reappearing threat to the state. The work of al-Mawardi should be mentioned here. His acceptance of the power of the state and his promotion of it by others as long as the state ensured religious practices for its citizens must be seen as a theologian's closeness to the state in whose *diwan* (council, office) he actually worked. As junior members of Islamic societies' elite classes, intermarrying with grand merchants and providing advice and legitimate discourses to often brutal rulers, the *'ulama'* had a stake in the continuation of various hegemonies throughout Islamic history. Whether as *muftis, qadis,* or exclusive exegetes, the stability of the state seems to have been a permanent discourse among them, though changing from period to period and place to place. *'Ulama'* could and often did play a role in opposition to the state and were often punished in retaliation. The case of al-Hallaj is perhaps the most extreme, as it united religious apostasy (*kufr*) from the dominant orthodox view of Islam together with political belligerence against the state. Another example is that of Shaikh al-Sha'arani who witnessed the invasion of Egypt by the Ottoman sultan Selim, attacked the Ottomans as infidels at first, and then, once their rule was established and his position ensured, became malleable and returned to the moral-oriented religious discourses that were usual for his class. In such positions as mamluk, janissary, or modern police and military personnel, the jobs were almost always male-oriented with a token representation of women as a symbol of a modernizing state.

A second hypothesis about gender difference in regards to particular jobs for men and women has to do with physical power. In fact, the first hypothesis presented above is itself based on this premise. The more physically demanding the job, the greater role to be played by men. Physically demanding does not necessarily mean more important or productive—after all, armies have always required physical power, but they are not very productive during times of peace when the military hierarchy becomes a consumer of a disproportionate portion of a country's income. Even in rural areas where men undertake the more physically demanding work such as breaking the ground and tilling, it is women and children who undertake or heavily participate in the more labor-intensive and continuous work of the land, such as weeding, watering, and removal of bugs and plant diseases. They participate in harvesting, thrashing the harvest, and collecting the grain. Among Bedouins, it is women who herd sheep and goats, feed them, weave the wool, make garments, fix the tents, and set up the dwellings. All these occupations are intensive and require perseverance, training, and practice rather than physical power. Yet states were built on physical power, and as long as armies play major roles in hegemonies, power will continue to gender society. As the following chapter will illustrate, the modern state, notwithstanding its adoption of discourses of modernity emphasizing human rights and women's liberation, has in fact increased the male orientation of "work" by increasing the state's administrative and centralizing functions. It is true that women were eventually mobilized to serve the state in Jordan, but as the chapter will illustrate, the laws guiding women's work make their work more token than real by framing it within parameters emphasizing "protection" and "temporariness."

4

Women and Work in Jordan Today

JORDAN was one of the earliest of the countries of the Middle East to undertake serious economic reforms aimed at liberalizing its trade, economic growth, macroeconomic stability, and growth of its financial market. The results of its twenty years' worth of efforts have been impressive given Jordan's small size and its lack of natural resources, its limited arable land measured at just over 10 percent of its total area, and its limited water supply. The stability of the political scene in Jordan and the consistency in its economic reform efforts are contributing factors to this relative success. Thus, Jordan has enjoyed a higher growth in income and jobs than most of its Arab neighbors. According to the World Bank: "Jordan and Tunisia are exceptional performers on virtually every indicator of human development—life expectancy, enrollment rates, and infant mortality." During 1990–1994, for example, Jordan's gross domestic product rate of growth was 0.39 percent, whereas Egypt's was -0.72 percent and Iran's -1.0 percent. Its export growth rate was 4.3 percent as compared to Egypt's 0.5 percent and Iran's -1.04 percent, and the inflation rate was 5.33 percent compared to Egypt's 14.80 percent and Iran's 20.50 percent. Other statistics speak well for Jordan: its literacy rate was measured at 82 percent in 1992, and the life expectancy of Jordanians is about seventy years.

This optimistic picture, however, is complicated by various problems facing the Jordanian economy. To begin, 50 percent of Jordan's population is quite young, under the age of sixteen, a problem Jordan shares with many other developing countries. At the same time, its high population growth rate, 3.4 percent, means that the trend will continue. Jordan will have to provide increasing numbers of jobs and economic opportunities if it is to maintain its standard of living and political stability. Today, because of its debt burden, increasing unemployment, loss of trade partners such as Iraq since the Gulf War, and greater dependence on foreign aid, Jordan needs to take critical steps to change the direction of its economy. One of the most important areas for economic growth in developing countries has been women's work. Recognizing that women constitute 50 percent of any country's population, and are thus an important labor reserve with, perhaps even more important, vast consumer potential, it has become essential for developing countries to stress women's work, encourage women to seek employment or open their own businesses, and open their markets for the employment of women. Jordan has taken steps in that direction, but so far the results have been rather limited.

Figures concerning women's employment in Jordan differ depending on the criteria used and the particular compilers. According to the Flynn-Oldham report, *Women's Economic Activities in Jordan*, "12.5 percent of Jordanian women 15 years of age or older are currently working in either short-term/seasonal activities, micro enterprise, agriculture, or salaried employment. Of the above group of currently working women, 12.4 percent are engaged in micro enterprise activities, which is equal to approximately 1.5 percent of the total population of Jordanian women. In 1998 estimates, this is equal to 33,000 women."

Another study estimates that women's participation in the economy does not exceed 16 percent.[1] The same study also found that the average working years for women does not exceed 3.7 years, and only a small percentage ever own their own businesses. This knowledge leaves a serious question as to why women do not stay employed. An obvious reason for leaving a job would be because of marriage, even though the Flynn-Oldham study does not give this cause too much importance.[2] The Konrad Adenauer Institute study calls attention to it:

> More than 90% of young Jordanian women marry, on average, by the age of 24.7 years. If it is the first marriage for both spouses, their husbands will be an average 3.5 years older than them. 42.5% of all married couples are first or second degree cousins or distant relatives. However, consanguineous marriages are declining proportionately with rising education levels amongst women. Many women stop working outside the home once they marry, or after the birth of their first or second child, unless both spouses are forced to work for economic reasons.[3]

These findings are interesting because they tell of the changing social scene. There seems to be a close corollary between education and women marrying later in life. There is also a smaller age disparity between husband and wife in later marriages.

My observations (based on lectures attended in three Jordanian girls schools, followed by question-and-answer sessions) confirm this trend and indicate a close connection with the particular class to which an individual woman belongs. Poorer women and women living outside of the center of Amman tend to marry earlier. Women who have recently moved to these areas also stop working to take care of their children and homes. Curiously, records of the Business and Professional Women's Club in Amman show another dimension. Better-educated women often marry lesser-educated men—sometimes substantially less educated—and quite often do not work or stop working because the husband wishes it. The records also show that women often opt to leave work after having given birth. The incentive to stay in work is not one that attracts women and makes them see it as essential to their welfare. Push factors, which will be discussed later, and social and marital expectations, to be discussed in chapter 6, are the main causes.

Equal Right to Work?

Women's "right to work" is clearly defined in the Jordan Constitution of 1952:

> Work is the right of all citizens (*al-ʿamal haqq li kul al-muwatinun*).
> Jobs are based on capability (*ʿala asas al-kafaʾat wal-muʾahilat*).
> All Jordanians are equal before the law. There will be no discrimination between [Jordanians] regarding rights and duties based on race, language or religion. (Article 6 of the Constitution)

Jordan's labor laws repeat and explain further. "By Jordanians are meant both men and women." Article 2 of the 1966 Labor Law still in force in Jordan confirms, "Owner of Business: any person . . . who employs in any way one person or more in exchange for wages," and the worker-laborer-employee (*ʿamil*) is defined as "each person, male or female, who performs a job in return for wages." These constitutional guarantees and labor laws are quite impressive in the overt and categorical equal rights they grant women, even though the antidiscrimination statement included in Jordan's Constitution refers only to discrimination based on "race, language or religion" and does not include gender as a category of discrimination.

In other words, Jordan's laws, like the laws of most modern countries, reflect basic principles of the right to work and equality for all its citizens. The actual laws and the fine print, however, present a picture of gender difference and patriarchy, notwithstanding declarations and intent. It is in the explanatory and executive parts of Jordan's laws that the patriarchal nature of the legal system becomes evident. Like the laws of other countries—including Arab and Islamic countries—the intent seems to contradict directly the actual laws and their execution. It is in the contradictions between what the principles set out and the actual laws that we find some of the basic difficulties and discriminations facing women who want to enter the job market and become financially independent. In Jordan, various legal codes (labor, personal status, citizenship, retirement, and criminal) peripheralize (*tahmish*) women by making them into male dependents and de facto deny women full legal competence (*ahliyya qanuniyya, ahliyya kamila*) even after they have reached the legal age of majority. This reality ensues through a combination of patriarchal family laws, state standardization and homogenization of the law, and the social belief that women need to be protected. The result is that, even though Jordan exerts efforts to allow women greater participation in public and business life, the laws act as a push factor forcing or encouraging women to leave the workplace.

Here we should turn to a discussion of the philosophical basis of Jordanian labor laws. These laws take into consideration the fact that labor relations are based on both legislation and *'urf.* Scholars of the law have therefore shifted between emphasizing the relations of production set up by these laws and the social significance of the laws.[4] This point is important for understanding how the social outlook toward gender is reflected in labor laws, notwithstanding the basic declaration of gender equality included in the Jordanian Constitution and labor laws. Because of the patriarchal outlook, an outlook based on acceptance of traditions as the basis for legislation, labor laws actually differentiate according to gender and on the basis of the need to protect women and allow a "moral" work environment. As will be discussed later, morality and a "moral," sexually segregated working situation in which women are protected represent the most important issues for people who are skeptical about women's employment. The widely accepted belief that women need protection has also been used by women's groups to define "problem areas" and to pressure successfully for benefits for women. Although this strategy has been important in achieving highly acclaimed "special benefits" for women—some that women all over the world have demanded and others that are special for Jordan—the philosophical basis of "women need protection" has in fact been at the very heart of continued discrimination that has undermined the constitutional guarantees of "equality" and "freedom" to choose, including the freedom to work.

It should be pointed out that many "special benefits" are sought by women workers everywhere. Here we can include the right to a ten-week maternity leave for the purpose of child care, of which six weeks must be allowed immediately following the birth of a child (Article 70 of the Labor Law). Also included is the requirement that any employer who employs twenty or more women must provide a child-care facility supervised by a qualified woman for the children of working mothers under the age of four, if there are at least ten children to care for (Article 71 of the Labor Law). Although Article 71 makes it easier for mothers who have no other possibilities of child care, thus allowing them to work, it is nevertheless a double-edged sword because it encourages employers not to employ twenty women at any one time or to employ women on a temporary rather than a permanent basis. Such benefits, however, should not have been considered "special benefits" for women; rather, they are social needs and family needs recognized as such by most countries because a child is a social and family responsibility and, according to Islamic law and *'urf*, is really the financial responsibility of the father.

The problem with "special benefit" laws is that they include some that are intended to lessen the work burden for women and to keep them safe from "dangerous" jobs. These laws work against equal access to job opportunity. Any denial of access to work opportunity is necessarily a stimulus for keeping women unemployed, particularly because the rules are based primarily on the idea that women are weaker biologically and of gentler constitution, therefore in need of protection. Interestingly, it is not only women who are extended "protection" according to the law, but also minors and juveniles. Minors in the labor force are defined as "each person, whether male or female, who is seventeen years old or less and not yet reached his eighteenth year." In other words, nonadult males are equated with adult women, both being in need of protection and having incomplete personal competence. Guarantees of equal job opportunities for women are thus severely undermined by the outlook toward what women can or cannot do, what they are allowed to do, and the essentialist perception of what it is that they *could not possibly be capable of.* Whereas the following chapters of this book will take up the social outlook and philosophy toward gender, this chapter focuses on the actual laws controlling women's work in Jordan and discusses in detail the impact of these laws in regards to women entering the job market. This chapter will point out particular sensitive areas that need solutions if greater participation of women in Jordan's economy is to be achieved.

A Husband's Prerogative

Perhaps the most glaring contradiction in Jordanian gender and labor laws has to do with the fact that Jordan's laws guarantee a woman an equal right to work yet insist that she cannot have that access unless she has her husband's approval. In fact, a wife can work only if she has spousal approval at the time the marriage is contracted, or if she was already working at the time the marriage was contracted without the bridegroom specifically forbidding her from working. Needless to say, the husband need not receive his wife's approval to work.

The necessity of a husband's approval is because of what is believed to be the requirement of the *shari'a* that a wife obey her husband, which is interpreted as giving him the right to confine her at home. Her obedience is in return for his financially supporting her and for other agreements in their marriage contract, including the payment of a dowry, which may or may not include jewelry and home furnishings (*tawabi' mahr*). Jordan's personal status laws and their application by its courts confirm this expectation. The validity of this argument will be taken up in chapter 6, when we turn our focus to marriage and divorce issues. Here, a number of points regarding the requirement that a husband approve his wife's work will be discussed. Of particular concern is the validity of this law and the basis on which it stands. Does the *shari'a* require a husband's consent, and does it give him the right to forbid his wife from working? What is the outlook of Islamic thinkers about women's work—is it the work of women that they frown upon or issues of gender mixing and morality? Given that such a law exists in Jordan, what is its impact on marital relations and in particular on the participation of women in the economy?

To begin, the Islamic *shari'a* does not discuss the issue of work or the right to work. It does not do so for men, and it does not do so for women. Rather, the *shari'a* focuses on matters of honesty, morality, and fairness in the workplace. In other words, there is no prohibition of the work of women according to the various sources of Islamic law, that is, the Qur'an and hadith. To the contrary, the Qur'an can be said to have taken the work of both men and women for granted: "[M]en have a share of what they have earned and women have a share of what they earned" (*"lil rijal nasib mima iktasabu wa lil-nisa' nasib miman iktasabna"*). Jordanian lawyer and former *shari'a* Court judge Ratib al-Zahir agrees that this statement is a clear approval of woman's work: "[W]ork is a way of making an income and Islam, which gave justice to women and gave her all the rights that fit with her humanity and pride, would not have stopped her from becoming an effective member in society. She is the sister of man, constitutes half of society and has energies of great use and benefit to her community."[5]

Even if we were to take the existing collections of *fiqh* as an accurate interpretation of what God wished, *fiqh* does not directly involve itself with whether a woman should work; as for *fiqh* and the public-private divide, as shown earlier, it was based on moral concerns of particular *fuqaha'* that were not discussing women and work but whose chief concern was with morality issues. Besides, *qadis* were not concerned with a husband's permission when dealing with cases involving a woman's professional or trade practice. Rather, as described in chapter 3, women worked and contributed to their families' and communities' welfare. They litigated in courts, knew their rights, and came in person to protect these rights. They sold and bought in the marketplace and were not willing to stay in marriages in which husbands demanded *ihtibas,* a demand usually associated with shopping. We do not see any court cases in which a husband demanded that his wife stop working or in which the divorce was because of his request that she stop working, even though quite often women were identified through the craft they practiced, such as *mashata, daya, dalala, mu'alima* (female master of trade), and so on.

Even among modern Islamic thinkers, there is no agreement as to the requirements for women's work or for a husband's approval before she can take a job. Rather, the discourse on women and work among modern *fuqaha'* seems to be focused on issues of gender mixing and morality, the same as their predecessors. Whereas the dominant discourse among people who oppose the work of women seems to be based on biological-nature arguments and other misogynistic ideas that a woman cannot do a job as well as a man, it is not the husband's approval or disapproval that seems to be of particular concern. Misogynistic attitudes consider women's abilities to be inferior to men's and dismiss the accomplishments of successful women who can "perform like a man" as exceptional. The Qur'an lines *"wa lil-rijal 'alayhima daraja"* ("and men are favored with a degree over them") (Surat al-Baqara 228) are used by Arab misogynists to establish man's inherent superiority over woman. 'Abbas Mahmud al-'Aqqad, the most influential Arab misogynist, opposes the work of women on the basis of women's biological nature and asks that all jobs be given to men, who would then support the women, whose role is determined by her nature, "including her [physical] capabilities and [inherent limited] ability to serve her kind . . . [h]er rights and duties within the family and society . . . [and s]ocial relations that are required by custom and public morality most of which are matters of traditions and manners."[6] Al-'Aqqad's conclusions continue to influence modern discourses and modern laws pertaining to women and work: that there are types of work they are capable or incapable of performing, that women need protection because of their weaker biological nature, and that it is society's responsibility to protect its moral standards, which is directly related to women in the public space. These issues are all based on principles that take the "nature" of woman as limiting her right to full equality and, though ensuring her legal competence as an adult, actually limit and frame this legal competence to make her legally dependent.

Interestingly, conservative Muslim clerics do not necessarily stand against women's work or demand that they must have their husbands' or guardians' permission before working. In his book *Huquq al-zawjiyya: Haqq al-mar'a fil-*

'amal, Sheikh Muhammad Mahdi Shams al-Din, the Lebanese Shi'i ayatollah, emphasizes that Islam does not take a stand against women's work in public and in the professions. He also delineates the moral issues involved. He begins by attacking people who claim that there are no rules regarding the work of women in *shari'a* or ones who demand that the *shari'a* be changed to catch up with the times:

> There are those who want to push [women] into the professions and the economy without any *shari'a* controls or rules because [t]he[y] are not concerned with the *shari'a,* or because [t]he[y] claim that such rules were not set up by the *shari'a,* or that these rules were suited for a society that no longer exists, and so we must change the *shari'a* to fit with the needs of our age, its knowledge and its needs. To those who make such claims, the *shari'a* is like an attire/dress whose size and style changes according to its wearer's appearance.[7]

The ayatollah then proceeds to attack people who claim that the *shari'a* does not allow a woman to leave her home or to work outside of her home, and believe that her only service is to her husband and children at home. "They claim that . . . allowing women to work is a transgression of the *shari'a,* and a transgression of God's laws [regarding women], and jeopardizes women toward dangers that threaten her chastity and her role within the family."[8] In answer to these "false" claims, the sheikh presents his interpretation of the *shari'a*'s outlook on women's work:

> The legality of woman's employment, her right to earn a living and enjoy the income of her work, and her right therefore to earn a salary equal to her contribution is the same as a man's right. Being a woman does not deny her that right. The legality of this has been proven by Islam, it is a God-given right that a woman does not have to struggle to achieve so as to save herself from the control of men and their power over her, or to prove her humanity and individuality as was the case in Western societies that did not recognize a woman's [inherent] right to work except after the social changes brought about by the Industrial Revolution and the need for working labor. . . . The economic independence of women is legally proven through the Islamic *shari'a,* she has her full economic competency. The husband, the father or the brother has no custody over her from that aspect.[9]

Asking, finally, why women should work, the ayatollah says, "[A woman should work] so as to utilize her energies and her time to enrich her community with her productive capacities rather than squandering energy and wasting time in *tarakhi wa kasal* [indolence and laziness]." [10] Because women have a responsibility toward their society and nation, it becomes the responsibility of the nation to train and prepare them to become partners in building it.

In other words, there are *shari'a* rules that must be followed, but they do not include the approval of a father or a husband. This approval is not what the *shari'a* is all about, according to the sheikh, whose findings are corroborated by medieval *fiqh* and by archival records, as pointed out earlier. But what are the *shari'a* concerns that need to be observed and seem to have been observed in the premodern period? The answer is gender mixing and morality. If a woman needs protection, it is from a workplace that includes gender mixing and therefore opens women to moral questions or harassment. Like most Muslim clergymen, Sheikh Shams al-Din does not condone mixing in the workplace and demands that women wear what is prescribed by Islam. He does, however, differentiate between normal modest wear and what is required by extremists that includes covering the face and making it almost impossible for women to function in the workplace. In other words, it is not the work of women that is in question, but the moral issues raised.

A middle position between people who encourage the work of women and the ones who want to prohibit it is presented by the Jordanian Islamic scholar Marwan Ibrahim al-Qisi who begins his study by decrying the condition under which Muslim women live. He attributes this situation to a lack of proper understanding of the words of the Qur'an and Sunna and the wrongful execution of the rules they set out. As part of this criticism he points to wrongful interpretations by *fuqaha'* and their dependence on weak traditions that are popular among the public; to public practices, particularly the wrongful treatment of women by men against God's laws; and to the wrong that women do unto themselves by not abiding by God's laws and the imitation of Western women. It is only by returning to a true interpretation of Islam and application of its laws that women will play the role to which they were intended and which would honor their rights and give them an ability to perform their duties. [11] Only if a woman recognizes her nature and abides by Islamic teachings will she live an honorable, productive life. Here using the *aya* of *"waqarin fi buyutakun"* (al-Ahzab 33) discussed earlier, al-Qisi reaches the following conclusions:

> 1. The husband has the right to stop his wife from leaving the home after having paid her advanced dowry. However, this right like any other right should not be misused by the man.
>
> 2. A Muslim woman should not go out too much, leaving her home must be for an important reason.

3. A Muslim woman should prefer to bear children and raise them, and watch out for her family's needs rather than work outside the home. However, there is nothing against her going out to work if there is a need as when there is no one to support her, but on condition that her work be according to conditions laid down by Islam, i.e. that this work be allowable by the *shari'a*, that said work does not take her away from her husband or children and that it not be in a situation where she would work with men.[12]

Al-Qisi completes the picture by allowing women to visit a doctor, preferably a woman doctor, but if not, then a decent male doctor and only in her husband's presence, and she is not to remove any unnecessary clothes. She could also practice sports but not in the presence of men, and she should be covered except for the "face, head, arms, and feet."[13] Al-Qisi's analysis is highly representative of conservative Arab society today and is well reflected in Jordan's laws. Even though he does not tie a woman's work to her husband's permission, he still requires a husband's permission for his wife to leave the home. Presumably, he means that she can take work into her home (for example, child care, which al-Qisi approves of), but leaving the home for any reason other than what is legitimate according to the *shari'a*—to run errands, visit parents, and so on—requires a husband's permission. Hence the strong connection between a woman's work, her husband's permission for her to work, and her obedience to him.

Although thinkers may differ on a husband's approval, all are directly concerned with issues of morality that seem to be completely focused on sexuality. Women, different from men by nature, should not in any way entice men to act indecently, nor should they be placed in a situation where they would be encouraged to act immorally. In other words, both men and women are reduced to their essential nature as potential sinners, an idea that is actually quite alien to Islam, which does not believe in original sin or blame Eve for the Fall. The fact that the Prophet's women companions went out publicly and his wives were active within their communities is usually explained as being possible because it was an ideal community when sin was the last thing on people's minds. That it is this "ideal community" that Muslims today should emulate seems to be a lost fact in this conservative gender discourse. The whole question on morality seems to be attached to particular *'urf* of certain societies during particular periods and is highly dependent on socioeconomic conditions.

There are social and legal repercussions involved in requiring a husband's consent for his wife to work. Personal status laws set a basis of gender difference and discrimination that has become reflected in social attitudes. Confirming that a wife must receive her spouse's approval for all her actions has been solidified into a social and cultural basis of gender in modern Jordanian society. This condition need not have been created. Spousal approval is by no means unique to Islamic society, because it characterizes marriage in premodern Europe and its colonial extensions in North and South Americas, Asia, and Africa. Here it was not a question of religion but rather of gender relations and culture. But it should also be remembered that in premodern Europe, women were guided by principles of *coverture*,[14] a term connoting the wife's being covered by her husband's name and power. Her dowry went to him, and he had full legal control of her person—at least theoretically; her property became his property, and he could incarcerate her if he so wished. That principle was not the case in Islamic societies: no *coverture* laws applied, a woman expected to be the recipient of a dowry, and her property remained her own. Furthermore, her allegiance continued to be toward her family, which was recognized by Islamic law as will be discussed in chapter 5. As example one needs only to point to the right of a wife to divorce her husband who moves her so that her family lives a distance greater than could be traveled in one day (*masafat al-qisar*) against her wishes or her family's wishes. The powers given to the husband vis-à-vis his wife by modern personal status laws are therefore greater than what he enjoyed earlier.

One of the social repercussions facing women who are believed to be disobedient to their husbands is the onus it places on her sisters and even female cousins. A disobedient wife is declared to be *nashiz,* which in legal terms really means that she no longer deserves his financial support, becoming in itself a basis for her to sue for divorce. But judges almost always rule against the wife and consider her at fault when she sues for divorce on the basis of "discord and conflict" (*shiqaq wa niza'*), even though it is the main legal method by which a wife can sue for divorce and hope to receive partial fulfillment of her financial rights. Who would want to marry into the family of a woman who has brought discord and conflict into her home and her husband's life? Issues such as her right to work, her wish to work, and even her family's need for her salary have little bearing in courts of law and consequently in society at large. The very name used for divorce cases seen by the court, *"shiqaq wa niza',"* and the fact that it is believed to be a wife's divorce, even though both husbands and wives have recourse to that method—particularly husbands who do not want to pay alimony—mean that women and their families are directly hurt if she is declared a disobedient wife. As *nashiz,* a wife is considered a shrew and is denied her right to her husband's financial assistance, and her whole family, especially her unmarried sisters and even cousins, is placed in a socially unfavorable situation.

As mentioned earlier, according to the *shari'a,* a wife expects her husband to financially support her as long as she is married to him and during the three-month *'idda* period following divorce. Specifics of this support differ among the various *fuqaha'*, and Jordanian courts have seen interesting cases in which wives sued husbands or ex-husbands for medical, schooling, or other specific expenses on the basis of their right to spousal support. An important question facing young Jordanians married to working wives or expecting to marry working wives has to do with spousal support. According to Personal Status Law 68, a wife who works without her husband's approval does not deserve *nafaqa* from him, even though she remains married to him and he lives with her. This law is interesting because it is not justifiable according to the *shari'a*. *Nafaqa* is paid not because the wife has no income to support herself according to Islamic law and *'urf*, but because she gives herself to her husband, sexually speaking. The idea is that working without his agreement means she is not obedient, which makes her *nashiz* and hence not deserving of his financial support because she is withholding herself from him. That interpretation is what *nashiz* really means in the law. But if they are living together, how could a wife be *nashiz?* The importance of this law is that it illustrates the legal method employed by legists to deal with a new problem by looking for *shari'a* justifications that are more like Gruyère cheese full of holes. In the above case, a way was looked for regarding disputes over the wife's income and the insistence of the husband that this income be integrated into the family income and the wife's refusal because it is his responsibility to support her, notwithstanding how wealthy she is. It should be mentioned that the couple always had the option to include in their marriage contract conditions regarding the question of financial support. But, in this situation favoring patriarchy, not including a condition is not used against the husband. Compare the case in which the court refused to accept the wife's evidence that her profession was included in the marriage contract and she continued to work after marriage. The court's finding was that she should have included his approval in the conditions in the contract, but because she had not her evidence did not matter.[15]

What if the husband agrees that his wife can work—does the wife deserve her husband's financial support when she receives an income from a job or a business she owns? Should she contribute to the family budget? According to the *shari'a*, a woman's income is her own and is not to be spent on the household, which is the husband's responsibility. Today, with the rising cost of living, such a situation is not even considered, and a working woman or one with income is usually expected to share expenses with her husband. In fact, it is quite common today among educated young men just starting out to look for young women who either have an independent income or hold a job. Young men with whom I discussed this issue voiced deep concern regarding the financial burden expected of a husband before and after marriage, including the dowry, attachments to the dowry (mainly jewelry and house furnishings), and the family budget. The latter in particular was a point of contention, especially in regards to working women who tend to wish to keep their own income. Because husbands consider it their right to allow or forbid their wives from working, they also consider it their right to control the income from that work. Several women who left their jobs because of this reason told me they saw no purpose in working given the difficulty of transportation, the added burden of family and housework, and the fact that they were not left with enough money to fulfill their own personal needs.

In Jordan, like other Arab countries, marital assets do not belong jointly to a husband and wife to be divided between them if a divorce should take place. This fact is based on the separate entities that a husband and wife represent, which is unlike the situation in Western countries. It is one of the reasons that women consider their income as belonging solely to them and quite often prefer to stop working altogether rather than turn over their salaries to husbands whose responsibility it is to support them in the first place. It is true that among the educated middle- and upper-class strata of society, married couples seem to be working on the basis of a joint family budget, but even here spouses hold their property separately, and there is consciousness among the women that what they buy or bring into the marriage should remain theirs. In Egypt, families of brides actually insist that the bridegroom sign a "list" itemizing all the goods that the bride is bringing into the marriage so if he divorces her, he has to deliver the items included in the "list" intact or else be prosecuted. Abuses of the "list" and how it is being used by brides' families today are proving to be an incentive for changing personal status laws in Egypt.

Personal status law gives the impression that once the husband has given his consent to his wife to work, he can no longer deny her. Actually, the situation is much more complicated, and this law in particular must be considered one of the most important hindrances to the entry of women into the workforce or to opening their own businesses because their continuation is dependent on "keeping the husband happy." The problems here are diverse. A man could refuse to pay his wife any financial support on the basis that he asked her to quit working and she refused and continued to work.[16] A husband could also deny his divorcée her rightful financial compensation because she worked without his permission. When the wife sues for these financial rights, which are often agreed upon at the time the marital contract was signed, the court asks her to prove that she had received his approval to work. Because such approval is almost always an oral agreement, it becomes very hard to prove, and the wife loses all financial rights, even what was agreed upon at the time of marriage and what was included in the marriage contract.[17]

Another interesting case was decided based on the fact that the wife worked in the armed forces and was not able to resign.[18] Here the husband had asked his wife to move with him to live in an area outside of Amman where he had lived continuously for a long time. Her move would have entailed quitting her job in the armed forces, which she was unwilling to do. In a *ta'a* case, the husband demanded that his wife be made to move and live with him. As the records state, the wife had worked in the armed forces before her marriage, and the fact that she continued to work after her marriage to him was evidence that he had approved of her working. Interestingly, the court never disputed the husband's right to demand that his wife quit and come live with him. Rather, all the court wanted the husband to prove was that the new home he had set up was acceptable, per *shari'a* requirements (that is, it was a legal house of a standard similar to ones of her same class). The court was also concerned that the wife worked in the armed forces and did not have the right to resign if she wished to do so. What this case tells us is that a husband's acceptance of a wife's work does not mean that he cannot later change his mind. It was because of the wife's inability to resign from the army that the court ultimately dismissed the case, not the wife's right to remain in her job once her husband had changed his mind.

Jordanian law, unlike most other Muslim countries, allows the inclusion of "prenuptial" conditions to marriage contracts. For some reason, probably social pressure (to be discussed in chapter 6), women hardly make use of this instrument to determine the form of their marriage relationship, including their freedom to work. The fact that they do not include such conditions weakens their situation once there is a dispute regarding their work. Interestingly, the inclusion of conditions to contracts was not as well known among women groups I met with as one would have expected, given that it is the most important way by which women are able to get out of an unwanted marriage without losing their financial rights and determine their living conditions with their spouses. The unwillingness of husbands to allow such conditions is one reason that this instrument is not used by women; another is a social discourse that discourages women from looking in such a direction so as not to limit their attractiveness as potential wives.

It is generally assumed that it is among the lesser-educated classes that disputes over a wife's work take place. Actually, this general situation seems to exist throughout Jordanian society. Thus, professional women face the same kind of marital control. A number of court cases indicate that teachers often face being declared *nashiz* because they refuse to give up their jobs on their husbands' demand. It should be pointed out that to be declared *nashiz* does not mean that a wife will be granted a divorce by her husband; he can keep her in that state indefinitely if he so wishes, unless she takes the case in front of the judge and goes through the expense and hassle of a *shiqaq wa niza'* court case, even though his nonpayment of financial support is enough reason for her to divorce him. In a 1980 Tamyiz Court case,[19] the wife, a teacher, was asked to prove that her husband approved that she worked. Given her education and the fact that she was already working at the time of her marriage, logic should have indicated that the husband must have married her knowing that she had a profession. Because he was the one denying that he had ever approved of her work, he should have been the one expected to produce evidence that he had indicated his refusal for her to continue working at the time of the marriage. The court, however, took the opposite stance and placed the onus of proof on the shoulders of the wife, notwithstanding the acknowledged *'urf* that written conditions by a wife regarding control of a husband's actions in marriage contracts are not acceptable socially and hence not practiced, even if the laws allow it. They are certainly not acceptable to husbands who could be considered wimps if they succumb to their wives' conditions. So according to *'urf*, such conditions are always oral, and the courts should be well aware of that fact. Obvious evidence, such as the wife's education, profession, or inclusion of her profession in the marriage contract, does not seem to make a difference in the court's decisions, as indicated in various similar marital disputes.

Work and Private Life

"Despite the fact that, as an often-cited statistic holds, women do two-thirds of the world's work, their achievements are very often invisible. Women work hard, but they often receive little credit for their accomplishments. Still rarely (relative to men) do they reach high-visibility positions of achievement and leadership."[20] With these words, Hilary Lips began her keynote address to the National Council of Women of New Zealand in which she discussed the contributions of women to their communities in public and private life that go unrecognized and unappreciated.

The most important reason for the lack of recognition is the nature of the work undertaken by women, which remains in an "invisible" area. Invisibility exists because her work is "expected of her." Thus, a woman's work at home in a domestic role as housekeeper and mother is looked at as what she is expected to do. Neither is her role in peasant societies—working in the fields beside her family or her husband and children, raising chicken and keeping a vegetable garden to supplement their income, or manufacturing boxes or baskets or other cash-generating items—taken into account, notwithstanding how important her contributions are to her family or community. The lack of recognition of women's work because it is associated with family or home is without doubt a basic reason for discriminating against her throughout the economic, political, and legal structures.

The lack of recognition also means that when women do take jobs, they are looked at as less capable than men in the same jobs. This fact is reflected in salary scales that constantly differentiate between the sexes at all levels and professions, whether we are talking about peasant labor or university professors. But it becomes a vicious circle: once regarded as less than her male colleague, once her contributions are taken for granted, she receives a lower salary, has a comparative lack of promotion potential, and is closed to particular jobs that are open to men. There is a basic outlook among men and women that women's labor can never be equal to men's. This belief is the case worldwide, even in the United States where women have achieved great steps toward nondiscrimination according to sex. "According to the U.S. Bureau of Labor Statistics women make up two-thirds of all minimum wage-earners, and during 1998, women in the United States earned 76 cents for every dollar earned by men. . . . Asian-American women earned 48 cents, and Hispanic women earned 48 cents." The reason, according to Lips, is "our long habits of thinking of women and the work they do as less important and impressive than men." [21]

Jordan is therefore not alone in social discrimination against the work of women. What makes the situation more difficult in Jordan is the moral discourse that associates a woman's duty at home with her religious duty toward God. Both the law and social discourses take it for granted that a woman's place is at home, that her primary loyalty is to her family, that she has to obey her father and her husband, and that it is up to the latter to agree that she can take a job. Thus, without familial approval, she cannot work, and this approval is usually dependent on family needs. Therefore, the social discourse stresses the idea that a woman works only because she needs to support her family or at least to help her husband cover the expenses for her and the children. The idea that a woman could be involved in a job or a trade for other reasons does not seem to be approved, and most women take jobs with the idea that they will not have to work as soon as the husband or family can afford for her to stay home. It comes as no surprise, therefore, that a number of studies regarding Jordanian women's work conclude that most unmarried working women plan to stop working after they marry, that 44 percent of married women intend to leave their jobs after having children, that 41 percent of women think seriously of stopping working, and that 25 percent of women with children have a hard time bearing their responsibilities as mothers and holding a job at the same time.

Young girls in Jordanian middle and high schools fit within this pattern. Asked about their chosen future professions, only one out of a class of fifty girls said that she hoped to go on to university and become a doctor. The rest intended to get married. When it was pointed out that being married is not a job and then asked what job they would take, a few agreed and indicated various occupations they would like, usually beautician or hairdresser. When asked why having a job could be important for a woman, they seemed to be aware of the importance of financial independence. Statements such as "So she could be financially independent," "will not need to ask her husband for money," or "if he dies then she can support herself and her children" show a keen awareness of the problems that wives often face. It is the contradiction between this awareness and the lack of enthusiasm at having a career that is surprising. Yet, on reflection, given the school curriculum, mass media, emphasis on the joy of a wedding, and the central role the bride plays in it—"it is her night" is the usual saying—it ceases to be so surprising. This point will be discussed in a later chapter regarding life and growing up in Jordan.

Class is important here. The three girls schools in which I posed these questions were all located in the more popular areas around Amman, and the students lived close to them. Records of the Business and Professional Women's Club of Amman confirm these findings. Although the women who resort to legal assistance at the club come from various classes of Jordanian society, the large majority originate from the poorer sectors of society who cannot afford legal assistance and whom the club advises and sometimes sponsors free of charge. Many women ask the club to help them find employment, and, in most cases, it is because these women no longer have anyone to support them or the alimony they are receiving is inadequate. Faced with supporting themselves and their children, they are willing to take any job, even though they may have completed their education and sometimes attended vocational school or even university. Having married, they were expected to stop working or not to work. It was only when the marriage fell apart or they were faced with financial need that the women looked for work and began to earn a living.

This situation is in contrast to middle-class women to whom a job appears to be an essential part of life, a natural continuation of their education from school to university and then on to a job. Actually, in Jordan as in other fast-changing urban centers of the Middle East experiencing significant population growth, increased consumerism, and upward mobility, it is becoming a requirement that a bride hold a job and have an income. If she is still a student, then she is expected to work after graduation. Otherwise, she is expected to receive financial support from her family or to have some other form of income from inheritance or property. This expectation is particularly prevalent among university students and graduates. Young men expect their wives to share in household expenses and work to better their material conditions and their future. As for upper-class women, there is a greater openness and choice. Although wealth allows women to stay home, they often opt to enter into business with their families or are made partners by their fathers. They may choose to become socially active in welfare projects and various forms of social and community services; they could enter the professions, particularly as doctors and lawyers, and an increasing number are opting to go into trade and open their own businesses.

No matter which class we are considering, however, the philosophical outlook toward women's work remains the same except perhaps for very wealthy families. Women's work is regarded as temporary and essential only because the family needs the money or because her earnings would help buy things for the family that they could otherwise not afford; that is, she works for the material well-being of the family. One consequence is that a woman becomes a "double-duty" person: not only does she hold a job with all its responsibilities, but once she comes home she still has to cook, clean, take care of the children, shop for household needs, and even do the children's homework with them. Her mother, if alive, helps when she is at work, but once home, she is expected to take over. Husbands of working wives usually help in all these household chores, but the help is considered "help," not responsibility. The working wife is under constant pressure to be the wife society expects her to be and her husband expects her to be even while holding her job and helping support the family. The psychological impact of this "dual role" and the social expectations are of severe impact on working women, yet this fact is not given due consideration, and she is placed under even greater scrutiny than a nonworking wife. Furthermore, if there is litigation between the husband and wife, it is almost always used against her that she is holding a job and therefore not fulfilling the duties expected of a wife.

As was shown earlier, there is nothing in Islam that forbids women from work, and women have in fact always participated in the economy. The nature of business and the labor market itself have changed, which has resulted in women losing out in areas where they competed earlier. As the nuclear family becomes the predominant form of family in Jordan, as it has in most of the world, society is bound to change its outlook toward the responsibilities of women in the home. Sharing the expenses of living, a responsibility placed solely on the shoulders of husbands according to the *shari'a*, should be reciprocated by a clear division of labor within the household, not only amicably as is usual between understanding spouses, but also in courts of law and in the philosophy regarding law and women's work.

Privileging Women

"Difference" provides a further basis for discrimination, notwithstanding how beneficial the difference is to weaker parties in the system. Jordanian labor laws determine areas of exceptionalism based on gender that continue the basic philosophy of gender discrimination. This fact is particularly true because the exceptionalism is not meant to be temporary to narrow an educational or social gap between two groups with different advantages or abilities. Here we are talking about permanent differences based on the nature of women and the inability of a woman to do a man's job. The exceptions made to the law extend the gap and help enlarge it. Other exceptions to the law are based on a woman's fragile and helpless nature and therefore the consequent need to protect her. Such an approach is at once the result of the dominant patriarchal outlook and a force extending that very outlook.

The following are examples of how some benefits work against women and how they strengthen the patriarchal discourse connecting women with marriage and dependency.

Night Work

Women cannot work at night jobs or in dangerous situations such as quarries, according to Article 69 of the Labor Law. Such a law would appear to be beneficial to women who prefer not to work at night and who would be protected from the unhealthy environment of quarries (stone, limestone, phosphates, and so on). But if working at night is so undesirable for women, then why put it in the form of a law? And although women could become abused in providing labor for quarries, such jobs are usually given to men. Protection from night work fits with society's concern with moral issues pointed out earlier. It is not so much the work of women that bothers most *fuqaha'* as the possible moral implications that could be caused by mixing the sexes in the workplace or women's work in an improper work environment. But if these concerns are legitimate, are women then given an advantage when it comes to working during the day and at jobs that do not include health hazards such as the ones she would face in a quarry? The answer is that no such preference is given, even in jobs located at the bottom of the salary scale, such as custodians and cleaning persons, in which situations men are still preferred—unless it is a girls school or other type of establishment for women—and the men are paid a higher salary than women holding the same job.

It is interesting that most of the laws protecting women use the basic arguments that women are the mothers of the future generations and as such their health and welfare should be guaranteed by the state. The argument itself is not a new one, nor is it unique to Jordan. In the Western world that argument was the very one used to create a situation of exceptionalism for mothers or potential mothers, which in turn allowed for patriarchal control and discrimination against women. Western labor laws introduced early in the century in non-Western countries under British control, for example, required that an employed woman who married resign her job. As for France, even today French women cannot work at night without their husbands' approval. Their laws, as explained in chapter 2, had diffused globally and became part of social *'urf* confused with the larger patriarchal picture.

The contradictions in the laws are another point of concern that put into question the validity of having such laws on the books, however worthy the intentions. Here I want to point to the exceptions to the law forbidding women from working at night, included in the codes and left to the Ministerial Council to mold as it sees fit. It was left up to the minister of labor to determine the industries prohibited to women and the hours of work. These rules were to be generalized according to government policy and "individual circumstances." In other words, the government recognized that these laws were not die-hard and were open to change depending on conditions and the needs of the country. This recognition is good, because it is possible to change these rules and make labor laws less discriminatory. This latter point is important particularly in the sense of applying a philosophy of equality by ending the conceptualization of law according to biological difference.

Exceptions to women's work at night at present include employment in hospitals and clinics, in restaurants and tourist establishments, as airline and airport staff, as personnel in industries for transportation of people and goods, in jobs requiring yearly inventories, in jobs preparing for beginning- and end-of-season retail sales, or in jobs where there is a fear of financial loss (for example, contamination of stored goods). These exceptions are so broad and diverse that the very law is curious and seems to be oriented toward the needs of the market rather than to the protection of women. When women are needed they are allowed to work at night, and when they are not needed they are forbidden from working. Thus, at times of inventory, sales, or increased tourist activity, women are allowed to work at night, but once the pressure is off, they are forbidden from doing so. This conclusion is supported by the limit for women's night work: thirty days per year, ten hours per day. Because extra work is compensated at 125 percent to 150 percent of pay according to the law, women who wish to increase their income by working overtime at night are virtually cut out except when job pressure requires it. Without doubt, this situation works to the advantage of men, and the law can be said to limit competition of women with men over scarce employment opportunities. The concept that men are the breadwinners and that women work only for financial need is important here. It is also the reason women are paid less than men.

To conclude, whether women prefer not to work at night or in dangerous jobs should not be determined by the authorities. Women work in the fields and continue to herd flocks in deserts under the most severe conditions, so it is not as though they are not capable. At any rate, ability should not be the basis of laws whose ultimate goal is equality. The matter should be left open to individual choice. Controlling job choices and setting rules based on biological and socially perceived roles strengthen gender difference and make women's helplessness and dependency a basis for legal interpretation.

Social Security

Jordan's Social Security Law for 1978 (amended in 1979) is comprehensive and is intended to benefit Jordanians and their families. The law is applicable to all employees to whom Jordan's labor laws apply as well as public employees in public service. Power over which sectors of society are to be covered by this law is given to the council of ministers, that is, the executive branch of the government, which can change the beneficiaries and the actual benefits depending on social conditions at any particular time. Inheritance of retirement benefits, however, is guided by the Islamic *shari'a* rules of inheritance. The law provides for financial assistance in the following situations:

- Injury at work and work-related illnesses.
- Insurance against old-age, incapacity, and death.
- Insurance against temporary incapacity due to sickness or giving birth.
- Health insurance to workers and their dependents.
- Unemployment. (Article 3 of Social Security Law)[22]

Although the law and coverage are as good as one can find in other countries, they do discriminate against women. The first problem with the social security law is that it does not cover jobs in which large numbers of women are employed. Thus, the law is not applicable to unregulated and temporary jobs. Women are highly involved in these types of jobs and do not have social security benefits—including retirement, health, and compensation for job-related injury, all of which are essential in today's society. Thus, they are at jeopardy in the workplace and have no support if laid off. Given the fact that retirement, health, and social security are some of the most important reasons that people go into public employment, extending social security to areas with a high employment rate of women should act as a pull factor for women to seek employment. As things stand, the incentive to work is that much less for women involved in these types of jobs, yet they are usually the ones in the greatest financial need.

Furthermore, the law does not apply to family members working for a family enterprise. This exclusion is particularly harmful to women who carry a substantial share of many such enterprises, whether as labor in fields, selling in family-owned shops, making goods to be sold in these shops, and so on. A woman's contribution to family enterprises remains "invisible"; she is not paid by her family, and her labor is not figured into any economic calculations. Whereas sons can draw salaries or at least draw funds from such enterprises, the same is not the case for wives or daughters whose financial support by the family is probably all they receive. Ownership of family enterprises usually belongs to the father, husband, or brother. If Jordan's laws regarding family ownership of businesses are uniformly enforced, then it would make sense, but what guarantees do women members of a family have, and what benefits can they expect in case of injury, unemployment, family disputes, or divorce? Clearly, there is an inconsistency in the application of these various laws.

Other forms of unregulated employment of particular significance to women include domestic help and "those within the same capacity." Most domestic help are women, and today a large percentage of people employed in domestic service, men and women, are non-Jordanians. The social security law does not apply to non-Jordanians, and abuses of foreign labor, whether Arab or Asian, are quite commonplace. Other countries, such as the United States, demand that employers of foreign labor pay social security for them so they can receive adequate coverage in case of injury, retirement, or unemployment. There is no reason Jordan's laws cannot take such an initiative to cover both Jordanian and non-Jordanian domestic labor.

Retirement

Benefits based on gender difference provide a basic contradiction to Jordanian constitutional laws about the equality of all Jordanians in regards to work opportunity and actual employment. Even though the benefits considered to be a gain for women and for which feminist groups have fought appear at first glance to be positive, on closer scrutiny they prove quite problematic if the goal is to increase women's participation in the economy. Besides, laws that are based on exceptionalism, biological or otherwise, only strengthen patriarchy and discrimination. I will begin by first discussing retirement benefits provided by Jordan's social security and retirement laws, and then proceed to explain the areas that are problematic in these laws.

Funds for the payment of retirement benefits are provided through monthly contributions paid by employers on the basis of 8 percent of the salaries of the employees, monthly contributions taken out at the rate of 5 percent of an employee's salary on the condition that the amount contributed by the employer not be less that five hundred fils, the amounts contributed by employees in return for (uncovered) periods worked earlier, and earnings from these contributions. In other words, the social security system of Jordan is funded much the same way as elsewhere, and it is part of the rights of workers when they are employed. Social security is supposed to cover everyone contributing to the system equally depending on the length of employment and the salary at the time of retirement. Given the equal contributions made by all employees according to their salaries, gender should not be a basis for paying out benefits, particularly because it is not a basis in contributions made by the employees. Yet, gender considerations are central to the system, and benefits differ according to gender in regards to:

- Period of employment needed to deserve retirement benefits.
- When benefits can be retrieved.
- Who has the right to benefits.
- Conditions required for providing benefits because of death of the employee.

It is not that regulations were meant to harm women; actually, they are mostly intended to make a woman's work easier, allowing her earlier retirement than men and facilitating her resignation from work while holding on to her benefits. But although the rules are generally considered to benefit women and were probably intended to make a woman's life and her family's life easier, in fact the differences in retirement benefits based on gender constitute a major form of discrimination against women and are without doubt a serious hindrance working against the sustained employment of women in the workforce.

The logic behind extending retirement privileges to women that are not available to men is the belief that women would rather not work if they had the choice and that, because the home is the natural place for women, the only reason women work is to support dependents or help supplement the family income. Once a woman marries, however, she will have her husband's support, and unless she needs to contribute to the household income, it is believed that she would then retire. Furthermore, it is also assumed that getting married, or having a son or daughter get married, is a costly affair and that mothers may prefer to receive early retirement to be able to afford such expenses. So privileges extended to women and not to men are intended as a benefit to women who expect to stay home after marriage or who choose early retirement. Whatever the intention, these "benefits" constitute a strong push factor for women to retire, especially when there is a financial need in the family, such as marriage of a son or daughter, sickness, or other forms of financial difficulty.

According to Article 14 of Jordan's labor laws: "Benefit payments deducted from the salary of an employed woman who resigns her job are to be returned to her" (*"tu'ad lil-muwazafa al-mustaqila al-'a'idat alati uqtuti'at min muratabiha"*), and "a woman has the right to leave her job and receive her end-of-service bonus at the time of her marriage" (*"yahiq l'il-mar'a al-'amila tark al-'ammal wal'husul 'ala mukafa'at nihayat al-khidma hal 'aqd zawajiha"*). In other words, if a woman resigns her job she can get back all the money she contributed to her retirement fund. It becomes a push factor encouraging women to stop working at times when her family is facing a financial crunch. If she is getting married, she is further rewarded in the form of an end-of-service bonus that she would normally receive only when she retires. This reward is problematic because it encourages women to leave their jobs, and, even more important, the connection between marriage and staying home is reinforced through laws that actually financially reward women for quitting their jobs. It is curious why a government would encourage women to work, offer them job equality through its constitution and labor laws, and at the same time make it rewarding for women to quit their jobs.

Needless to say, men do not receive the same options as women when they get married. Gender difference is reflected further in retirement laws. According to Article 41 of the Social Security Law: "Retirement entitlements are due to the insured man when he reaches the age of sixty and to the insured woman when she reaches the age of 55." Furthermore, men can retire after twenty years of service, whereas women can retire after fifteen. Because the amount of retirement is based on the last two years of employment, women tend to retire at much lower pensions than men for the very same job (Article 43b). If a woman wishes to retire earlier than fifty-five—which the law allows as indicated above—she is reimbursed the monthly deductions for retirement and other benefits that were taken out of her monthly salary while employed. Early retirement and early receipt of benefits can be considered a way by which women could save a nest egg through which to begin a business. However, the amount she would receive would hardly be adequate because it is only her contribution to the retirement fund that is in question. In most cases, funds received from early retirement go toward paying for a wedding or family emergency.

Gender difference is also applied in cases of mandatory early retirement. Article 15 of Jordan's labor laws reads: "The Ministerial Council can decide to retire an employee if he has completed 20 years of work and the woman employee if she has completed 15 years of work." This article is further emphasized in Article 17: "Keeping in consideration Article 26 of this law, he is considered retired by decree any employee whose service is terminated without resignation or by losing his job if he completed 20 years and the woman employee if she has completed 15 years."

Social security and retirement laws can be said to discriminate indirectly and unintentionally, that is, they were actually meant to assist women and were built on a conception of women as more frail by nature and that they work only because circumstances compel them to. Other forms of legal discrimination, however, are quite overt and direct. An obvious example has to do with the situation in which a woman employee dies while still in service. In such a situation, her pension would go to her family *only if* the family (children, husband, mother, father) can prove that they are destitute and need the pension or that she was their direct financial provider while alive. Article 52 of the Social Security Law concerning beneficiaries states: "In fulfillment of the intent from this law, beneficiaries are those family members of the insured . . . who fit the following [categories]: a. His widow; b. His children and those of his brothers and sisters whom he supports; c. His widowed and divorced daughters; d. The husband of the deceased insured [woman]." [23]

This law equalized widower and widow of deceased employees but places them in two separate categories because the actual treatment of each differs. Whereas a widow and dependents of a deceased employed male need prove only their relationship to him and that he is deceased, the requirements for the family of a deceased woman employee make it almost impossible for them to receive any of the retirement due her by law. It must be remembered that the employee paid for this privilege through monthly deductions from her salary and that contributions by the employee were part of the contract according to which she was employed. Therefore, social security benefits are not a "grant" from the government that administers the service, and it is not up to the government to differentiate between recipients according to gender of the employee.

But differences also exist when it is the husband or the wife of a deceased employee who is receiving the pension. Article 56 of the Social Security Law, titled "Conditions for Paying Retirement Pension to the Husband," states: "It is a condition for the husband to receive the pension due him because of his deceased insured wife, that he be completely incapacitated, that he have no private income equal to the amount of pension due him [from social security]. . . . [I]f that income is less than what he is due, then he is to be paid the difference and the rest is to be divided among the other beneficiaries."[24] Add to the above the fact that only those beneficiaries who have no other means of support are deserving of the pension of a deceased insured woman employee. Article 34 of the Labor Law for 1996 states: If a woman employee who has gained a pension "dies, her pension is transferred to her beneficiaries according to this law if their need is proven and if it was also proven that the employee was directly responsible for their support." This statement means that unless her family can prove that they have no one to support them and no other means of support, that "she was directly responsible for their support," they would not receive her pension. In other words, it is very hard for the family of a deceased female employee to receive the pension that was due her from the benefits that she was obliged to pay by law throughout her employment. Given this fact, there is no reason for a woman to continue until her age of retirement. These laws are very serious and are at the heart of the perception of women as peripheral to the workplace, limit their promotion, and reduce their incentive to remain employed.

One last point that needs to be raised about laws of retirement has to do with the connection between polygamy and pension. Jordan, like other Muslim countries—exceptions include Turkey and Tunisia—allows a man to be married to four wives at any one time. The choice is his, and the approval of his existing wife or wives does not come to bear on the validity of his new marriage (this matter will be discussed in more detail in chapter 5). However, even though wives are almost universally against a husband's taking a second wife for emotional, financial, and other reasons, it is the wife who has to carry the burden of the husband's actions when it comes to receiving a widow's pension. Whereas a husband does not share the pension of his deceased wife with another man because a wife is not allowed to be married to more than one man at any time, the wife has to share her deceased husband's pension with his other wives if he is a polygamist. The same goes to the children of a deceased employee: they have to share his pension with children from his other marriages.

It is in the finer details regarding who deserves pension and the percentages due various members of the family regarding pension from a deceased provider that this form of discrimination becomes clear. It is also directly connected with personal status laws regarding wives of deceased employees. It does not apply to a man receiving his own pension or who is beneficiary of his wife's pension. The tables explaining benefits to various beneficiaries of pensions published by the Lawyers' Syndicate show that although percentages due to spouses may differ depending on whether the parents of the deceased insured employee are still alive, in all cases the wives share the same portion that one single wife would have received had the husband not been a polygamist.[25] Thus, when a husband has more than one wife the result is that on his death, the pension that should have been due one wife is divided among two to four, as the case may be. The same goes for the children. The more wives the more children, and the lesser the amount that each child will receive. Given the fact that social security benefits are pegged to a minimum standard of living that increases only when the amounts received are not adequate to meet the minimum needs of life, it is obvious that subdividing pensions among wives can be only a source of hardship and harm.

If the right to more than one wife is religiously sanctioned and inheritance laws are based on the Islamic *shari'a* that gives the man double what the woman receives at every level of the relationship between heir and deceased, it should have little to do with social security benefits by which an employee's family expects to be supported on the basis of at least the minimum required to survive. When a husband takes a second wife he is taking on a financial burden that he feels he can support. Why, then, should it be any different in regards to the pension his survivors would receive? Why should his wife and children have to suffer from an act that he took unilaterally, particularly when his pension becomes their only source of income and it is pegged to the poverty scale? As a way of not encouraging polygamy and to make sure that widows receive a pension that would allow them a respectful life without having to fall back on charity, why should not husbands who take a second wife be required to contribute more of their salaries into the social security fund? Whether the employers should contribute as well or the husbands should have to carry the employer's share can be discussed. But doing so would be fair for wives who had no say in their husband's taking a second wife. An alternative would be that only the first wife would benefit from a deceased employee's pension, except if it is she who initiates the divorce, and depending on how long she has lived with him her benefits would not cease because of his repudiation or unilateral divorce. A second wife could then be covered by social security only if the first wife is deceased or if the husband adds to his monthly contributions to the social security fund. This method would discourage second marriages and unilateral divorce for no fault of the wife. It would also discourage women from marrying a man with an already existing wife. Just as important, it would recognize the participation of a wife as homemaker and partner in the Jordanian home. Ironically, Jordanian laws may emphasize family and a wife's primary job as being in the home, but it is not reflected in the laws regarding financial benefits, which reverse the concept to see the wife as an individual and not a member of a family.

Laws Not on the Books

Missing laws, that is, laws to regulate important aspects of employment, constitute a major hindrance for women's work, discouraging them from entering the job market. They also constitute an effective push factor for women to leave the job market. Jordanian labor laws are inadequate in these areas. Here some of the laws are implicit, that is, they do not exist and are not taken into consideration, whereas others are very explicit, and even though they may be harmful to both men and women, they are particularly negative to women because women happen to constitute a large percentage of employees in sectors of the economy that can be described as unregulated. I will first discuss explicit laws and then move on to implicit or nonexisting ones.

Explicit Laws

Jordanian laws explicitly exclude large sectors of the workforce. According to Article 3 of the Labor Law for 1966:

> Keeping in mind rules set out in item G of Article 12 of this law [amended by Article 2 of Regulatory Law 12 for 1977], this law is to be applied to all workers and owners of business with the exception of:
>
> - Public employees and municipal employees.
> - Members of owner's family who work in his projects without receiving pay.
> - Domestic labor (servants), gardeners, cooks, and those in the same capacity.
> - Agriculture labor except for those specifically included by the council of ministers/cabinet.[26]

These *unregulated jobs* are performed by both men and women. But women constitute a significant majority of domestic labor. Furthermore, women constitute a significant portion of agricultural labor, as part of family activity. Here gender ties based on personal status laws (to be discussed later) act to deny women the possibility of independent wealth, even though ownership of property is a guarantee for women in Jordan as it is in all Islamic countries. Furthermore, although most civil servants are men, most women who take white-collar jobs happen to work for the government.

As pointed out in chapter 2, it is *'urf* that guides the fact that members of a family working for a family business do not get paid for their labor. But here it is the women who end up with nothing because the family business is usually owned by males and inherited by them. A woman who does not "tow the line" would find herself outside the family business with no supporter. Jordanian laws do take the "family business" into consideration and legislate for it. The problem is that such legislation is not enforced and put into action. Section 1061 of the Jordan Civil Code states: "The members of the same family who have common work or interest may agree in writing to create a family ownership and this ownership shall consist either of an estate to which they succeeded and agree to subject it in all or in part to a family ownership, or of any other property owned by them and they agree to include it in the said ownership."

It is the Ministerial Council that has the authority to regulate and shape the legal definition of groups such as family businesses. Therefore, extending the protection of the law to family members involved in family businesses—for example, health and social security—can be achieved through executive action. Of course, it is difficult because of the resistance of family members to government regulations of any kind, as the relationship between government and the public appears to be a one-way affiliation in which, through regulations of all sorts, members of the public find themselves paying taxes of one type or another, a fact that they resist to the best of their abilities. This situation is not unique to Jordan, but is to be found throughout the world. Small family businesses in many cases could not survive government regulations, and women and men stand firmly together to withstand any such pressure.

Another explicit law that discriminates against women has to do with taxation. Tax exemptions provided by Jordanian laws benefit men and discriminate against women. Article 13 gives the husband the right to five hundred dinars' exemption for his wife, for each of his children, and any parents he supports. The wife does not have the right to claim the same exemptions, even though the law considers a husband and his wife independent taxpayers. Women can claim exemptions only if the husband demands explicitly that she be granted these exemptions or if she is the only supporter of the family (Article 4c).

Missing Laws

The most serious law missing from Jordan's labor laws is an explicit law forbidding discrimination against women in job opportunities or in the workplace. Yet Jordan is signatory to international agreements that make equality between women and men explicit. Given the fact that many of the labor laws are designed to benefit women no matter what their results, a law explicitly forbidding discrimination on the basis of gender would also benefit men who might wish to take advantage of, for example, early retirement.

The lack of a law stressing equal salaries for men and women who hold the same or equal jobs and a law establishing minimum wages is also problematic. Because women generally hold the lowest-paying jobs and are usually paid less than their male counterparts performing the same job, the lack of such a law clearly works against them. It is estimated that women are paid on average 20 percent less than men and receive higher pay in low-paying jobs only in the service sector or as clerks.[27] At the same time, even though Jordanian laws guarantee equality of promotion on the basis of educational level, training, or capability, only a few women reach higher levels in either the public or the private sector, and men are promoted much faster. A glass ceiling is therefore an impregnable reality in Jordan.

Even though Jordanian *'urf* stresses the need to protect women, and this belief is at the heart of many of the laws that discriminate against them, curiously there is no explicit law defining and forbidding sexual harassment in the workplace, on university campuses, or in other public areas. The assumption is that sexual harassment is part of Western culture and does not exist in Islamic countries. The reality is quite different, a fact recognized by the *fuqaha'* who see the need for a moral environment for women to work in. The legal record shows that, like other countries, sexual harassment does exist in the workplace in Jordan, if presented differently. Records of the hot line of the Itihad al-Mar'a al-Urduniyya shows that sexual crimes, including sexual harassment in the workplace, constitute 5 percent of the complaints brought to their attention by women who ask for legal assistance. The Itihad's findings indicate that sexual harassment occurs frequently in offices and companies, and that the frequency is particularly high in offices where there is a boss and a secretary. A case handled by the Tamyiz Court demonstrates the findings of the Itihad. In this case, a male employee found a secretary alone, fondled her, and would have done more had she not started screaming. He was a much older man and was her superior at work. Unlike most women who suffer sexual harassment in silence the world over, she brought charges against him and proved her case. Unfortunately, the punishment he received was three months in prison and expenses. She got no compensation and probably suffered consequences that the case did not report.[28]

Although women employees in Jordan and other Islamic countries speak of the continuous harassment they face—a theme often covered on television programs, in soap operas, and in novels—it is only when a physical attack on their person occurs that they bring charges. Constant harassment in the form of flirtation and demands that the female employee "go out on a date," or, as in another court case, demands that "she marry him," is a daily affair. No laws exist in Jordan to stop a constant crime that can easily be placed under the title of *hatk 'ird*, that is, offending modesty. Women, however, find it difficult to raise such issues because doing so may cause their families to force them to stop working. Besides, given the numerous honor crimes heard about in Jordan at the present time, the fear of becoming a potential victim causes women to stop working rather than face harassment that may lead to greater problems. It is strange that such matters can continue in Jordan where protection of women is so important and social conservatism frowns on any such actions.

To conclude, most of the legal points discriminating against women in the workplace come under the responsibility of the executive branch of Jordan's government. Thus, it is not a question of constitutional change, nor does it need congressional action or the approval of the clergy. Rather, there needs to be executive action on the ministerial level. Excuses for continued discrimination based on Islam or *'urf* do not stand up to scrutiny. For example, according to Article 69 of the Labor Law, it is the minister of justice, after consultation with the pertinent official departments, who determines:

- The trades and work that forbid the employment of women.
- The hours during which women are not permitted to work and the situations in which an exception to the rule may be applied.
- Pensions, promotions, and criteria for hiring, firing, and promotions.

As explained in this chapter, all these areas are of particular significance when discussing inequality in the workplace. If it is a ministerial decision that is required to change the jobs forbidden to women or the hours in which they can work, and the pensions, promotion, and so on, then why do these differences remain on the books in Jordan? Changing these rules depends on executive action and does not require passage of laws.

Here I am not suggesting that women be forced to work in all jobs and all times; rather, the option should be open to them, especially given the financial incentives. Defining job opportunity based on gender and using the state's power to enforce employment discrimination give an absolutist philosophy to the whole system, defining areas of work in which women cannot trespass. Laws do recognize the ability of women to perform during hours and at jobs forbidden to them by allowing exceptions to the rules during times when there is a great need. This fact contradicts the division of labor envisioned by Jordanian laws, which become applicable according to market needs. Such rules and regulations that obviously favor male employees need to be reconsidered.

Jordanian laws actually go further in opening the door for women into areas that other Muslim countries have not allowed, as yet. Here particular mention should be made of Jordan's recognition of women's ability to work as judges in civil courts. There are four women judges serving on the bench in Jordan today, whereas other countries considered to be more advanced in women's rights—for example, Egypt—have so far refused such recognition.[29] From what I have seen, the number of women judges should grow in the future, although there does not seem to be any effort toward including women in *shari'a* courts, which come under the power of the office of the chief *shari'a* court, *Qadi* (*Qadi al-Quda*). This fact is curious because it is in *shari'a* courts that personal status laws are practiced, and patriarchy continues to make it an exclusive arena for men. This area of concern needs to be pointed out.

5

Laws of Guardianship and the Construction of Gender

'URF is a recognized source of Islamic law. According to one interpretation, rules of evidence in *shari'a* law are divisible into "textual evidence" (*adila naqliyya*) and "derivative evidence" (*adila tab'iyya*). Textual evidence is defined as:

> What is transmitted without any contribution of *ijtihad* in its transmission or its formulation, such as the Qur'an, *Sunna,* and *ijma'* when its supporting evidence is textual. *'Urf* [is also included] because the formation of *'urf* is due to repetition of traditions (*'adat*) so that they gain the quality of moral obligations (*al-ilzam al-adabi*) inherited from one generation to the other thereby becoming a binding source when used by the judge in rendering a judgment. . . . [Legally] *'urf* is [constituted of] actions and words that are repeated until they gain security in people's hearts (*nufus*), acceptance in their minds (*'uqul*), and consequence (*ri'aya*) in their behavior (*tasarufat*).[1]

Anything that does not gain permanency in hearts, minds, and usual practice is labeled "exceptional" and rare and cannot be considered *'urf* with any legal validity.

Two types of *'urf* are distinguishable: vocal or oral *'urf* and legal *'urf.* The first consists of words and meanings of words that could have had an original meaning that has changed with time. For example, the word *"walad"* linguistically designated both girls and boys but is today used to denote boys only. The word *"lahm,"* which linguistically includes all flesh, is today used to denote animal or chicken meat with the exclusion of fish meat, which is referred to as fish and never as meat. As for legal *'urf* (*'urf qanuni*), the word denotes terms that have moved from general practice to become legal terms such as *"jarima,"* (crime),

which usually means a murder to be dealt with through particular legal procedures, investigations, police, court, and legal codes determining exact punishments. Publicly, the word *"jarima"* has much wider meanings and connotations
that differ from place to place and time to time. In the contemporary world, one
has to also include international *'urf* that may at one time have referred to political matters and imperial relations, but has evolved to include nationality questions, trade protocols, and, as the world becomes smaller and more interrelated,
human rights issues, particularly concerning religious freedom, freedom to
work, freedom of movement, right to life, freedom of thought, and security of
person and property.[2]

Because security of person and property is ultimately intertwined with trade
and international relations, diffusion of national and local *'urf* from one area of
the world to the other, once controllable, has today become a reality causing
complications and contradictions within states subjected to the impact of international legal pressures. Because of the new world order that is becoming a reality today and has been evolving for some time, the necessity to homogenize
world trade systems to facilitate exchange has caused increased pressure to homogenize legal and political systems worldwide. This need to homogenize, however, is growing at a much faster rate than the ability of societies and
communities to move away from what can be called particular *'urf*. By *particular,*
I do not mean *shari'a* law, as in fact it has been evolving and changing with
greater structural and cultural adjustments, but the specific traditions that have
become the norm for communities and have been today translated into state
laws or into an attitude applied by the judge in court as his interpretation of state
laws.

This chapter discusses the connection between *'urf,* shaping the individual
Jordanian woman, and the concepts that guide social attitudes in the construction of gender in Jordan. Schools, television, and other forms of communication
and media all play an important role in the formation of the individual. The
chapter will point out some of the most problematic aspects that create a dependent woman even though Jordan's laws, at least theoretically, are directed toward creating a woman with full legal competence expected to carry her burden
in building the nation's economy and society. The chapter will also make suggestions as to what areas could be changed to give a push to transforming both oral
and legal *'urf*. Because creation of *'urf* entails the transformation of what is really
derivative evidence into what becomes acceptable as "textual evidence," thereby
gaining the legitimacy of the sacredness of "textual evidence," it is important
that *'urf* be deconstructed to show how patriarchy is actually built through so-

cial, educational, and other practices. Without changing social practices, there is little hope that a fast resolution to attitudes toward women and work will meet with development ambitions in Jordan. The chapter begins by detailing the early expectations of young Jordanian girls; their life within the family and relationships with mother, father, and siblings; what is expected of them; and what they expect in return. It also discusses the contradictions a girl faces during her everyday life and the fears with which she grows up. The chapter then moves to discuss the role of the father in a girl's life. As *waliy*, his legal powers are significant throughout his daughter's life. When he dies, he is replaced by another male member of the family who acts as *waliy*. It could be a grandfather whose powers are close to the father's, or an uncle or brother, whose powers are significantly less than a father's. The important point is that a woman remains under the *wilaya* of a male member of her family almost throughout her life, whether according to the law or to *'urf* constructed over time on "derivative evidence" that has gained "textual" credibility. She is therefore never completely independent or fully legally competent, no matter that the Jordanian Constitution says otherwise. Through a discussion of the issue of *wilaya* as interpreted by the different Muslim schools of law, it will be made clear that even though personal status laws are said to be based on the Hanafi code, in fact they are a modern product of various Muslim schools, tribal laws, and modern Western laws, and therefore gender constructs reflected in and applied by Jordan's laws today are in fact state laws that could be changed and amended by the state without impinging on Islamic beliefs and laws.

Constructing gender is based largely on discourses of morality and duty, pride, and fear. It is no different with Jordanian women. The educational system in Jordan, the curricula and administration of classrooms in particular and schools in general, as well as the philosophy presented by teachers in the classroom and by government-assigned textbooks all create gender difference and outline particular functions for women that help keep them in a position of dependency and obedience to father, brother, family, and clan. It is achieved through models of Islamic morality, coupled with pride in heritage, into a potent if contradictory formula, which works effectively. By comparisons between Jordanian laws and legal and educational practices, this chapter shows the commonalities between Jordan and other Arab countries in the past and present, and the differences that are largely based on *'urf*. By deconstructing these images, it is hoped that sources of gender discrimination will be made clearer and hence addressed as discourses with the power to create and hold on to power relations unless they are changed.

Expectations, Contradictions, and Fears

"Once, it was the foot in modernity that was tentative and hesitant, now it is the traditional way of life, though valued and nostalgic, that has all but disappeared. While in the beginning modernity was viewed with suspicion as perhaps too indulgent, too luxurious, it later became a necessity of life. Life, all around, was changing and in order to compete and survive, the Bedouin had to change. Change or perish." These words are used to launch a stimulating study of the changes experienced by the Bedouins of Jordan because of the impact of modernization. Once central to the population of Jordan, life in the *Badya* today constitutes less than 1 percent of its total population. As the authors explain, "the nomads, traversing the desert with their goat hair tents, have disappeared, though Bedouinism as a cultural identity remains."[3] Similarly, Jordan today has a highly urbanized society with modern amenities and laws that attempt to embrace principles of human equality and rights. Yet, the expectations of life based on its cultural and legal *'urf* continue to be much what they were before. This fact is particularly true among poorer classes who have not had exposure or the financial freedom to enjoy greater social equality and political democratic participation. Although it is less so among the richer and more Westernized classes, the moral code and respect for *'urf* are the same, if actions and extremism are lacking. One can in fact state that *'urf* in the sense of what is acceptable to majorities constitutes the fabric by which society holds itself together and at the same time allows hegemonies to rule. *'Urf* changes with time but only with greater socioeconomic transformations that touch upon and open up class structures to greater change and equality.

The expectations of life are for the most part determined by traditions. Roles are determined by both traditions and socioeconomic conditions. Changes in the one lead to changes in the other. If at one time middle-class women were educated at home and did not expect to take up white-collar work in government civil service, today a university education almost always means an intent or at least a wish to have some sort of job, preferably one guaranteed by the government with ensured benefits. The country's economy had to change to make available such a job, the political system had to change to require a bigger and more efficient civil service, and poverty made families more acceptable of having their daughters work in the same offices as men. Furthermore, international conditions and greater homogenization of laws and philosophy of men and human rights pushed governments to become more interested in the welfare of their citizens and to adopt principles of women's equality of opportunity. To be a viable state in a greater interdependent world meant to abide by laws established by world institutions, without which countries would find it more difficult to guarantee their international trade, receive international assistance, and secure their borders as well as recognition of the sovereignty of the ruling class. And so expectations change, with new expectations not necessarily replacing old ones completely, at least not at first, but rather being superimposed on older expectations.

Engendering takes place from the very early days of a boy's or girl's life in Jordan. Here it is not a question of who is more beloved to the parents or cultural inequality as much as it is a question of roles and power. From the day of his birth, a boy is treated as holding special importance to his immediate family and his wider clan. Expectations for the future are defined from these early beginnings. What boys and girls expect from their lives as well as what their family, clan, and society expect from them are constructed early indeed. Realities often conflict with these expectations as boys and girls grow older, living through adjustments, fears, and the pains of success and failure in meeting these expectations, experiences normal to children growing up in all societies.

In Jordan, when a boy is born, it is an occasion of great celebration and congratulations to his parents. Popular proverbs repeated by visitors at the time of his birth include, "the boy, even if as tiny as a key, fills the home with joy" (*il walad law qad al-muftah biy'abi al-dar afrah*) and "fly away you are your father's helper" (*tih inta mu'in li-abuk*). Parents are congratulated with such words as "God willing he will be raised with your glory" (*inshallah yitraba bi'izak*). In contrast, a newborn girl, particularly if the couple already has one daughter or more, could be met with hushed congratulations and proverbs that present her as a burden in contrast to her brother. "The girl, if as small as a pillow, depresses the home" (*al-bint law inaha qad al-makhkhada, bitinzil 'ala al-dar khamda*) contrasts strikingly with proverbs about a boy's birth. To protect a young boy from the evil eye, he is sometimes dressed in a girl's clothes in the belief that no one would jinx a girl child. Furthermore, the mother of a newborn daughter could be greeted with "thanks be to God for the safe delivery of the mother" (*al-hamdu li-Allah 'ala salamat al-walida*), and if the infant girl dies, the proverb "a girl's death is a shield [of honor]" (*mawt al-bint satr*) could be used.[4] The last proverb illustrates the place tribal *'urf* places on honor and the ultimate fear of dishonor that could be brought about by the misconduct of a daughter as being worse than death, honor being placed squarely on female shoulders.

This popular picture regarding a family's attitude toward girls and boys should not be exaggerated, however, and certainly does not give credit to the importance of the daughter within her family. For one thing, Jordanian proverbs are not exclusively favorable to boys. "A pretty girl rather than a scandalous son" (*bint maliha wala walad fidiha*) points to the preference of girls to boys, and "a daughter's house is a house of plenty" (*bayt al-bint bayt al-barakat*) illustrates that a daughter's house is always welcoming to her family and that having daughters dispenses with the need for sons.[5] Daughters in Jordanian society as well as other Arab ones have always been dear to parents, particularly mothers who see in the daughter a friend, a companion, loyalty, and love. A poem written by a mother lamenting the death of her daughter helps illustrate this special relationship between an Arab mother and her daughter.

> I want my daughter to wash my corpse,
> To drape my garment and arrange the shroud.
> I want her to reach my age: she will rest
> My head on her lap, and she will groom me.
> I want my daughter to turn
> My dead body piously toward Mecca;
> Pain came to me filling my ribs.
> My beloved cannot hear my complaint,
> She does not know my loss.
> I dressed her in red and she exhaled
> The fragrance of rose. I made her beautiful.[6]

That the firstborn is a girl could be a cause for celebration for many reasons. An important one is that an older sister becomes the right hand of the mother, helping in housekeeping and child rearing, sometimes becoming a second mother to her younger siblings. As more children are born—which is traditional in Jordanian society, an ideal number of children being four or five with at least two sons—older daughters become very important and remain so until they marry and leave the home. The particular relationship she forms with the brother or sister she helped raise continues throughout her life, forming a very strong connection between them. All children, boys and girls alike, are expected to work within the family. Boys stand in their fathers' shops after school to help in sales. They are sent on errands and entrusted with their sisters' supervision and security very early on, a responsibility that could be taken too seriously and lead to violence against a sister when the brother disapproves of her conduct. Girls are expected to carry their mother's or sister's newborn child and baby-sit as early as the age of four or five and certainly by the age of ten. Although children are expected to play and have fun—villages and supervised town quarters allowing them security and hence relative freedom in comparison to large urban centers—boys and girls are still expected to contribute to the family's economy early on. Once in school, a child's contribution may decrease, but older sisters will be left responsible for the home and her siblings when the mother goes out. As she reaches adolescence, a daughter's contributions to the family become solidified even when she is attending school. These responsibilities are mostly inside the home, and she is conditioned to fit within the housekeeping and nurturing needs of the family such as washing clothes, cleaning the house, cooking, and helping to raise children. Because Jordanians tend to have large families, the help of a daughter is almost essential as the mother becomes busy with the birth of one child before the other is fully grown.

As for boys, as students they are expected to contribute less to the home so as to focus on schoolwork. A son continues to contribute to the family's economy by helping in the family business if one exists, but even then his primary responsibility is to study and succeed. As he grows older, he may take up his father's craft and follow his footsteps, but if he decides to continue with his schooling, it becomes his primary objective. When the father is a white-collar worker, sons are almost always expected to go on to college. Families short of funds tend to focus their financial resources on educating their sons rather than their daughters.

Greater weight may be placed on the birth of a son because of the help he could give his family; he may take over the father's craft or business, and will bring his wife home and continue to contribute to the family's income. As one Jordanian woman put it to me, "sons bring their wives home and contribute to the family's support but daughters move to their husbands' homes and no longer contribute to their families."[7] As his parents grow older, a son becomes something of their "social security" because social security exists only for laborers in government service or private businesses covered by social security laws. The burden placed on the son's shoulders from the day of his birth continues until his death. If he does not fulfill his family's expectations, he disappoints them and is despised by his community. As an emigrant or migrant laborer working overseas, the son is still expected to send money home to contribute to the family's income. Clan reach and responsibilities to the extended family do not recognize borders. This type of solidarity has in fact been an important reason for economic stability where predictions assumed different outcomes in Jordan and other Arab countries. Family needs and solidarity are the basis of the economy rather than profit and consumerism.

Umm Khalid who lives in a *mukhayyam* (Palestinian refugee camp) outside of Amman was enlightening on social attitudes toward sons and daughters. Having given birth to eighteen children altogether, half of them boys, she was very effusive about the importance of her sons. Yet, two of her daughters were living with her, and she sponsored them for loans with a microfinancial bank, one to do needlework and the other to operate her own grocery. The relationship with her daughters was quite close, but her sons were a real source of pride. "To know that you have grown sons out there in the world is the greatest of feelings," she assured me. Not that they support her; rather, she was the main financial supporter of her family from the grocery store she owned through small microfinancial loans. As to her daughters-in-law, she saw them as taking care of her sons' children. When asked if these children were not the daughters-in-law's too, Umm Khalid explained that no, children belonged to the man. As for the mother, Umm Khalid likened her to a cooking pot: the food may be cooked in it, but the ingredients and the final results did not belong to the pot! She herself found nothing wrong with the picture and saw no reason she herself, as a "cooking pot," should not love and be loved by her children. Her attitude reminded me of the sarcasm of a woman entrepreneur at the Business and Professional Women's Club of Amman who said, "We bear them, carry them for nine months, give birth to them and then raise them only to be told that they belong to the husband." In his study of the village of Baytin, Abdulla Lutfiyya explained the attitude toward sons and daughters through the names that parents choose to designate themselves:

> Once a child is born to a young couple, the people of the village stop referring to the parents by their first names, as is customary, and begin calling them after the name of their child . . . even if the first child is a female. But, if a son is born after the first daughter, there is a change. The parents are then called after the first son and drop the identification with their first daughter. . . . Should the first boy die during his father's lifetime, the father is named after the second son. However, if no second son is born, the father retains the name of his deceased son for the rest of his life.[8]

In other words, a first daughter is important but never as important as a son. It is not that having a daughter is not a source of happiness, but real pride is placed on having a son whose name becomes the form of designation of the parents as *Umm* or *Abu* So-and-so.

Constructing the modern Jordanian therefore begins very early within the home and fits with the actual conditions and needs of a Jordanian family. The roles played by males and females reinforce social cohesion; aberrations cause confusion and dislocations. But roles change with time, and the importance of women as breadwinners in their families is today gaining strength. As a member of her tribe she is invaluable not only as a wife, mother, and homemaker, but also as a shepherdess, builder of the tent home, worker of animal skins and leather, and spinner and weaver of wool. As a peasant wife, she is invaluable in assisting her husband in irrigating, weeding, and other wearying, backbreaking jobs without which agriculture would fail. She grows vegetables for the table and for sale in local markets, raises chickens, milks cows and goats, and produces milk products for home consumption and sale to supplement the family's cash. It is also the wife who runs the household if it is a single household, or becomes an active member of the wider household if she is living with her husband's family. Raising children is entirely a woman's affair, with the father interfering when she asks or when discipline is required. This situation begins to change by the age of three when fathers are brought into the picture, and by the age of seven, the father becomes the "important disciplinarian" in a child's life.[9]

The power of the father over his daughter remains unquestioned throughout her life, even after her marriage. In other Arab countries where the work of women is widely accepted and girls work from a very early age, fathers have come to depend on their daughters' income from their work as domestic servants in urban homes, as factory workers, or as day laborers in such unexpected labor-intensive jobs as breaking and carrying stones, mixing cement on construction sites, and brick making. Because fathers are in full legal control of daughters and a father's power to discipline does not raise anyone's eyebrows, young girls have today become a new source of income for their families in countries whose populations are experiencing increasing poverty such as Egypt, Sudan, and Iraq. Even in Jordan, fathers will allow a girl to work but will mortgage her wages for years to come by having her sign a bank loan that the father receives in advance and the daughter guarantees with her wages. In other cases where girls work, they are kept unmarried for long periods, whereas their brothers are married early, and it is the income from the daughter's labor that supports the wider family. This situation, however, is not as widespread in Jordan as it is in other poor countries. Jordanian men are still expected to support the family, and a woman's labor is expected only if there is no male provider. As economic hardships increase, this situation is changing, and more women are becoming the chief and sometimes only breadwinners.

It is not surprising that young Jordanian girls' expectations continue to revolve mainly around marriage, notwithstanding the existence of compulsory school education and greater job opportunities. Their families' expectations for them also revolve around marriage. Their society's expectations are the same. It has not changed, even though today more women are entering universities and working. In fact, if there is one constant fear in the life of a Jordanian girl it is that she will never be married. Spinsterhood seems to represent the worse fate that a young woman can imagine for herself. It seems to symbolize something wrong with the girl, her family, her looks, her mental and physical capabilities, or her morals. In the short story "Saya'ti" ("He will come"), a young woman whose bad luck is symbolized by her inheritance of her father's "ugly face" is consumed with jealousy and pain at her continued lack of prospects while her brother marries and her sister is betrothed. "He will come, he will come, to relinquish all my pains, drive away my sorrow, wipe out my lonely fires," she sings while dreaming of a "dark knight" who will come to her on his white steed.[10] She is faced with her brother's cruel wife who keeps reminding her of her spinsterhood, and her sister's fiancé who "rubs it in," hoping to get rid of her as a chaperone so he can be alone with her sister. Similar images and stories can be found in Arabic literature from other countries; marriage continues to be part of expectations of women everywhere, if not with this intensity and extremism. To be "left behind," notwithstanding how much of an individual choice it may be, is cause for sympathy and pity, and at the least demands an explanation. Only among the very educated, wealthy, or independent professional and businesswomen is there understanding and acceptance that it may have been a matter of choice and not because a bridegroom was lacking. Even then, the unmarried woman is sensitive about how her family and colleagues perceive her.

Social conditioning that makes marriage and family the ultimate goal for a woman begins very early as she plays the role of her mother's helper; it is strengthened at every step of a woman's life. When a man or woman marries, it is not a simple individual act, but is considered an alliance between clans and families. Because of interdependence of family members, it is very hard for a person to marry against their family's wishes. This situation is especially true for women who have no one to fall back on, nowhere to go, if their marriages break down. According to Elizabeth Fernea:

> The crucial test of allegiance came at the time of marriage, when the man or woman either acceded to or rebelled against the wishes of the family in preparing to extend the family unit into another generation, for marriage in the system was not officially perceived as an emotional attachment between individuals (though this might develop later) but as an economic and social contract between two family groups, a contract that was to benefit both.[11]

To be married, to be well regarded in the community, and to live in harmony with the family, particularly its male members, require modesty. Modesty means many things to many people. Basically, it points to a need not to stand out in ostentation, not to be dressed vulgarly, and to respect the privacy of others and not ogle them (hence, it is best to keep the eyes lowered). To more conservative elements it means dressing conservatively, with longer skirts, looser clothing, and covered arms. To the more strictly religious it means wearing the Islamic garb that in Jordan is usually in the form of a coat-style dress covering the body to the ankles and the arms to the wrists. The dress may be colorful, although more sedate solid colors are expected, and the hair cover may be of silk, cotton, or polyester depending on economic ability. The hair cover is usually solid in color but might be quite colorful and beautiful. It is really in the area of modesty that the class gap appears most clearly and the contradictions between discourses and reality become most glaring. Although wearing jeans and shirts is common among boys who also often use jewelry and wear colorful silky-style shirts and skin-tight T-shirts, their actions may be objectionable to parents, but nothing much is done about it. The double standard here is obvious, because the same family with a jeans-wearing son will not allow their daughter out with trousers or without a head cover. It is only among the richer Westernized classes that there is no double standard, if only in connection with dress. The rest of Jordanian society does not seem to see anything wrong with rich Jordanian girls wearing Westernized clothing but forbids their own daughters from wearing the same.

As chapter 3 of this book has shown, the idea that women were totally secluded in the Islamic past is insupportable by facts. During the early days of Islam, women went to war, traveled, went to the mosque, and were expected to give their opinion regarding political events by rendering their *bay'a.* Court records from the medieval period illustrate the activities of women in public, in the marketplace, as midwives, shopkeepers, *awqaf* administrators, and official witnesses in court. The idea of seclusion was theoretical at best and was more a matter of wishful thinking of certain *fuqaha'* who had their own ideas regarding moral *istihsan* (discretion; application of discretion in a legal decision), which, however, did not seem to be the commonly accepted view of the people at large but was perhaps fashionable among richer women who were not expected to mingle with the common people, as is the case today in most Arab countries where the rich drive cars and shop either abroad or in particular areas. Therefore, modesty has little to do with seclusion; rather, it is a state of being expected of women at all times and particularly in public where there is possible interaction with men. Accordingly, Islam expects modesty of men as much as it expects it of women. According to an often-quoted tradition of the prophet Muhammad: Jarir recounted, "I asked the Prophet what to do if my eyes fell on a woman by chance. The Prophet answered, 'turn away your eyes.'" So it is not only the woman who should be modest and not look at men; men are expected to do the same. This admonition is the subject of Qur'an *ayas:* "Say to the believing men that they should lower their gaze and guard their modesty. That will make for greater purity for them and God is well aware of what they do / And say to the believing women that they should lower their gaze and guard their modesty, that they should not display their beauty and ornaments except what usually shows of them" (Surat al-Nur, 24:31–32).

Yet here again, "derivative evidence" has been used to create *'urf* endowed with textual relevance. Whereas the first *aya* in the above quote is often quoted by people who call upon women to be modest, the second *aya* is hardly mentioned; instead, other forms of evidence are used to supplement the significance of the first *aya* to come up with an "Islamic" requirement for women to veil as a form of modesty and place possible immorality on the shoulders of women who do not heed. At the same time, a man's immodesty is not really weighed against him, as are suspicions of a woman's immodesty. The contradiction between what Islamic moral discourses tell women Islam expects of all Muslims and the realities of life that narrow these demands to women forms one of the basic confusions of women's lives, leading to a lack of self-esteem and fear of doing wrong in the eyes of God and society without a clear differentiation between the two.

There are a number of contradictions faced by Jordanian women today in regards to what their families expect from them and what they expect from their families. On the one hand, love marriages occur much more widely today, especially in urban centers. A girl could meet with a fellow student in college, fall in love, and wish to marry him, but her family refuses. The relationship would have to remain hidden for fear of repercussions if the family were to find out. Before the young man she commits herself to is able to establish himself and ask her family for her hand in marriage, her marriage could already have been arranged, and she has no choice but to accept. It is true that Jordanian laws require the approval of the bride in any marriage, but family pressures of various kinds from physical to mental could be brought to bear on the daughter by her mother, father, and siblings whom she accepts as having her good at heart and are therefore acting on the basis of that belief, which in fact they usually are. Besides, the approval of a girl's *waliy* (guardian) seems to be more important to the authorities than her consent, as the transacting official can accept a girl's silence as acquiescence according to the law, but will not perform the marriage if her father is against it.[12]

The most important reason for a girl's acceptance of her family's wishes is that they provide her with perhaps the only support and security system in a culture that gives husbands unlimited right to divorce and patriarchal powers. Today, however, even if the daughter follows the wishes of her family in regards to marriage and choice of husband, it does not guarantee family support. Perhaps because economic conditions are not what they once were, families are not always able to support their "returned" or divorced daughter as would at one time have been taken for granted. This situation is particularly true if the patriarch, her father, is deceased and she would have to fall back on the assistance of a brother who has his own wife and children to support. Records of the BPWC in Amman illustrate case after case of women coming to ask for assistance from the club's lawyers in pursuit of restitution from husbands who do not pay alimony or child support. Having no place to go once divorced, wives look for any help they can find. Some have school and higher degrees, but have not held a job since graduation or since they were married. They often ask the club to help them get employment. Insecurity regarding her fate and her children's fate constitutes one of the most important contradictions in a woman's life. As Jordanian society changes and the family structure moves further toward the nuclear family, women are caught between what they expect of life, what their families expect of them, and changing socioeconomic realities.

There are other important contradictions in women's lives that question their expectations to be a wife and mother in fulfillment of a woman's role as defined by the social and religious discourse. These contradictions constitute fears with which women have to live, but the type of fears discussed here need to be distinguished from feelings of "guilt," which may provide similar controls and inhibitions in Western societies. A good example here has to do with financial support and marital security. Whereas a woman expects support from her family and her husband as long as she is obedient and follows the moral code expected of her, she could face a situation where her husband may decide to take a second wife. He could also decide to divorce her and "return" her to her family. Her family in turn may take her in willingly or may do so under duress and make her and her children feel their rancor, forcing her to finally leave. Furthermore, although society, reinforced by religious discourse, tells her that the home is a woman's castle where she can be happy with her husband and children, very often she finds herself living with her mother-in-law who is the actual ruler of the household. So it is not simple obedience to her husband that is required; she finds she is at the bottom of the scale and has to satisfy her husband's family if she hopes for the success of the marriage.

These conditions do not mean that all Jordanian women actually face displacement by a new wife or destitution after divorce. Fear of what could happen is in itself a source of instability, especially when what is feared or imagined is not only legally possible but occurs frequently to others. These fears are therefore a source of power in the hands of men who could make them a reality. Such power is usually in the hands of husbands who could bring another wife home or a brother at whose hands she could suffer violence if he were to misconstrue her actions. Because the legal system takes these types of motives based on traditional expectations into consideration, the fears are real and creditable, causing women to prefer subservience and peripheralization.

As pointed out earlier, not getting married and remaining a spinster represents a true fear among young women. Students at a girls middle school in Amman to whom I put the question "What do you hope to do in the future?" answered, "Get married" and did not seem to differentiate between having a job and marriage. When this fact was pointed out to them, only two of the girls came forth to indicate that they would also like to take a job as well as be married. Dropping out of school to be married is quite common, and unlike other countries where pregnant women are not allowed to come back and continue their education, Jordan does not see anything wrong with allowing them to do so. When an acceptable bridegroom proposes to the family and the daughter is of age, there is no reason to delay. Cousin marriages and other forms of arranged marriages continue to be common, if less so among the educated. Such marriages are something of an agreement between families rather than individuals, at least theoretically, as family proximity allows cousins to get to know and desire each other. "Marriage" is therefore the dominant discourse with which girls live, and by the time they finish school, many are already betrothed and are married soon after graduation. In a couple of cases at the schools I visited, married girls continued to be enrolled even though at least one was pregnant.

Not having children becomes another source of fear following marriage. This fear is particularly prevalent among popular classes who see a delay in pregnancy as a deep cause for concern. The blame is usually placed on the shoulders of the wife, and a husband could be induced to divorce his wife or take another one. Rarely and only in the case of enlightened men do they begin by looking into possible physical problems with themselves. It is almost always the wife who has to get a medical checkup to determine her ability to conceive, and even when it is proved that nothing is wrong with her, she could still be repudiated for not having borne her husband children, or he may decide to bring another wife home in the hope or with the excuse that he wants a son. Although these actions are to be expected more among popular classes, they exist at all levels of society, if in different ways; for example, a middle-class or rich husband could take a second wife in secret and not announce it until she gives him a son, if he announces it at all. Very often a husband is actually advised to take another wife who could give him sons rather than told that a child's gender is a man's biological responsibility. The mother of girls may defer to amulets and various forms of popular spells and traditions so as to give birth to boys. Among popular classes, for example, immediately after giving birth to a daughter, a woman is sometimes fed veal meat so as not to beget any more girls.[13] Interestingly, when it comes to birth control, it is the wife who is the focus of control rather than the husband. According to Dr. Sireen Musmar, director of Jam'iyyat al-Umma wal Tufula of the Ministry of Health, men are very resistant to using any form of contraception, and birth control is mainly a wife's responsibility. The subject of sterilization is rarely broached in the Jam'iyyat's efforts to control birth because of the negative repercussions that it may have on its activities among the Jordanian public.

The possibility that a husband could take another wife is without doubt a most important source of fear to women, a fear that "keeps her on her toes," so to speak. The threat is always present, something to be apprehensive about, notwithstanding how solid the marriage. Arabic fiction is full of stories of a wife who learns about her husband's second wife and the humiliation that follows. Movie after movie present the same story, often with an *'urfi* wife (common-law wife) who remains hidden for fear of social recrimination. Even though the religious discourse justifies such actions as determined by God and therefore could not constitute harm to believers and whole books have been written to show God's wisdom in allowing men to take a second, third, and fourth wife, except for the odd case, Muslim women have never found polygamy acceptable. Interestingly, polygamy is given some modern justifications that are presented as "Islamic" to show how beneficial polygamy is to Islamic society and even how privileged women are because of it. Women are told that men die in war, and without polygamy some women would be left husbandless and only a few would have husbands, an unfair situation for the rest. Besides, if a wife could not have children or if she is sick, is it not better for her to remain an honored wife in her husband's home while he takes another wife than if he divorces her and she becomes destitute?

The justifications even include a husband's desire for another particular woman, and here the West is always brought in to compare the superiority of polygamy to extramarital relations and the taking of mistresses in Western societies. Is it not better for a wife to remain in her husband's home, cherished and respected, than for him to divorce her and take another wife whom he desires? Or even worse, take that woman as a mistress? The contradictions between these arguments are lost in the face of a wife's helplessness to stop her husband from taking a second wife. He could and many do. But the justifications are based on basic fears of women who find refuge in accepting the husband's prerogative to take more than one wife as religiously sanctioned, a way of overcoming the pain of disillusion, betrayal, and heartbreak. There is no honor in having your husband take a second and third wife, only humiliation, no matter what the discourse says. But because women are completely dependent on their husbands for financial support, they would lose their children in custody battles, and would lose their financial rights in *shiqaq wa niza'* courts that would see a wife's wish to separate from a polygamous husband as the wife's fault because the husband has an unquestionable right to take as many as four wives without having to show any of the excuses justifying polygamy by *'urf.* Having left school early, or left her job to be married or have children, a woman becomes hostage to her dependent situation, and there are few alternatives for her other than to accept her husband's polygamous actions. The fear is constant that she and her children will become destitute because of the influence of the new and often younger wife and the economic pressures on the husband that may bring about her repudiation at the least provocation.

Yet some actually still claim that women find nothing wrong with polygamy and that a woman could actually choose the new *durra* (second wife), especially if she is older, in poor health, or needs someone to help with household chores. If this allegation is true, why is it that archival records show us that the most important demand made by wives when signing marriage contracts is that they have the right to terminate a marriage if a husband decides to take another wife?

Jordanian laws have taken this aversion to polygamy among women into consideration. Thus, they allow women to include conditions in their marriage contracts as long as said conditions do not contradict Islamic principles. Unlike most Muslim countries, Jordanian laws and courts do not regard a condition controlling the husband's ability to take a second wife to be against Islamic principles. Jordan's laws are quite advanced in this area in comparison to other countries such as Syria, Saudi Arabia, or Egypt, which refuse to put any controls on a husband's polygamous rights. This issue will be discussed in chapter 6, but it is important to point out here that, notwithstanding the existence of this right to include conditions, hardly any Jordanian women take advantage of it. Reasons for this fact must be looked for in the hesitation of a bride or her family to appear too "tough," perhaps thereby chasing away the bridegroom, a real possibility given the patriarchal order and male pride. More important, however, is the fact that most women are not aware of the existence of such a right. Even though the laws require that the *ma'dhun* (officiating cleric) explain the marriage certificate, requirements, and every aspect of the marriage, most Jordanian women do not know that they can include conditions in their marriage contract and certainly not a condition that would limit the right of a husband to take a second wife. Such a condition would in fact introduce leverage within the marriage, and a husband would have to think twice before taking a step that would mean losing his first wife and breaking up his home. At least it would reassure a wife of a way out with full financial benefits in case it happens to her.

Perhaps the greatest contradiction in a Muslim woman's life in Jordan and elsewhere is the Islamic emphasis on equality that places her at the same level as men in God's eyes. The *shahada* profession of faith, praying five times a day, fasting Ramadan, going on the Hajj at least once in a lifetime, and paying the *zakat,* is equally required of men and women. The Hajj rituals are also the same, as are the actual steps taken in ablution and prayer. "All Muslims, women and men alike, are equal in the eyes of God" is a statement with which Muslims have grown up believing, one that is repeated often in school, on television, in books, and by politicians and clerics. This statement with which young Muslim women have grown up since early childhood is confirmed by the Qur'an. In discussing genesis the Qur'an states,

> O mankind: Reverence your Guardian Lord Who created you from a single soul/person (*nafs*) created of like nature its mate and from them twain scattered [like seeds] countless men and women; revere God through whom you demand your mutual [rights] and [revere] the wombs [that bore you]: for Allah ever watches over you. [Qur'an, Surat al-Nisa', 4:1]
>
> It is He who created you from a single soul/person and made its mate of like nature in order that he might dwell with her [in love]. When they are united she bears a light burden and carries it about [unnoticed]. When she grows heavy they both pray to Allah their Lord [saying]: "If You give us a goodly child we vow we shall [ever] be grateful." (Qur'an 7:189)

It is a clear declaration of equality, as all Muslims believe. Yet, in a society that is Islamic for all intents and purposes, this image of equality seems to have been lost except when the people are reminded that they are Muslims and the followers of "the most just of all religions."

Wilaya (Guardianship)

Jordan's personal status code sets out a tight framework regarding the powers of a *waliy,* and the courts follow closely in their application of these laws. If anything, guardianship laws concord with Jordanian social *'urf* more than other elements of the Jordanian legal system. The contradictions between what the law states and sets out to do and how the state and its courts apply these laws are minimal when compared to other issues such as marriage, divorce, rape, or honor crimes. This concordance is in itself problematic because the *'urf* upon which laws of guardianship are based is in fact outdated, coming from a time when the majority of Jordan's population lived under tribal conditions. The Ottoman Family Code did bring in a more structured and state-controlled form of patriarchy and declared the Hanafi *madhhab* as the main source of personal laws. These new measures, however, did not actually replace the preceding system but were rather added to the already existing tribal patriarchy that was closer to the Maliki school of law than other *madhahib*. The overlayering and combining of different legal codes and legal philosophies resulted in strengthening a *waliy*'s powers by making the state a participant with new forms of control. Today, as Jordanian society undergoes deep structural transformations by moving away from a tribal makeup to modes of production more attuned with urbanized, service-oriented, industrialized, and commercialized societies, laws of guardianship stand as a hindrance to "opening up" the system to allow for greater participation in the country's development and future.

Guardianship usually involves the powers of a father over his children, boys and girls alike. The relationship between a father and a daughter is built on strict respect and authority, deep pride and love, and fear of the father's authority. As pointed out earlier, it is the mother who raises the children, and the father is there to protect and financially support and provide for the family, but he also holds the power and responsibility for discipline. "The love for and the fear of the father becomes mixed together in the child's self. The youngster learns early in life to obey the father's orders without questioning them and looks at his father as the mighty giant who rules unchallenged in the family's world." [14]

Whereas both girls and boys are raised to respect and give unquestioning obedience to their fathers, the girl continues under the father's control much longer, practically until she is married, and even then he does not lose his actual if not legal control over her. The legal authority of the father differs according to the gender and age of the child. The authority is almost absolute over minors and changes, at least theoretically, as the child grows older. However, because of the nature of clan and family relations in Jordan, the powers of the father over his children, particularly the daughter, continue throughout her life. When the father is dead, a substitute *waliy*, such as an uncle, does not hold the same powers as did the father or grandfather. Although the legal minimum age for marriage is fifteen for girls and sixteen for boys, the age for legal majority in Jordan is eighteen, according to the Jordan Civil Code, Section 43. "Every person who attains full age, enjoys his mental powers and is not forbidden shall have full capacity to exercise his civil rights. The age of majority shall be eighteen full solar years."

Here the discrepancy illustrates the *talfiq* of modern Western laws together with Islamic law and *'urf*. The age of eighteen became the legal practice in Europe following the Napoleonic Code. [15] In contrast, the minimum age for marriage is theoretically based on a particular interpretation of the Hanafi *madhhab*.

Actually, none of the *madhahib* set a particular minimum age for marriage or for reaching majority. Rather, they spoke in generalizations as to what is preferred. For the Hanafis, majority was determined according to rational behavior, maturity, and puberty. Establishing a standardized legal minimum age for marriage to be applied homogeneously throughout a country is part of normal state structures accompanying centralization. In other words, notwithstanding the claim that personal status laws in Jordan stem from the *shari'a* according to the Hanafi *madhhab,* in fact, whether the minimum age for the marriage of girls is set at fifteen as it is at present or eighteen as Jordanian feminists and activists demand, the particular age would have little to do with Islamic law or practices. The state can raise or lower the minimum age for marriage as it wills. Keeping the minimum age of marriage low at fifteen for girls has meant a much shorter period during which girls can be educated or trained in a craft, particularly as they tend to be married quite young. The median age of marriage for girls in Jordan is eighteen years, including remarriages.

One of the most important powers a father has over his daughter is the requirement that he consent to her marriage, *"la nikah bi dun waliy"* ("no marriage without a guardian"). According to Jordan's laws no marriage can take place without a male guardian's consent, regardless of the daughter's age. Only if the daughter has been previously married is she then able to transact another marriage without the approval of a *waliy.* Article 13a of Jordan's personal status code states: "The consent of the guardian shall not be required for the marriage of a woman who has been previously married (*thayib*) who is of sound mind and who is more than eighteen years old." Accordingly, women who reach the age of majority and do not suffer from "idiocy or lunacy" (Section 44) are supposed to enjoy full personal freedom and capacity to exercise their civil rights.[16] Interestingly, the same type of right is extended to marriage so that once a girl has reached the age of eighteen she can ask the judge to marry her to the man of her choice, and the guardian would have to present legal reasons to the judge to stop him from performing the marriage. In other words, competence of a woman to handle her own affairs is based on her experience. Once she has experienced the state of matrimony, then she is considered competent in choosing a husband. This approach has little to do with the Hanafi *madhhab* that considers competence to exist with *'aql* when a young person reaches puberty and maturity. Thus, experience in life, such as through education or work, would count, but it is her reaching rationality and puberty that is the measure according to the Hanafi code, yet that is not how Jordan's laws are applied, notwithstanding that the stated source happens to be the Hanafi code. In contrast, the Malikis do not consider a woman to have reached majority unless she has been married and gained the experience necessary for legal competence, which tells us that at least in this point, the Maliki code extends into Jordan's laws to increase patriarchal control beyond what the Hanafi code allows. The opposite happens wherever necessary.

Glaring contradictions in gender laws are demonstrated by Article 22, which denies women the very rights that it granted them in Article 13a. It does so by bringing in the Hanafi interpretation of *kafa'a* as a means of limiting a daughter's or granddaughter's (girl's or woman's) right to choose her own husband no matter how old she is, that she is mature or of the required age set up by Jordan's personal status codes.

If a virgin or a woman who has been previously married and has reached eighteen years of age denies that she has a guardian and marries herself and it is later discovered that she has a guardian, then the case shall be examined, and if she has married a man of equal status, the contract shall be binding even if the dower is less than proper. If she has married a man who is *not of equal status,* then the guardian shall be entitled to apply to the judge to request dissolution of the marriage.

In other words, even when a girl reaches the age of eighteen, the official age of legal competence, she could still have a guardian. But there are conditions to this rule that tell us something about the philosophy behind the law. It is not a girl who has reached legal competence who cannot marry herself, because this article assumes that she could so in the situation where she has no guardian. It is when she *does* have a guardian and she hides that fact to facilitate her marriage that it becomes problematic. But why should a person who reached majority be expected to have a guardian only because such a guardian, like a father or grandfather, is alive, whereas another whose father is not alive is not required to get the approval of a guardian to the marriage? Obviously, this article is meant to suit circumstances in which there is a father or other guardian who claims authority over the female—woman or girl—and then his word supercedes hers. This situation is fairly traditional in Maliki law, which claims that a woman must have a *waliy* except if she has no protector, is of low morals, or is ugly. To give the guardian a basis upon which to object in case the marriage has already taken place, the Hanafi *madhhab* ensures that the strictest interpretation of *kafa'a* is applied. Whereas all of the *madhahib* require *kafa'a,* the Malikis and Shaf'is accept the marriage of a girl to someone who is not her social equal once the marriage has been consummated. But the same is not true with Jordan's laws that use the Hanafi *madhhab* to allow the judge to annul a marriage on the basis of *kafa'a* at the request of a guardian unless the wife is pregnant or a child has been born from the marriage.

Clearly, Jordanian laws see the guardian as the father: if he is alive, he has extensive powers; if not, then his replacement's powers become limited. Article 6 of Jordan's personal status laws states:

A judge may, upon request, give in marriage a virgin who has reached fifteen years of age to a man who is of equal social status and where her guardian, other than her father or grandfather, opposes the marriage without lawful justification. If the opposition is on the part of the father or grandfather, the claim of the woman shall not be heard unless she has attained eighteen years of age and the opposition is without lawful reason. But the father could still stop this marriage on the basis of *kafa'a* [social parity].

Add to this statement the fact that a married woman who is less than forty years of age cannot come to court to sue for divorce from her husband without the presence of her father if he is alive and a male *waliy* if deceased, and it becomes clear that women are considered under the control of their fathers (or grandfathers) as long as the father is alive. Similarly, a girl who is still considered a minor under eighteen years of age cannot ask her husband for a *khul'* without the approval of her guardian.[17] Having reached the age of eighteen, a daughter can ask a judge to marry her to the man of her choice, but the father can stop the judge from performing the marriage on the basis of a lack of *kafa'a*. The father therefore chooses his daughter's first husband and must approve her divorce and her remarriage; the husband must be of equal social status or the judge could annul the marriage at the demand of the guardian. At fifteen she does not choose her own husband, although her consent is required. Theoretically, she has to give her consent, but practically speaking, the pressure brought to bear on her is such that her refusal gets lost. As In'am 'Asha, a well-known journalist and TV personality, related to me, she is the eldest of eight girls and was told her refusal to marry was an obstruction of the marriage of her sisters. No one bothered with her wish to continue her education, and her marriage to her cousin took place when she was aged fourteen and eight months. The usual certification of age issued by local health offices was presented to prove she was fifteen years old, the minimum legal age of marriage for girls.

These laws are said to be Islamic and specifically Hanafi. How true is this assumption? If it is accurate, then there is no doubt that practices dating from earlier periods would illustrate the same laws and practices as do Jordanian laws and courts today. Studying court records dating from before the introduction of

Jordan's personal status laws, however, shows that there are significant differences between laws and practices today and then. The differences that are of concern to this chapter involve in particular the issue of *wilaya*. Simply put, although there is usually a *waliy* present to stand by the bride, it is only in the case of minors or *bikrs* (virgins) that a *waliy* has to be present. An adult virgin could marry herself without the presence of any male to represent her in front of the Hanafi judge. Furthermore, even though it was more traditional that the guardian of a minor be a male relative, often designated by the father but usually chosen by the judge when the father dies before designating anyone, the mother was often made the *wasi* over her minor children with authority over the child and his or her property.[18] Mothers who acted as *wasis* to their minor children were recognized in that capacity by judges when they represented their children in court. For example, take the case of a mother who sued a man who owed her and her children twenty-eight jars of oil that he had previously owed her deceased husband. The case record refers to her as the legal *wasi* over her children.[19] Another case from nineteenth-century al-Salt also illustrates that women were assigned as *wasis* even when they were not the mothers. In this case a woman took another to court because she continued to live in a house that she and her brother's children had inherited from him. "Since Fatma al-Shamiyya, the named defendant has seized the named building without any legal rights, I ask that she take her hand off my share of the building and the share of Mu'mina, the minor who is under my *wisaya* and to deliver the share of Mu'mina to me since I am her legal *wasi* as established by the legal document in my hand."[20]

When the *wasi* was a man, the mother was still often considered the more important guardian, as in the following case from sixteenth-century Jerusalem in which the mother complained that the legal guardian—chosen by the deceased father or by the court—was not doing enough in regards to her children's extensive inheritance from their deceased wealthy merchant father. The court found for her: "Since his honor . . . the sheikh Ahmad . . . the legal *wasi* over the named orphans, children of . . . and the *nazir* [guardian] over them . . . is to take no general or specific action regarding the property of the orphans named above except with the knowledge of the named *nazira* [female supervisor/guardian], and the *mawlana al-hakim* [judge] gave her his permission in regards to this matter."[21] More important perhaps, in premodern courts mothers also had the powers of *wilaya* over their minor children so that they could transact their marriages and divorces through *wilayat al-ijbar* (the right to force) over minors; that is, a mother had the same powers as did the father when alive. This fact is not recognized by Jordanian law today.

Education and Discourses of Gender

The prophet Muhammad is reported to have indicated that seeking knowledge was mandatory to all Muslims and was not a matter of choice. *Kuttabs* (mosque schools for children) have for a long time provided basic education to children in essential subjects such as religion, Arabic language, and mathematics. Endowing a *kuttab* or *madrasa* with a *waqf* to ensure its future income was always considered an act of great charity to be rewarded in heaven. Beyond the *kuttab*, it was normal for boys who were exceptional, or who could afford it, to study at higher *madrasas* in important urban centers, which did not mean that all girls were cut off from education. Rather, the education of girls, mostly members of the middle classes, continued in the home, and some achieved a high degree of learning and even became teachers and narrators of Islamic traditions.[22] The Qur'an supports this right of women to learn and to enter into religious debates based on this learning. Surat "Al-Mujadilah" (the debating woman) states, "Allah has heard and accepted the statement of the woman who pleads with you [the Prophet] concerning her husband and carries her complaint to Allah, and Allah hears the arguments between both of you for Allah hears and sees all things" (58:1). Women are then encouraged to seek knowledge so as to be able to handle life with their husbands and within their communities. This *aya* is an important statement, and its context tells us that a woman is not expected to simply accept the interpretation of Islamic law that her husband endorses.

The history of women and work, discussed in chapter 3, illustrates how knowledgeable women actually were regarding their rights and the actions they took to protect them. Women came to court all the time to be declared *wasis* over their children and were the most reliable in safeguarding their children's wealth;[23] they demanded their inheritance and made sure that their portions were registered in court; and they demanded *khul'* from their husbands, and when a husband was reluctant, they came to the *qadi* and presented their cases and got what they wanted.[24] The important thing is that they knew legal procedures, and it was not unusual for them to come to court alone without a male representative such as a father or brother, even when it came to marriage and divorce.[25] Modern codification of the law and the requirement of legal representation by lawyers would, of course, limit the ability of women to handle their own affairs, particularly as the new legal codes were no longer as clear or familiar to the population at large. The wisdom of the Prophet in requiring knowledge for all Muslims cannot be dismissed in the face of these facts.

The modern period saw serious efforts on the part of Jordan's government to educate women. Jordan, like other Arab countries with their populations of nearly 150 million stretching from Mauritania and Morocco in the West to Iraq in the East, has adopted education as an essential route to modernization of its society to achieve a higher standard of living and to secure wealth, security, and a better life in the future. The education of women received serious attention. Educating women, because they are mothers and potential members of the workforce, has been on the agenda of all Arab countries, including Jordan's, which has achieved significant results. Even though Jordan's modern educational plans for women are quite recent when compared to other Arab countries—Egypt being the first with modern schools for girls in 1829, followed by Lebanon in 1835 and Iraq in 1898—its high literacy rate among women stands out as a significant achievement. Government statistics dating from 1994 indicate that illiteracy rates were 9.8 percent and 20.7 percent for men and women, respectively. Formal education is available and open to all Jordanian women, except for the more rural areas where such facilities are a luxury to everyone. The important point, however, is that when it comes to formal education, the school system does not discriminate in providing facilities for men and women; the discrimination comes in other ways, such as differences in facilities provided to girls schools versus boys schools: for example, computers do not seem to find their way to schools for girls. In 2000, Jordan's government launched a plan to provide computer and technological education to all schools in Jordan. It remains to be seen what role gender will play in this new plan, given the gendered results of Jordan's $1 billion plan launched in 1988 to reform education.

Jordan's accomplishments in the field of education are rather startling given the fact that such a system was hardly in evidence when the area that later became the Hashemite Kingdom of Jordan was first established in the 1920s. The centrality of education in government plans certainly played an important role in these accomplishments. According to government statistics, "today there are 2787 government schools, 1493 private schools, 48 community colleges, and 19 universities." Government plans extended to the countryside, providing a school for every village with ten or more school-age children. Enrollment is high, at 95 percent of students eligible compared to only 47 percent in 1960, urban and rural attendance being close. These figures gain significance given that today 42.2 percent of Jordan's population is fourteen years old or younger and another 31.4 percent is aged fifteen to twenty-nine, which means that Jordan is potentially enrolling one-third of its citizens in educational facilities. These numbers are significant and show the critical importance of education in determining the future of Jordan. If the educational system is molded more toward greater gender equality, a strong work ethic, and business and the market, it would prove quite dramatic and perhaps provide the best means for Jordan to modernize and catch up with the productivity expected of a new world order.

What makes this prediction even more plausible is the fact that education is free for all primary and secondary school students in Jordan. Even more important, education is compulsory for all children up to the age of fifteen. This requirement is at once encouraging and problematic. It is encouraging because the educational system has virtually a "captive" audience to be molded through the classroom, curricula, and schoolbooks. It becomes problematic for a number of reasons involving teachers and the quality of teaching, the facilities provided to various schools, and the structure and paradigms upon which the curricula and schoolbooks are based, particularly because of the universal application of these paradigms in all Jordanian schools through the powers of the Ministry of Education.

Perhaps the first problem with the system has to do with the unequal quality of education. Of the 1,346,178 children who attended elementary and secondary schools during 1997–1998, 951,831 attended public schools, and 229,487 attended private schools. Another 143,893 attended schools run by the United Nations Relief and Works Agency, and another 20,967 attended other types of government-run schools. The above figures point to the fundamental split in Jordan's educational system, that is, between public and private education, which gains great significance in the creation of culture in Jordan. The split not only is between rich and poor but also has important social and cultural repercussions that are immediately tied to political and economic problems. Not only are schools equipped differently, but the quality of the teachers is also disparate. For example, some private schools refuse to hire veiled women teachers even if it is against the law. The opposite goes for other schools with particular religious leniency. Association with the way a person is dressed is significant in a teacher-student relationship and is of the greatest importance in cultural construction. Another example involves coeducation. Private schools have coeducation, whereas public schools do not. But even in private schools that do have coeducation, the tendency is to have the boys sit in one part of the class and the girls in another. Gender segregation is thereby enforced and is probably what the parents expect. Most important, whereas one sector produces Western-educated, professionally oriented graduates to staff the country's higher government offices, including important posts in the Ministries of Foreign Affairs, Culture, and Economics, the other sector provides lower-level graduates, potential army and police officers, and the general student body in Jordanian public universities. As for market-oriented education, it has little bearing in Jordan's educational system in either the private or the public schools.

Statistics for the secondary schools are illustrative of the lack of importance that women give to practical and work-oriented education, a reflection in itself of the education they are exposed to at the primary level. Whereas 38.59 percent of male students were enrolled in vocational education in 1995–1997, only 17.58 percent of female students were. The rest were enrolled in academic education in science, arts, or religion.[26] This disparity is serious because not only does vocational education prepare students who have no interest in pursuing higher studies in crafts that they could later make into a career, but the years spent in vocational training also provide an apprentice program following which a graduate becomes a skilled craftsman ready to join a business or to work privately. Women do not seem to be encouraged to join vocational training, the most important reason being that schools for girls do not provide such training and the ones that do focus almost completely on traditional handicrafts and food making. A good example of the latter is a school in Hayy Nazal where an impressive program of traditional handicrafts is offered and where students are trained to cook in large, well-equipped kitchens. There are also facilities to learn how to sew and knit. But there are no workshops or any form of training in "men's occupations," which include carpentry, electricity, and computers.

These cultural problems cannot be underestimated, according to Nawal Hashisho, a well-seasoned, exceptional educator who is director-general of the "Modern Schools," one of Amman's better private schools. She agrees that class is a basic problem of the educational system that actually emphasizes class and gender differences even though the curricula of all schools are standardized and controlled by the Jordanian government. Given the power of the schoolroom, Hashisho wonders at the continued dependence on old educational paradigms when Jordan's educational plans are expected to advance scientific, technological, and business education. "There is no effort at the government level to change a paradigm which is gender based, patriarchal and repetitive of traditional culture."[27] The centralization of education and central control over textbooks and curricula could work toward introducing change, but as long as the same philosophy and outlook underlie the material presented, there can be very little change. This same problem extends to computers: simply providing schools with computers is a first step, but what will be taught through the computers is another thing altogether.

One has only to look at the basic education curriculum and study plan for Jordanian schools to understand what Hashisho is talking about. For 1997–1998, for example, it is only at the tenth grade that students begin computer education and even then for only one hour per week. Yet, civics and social studies (*al-tarbiyya al-Ijtima'iyya wal-wataniyya*) begin in first grade for two to three hours per week, and "music and anthems" begin in first grade at the consistent rate of one hour per week each. Islamic education and culture begin in first grade and continue until tenth grade at three hours per week. Even more serious, physics, biology, and chemistry begin only in ninth grade at two hours per week each. The largest number of hours spent at this level are learning Arabic and math (nine hours for Arabic per week and five for mathematics beginning in the first grade),[28] both of which are very important but seem to continue the same tradition as the *kuttab* system that was almost completely focused on learning the Qur'an and Islam, Arabic language and grammar, and mathematics.

The emphasis on civics and Islamic culture is important for nationalism and constructing a culture of belonging and loyalty to Jordan. But the way the material is presented is quite deductive, information presented in absolutist and conformist ways that do not lead to interpretation and questioning. It is true that the schoolbooks contain questions for students to exercise their knowledge about the material presented. The problem is that the questions are regurgitative, intended to build nationalism, but do not lead to an appreciation of concepts such as freedom, democracy, and historical change, even though there are definitions for freedom given in these textbooks. More important, there is a lack of effort in trying to make connections between the historical period and the historical context. A schoolbook at the primary level of education may begin with the Arab history of modern Jordan and end with the history of Islam, with a particular focus on the prophet Muhammad. The idea is to extend national consciousness back to the Islamic roots of the Hashemites, to show a long historical continuity and give a particular role for Jordan as continuing the Prophet's tradition of unifying the Islamic and Arab Umma. There is nothing wrong with such a national narrative—it is what all countries do and is certainly the same approach of schools in the United States at the primary and middle school levels, a perfect time to mold kids through national and civic indoctrination. The problem with the way the material is presented to primary school kids in Jordan is that there is no encouragement of speculation among students; they are expected to accept and memorize. No connection is made between history and historical context, between power and social structure, and issues of class and gender are hardly touched upon in either the curricula or the textbooks.

A few examples will illustrate this point. Take social studies and civics schoolbooks (*al-tarbiyya al-Ijtima'iyya wal-wataniyya*) for elementary schools. Social studies and civics are supposed to introduce a student to the history and culture of her country. To be a good citizen, a person must know about his country's government, institutions, affiliations, loyalties, legal system, social structure, and so on. It becomes a subject of both political indoctrination and culture construction. A survey of textbooks for primary education illustrates how traditional cultural norms, including political and social patriarchy, can be reinforced by textbooks. The subject matter covered by schoolbooks can be divided into five main parts: Jordan's history, particularly that of the Jordanian royal family and its accomplishments; Islamic history, particularly the founding period of Islam and the history of the prophet Muhammad; the geography of Jordan and the Arab world; correct or logical thinking and what makes a good citizen; and Jordanian society and culture. In other words, the subjects cover a wide range of material as expected from this type of class.[29] The structure of the schoolbooks and presentation of material are also impressive, although the historical material, especially regarding the Ottoman period, generalizes nationalist impressions that are not entirely accurate. The schoolbooks also try to present a gender-free narrative and do mention at least one woman in the context of fighters in early Islam.

But there are serious problems with these schoolbooks that reconfirm attitudes toward women already dominant in Jordanian *'urf.* This situation exists even though as Hashisho stressed, there is a sincere effort to do away with such discrimination. For one thing, most of the pictures in the schoolbooks are of men, whether we are talking about cartoons or photographs. They include men working in fields, herding sheep and goats in the desert, sitting in their tents, or eating in restaurants. It is the men who are depicted as playing the active role. It is the men who are dressed as members of the army protecting Jordan's borders, the men who appear as policemen keeping order on the streets, the men who appear as teachers and as industrial workers. In discussion of tribal life, it is the men who appear in all the pictures, herding or even as children holding sheep. Even in economic activities where women are vital, such as agricultural production, women remain invisible. In lesson 10 for fourth grade titled "Characteristics of a Good Citizen," one of these characteristics is identified as working energetically. Three pictures are presented as examples, and one of the main questions asked of the students following that lesson is "What are the similarities between these three pictures?" Looking at the picture it becomes obvious that it is men who are at the center. One picture is about agricultural workers, the second about industrial workers, and the third is a traffic officer stopping cars on the street. They are all active, working vigorously, and they are men. Just to reconfirm the impression, the students are asked, "Give three examples of persons who work with seriousness and energy."[30]

As for the women, they appear a few times in schoolbooks, once as a doctor, once as a nurse, a picture of Princess Basma bint Talal, girls standing in line in a school courtyard, women officers dressed and walking in a parade probably on independence day, and a drawing of women meeting the Prophet on his arrival at Medina from Mecca following his Hijra (A.D. 622). Almost all of the other pictures are of men, whether we are talking about the past or the present. Except for Princess Basma, the parading army officers, and a couple of students in group pictures, all the women are wearing head covers. Even the doctor is wearing a veil.[31] There are no pictures of women actively involved except for the nurse, who appears to be a mother hovering over a young girl. Why not depict the parading officers in some sort of activity rather than as showpieces?[32]

Needless to say, all the historical personalities discussed in these books are men, whether we are talking about the early Islamic period or the modern period. Though one woman is mentioned, Umm 'Amara Nusayba b. Ka'ab, she appears to be rather exceptional and unimportant because few details are given about her contributions.[33]

Perhaps one of the reasons for this state of affairs has to do with the approach to social studies and civics. Here we do not see any great interest beyond a nationalist discourse in which Jordan is depicted as fighting a battle for Islam since the time of the Prophet, then against colonialism, and finally today to unify Jordan for its people. This stance is to be expected from countries that experienced colonialism. The past has to be used as a heritage to unify it with the present and to create a cultural discourse that will confirm the existing hegemony; in this case the Islamic heritage is fundamental. There is also an inordinate amount of coverage of the Jordanian armed forces, placing stress on the aggressive image of man and the essentialness of that image as part of Jordan's security and welfare. The image of the macho male is strengthened and modernized.

Engendering is subtle at its best. Schoolbooks are not intentionally gender discriminatory, but the message of gender difference is brought home in more subliminal ways. A good example comes out of the "logic" exercises that are very valuable in themselves because they teach children how to address questions, research them, and come up with possible answers. In the social science and civics schoolbook for fifth grade, the following story is given. "Basil reorganized the house-furniture while his mother was traveling. He changed the places of the bedrooms and the living room. When his mother returned she was surprised and said: this is a new house!" Students were then asked the following questions: "What did Basil do? Did he buy new furniture? Why was the mother surprised?" The message here is intriguing, notwithstanding the intent of the lesson. A boy can actually change the organization of the house without his mother's permission while she is away, and the mother is simply surprised and has little to say about the actions of her son. Active and aggressive son, passive and compliant mother. Would it have been acceptable to the people who put this story together to put the father in place of the mother? Probably not, because a father, unlike a mother, cannot be bypassed when a son decides to do what he wants with the family home.

What is missing from these schoolbooks is as important in forming the future Jordanian as what is included. For example, nowhere is there a discussion of concepts such as sovereignty, power, gender, or class. The role of environment (*bi'a*) in forming different groups such as Bedouins or peasants is discussed, but there is no discussion of money, property, or class. It may be asking too much to cover a large variety of concepts, but at least the basic concepts with which students should be familiar have to be covered. Here the experience of Sitt Hind 'Abdel-Jaber comes to mind. She attributes her success as a professional businesswoman to the atmosphere in which she was raised: a family where the language of business and trade was quite familiar. She stresses the importance of an early introduction to business education and an understanding of concepts of market forces, buying, and selling, to which students are introduced quite early in the United States and which Arab society was familiar with at one time when commerce was the main activity of most of the population. She is correct: there is no reference in textbooks or curricula about the role of commerce, business, and banking; how such institutions work; or any approach to the importance of savings and enterprise. In other words, no work ethic is being built into the young Jordanian to teach him or her the importance of working for pay, what to do with this pay, or connections between what they do as children and what they will do as adults. There is also little effort to build symbols, heroes, and heroines modeled after ordinary Jordanians and their accomplishments as writers, as athletes, or in other capacities. The only heroes depicted are members of the royal family, past and present. Cultures need symbols that are widely representative. How can a society begin to appreciate possible equality between its men and women when women are completely invisible except if they are royalty?

Students in fifth grade begin to learn about international organizations, international relations, and human rights. The coverage in the schoolbook assigned is comprehensive. Part of what is discussed includes the meaning of discrimination, and examples from history and the contemporary world are presented. Universal equality is also emphasized: "People are born free and they are equal in rights, dignity, and humanity notwithstanding differences in color, race/sex [*jins* could be either], language, religion, political inclination, or wealth." Even though the word "jins" could mean sex or race, given the other issues referred to it most probably means race in this instance. This belief is confirmed by the fact that the pictures and discussions in this section of the book do not present women or women's issues even once. Yet here is an excellent opportunity to introduce some of the fundamental problems recognized by the world community, such as discrimination and violence against women, which are the focus of great international activism and treaties to which Jordan is a signatory.

Classrooms are perhaps even more important in forming the young individual than schoolbooks. As any teacher knows, there is great leverage privileging the teacher in a student-teacher relationship. Not only is a teacher the authority in the classroom, but she is also seen as an example and a guide. The power to grade and to punish is not lost on young students, the earlier years being even more important than later years, so that by the time a student graduates and goes to college, ambitions and expectations have all but been formed. College can only help redirect or emphasize certain attributes gained by students at the school level, given the fact that in Jordan specialization takes place at the secondary school level when students are divided into sciences (*'ilmi*), literature (*adabi*), religion (*shari'a*), and vocation (industrial, commercial, agricultural, nursing, hotel management, and home economics). Thus, even future career orientation of Jordanian students is set before they graduate and go to college. In other words, schoolteachers in Jordan have greater powers than their counterparts outside the Arab world. Add to this fact that school is perhaps the only place where girls come into contact with people other than members of their own families, as movement of girls is limited outside of the home without the accompaniment of a family member. The ability of the school and its teachers to mold the future Jordanian woman can therefore not be undermined. Given these facts, schoolteachers can either become a force reinforcing conservatism and traditional expectations from girls in Jordanian society or instill a different outlook that need not conflict with expectations but could help widen spheres and possibilities.

Observations from visiting four Jordanian schools for girls were not encouraging when it came to the culture in the classroom, which emphasized gender difference and expected gender roles. Intissar al-Qihwi, headmistress of a secondary girls school in Amman, perhaps one of the most impressive and dynamic educators I have met, explained a great deal about these problems. She understood not only the significance of education but also the serious need to reorient it in a more dynamic, goal-oriented direction in which girls understand they have wider options in life and are given the ability to consider these options. But the first problem that is faced, according to her, has to do with the parents who look at their daughters as "spending time" in school until they get married. As she pointed out, girls begin to drop out around the age of fifteen as their families accept proposals of marriage and the girls are required to drop out. Al-Qihwi finds this situation to be a source of great distress, and tries her best to convince parents to keep their daughters in school even after they are married, notwithstanding how difficult it is at every level. There were two married pregnant girls at the school at the time of my visit, but al-Qihwi insisted that they complete their school education so that they would have a weapon, as no one knew what the future would bring their way.

My conversation with al-Qihwi added emphasis to the demands of Jordanian feminists that the age of marriage be raised to eighteen to allow girls to mature, to complete their school education, and to realize the options that could be open to them. As long as the age of marriage remains fifteen, there seems little that can be done to allow girls to mature beyond the domestic scene. Early marriage only emphasizes Jordanian society's engendering of roles. Not that early marriage is anything new in Jordan, as archival records show that boys and girls were married quite early in Islamic tradition.[34] But the concern here is to allow for early sexual relations within a legal framework, which happens to be one of the major reasons there is opposition to raising the age of marriage among girls from fifteen to eighteen, especially among the more rural and tribal populations of Jordan. Because children who want to break the rules do so anyway and girls from rural and tribal areas are married even before reaching the age of fifteen—a medical certificate attesting to their having reached that age is all that is required—there is no reason that the minimum age for marriage could not be raised. In fact, if Jordan has future hopes for its women as educated citizens contributing to economic development and growth, raising the minimum age is imperative.

I would like to end this discussion by presenting a cartoon of the typical home scene as presented to students.

The caption below the picture reads: "After washing their hands and brushing their teeth, the family sits in the living room. The father reads the newspaper. The mother knits. The older sister does needlepoint. Suna plays with her dolls. And Jinn Ali looks at the pictures in the books."[35] This scene comes from a Turk-

ish textbook and is representative of similar scenes that appear in textbooks from schools in Jordan and all over the Islamic world. My selection of a Turkish textbook is to call into question the belief that Turkey has managed to change its patriarchal structure by simply changing its gender laws. The laws in Turkey may have changed but not the outlook toward gender and patriarchy, which is repeated through *'urf* to the point of being given "textual" authenticity equated with religion, faith, and expected traditions. For things to change, it is this image that has to be attacked and transformed before a new generation continues the same patriarchal patterns of their fathers and grandfathers before them. New *'urf* is needed, and questioning existing *'urf* built on "textual" constructions must be encouraged.

One can conclude that gendering takes place very early in life. Through family, society, and schoolroom young girls and boys are educated into a culture in which basic human relations are integral. Social roles begin to be learned soon after birth through attitudes toward children of different sexes. Expectations toward girls in Jordan are different from attitudes toward boys. So are expectations of boys from their families and societies different from the expectations of girls. As this chapter has shown, the adult woman is formed early on, through relationships with her mother, father, and siblings. From the beginning she is aware that because she is a girl she is lacking in some way. Her family may love her, but there is not as much celebration or pride in her accomplishments as there is in the arrival and accomplishments of her brother. Financial allocations of the family are directed first toward ensuring her brother's future; she always comes last. Her main job in life, she is told from her very early years, is to be a housewife and a mother. She must learn modesty, not be heard or seen. The image may not fit with her mother's relationship with her father or her brothers, for very often Jordanian and Palestinian mothers are the actual power in the home, but even her mother is the first to impress on her the superior importance of the brother and the need to cater to his needs. As she grows older she is increasingly faced with the power of her father. Not only is he the source of discipline and hence of fear, but he is also the one with absolute legal power over her. She cannot do much without his permission, and at the same time he represents security and the source of financial support without which the family cannot survive. And so develops the love-hate relationship between the father and daughter. No one is more beloved to her, yet she is in constant fear of angering him, of acting immodest, or of doing something that would be misunderstood as disrespectful or immoral. The merging of fear and respect is shared by the sons, but sons know that they will soon get out from under parental authority and be free to develop and grow. For the girls, the only way to "get out" is through marriage, which is every girl's dream, what she expects, and what is expected of her. Once married, however, she discovers that she has moved from one type of patriarchal authority, the father, to another, the husband. She cannot go out without his permission and cannot even take a job unless he agrees. The power of the father does not end there; her brother's authority also continues even after she is married. After all, she is considered a member of her clan, and as such her moral attitude reflects on them, so her male relatives continue to form a real authority in her life. She can sue for divorce only with her father or a *waliy* present, although she can do so alone if she is over forty years of age; otherwise, the judge may refuse to hear her case. Educated or not, owner of business or not, doctor, lawyer, what have you, she still cannot get married without her father's permission or divorce without his approval. She could appeal to the judge if she is an adult over eighteen years of age, but why appeal to a complete stranger when she is already considered an adult and could in fact marry, have her own home, and be trusted with raising children at the age of fifteen? The contradictions of a girl's life develop into the incongruities of a woman's.

When married and in her home she expects to be the queen, as she has always been told. According to the Islamic discourse that she was told should guide her life, she should have her own home separate from her husband's family. When it does not happen, she finds she has no one to support her in her bid for a separate home, even though the law should stand with her. The alternative is divorce, but she soon learns that there is "something wrong" with a divorced woman. In school she was supposed to be educated and look forward to a more active and productive future, but the school only reemphasized the lessons of her early youth, that is, the passivity of women, the activeness and even aggression of men, and the importance of patriarchy. As this chapter has shown, for Jordanian women to be expected to take a greater role and interest in their country, its development and its economic activity, there will have to be basic changes in attitudes in regards to bringing up children, to school curricula, to teaching in the classroom, and finally the legal system that sanctions patriarchal power and makes women into passive dependents.

6

Marriage, Obedience, and Work

THE Islamic marriage contract defines the relationship and mutual obligations of husband and wife. The contract as applied in Jordan allows husband and wife to include conditions that they consider of particular importance for the success of their marriage and their willingness to remain in it. As long as these conditions are within the bounds of what is acceptable to the *shari'a*, courts find them to be legitimate, and either party can sue for divorce if the other breaks the condition and is therefore in a situation of breach of contract.

At the heart of marriage are a number of assumptions that are not written out but are socially accepted and legally recognized by the law and courts. Most important is the responsibility of a husband to support his wife financially. Schools of law have differed on exactly what constitutes support—for example, does it include medical expenses? Notwithstanding differences, all agree that by becoming married, a wife expects to be supported by a husband and that this support should be according to the social level that she was used to while still in her father's home. Jordan's laws recognize a husband's responsibility to support his wife and take a wide comprehensive outlook that grants the wife the most important needs itemized by *shari'a*: "A wife's *nafaqa* includes food, clothing, housing, medical needs within the known bounds, and [a servant] to serve the wife whose social equals have servants."[1] The woman's own money that she may receive from inheritance, investment of her dowry, or any other means is considered hers according to the Islamic *shari'a* and not the household's or family's. The exception to these rules in Jordanian laws involves the working wife: "There is no *nafaqa* for the wife who works outside the home without the husband's approval."[2] This statement does not fit with the Islamic *shari'a* but is a modern addition based on the *shari'a* idea that a wife who leaves the marriage home without her husband's approval does not deserve his *nafaqa*. That "leaving the home" really meant abandoning the marriage and not living with the husband and not simply going out of the house has been forgotten. Although Christians have a different form of marriage and marriage contract, nevertheless the same expectations regarding the husband's responsibility for the financial support of his wife apply.

What does the wife owe in return? Here the law is interpreted differently, but it is generally accepted that the wife's obedience to her husband is expected in return for his financial support. When she is disobedient, then he has the right to withdraw his financial support or to divorce her without compensation or payment of the agreed upon financial rights defined by their marriage contract. What constitutes disobedience is problematic and, according to court records, very often contradicts Jordanian laws. The question of a wife's right to work without a husband's permission figures prominently here. Given the *shari'a* outlook toward women's work, it is not surprising that modern *shari'a* court judges seem to vacillate about this matter. A judge's decision that the "work of a wife with or without the husband's permission does not deny her a *nafaqa*" was overturned by *shari'a* court decision number 18900 in which the judge concluded, "I say that that decision is contrary to what article 68 of the law states."[3] Jordanian judges have also vacillated in cases before the court involving family disputes over a wife's work when the husband did accept her work. Here questions revolved around proving that he did approve, and if this fact is proved, does he have the right to withdraw his approval later? What if he married her knowing that she was already holding a job or involved in business? Does that constitute approval?

Personal status law gives the impression that once the husband has acquiesced in regards to his wife's work, he can no longer deny her. Actually, the situation is much more complicated, and this law in particular must be considered one of the most important hindrances to the entry of women into the workforce or of opening their own businesses as their continuation in either is dependent on "keeping her husband happy." The problems here are diverse. A man could refuse to pay his wife any financial support on the basis that he asked her to quit working and she refused and continued to work.[4] A husband could also deny his divorcée her rightful financial compensation because he is divorcing her on the basis that she worked without his permission. When the wife sues for these financial rights that are often agreed upon at the time the marital contract was signed, the court asks her to prove that she had received his approval that she could work. Because such approval is almost always an oral agreement, it becomes very hard to prove.[5] Another interesting case, as discussed in chapter 4, was decided on the basis that the wife worked in the armed forces and would not be able to resign. Here the husband moved his wife to an area to live outside of Amman where she had lived continuously for a long time. In a *ta'a* case he de-

manded that his wife move there with him. As the records state, the wife worked
in the armed forces before her marriage, and because she continued to work after
being married to him, it is clear that he must have approved of her work. Yet the
court did not dispute the husband's right to demand that his wife quit and come
live with him; rather, it asked that he prove that the new home he set up was acceptable per *shari'a* requirements and also indicated that because the wife
worked in the armed forces she did not have the right to resign even if she wished
to do so. So the husband's acceptance of a wife's work did not mean that he could
not change his mind later, and it was the wife's inability to resign rather than her
husband's right to demand that she stop working that was of substance to the
court, which turned down the husband's legal action.[6]

Women in professions considered quite respectable in Jordan also face the
same kind of marital control. A number of cases indicate that teachers often face
being declared *nashiz* because they refuse to give up their jobs on the husband's
demand. *Nashiz* is a condition in which a wife is considered disobedient and not
deserving of financial support from her husband. Being declared *nashiz* did not
mean that a wife would be granted divorce by her husband; he could keep her in
that state indefinitely if he so wished, unless she took the case in front of the
judge and went through the expense and hassle of *shiqaq wa niza'*, as discussed
elsewhere in this report. In Tamyiz Court case 21332, dated December 4, 1980,
the wife, a teacher, was asked to prove that her husband approved that she
worked. Given her education and the fact that she was already in the profession,
logic should have dictated that the husband must have married her knowing that
she had a profession. Because it was he who questioned her right to work, the
burden of proof that he never approved of her work should have been placed on
his shoulders. It, however, was not so in this case, nor in any of the cases sur-
veyed; the onus of proof was laid at the feet of the wife, notwithstanding the acknowledged *'urf* that written conditions in the marriage contract are not
acceptable socially. They are certainly not acceptable to husbands who could be
considered wimps if they succumb to their wives' conditions. So according to
'urf such conditions are always oral, as the courts should be well aware. Continuing and well-known realities, including a wife's education, profession, or inclusion of her profession in the marriage contract, often does not make a difference
in a judge's rulings. Because Jordanian marriage contracts allow for the inclusion
of conditions, women should be advised to insist on the inclusion of such oral
agreements in the written contract, particularly because Jordanian *'urf* accepts
the idea that a husband has a right to allow or refuse his wife the right to leave the
home or to work.

Complicating the issues more is the fact that today husbands whose wives work with their approval question their responsibility for supporting them. Other husbands claim the wife's income as a family income to be spent by the husband as the financial supporter of the family. Jordanian law strengthens such arguments by allowing a wife's right to her husband's financial support to fall if she works without his permission, which has given husbands leverage to control the wife's income in return for giving them the right to work. Being the head of the household means controlling the budget; a working woman then has to abide by her husband's control of where her money is to be spent. Women have left jobs because of these reasons. As one woman told me, "I became tired of my husband changing his car every year while I continued wearing the same clothes from my trousseau." Another told me that her brother-in-law sat in her dentist sister's clinic after work to receive the fee of her customers and nightly counted the income for the day, which he then pocketed. Although these cases may not be typical, control of a wife's income does not sit well with wives and discourages them from opening their own businesses because ultimately they have no control over their own income or ability to continue working if the husband changes his mind.

This chapter will detail these problems and draw upon actual court records that show the dilemma faced today by young men and women whose needs no longer conform with what Jordan's personal status laws defined early in the twentieth century. Given the expectation that a wife's obedience is reciprocated by a husband's financial support, a wife's income from a job or business is a particular point of contention. What is involved in an Islamic marriage? What does paying of *nafaqa* entail for the husband, and what is its connection with the definition of marriage according to the *shari'a*, as compared to how personal status laws define the institution? Should the wife be an equal supporter? Should the husband be in control of her money, as is expected of the head of a household whom traditions recognize as the sole or at least main financial supporter of the family? What happens to the whole question of *qiwama* (guardianship or support) when a wife contributes to the household income? Today, couples are moving increasingly to form joint decision-type marriages in which both work, bring income home, and spend it together for mutual needs. Although this move is positive, the laws do not protect the woman once the marriage begins to fall apart. A woman who works is regarded as not fulfilling her full marital obligations. A wife who "wants out" of a marriage has a very hard time getting divorced and almost always loses a good portion of her financial rights—including property she and her husband bought together—in return for ending the marriage. Therefore, it is important to try to understand the significance of the law requiring a husband's permission before his wife can work. Such laws appeared only in the modern period, and they are by no means unique to the Islamic world. As discussed earlier, French women still cannot work at night without their husbands' permission. Other questions to be addressed in the chapter include the wife's *ta'a* (obedience). Is it contingent on the husband's payment of *nafaqa*? What does *ta'a* involve, and how is it connected with the meaning and purpose of marriage in Islam? If the wife contributes equally to the household income, should not then obedience change in meaning since it is reciprocated by a husband's financial support? At the heart of these questions are laws and traditions regarding marriage that are controlled by personal status laws, already extensively referred to throughout the book. Here we will focus on personal status laws pertaining to marriage in its various aspects, including financial support, obedience, and women's work. Because of the importance of divorce and court procedures regarding marriage and divorce in constructing gender relations and the power of patriarchy, they will be covered as well. The approach follows the methodology outlined for this book: looking at today's laws as a construction of various legal traditions that can be deconstructed and new ones introduced more fitting with Jordan's needs today without really touching on the central social concerns regarding morality and honor.

Defining Marriage

A prenuptial condition in a marriage contract is undoubtedly one of the most important instruments that women in Islamic societies at one time used to ensure control over marriage, a wife's position within her husband's home, financial support expected from her husband, and even intimate details involving the marriage.

Modern Jordanian women do make use of this right to a certain extent but nowhere close to its potential or to how well their sisters did before the beginning of legal transformations by the Ottoman Empire during the nineteenth century. Earlier conditions were quite comprehensive and sometimes included circumstances that were particular to the couple being married. Some of the more general conditions that repeat themselves often included a husband's not taking a second wife, that he not beat her, not move her away from her family, provide her with particular luxuries and items of clothing, and so on. Today, Jordanian women make little use of prenuptial agreements, even though they could give them leverage and empower them in relation to their husbands. Ignorance of this right among both men and women and the general unwillingness of the bride and her family to "act tough" toward a bridegroom and thereby lose him have curbed the potential of this instrument guaranteed by law and of long-standing existence in Islamic societies. Furthermore, the meaning of prenuptial agreements has changed significantly in modern law. That they should not contradict with Islam is a general rule applied before and after the modernization of law. But it is in the interpretation of what does or does not constitute "Islamic rules" in a marital relationship that the differences between earlier practices and today's practices illustrate the confining of the woman's agency in negotiating her life and the greater power that has been handed to a husband by modern law.

As for ignorance of the law, it seems to be widespread among Jordanian women and constitutes a serious problem in regards to their knowing whatever rights they have today. For example, all Jordanian women know that a wife has the right to hold the *'isma* (marital knot) if it is agreed upon at the time the marriage is contracted. They also know that holding the *'isma* gives the wife the ability to divorce her husband. However, most Jordanians think that if at the time of the marriage contract a woman is given the *'isma,* it means that only the wife retains that power and the husband loses it. This belief is incorrect because despite whether a wife holds the *'isma,* the husband never loses his absolute power to divorce her at will. But it is the perception that matters. Brides are not willing to "steal a husband's manhood" by asking him to turn over the prerogative of divorce. Given the centrality of marriage in a woman's life and the fear of spinsterhood, it is important that the husband be appeased and not frightened away from the marriage. It is true that the *ma'dhun* is required to discuss all aspects of marriage and the marriage contract with the bride and bridegroom, but it never takes place because it is not traditional for the *ma'dhun* to do so and because the bride is usually absent at the signing ceremony (*katb al-kitab*).

What is "Islamic" and therefore not open for negotiation in a marriage contract is actually dependent on the definition of marriage, a definition that has changed significantly with modernity, as happens with most institutions, largely because of sociopolitical conditions. Article 2 of Jordan's personal status laws defines marriage as "a contract between a man and a woman who is legally available to him with the object of forming a family and producing children."[7] This definition, like the rest of Jordan's personal status laws, is based on the Ottoman Family Code of 1917 that was adopted by Jordan and was in turn supposedly based on earlier *shari'a* practices. That statement, however, is not the truth of the matter. Furthermore, even though it is widely believed that all Muslim countries follow the same philosophy of marriage, that situation is also not the case. Other Muslim countries do not conclude that the purpose of marriage is to form a family and reproduce. For example, Article 1 of Kuwait's 1984 personal status code states: "Marriage is a contract between a man and a woman who is lawfully permitted to him, the aim of which is cohabitation, chastity and national strength."

Article 2 of Libya's 1984 marriage laws defines marriage as "a lawful pact which is based on a foundation of love, compassion and tranquility which makes lawful the relationship between a man and a woman neither of whom is forbidden in marriage to the other." In contrast, definitions of marriage similar to the Jordanian one appear in the personal status laws of Syria and Egypt. The Syrian definition is: "Marriage is a contract between a man and woman to whom she is legal whose purpose is to create common life ties and procreation" ("*al-zawaj 'aqd bayn rajul wa-imra'a tuhil lahu shar'an ghayatihi insha' rabitah lil-haya al-mushtaraka wal-nasl.*")[8] Almost the exact same definition of marriage in the Syrian code appears in Iraq's.[9] Algeria's personal status laws define marriage in a similar way: "[M]arriage is a contract that takes place between a man and a woman according to the *Shar'*. Of its goals is the formation of a family based on affection, sympathy, cooperation, and morality of the couple and the protection of posterity [*ansab*]."[10]

The comparison between the Kuwaiti and Libyan definitions of marriage, on the one hand, and Jordan's, Syria's, Iraq's, and Algeria's, on the other, is important. The most important difference has to do with the formation of family and procreation. Neither Kuwait nor Libya were subjected to French or British rule, as was the case of the rest, nor did they experience direct diffusion of Western concepts of family and marital relations, as did countries whose legal systems were reconstructed and modernized under European tutelage. It is therefore not surprising that Kuwaiti and Libyan definitions of marriage are closer to the Qur'an's definition of marriage. The importance of "family" and children as a "purpose" of marriage is more attuned with European Victorianism than with Islamic traditions. Although Islam looked on children as one of the great prizes of life, marriage constituted a different relationship within Islamic tradition. After all, divorce was allowed, and as court records illustrate, people divorced and married others quite often, and they continue to do so today. Furthermore, we do not see "not having children" as an important reason for divorcing wives in Ottoman court archives, although that type of reasoning is an important cause for divorce in modern courts. Yet inability to consummate marriage was an important reason for a woman to sue for divorce in Ottoman courts, consummation being the purpose of the marriage and therefore nonconsummation one of the most accepted reasons for divorce according to all the *madhahib*. Ratib al-Zahir points out that Jordan's personal status laws as a whole and the definition of marriage specifically do not fit with the most acceptable interpretations of marriage among *fuqaha'* as determined by their reading of the *shari'a*.

It is important to question the definition of marriage because of the basic division of labor based on gender that Jordan's personal status laws legitimate. If marriage is transacted to form a family and procreate, a wife's primary function becomes bearing her husband's children and taking care of them at home. She provides the service at home, that is, cleaning, cooking, and so on. Her marital obligations toward her husband are to obey him, which includes not going out of the marital home without his permission. In return, it is the husband's responsibility to financially support her and their children. This type of basic relationship between husband and wife predominates globally and continues to be the most acceptable way by which people look at marriage and roles of husband and wife. It is codifying these roles that carry consequences for a woman that is in question here. The definition places the woman in the home, and "going out" becomes a breach of her marriage contract if she has not received his prior approval. The many cases that were brought to Ottoman courts in which a husband demanded that his wife "not go out" or his wish to divorce her because she went out too much show that women went out at will and that the question of a husband's approval was probably more complicated.

A nineteenth-century declaration of divorce recorded in the *shari'a* court of Nablus illustrates the attitude toward a wife's going out without a husband's prior permission. "In front of the honorable *shari'a qadi* . . . [man's name] appeared and declared that he took an oath in regards to his wife Fatima . . . that if you were to go out of this house then you are divorced a triple divorce with no going back. After his oath she left the house and was [thereby] divorced. The *hakim* declared that he owed her all her financial rights including her delayed dowry and had him pay her delayed dowry of 25 qirsh." [11] It is important to point out here that the wife received her full financial compensation and that leaving the home without her husband's permission was not considered cause for divorce on her part, which would have given her husband the right to renege on his financial obligations toward her. A husband's financial obligations toward his wife could amount to an impressive nest egg for the wife, as they include her delayed dowry agreed upon at the time the marriage was contracted, her alimony usually assessed as one year's support after divorce unless she gets remarried, her *'idda* allowance that includes housing and living expenses, and possibly a *mut'a* (compensation of supplies or entertainment) allowance because the marriage was ended not of her choice, even though the wife may have left the home to enforce her husband's oath to divorce her.

The outlook of courts has changed. Today's courts look at the wife as the section of the "family" that belongs in the home; her leaving the home for any reason then constitutes a form of "harm" to the family. Therefore, in determining the causes of divorce, a wife's work figures strongly against her, and she suffers accordingly through substantial reduction of her alimony in *shiqaq wa niza'* courts. Working wives know it, and the social pressures on them are a great hardship because they are still expected to be full-time people at home yet carry job responsibilities. At the least appearance of problem within the marriage, it is the working wife who receives the censure of society and the law.

One should also point out the inconsistency in personal status laws that may establish a division of labor between husband and wife, but do not take this division into consideration when it comes to compensating a wife for her years of marriage when divorce takes place or when the husband dies. His property and all assets accumulated during the marriage that are written in his name—which is the norm—stay with him at the time of divorce or are inheritable according to Islamic law when he dies. The wife's share in the first is zero and in the second it is one-eighth if she has children with him and one-quarter if she does not. In other words, if the purpose of marriage is to create a family, the laws that follow from such a basis are not consistent with the meaning of a family. This fact is particularly apparent given the ease with which a husband can divorce at any time and at will. Notwithstanding how much time a wife may have given the "family," she has little leverage or rights normally associated with "family," such as half of all marital assets or the right to a husband's full pension in case of his death, as is normally the case where the principle of "family" is a basis for defining laws of property, taxation, social security, and so on. In fact, the whole idea of "family" seems to be applied only when it comes to the definition of marriage and the division of labor between husband and wife. Two laws in particular prove this point. The first law has to do with nationality. According to the Jordanian Civil Code, Section 33, "Jordanian nationality shall be governed by a special law." Section 34 defines who has this right by detailing who is included in a family: "1. The family of a person shall consist of his relatives. 2. Persons shall be deemed to be relatives if they have a common ancestor." [12] Nationality, however, is not granted according to this definition of family. Not all relatives have a right to enjoy Jordanian nationality, only people with a Jordanian father. This contradiction in the law is but another way to effectively deny women equal rights and put into question the fate of any property owned by women who are married to non-Jordanians. Security of nationality and property is essential for any type of economic growth. The second law involves taxation. Tax exemptions provided by Jordanian laws benefit men and discriminate against women. Article 13 gives the husband the right to five hundred dinars' exemption for his wife, for each of his children, and for parents he supports. The wife does not have the right to claim the same exemptions, even though the law considers a husband and his wife independent taxpayers. Women can claim exemptions only if the husband demands explicitly for her to be granted these exemptions or if the wife is the only supporter of the family (Article 4c). In other words, we are not talking about a "family" unit in which all its members expect equal protection and support but rather a patriarchal unit based on male custody over female. Women's groups I met with and whose reports I read referred to these two laws that they considered to have severe impacts on women. Although these laws may not appear to be immediately pertinent as constraints on women and work, in fact they are.

So what is marriage according to the *shari'a*? Actually, marriage in Islam is based on a contract that is quite similar to any other type of contract that sets out the basis upon which the parties involved reach mutual agreement. The very wording of the definition of marriage in Jordan's personal status laws confirms the contractual nature of marriage. As Ratib al-Zahir points out, "a sales contract for example can take place between a man and a woman who is legal to him (*tahilu lahu shar'an*). A rental contract as well could be between a man and a woman who is legal to him." More important, al-Zahir regards the definition of marriage as hedging the interpretation given to it by the *fuqaha*'. Modern lawgivers kept away or shied away from the idea that a marriage contract allowed a man to enjoy a woman sexually. Rather, they tried to show noble intentions for marriage, with "lofty goals such as building the good society that assured chastity and virtue." [13] Put differently, one can conclude that modern marriage is defined according to the historical context presented by the twentieth century with a strong dosage of leftover nineteenth-century Victorianism with its emphasis on the nuclear family, the wife's domesticity, and a "home, sweet home" attitude. Seen this way, the philosophical outlook regarding marriage and gender actually has little to do with the *shari'a* as practiced earlier before the modernization of law and must be seen as a modern state-constructed system that can be changed by the state the same way it was created by the state.

The linguistic meaning of the word *zawaj* [marriage], points to the joining of one thing with another after each was separate on its own. The word became known by its association with the act of joining a man with a woman in particular so that the word when pronounced came to have only that one meaning. In *fiqh*, marriage was defined by the *fuqaha*' in many ways, similar to one another, all of which revolved around its purpose and that giving the right to the man to enjoy a woman. . . . According to contemporary Hanafi theologians [however]—for example Sheikh Mustafa al-Zarqa'—marriage is defined as a contract between a man and a woman whose purpose is to legalize sexual enjoyment between them with the purpose of procreation and formation of a family.[14]

Here al-Zahir takes issue with the contemporary Hanafi definition of marriage and points out that Sheikh al-Zarqa' and other theologians of the modern period have mixed up the *purpose* of marriage (sexual enjoyment) and the *results* of marriage (procreation). He also points out that the definition of marriage in Jordanian law is linguistically incorrect. Marriage cannot be between a man and woman "who is legal to him" (*tuhilu lahu shar'an*) for the purpose of procreation, because she is not legal to him until she is married, and it is the contract that makes this possible. One can conclude that linguistically, the definition of the contract is faulty, and as it stands it is but a construct emphasizing the possible results of the marriage, that is, family and procreation, as seen by state legislators, rather than an Islamic purpose of marriage. The reasons for entering into a marriage contract, then, should not be confused with the possible results of the contract, yet that is what personal status laws have done.

Court records seem to confirm this definition of marriage as allowing the husband exclusive intercourse with a woman, that being the purpose of the marriage. This case comes from Ma'an *shari'a* court and dates from 1932:

Majlis al-shar'i at the *shari'a* court of Ma'an met with me, 'Abdal-Majid Mihyad acting as presiding judge. The adult woman Thuraya bint 'Awda al-Hasanat came and with her husband Salim Badah Ibrahim al-Hasanat who are known to Salim b. Khalil al-Hasanat and 'Amid Badah Huwaimil al-Hasanat, all of whom are inhabitants of Wadi Musa, and Khashman Bada 'Ayyid Abu Krayki from Ma'an. The mentioned Thuraya asked her mentioned husband Salim to remove her (*yukhli'ha*) from his marriage-knot (*'ismatihu*) and marriage contract against fifteen Palestinian pounds as replacement for *khul'* that she would pay him when she is married to another man and against renouncing all his duties toward her because of their marriage, and renouncing the *nafaqa* due her for the *'idda* period. The mentioned husband accepted this and [divorced her through] *khul'* by using the words *"khali'tik"* from my *'isma* and marriage contract against an amount of fifteen Palestinian pounds that you are to pay me when you marry another man and against all what is due you from me pertaining to our marriage and your *nafaqa* due you for the *'idda* period. Thuraya agreed and committed herself to paying him the substitute for *khul'* when she marries another. . . . Accordingly I explained to the mentioned [man] that his mentioned wife is now divorced (*banat*) from him a *baynuna sughra* (irrevocable divorce) and is not legal for him to remarry except with a new contract and new dowry . . . and I explained to the divorced (*makhlu'a*) that she has the right to marry whoever she wished and that when she does get married she has to pay the agreed upon amount. Written and signed on the 27th of Sha'ban which is equivalent to 25/12/1932.[15]

This rather rare case (I have seen it only once before) is signed by all the parties concerned, including the wife who must have been literate because there is no indication that she included a sign next to her name. The inclusion of a condition that her divorce is contingent on her compensating her husband in case she marries another man illustrates the rights the husband saw from this marriage and the acceptance of the court for conditions that go beyond what we know today as the norm. Certainly, there is nothing in personal status laws that would allow a judge to allow such a condition today, nor would it constitute part of acceptable social practices. Yet, the demand of the husband, the commitment of the wife, and the instructions of the judge show there was nothing wrong in the eyes of either the court or society that two persons can include whatever conditions that suited them whether in marriage or divorce. Moreover, the case shows that it is the sexual aspect of the relationship that is the mainstay of the marriage. After all, the couple is being divorced, yet the husband still wants a hold on the wife and demands compensation for delivering his sexual rights to a new man. He does not expect to take her back without paying her a new dowry because divorce by *khul'* is irrevocable. She is no longer going to live with him, and there is no expectation of children. So the only hold left is her compensation for giving herself to another man, and it will presumably be through the dowry she receives from the new man that she will purchase her own freedom from her first husband.

This arrangement does not mean that children were unimportant to marriage; on the contrary, as very early marriage contracts show, one of the pleasures of marriage is to have children. But hoping for children is a far cry from legal codification that makes out the purpose of marriage to be "having children." In Islamic history, children were born from slave women and were recognized by fathers who then usually manumitted the mother as an *umm al-walad* (mother of the boy) without there being any marriage. Besides, we do not see medieval *fuqaha'* spending time discussing not having children as one of the reasons for a husband to divorce his wife or for taking a second wife. Such excuses are part of modern discourses on gender and had little validity to Islamic *fiqh*. What interested *fiqh* were a husband's virility and his ability to consummate the marriage. The husband's impotency is one of the reasons that all the *madhahib* adopt for *faskh* (annulment) of marriage or for granting the wife divorce with full compensation. Yet among contemporary Islamic thinkers, *muftis* and *fuqaha'*, not having children has constituted an important excuse for divorcing a wife or a husband. As explained in chapter 2 of this book, *fiqh* is closely connected with social and moral discourse and can therefore be seen as a good reflection of the socioeconomic forces producing culture from within particular contexts.

Contracting Marriage

The method of transacting marriage and the content of contracts belonged to the two parties involved. Any condition was permissible as long as it was acceptable to the *shari'a*. The important thing to realize is that many issues included in Muslim marriage contracts that are accepted as purely Islamic were really there as a normal part of local *'urf*. Comparing marriage contracts dating from before the reform of laws and courts and contemporary Jordanian marriage contracts will help illustrate what basic "Islamic requirements" have been most consistently followed and what was more *'urf* than Islamic. Both the shape and the content of marriage documents differ from the premodern to the modern period. Whereas the prereform marriage contract can best be described as a "blank sheet" into which the contracting parties representing bride and bridegroom entered the acceptable formulas for marriage contracts for that particular town and *madhhab* and conditions that may have been agreed upon, the modern contract is more like a "fill-in-the-blank" form in which particular information has to be entered. The basic information required is the same for modern and premodern contracts, but they are significantly different in other ways. Thus, all contracts required the inclusion of the names of the bride and bridegroom, their fathers' names, location or address, the name of the official contracting the marriage (a *qadi* or *ma'dhun*), and a statement that the wife is free to marry, which really means that she does not already have a husband or that she has completed her *'idda* if divorced or widowed. The consent of the bride has to be noted in the contract, and the name of her *waliy* or *wakil* is also included. Sometimes the husband is represented by a *wakil*, and if the bride or bridegroom happens to be a minor, as is often the case in premodern contracts, then the names of the people marrying them must be recorded. A dowry is expected in these contracts, as is some *ijab wa qubul* statement, which is something like an exchange of vows. Other required information includes the status of the bride, whether she is a *bikr* or *thayib*, also referred to by the words *hurma* or *mar'a* (both mean "married woman"). The name of her previous husband is included and when she was divorced from him, if relevant. The same information is not required of the husband, except in premodern contracts if the bridegroom was a minor, in which case his *waliy* would be acting on his behalf.

Another requirement normally included in all marriage contracts is the *mahr* (dowry), and here the form in which it appears differs greatly according to *'urf* and socioeconomic standards. Although fulfilling the requirement of the *shari'a* that the bride must receive a dowry that is hers to keep, each community and family negotiates the best form that this dowry should take. Usually the dowry is divided into a *muqaddam* and a *mu'akhkhar* (which are supposed to mean advanced dowry paid at the time of the marriage and a delayed dowry to be paid at the time of divorce or the husband's death). Today, the dowry takes the classical form, but that way was not the case earlier for many parts of the Ottoman Empire where varied practices by which the dowry was paid existed. A typical *khul'* case showing the issues involved reads:

> [T]he woman Laila . . . present [in court] identified by . . . and Karim . . . her neighbor, asked her husband the man called Hassan . . . here present with her in the *majlis* to divorce her [*yukhli'ha*] from his *'isma* and *'uqdat nikahihi* [marriage knot] on condition that she relinquish the *mu'ajjal* [delayed dowry] of her dowry amounting to fifteen qirsh and the rest of her *mu'ajjal* [advanced dowry] amounting to twenty qirsh and from the *nafaqa* of her *'idda* and her housing expenses and that the *nafaqa* of her infant suckling daughter Amna and her clothing allowance and the *nafaqa* for her pregnancy from him from which she will be delivered for five years from today.[16]

This case illustrates that a bride did not necessarily receive the full amount of her dowry before the marriage was consummated; rather, a larger amount was reserved to be paid later during the marriage than the *mu'akhkhar*—referred to as *mu'ajjal* in this case—that she would receive in case of divorce or the husband's death. Another interesting issue has to do with the five years during which the husband pledged his support to his children, if not the ex-wife. This condition may have been part of their original marriage contract or part of the divorce settlement.

A marriage contract from the Upper Egyptian town of Isna explains the flexibility of marriage and divorce decisions further. Here the agreed upon *sadaq* was not paid as a lump sum but was divided into a *mu'ajjal*, paid immediately at the time of betrothal; an *'idda* compensation that included clothing and furnishings whose cost is calculated and paid to the bride's family as a cash sum; and the *hal*, which is due before the consummation of the marriage. As for the *mu'akhkhar* part of the dowry that could constitute up to 70 percent of the total amount, it was often paid in installments over long years during the marriage and not at its termination,[17] and sometimes other arrangements were made by which the *muqaddam* and *mu'akhkhar* were more traditionally paid.[18] Theoretically, the money went directly to the bride, and it was a debt owed by the husband unless it was negotiated as part of a divorce settlement. Although it was not unusual to pay the *muqaddam* in installments often reaching twenty years,[19] in richer commercial towns the *muqaddam* was always paid in advance and quite often paid directly to the bride or to her *wakil* in her presence.

Differences in marriage practices show that social practices are geographically based and are linked to socioeconomic conditions. They also indicate that we should not generalize about the status of women without consideration of the specifics of the particular historical context. For example, one widely accepted conclusion about Islamic society is that divorced women are frowned upon by their communities and have a hard time getting remarried. The archives show a completely different picture. Second marriages were entered into quite easily by women, more so in certain areas than others. The women of al-Salt, for example, did not seem to have any problem marrying, divorcing, and remarrying. A girl or a woman would come to court with her betrothed and ask that the judge officiate their marriage; no shyness seemed to obstruct her from doing so, nor did she need the intervention of a male relative to speak on her behalf, even though she often had a man acting as *wakil* to "give her away" as a form of respect and acknowledgment of her status as a protected woman. Often the *wakil* was not a member of her family.

Interestingly, when a woman was embarking on a second or third marriage, she was not only usually present when the marriage was being contracted, but also received the dowry personally. Women also often demanded that they receive the full amount of the dowry in advance and not in portions of advanced, delayed, or installments. In other words, previously married women who were marrying again or were remarrying their divorcées showed a greater wish to control their marriages. This fact tells us that she may have had to give up a large portion of her dowry in return for divorce or that her guardian had in fact acquired the dowry and she was cheated of all or part of it. Studying dowries in marriage contracts illustrates the negotiations that went on between the different parties to a marriage, in particular the role played by women as active participants in deciding what their marriage would be like and how the financial obligations that involved her would be decided. The picture is far from the passive woman being forced into a marriage that modern society envisions about Muslim women before the modernization of laws and courts.

Marital obligations in marriage contracts dating from the Ottoman period and earlier included certain obligations expected from the husband as well as promises made by him that appear in a large number of the contracts with certain differences. One usual obligation is in regards to the husband's responsibility to support his wife and to provide her with an adequate wardrobe or a sum of money to cover her clothing expenses. The usual promise the husband made was to provide his wife with a wardrobe (*kiswa*) for winter and for summer (*kiswat al-sayf wal shita'*). But there were other formulas indicating that negotiations were involved in determining what that *kiswa* was going to be. In marriage contracts of many towns there was no inclusion of a clothing allowance, perhaps because it was taken for granted that a husband supported his wife, or perhaps because clothing was not expected of the husband or clothing was not such an important issue. Even though modern Jordanian laws consider the *kiswa* to be part of *nafaqa,* actually Islamic *fiqh* saw it as a separate obligation. The same went for the fee to be paid by the father for breast-feeding his child. The way the modern understanding of these concepts works is that the judge makes a *nafaqa* allowance based on a particular sum that glosses over all of the rest because they become automatically included. The latter is why a divorced woman ends up with such a small alimony, including minuscule amounts for breast-feeding, often no more than five dinars per month, insufficient for a few days' nourishment.

Details regarding *kiswa* included in premodern marriage contracts were one way by which a wife's family ensured the welfare of their daughter in her new home. Conditions were widely used for the purpose of obligating the husband to provide certain assurances about the marriage that if left unfulfilled would constitute a "breach of contract." The injured party could then consider herself divorced, ask for divorce from the *qadi,* or, as in most cases, renegotiate the contract completely based on the new situation. Whereas both husband and wife could and did include conditions in the contract, these conditions were more important for the wife and constituted a safeguard against future abuse at the hand of her husband. The reason has to do with the system of divorce in Islam. Whereas a Muslim husband has an absolute right to divorce his wife at will, the wife does not have that right but has to appeal to the judge to be granted a divorce. Setting conditions for the marriage contract at the time the marriage took place when the parties were still *'ala al-barr* ("on the shore," not yet embarked) gives her a way out of the marriage later or at least the ability to renegotiate her marriage from a position of strength when it becomes obvious that the marriage is not in her best interest. So what are the most usual conditions that wives included in marriage contracts before the establishment of modern personal status laws?

"No" to Polygamy

Interestingly, and perhaps not surprising, the most widely included condition has to do with polygamy. This point is very important because notwithstanding what the *shari'a* says about how many wives a man has the right to take, the courts allowed marital conditions limiting the husband to one wife. Court records show us that wives used their right to divorce or to renegotiate their contracts when the husband broke the condition. Courts treated husbands who took a second wife after having agreed not to in the marriage contract as having committed a breach of contract. Whether the *shari'a* gave the husband the right to take more than one wife was not the court's concern; the agreements he entered into when he contracted the marriage concerned the court. In short, the court did not decide what did or did not constitute *shari'a* and insisted that contractual conditions be adhered to, even if it was contrary to the agreement between husband and wife.

That a husband not acquire a slave concubine (*tasari*) was also high on the list of conditions. *Tasari* gives us pause because of the changes in the interpretation and application of the *shari'a* given historical transformations. Whereas it was very normal for men to own slave concubines, it became legally unacceptable by modern law following the emancipation of slaves and the push to end slavery undertaken by the British Empire and followed by its colonies and dependencies, including countries such as Sudan where slavery was a mainstay of the economy. Even though the *shari'a* never forbade slavery and slavery continued in practice until forbidden by the modern state, the *shari'a* did frown upon it, which gave modern Muslim governments an excuse for forbidding it. But *shari'a* also frowned on divorce, declaring it "the greatest of legal evils." Yet *talaq* (a husband's unlimited right to repudiate his wife for whatever reason) was never forbidden by modern law.

Tasari therefore gives us a good idea about how the *shari'a* has adjusted from age to age depending on who is interpreting it. Even though the right to sexual intercourse with slave women was sanctioned by the *shari'a* as practiced during the Ottoman period, it is certainly not sanctioned by the *shari'a* today because slavery was made illegal by the modern state. So here again we see the flexibility of the *shari'a* and the changes that it can incorporate in answer to new demands. The expectation is, of course, that change toward "better" interpretations and laws would provide greater human dignity as was the case with slavery, but unfortunately it has not happened when it comes to women's rights.

Wife Beating

The second condition most widely included by women in marriage contracts involves wife beating and abuses of various kinds. Women were at the mercy of husbands who could be abusive, and because a bride and bridegroom did not really know each other before marriage in any concrete way that could inform her of the potential violence of the husband, it was clear from the frequent appearance of conditions against wife beating and abuse that women of all levels of society refused such treatment and gave themselves the option to get out of abusive marriages.

The above does not mean that for a wife to be divorced because of abuse or beating that she had to have had a codicil against marital abuse in her marriage contract. When abused or feeling that she suffered abuse of some sort, a wife came to court and demanded that her husband cease his abuse, that he be punished, that he pay her compensation, or that she be divorced from him. To receive justice, she had to prove her case, usually through the presentation of witnesses or evidence to the satisfaction of the judge. When abuse was proved, the judge would defer to the wife's wishes but would not automatically grant her a divorce, preferring reconciliation between her and her husband if only on a trial basis. If she insisted on divorce, the *qadi* could not force her to stay with her husband against her will and usually offered her *khul'* as a means of immediate divorce from her husband. If it was a repeat complaint or if the abuse was excessive, the *qadi* could opt to divorce her, thereby guaranteeing her financial rights. She lost such financial rights through a *khul'* divorce.[20] A typical nineteenth-century case details a situation in which the husband had previously taken an oath that he would divorce his wife if he were to beat her again. He did beat her, she sued for divorce, and the judge granted it despite the husband's denial. Because the divorce was a "triple divorce," the only way he could ever remarry her according to the *shari'a* was if she were to marry another man first and consummate the marriage with him.[21] (A husband can divorce his wife two times. After the third divorce, she must marry another man, and the marriage must be consummated before she can be remarried to her first husband. This rule is meant as punishment to a husband who abuses his divorce rights. It is probably also a way of giving the wife a chance with another man before going back to the first husband.) The welfare and safety of the wife seemed to be the primary concern of *qadi* courts, as the following wife-beating case shows:

> It has been proven through legal methods following the legal suit [presented in court] and acceptable witnesses that Nassir b. Hajj Sa'id from the village of Marda . . . is not to be trusted (*ghayr ma'mun 'alayha*) in regards to his wife, the woman Sa'ida . . . of the village of Bishta. He constantly punches her and hurts her through beatings, insults and so on. Therefore, the *hakim al-shar'i* [head of court or legal council] has forbidden him from moving his wife from her village

since he is not to be trusted but he is to continue supporting her financially and that he live with her in the ways acceptable to the *shari'a*.[22]

Including a condition to the marriage contract against abuse made things easier for a number of reasons. First, the husband was forewarned, and, significantly, many contracts that included a condition against wife beating were re-marriages in which the wife made her marriage "airtight" to control the abuse of the husband she was remarrying as well as to give herself an immediate way out of the marriage while safeguarding her financial rights. Second, whereas some "abuse" conditions were straightforward, others tended to be very specific as to exactly what constituted abuse. This way it was not left up to the judge to decide whether the beating the wife suffered or other form of abuse sufficed her demands in court. Last, wives were careful to include details as to what would happen and what compensation she would expect, often including divorce, if the husband treated her in an abusive pattern. By agreeing to these conditions, the husband could not depend on the court's gender outlook in determining the outcome when and if he abused his wife. Courts often took other matters into consideration, including the character of the couple and who vouched for them within the community. So even in cases of physical abuse, a husband's words can be used against his wife to justify the abuse. By beating her for any reason, regardless of whether it was acceptable to society and whether the man was of unimpeachable standing in the community, the husband was in breach of contract and a wife would get an automatic divorce if she wished. Given the daily cases of wife beating and abuse, most of which go unreported and when reported are disregarded by the police, and even when brought to court justifications are found for wife beating, premodern marital conditions against wife beating and abuse were certainly much more superior in protecting women than state laws that remain ink on paper today.

A Husband's Absence

Another important condition that is mostly tied with the location in which the marriage took place and the husband's occupation has to do with travel. This condition is particularly prevalent in contracts from cities such as Nablus, Jerusalem, Aleppo, or Alexandria where large transit communities lived, such as communities of *maghribis*. Contracts from these towns illustrate that it was common for marriages transacted with merchants that a codicil be included divorcing the wife when the husband traveled for a specific period of time. Sometimes the codicil indicated that if he left her "without any financial support" for a specific period of time then she had the right to ask the *qadi* to divorce her. Given such prenuptial agreements, when women came to court asking to be divorced, no one could or did object to granting it to them. There was no specific waiting period demanded of her as that period had already been set by the contract. "In her suit against her husband Muhammad . . . the woman Sharafiyya . . . claimed that her husband had taken as a condition ('*allaq*) her divorce over supplies/enjoyment ('*ala mut'a*), that if he was to be absent from her in al-Quds al-Sharif town a period of months and left her without any *nafaqa* and no legal provider then she becomes divorced from him." [23] In this sixteenth-century case from Jerusalem, the courts divorced the wife, but the husband returned and claimed that she lied and he had never taken such a promise upon himself. The wife provided reliable witnesses, and the divorce stood. Thus, the condition was actually an oral one undertaken at the time of marriage and was not necessarily included in the marriage contract. As mentioned earlier, cases in which a wife claimed the oral acceptance of a husband that she could work after her marriage have been denied by modern Jordanian courts.

When there was no "absence" condition in the contract, women asked to be divorced from husbands who had left them for a period of time that was beyond what was considered acceptable. In such cases, *qadis* did make an effort to ask women to be patient and wait for the husband to return. Some women did take the *qadi*'s or *shaikh*'s advice at least for a while, but there was no forcing the decision on them, and most women had already made up their minds to divorce before coming to court. A "husband's absence case" ending with the wife's divorce dating from A.H. 785 (A.D. 1385) reads as follows: "Bismillah . . . according to the here-signed witnesses . . . they testify to legally binding knowledge of Hajj Muhammad al-Karki al-Jammal who married Buthaina Khalil b. Ghazi of Nablus a legal marriage and that he was absent before the marriage was consummated and his whereabouts were not known after his wedding. He left no financial support (*nafaqa*) and no one to support her and he is unable to pay her dowry." [24] In this case, it was enough to prove that the husband had left his wife without support and that he was absent for some time for the court to give her the divorce she was seeking.

Other important conditions were that he not travel far away and leave her for a long period of time, and often the period was specified as one year, six months, or even less. In a contract from sixteenth-century Cairo, the wife included a specific condition that if her husband mistreated her or moved her far from her family or took a second wife, then she had the right to be divorced if she so wished. [25]

This type of contract is quite typical and reflects common gender concerns that go beyond time and space.

Another situation in regards to travel involves the bride's demand that the husband not travel with her or take her to live far away from her family for any extended period or move their residence to another town. Modern law has included this situation as one reason for which a wife can ask her husband for a divorce. The term to indicate the distance beyond which a husband could not take his wife is *"masafat al-qisa."*

To conclude, conditions included in marriage contracts were binding to its signatories. Breaking a condition constituted a basis for divorce, and because a husband automatically had the right to divorce his wife, including conditions in the contract benefited the wife more than the husband, as his "breach of contract" allowed her to sue for divorce without losing her financial rights. The contract's flexibility allowed women to include all sorts of conditions, some of which were discussed above. Sometimes the conditions included were very specific and even unique. Wives could include the specific place where they wished to live, that the marriage home be near her family, or that she not live with his family because her traditional authority over the household would be minimized. Other wives asked to be provided with specific comforts such as house help, slaves, or jewelry. Still others included details regarding the specific quantity and quality of the *kiswa* he was to provide her or that she be provided with certain funds or pocket money beyond the agreed dowry.

Modern marriage contracts differ significantly from the premodern ones discussed above. Although they too fulfill Islamic requirements, they vary in their form and function. One significant difference has to do with the inclusion of a line in the modern marriage contracts that requires the addition of the wife's profession. Whereas a woman's craft was sometimes added next to her name in court records if that was how she identified herself or the matter for which she came to court involved her craft during the premodern period, it was not usual for a wife's profession to be included in the marriage document, and neither was the bridegroom's most of the time. Furthermore, wives did not include conditions in premodern contracts giving them the right to work or handle their own money, but this important condition is included sometimes, if not enough, by modern wives. Because women have always worked or invested their money, the noninclusion of conditions in premodern contracts and their inclusion in modern contracts are closely related to the marriage and family laws of the two periods. The inclusion of conditions allowing the wife to work after her marriage was a way of handling the law according to which a wife had to receive her husband's approval to be able to work. Because there was no such law before the modernization of the legal system and the introduction of personal status laws, there did not seem to be any need to include a condition allowing a wife to work, even though wives did work, as chapter 3 has illustrated. In other words, a husband's control over whether his wife could work is really a modern invention. Legists introduced and codified into law questions of little relevance earlier, thereby establishing gender controls and enforcing them through the powers of the state acting in the role of patriarch.

Finally, a minimum age for marriage was an innovation of the modern state. It is true that *fiqh* had a great deal to say about the proper age for marriage, and that there seemed to be generally accepted patterns regarding the age question, particularly when it involved the *dukhla* (consummation of a marriage) that could have been contracted much earlier. Thus, it was almost unheard of that a *dukhla* take place before the girl or boy reached *bulugh*. Rather, even when minors were married, the marriage was contracted, but the girl stayed with her family until she was physically able to consummate the marriage. Often the husband asked or was required by her family to support her while she stayed with her family. Majority today is determined on the basis of a predetermined age established by the modern state following traditions in the West. As explained in chapter 5, a minimum age requirement for marriage, fifteen and sixteen for girls and boys, respectively, has no precedence in premodern marriages, nor are the ages of particular relevance for any of the *madhahib*. Furthermore, twenty-one as an age of majority when the son or daughter is no longer under the guardianship of his or her parents and is considered competent to control his or her own life has no bearing in *shari'a* law but comes directly from French law. Giving sons the right to handle their own property when they reach the age of eighteen has little to do with Hanafi law, which determines majority based on mental maturity and puberty and does not give an exact date. Rather, the *madhahib* spoke in ranges, and the courts turned over the managing of property to boys who were much younger because they proved they had reached *rushd* (majority). The point I am making here is that marriage contracts are a result of more than the actual formality of taking a wife according to the dictates of a particular religion. The shape of the contract and hence its ultimate impact on the two signing it are defined according to particular conditions at the time the marriage is being contracted.

Modern marriage contracts require the inclusion of who holds the *'isma* (right to divorce). Giving the wife that right did not deny the husband the same right, but simply allowed the wife to divorce as well. If the wife is not indicated as holding the *'isma,* then it would be the husband's sole prerogative to divorce.

Holding the *'isma* was also built on the idea that the husband could delegate his right to divorce to his wife and was not seen as a condition included by the wife according to which she was willing to enter into the marriage. The interpretation is quite patriarchal and is built on the assumption that the husband is the only party with a "will to act" within the marriage, itself a concept foreign to *shari'a*, which judges each individual according to his or her actions and gives women the right to manage their lives and finances. It does, however, reflect the philosophy behind Western patriarchy before the gender revolution that took place as part of the social upheavals accompanying the Industrial Revolution, end of the ancien régimes, and two world wars. This point is important because before the reforms, the right of divorce was not indicated in the contract, which did not deny the husband the right to divorce his wife whenever he wished, but also allowed the wife to sue for divorce for whatever reason. Because the modern social discourse belittled a husband who allowed his wife to hold the *'isma,* this method of security for the wife is hardly resorted to except in marriages involving very wealthy or experienced women, women of the "aristocratic" classes, or famous artists. Interestingly, when Muslim women are asked about holding the *'isma,* they consider it an unacceptable practice and demeaning to the man. When questioned further, it becomes clear that most do not know that when a woman holds the *'isma* the man can still divorce her if he wants. The fiction is that she takes that right away from him, thereby denying his manhood.

Courts and Procedures in Contemporary Jordan

Jordan's modern *shari'a* courts were created by Law 41 for 1951, later replaced by Law 19 for 1972.[26] The head of the *shari'a* court system is the *qadi al-quda,* and the courts are formed of first-instance courts in various parts of the country, each headed by a single *qadi,* and an appeals court headed by three *qadis,* one acting as head. The rulings of the appeals court are final. Among the functions of the *shari'a* courts pertinent to women and gender are: *hadana* (custody of infants); *wilaya* and *wisaya;* marriage, including the marital contract and all matters involved in marriage; divorce and disputes stemming from marriage; the dowry in its different types, including *tawabi' mahr; nafaqa* due from the husband to his wife and children during the marriage and after divorce; and paternity of children.

The real significance of courts and court procedures usually becomes apparent to a woman only when she is faced with dissolution of her marriage. She may have to appeal to a judge to approve of her marriage when her father refuses to give his consent or to divorce her from a husband to whom she no longer wishes to be married, or she may have to appear in court to ask for her and her children's financial rights from a husband who has abandoned or divorced her and does not pay *nafaqa*. She may also appeal to the courts for custody of her children or for various forms of settlements dealing with her marriage. It is no exaggeration to describe the usual experience that women get out of *shari'a* courts today as traumatic. The breakdown of the marriage is usually blamed on her, except in situations in which the husband's reputation is unredeemable. She is often without any funds, her husband having divorced her and walked out, leaving her destitute, yet she is expected to come to court and pay for a lawyer to represent her. Expecting to receive financial rights as stated in her marriage contract, particularly her delayed dowry, she soon realizes that she is lucky if she gets out with a fraction of what she expected, out of which she still has to pay court costs and lawyer fees. Lacking financial resources, even the cost of transportation to and from court becomes difficult. Lawyer Manal Shamut, an experienced *shari'a* court lawyer, described these difficulties and how unwilling judges are to expedite cases so that wives do not have to struggle to come to court, leaving daily jobs and losing wages, and paying for transportation they can ill afford. Ratib al-Zahir, who is a practicing *shari'a* court lawyer and was previously a judge in *shari'a* courts of Jordan, confirmed Shamut's assessment of the difficulties faced by women who come to *shari'a* courts, as did a leading male lawyer-activist who censured Jordan's judges for making the situation even harder on both women and men than it need be.

One main reason for which women come to court today is to sue for divorce. Divorce would allow a wife to keep her financial rights; otherwise, she would be expected to relinquish all such rights by asking her husband for *khul'*. To be able to sue for divorce, a wife has to prove that the marriage is causing her harm, defined according to a list that was put together by the committees that write Jordan's personal status laws. The list, which includes nonsupport, wife beating causing severe bodily harm, and irreversible impotency of the husband, is based on the *shari'a* as represented by medieval *fiqh*. However, books of *fiqh* never presented a list of what constitutes reasons for divorce that must be applicable if the wife is to be granted divorce, as is the case in Jordan today. Rather, *fiqh* discussed what the *fuqaha'* considered to be problems brought to their attention in their capacity as Islamic thinkers, *muftis,* or judges. They thought about particular situations that presented themselves and did not set out to define the *only* Islamic reasons for divorce. Such narrowing of reasons was the prerogative of the modern state in its efforts to standardize its systems as well as a new moral attitude to try to keep the nuclear family together through limiting access to divorce by placing the wife under greater control of her husband. This patriarchal attitude meant that a husband's right to divorce would not be curbed or controlled in any way.

Khul, also known as *ibra* (wherein the wife frees her husband from any financial obligations toward her), is open to the wife in case she cannot receive a divorce decision from the judge. However, according to the way *khul* is interpreted in Jordanian courts, it is not a direct right of the wife; instead, the husband has to agree, and he could ask for financial compensation before he agrees to let her go. The alternative would be a divorce case in *shiqaq wa niza* courts that could last a long time. Wives are more than willing to simply give up their rights to get out of a marriage, especially when it is abusive to her yet perhaps not abusive enough to convince the court or the abuse may not fit within the parameters of "harm" as defined by the law.

Shiqaq wa niza is the name of the court that a woman has to apply to for divorce from her husband in Jordan. It is there that the wife must prove that there are such severe problems between her and her husband as to warrant the divorce. A husband can bring a *shiqaq wa niza* case as well in his effort to divorce her without having to pay her full financial rights (alimony, *'idda* alimony, or *mu'akhkhar*). Invariably, what is at stake are the wife's financial rights, financial rights that were guaranteed to her at the time of her marriage in case her marriage did not work out. So we are not talking about taking more out of the husband, except for a *mut'a* allowance that would be decided by the judge if the husband is clearly in the wrong and the divorce would mean the wife would be denied future benefits that she had expected from the marriage. The law is very specific about the reasons allowing the *qadi* to grant a wife a divorce. She could be granted a divorce for nonsupport, but she would first have to prove that her husband is not supporting her, that there is no member of his family—for example, his father—who is willing to support her, and that the husband is destitute and there is no hope of such support. To prove all these points she usually has to wait a long period of time. Other causes of divorce could be marital abuse in which her husband beats her excessively enough to break a limb or leave obvious physical harm on her body. Even then, she may not be granted a divorce immediately because wife beating is sometimes acceptable to the court depending on the social background from which the husband and wife originate. Otherwise it becomes a *shiqaq wa niza* case. A husband's impotency is one of the reasons a wife is allowed to sue for divorce. But proving a husband's impotency is not a simple matter and is not always sufficient to receive a divorce judgment. Not only must there be medical evidence of his impotence, but the wife has to prove that she had no previous knowledge of his condition before agreeing to the marriage and that she did not agree to live with him after knowing about it. Interestingly, her shyness in this matter is not taken into consideration as it is when her marriage is performed without her vocal approval. Besides, even after the husband's impotency is proved, he is given one year according to the Hanafi *madhhab* in which to get cured. In other words, a wife would have to go on living with a husband whom she has taken to court and whose impotency she has proved, notwithstanding what emotional and physical hardship it might cause her. The following case from turn-of-the-century Ma'an illustrates the handling of cases of impotency by *shari'a* courts even before the introduction of personal status laws but after the changes introduced with the Ottoman Mejelle and the application of the Hanafi code. One interesting aspect of this case is that the wife's complaint did not include her husband's inability to give her children as a reason for suing for divorce. Rather, it was the lack of the consummation of the marriage that was in question:

> In the Majlis al-Sharif of the Court of Ma'an district in *liwa'* (region) of Karak, in Governerate of Syria . . . appeared the woman Fatima . . . and claimed that her husband *al-dakhil biha* [cohabit, marriage consummated], Muqbil . . . here present with her in the Majlis as witnessed by. . . . All from the village of al-Shawbak, stated that her mentioned husband Muqbil, had since one year and four months married her and cohabited (*dakhal*), but that until this day he has not had intercourse with her and was not able to get an arousal and she asked to be divorced. . . . The husband was asked about what she claimed and he confessed that they are married but he was not able to have an erection and asked that he be given a year according to *shari'a* law, and accordingly we granted him a year in accordance to the *shari'a* and ordered her to live with him for one year and at the end of the year if he had not been able to have intercourse with her and was not able to have an erection (*intishar alatihu*), she should then come before the judge.[27]

In *shiqaq wa niza'* cases, the judge chooses two arbitrators who could be—but are not always—from the couple's families. The arbitrators' first objective would be to save the marriage and report back to the judge. If they succeed, all is settled. If not, then they have to report back to the judge whom each arbitrator believes is at fault in the breakup of the marriage. They also have to give him estimates of the percentages of her financial rights that they feel should be paid to the wife. They are expected to take the husband's financial ability into consideration in making these estimates. The judge then considers their suggestions and reaches his own decision, keeping the husband's financial abilities in mind. The process sounds fair, but what is at stake here is not a determination of how much alimony she would receive, as is the case in American courts, but how much to take out of the already agreed upon financial rights of the wife. This amount includes her delayed dowry that was agreed upon and contracted at the time of marriage and is legally due to her at the time of divorce or the husband's death; her alimony for one year that should be calculated as the full amount afforded by the husband and not a percentage of it; and possible *mut'a* compensation, as she will be getting very little out of a marriage that she expected would last a long time and that may be breaking up for "irreconcilable differences" and through no fault of hers. Depending on the status of the marriage, gifts the husband gave her could also be in issue. So the wife has much at stake, whereas the husband can only gain from this type of arbitration. In effect, a wife who does not wish to stay in a marriage has to buy her way out and is left harmed by the procedures and quite often destitute. Undoubtedly, this situation in not one in which she could be economically productive.

Therefore, in *shiqaq wa niza'* courts, whether it is the husband or the wife who sues for divorce, the result is almost always against the wife in the sense of reduction of her financial rights and compensation. As for *mut'a* compensation, it was almost automatically provided to a wife in medieval courts and was assessed quite separately from the *kiswa* and *nafaqa*.[28] In a court case from Jerusalem dated A.H. 795 (A.D. 1396), the *qadi* agreed to a divorced wife's demands for financial rights. After questioning the husband as to his profession and income for the past year—the husband was a mortician—the *qadi* granted her 10 percent of the two hundred thousand dirhams the husband had earned that year as *mut'a* compensation and 5 percent for her *kiswa* for that year.[29] It should be mentioned that this document dates from before the Ottoman period; *mut'a* compensation was not frequently awarded in Ottoman courts. Today, however, more women are demanding *mut'a* compensation, and courts are awarding it. The revival of these old medieval traditions is part of the Islamic movement that is reviving books of *turath* that are being reread and reintroduced into Islamic legal *'urf.* Qadis today award *mut'a* compensation in cases where there is flagrant abuse by a husband of his divorce rights, and in particular when the husband is wealthy and the wife is losing out in the divorce.

Procedures used in "family dispute" cases are modeled according to the Qur'an, which frowns on divorce and requires that two reliable people, one from the husband's kin and the other from the wife's kin, be assigned the job of reconciling the couple. A number of issues are not taken into consideration in these arbitration procedures. The most important is the fact that *fiqh* has interpreted divorce as being the sole prerogative of men; when the wife holds the *'isma,* it is seen as a husband delegating his right of divorce to her. He could also take her back at will during the *'idda* period unless it was a final divorce. But if divorce is a man's prerogative and Islam frowns on divorce as being the "legal act least dear to God," one would assume that the arbitration system was intended to be applied in case the husband wished to divorce. But it is only when the wife asks the judge to divorce her (*tatliq*) or when the husband brings his divorce to *shiqaq wa niza'* court in an effort to reduce his financial obligations to his wife that arbitration is used. So arbitration in no way affects him. Yet the Qur'anic basis of arbitration pointed above does not indicate that it is to be applied in a case in which it is the wife and not the husband who wishes to be divorced; rather, the Qur'an talks about the requirement for arbitration in any situation where divorce is contemplated by either the husband or the wife. The arbitration *aya* is not gendered: "If you fear a breach between them, appoint two arbitrators, one from his family and the other from hers. If they wish for peace, Allah will cause their reconciliation. For Allah has full knowledge, and is acquainted with all things" (Qur'an 4:35). Because wives wishing to divorce usually remain adamant, whereas the husband can afford to be patient because of his right to divorce at any time, "family dispute" cases always end up with a wife staying with a husband she does not want to remain married to or being "cheated" by preferring to lose all rather than remain with a husband who is abusive, who took a second wife, or who was someone she simply did not wish to stay married to.

One of the biggest problems that women face in *shari'a* courts has to do with delay in procedures. For example, a *qadi* is often dissatisfied with the results of the two arbitrators he chose; he may and often does call upon a third to join them and may also disagree with the findings of the third because of the disparity among arbitrators. Add the fact that the husband almost always appeals decisions when they work against him, which causes further delay in the court's reaching a decision. Meanwhile, the wife may have no financial support and is under pressure to remain under the power of a man she wishes to divorce. Because a husband has the prerogative to divorce a wife, does not have to wait for divorce to take another wife, and it is he who is to pay the compensation, a delay is as consequential to him as to the wife, but given the possibility that the delay will determine how much less he has pay his wife, it is in fact welcome. The inequality in regards to divorce is therefore clear and is a major cause for women's suffering today.

As pointed out earlier, various Jordanian codes contradict each other in regards to gender. Different presumptions are used to justify laws in different codes. Some are more obvious than others. Such contradictions could be handled by judges and procedural regulations of the courts, which, however, does not happen. For example, the Jordanian Civil Code is the final arbiter when it comes to disputes between various legal codes. Section 11 of the civil code states: "Jordan's civil law shall be the reference in regulating relationships when their nature is required to be determined in a case where there is conflict of laws in order to ascertain the applicable law among them." At the same time, Section 62 of the civil code declares itself against harm in the law: "Injury does not justify injury and damage shall be abated" (*"la darar wa la dirar wal-darar yuzal"*).[30]

Given these two articles, one would imagine that the important principle of comparative advantage (based on the Islamic principle of *maslaha* [promoting advantage or the common good]) would apply here.[31] But comparative advantage is not applied in situations when it involves harm to the wife. Thus, the *qadi* does not take into consideration the harm to a wife when compared to the advantages of a husband who wishes her to remain married to him or who refuses her wish to take a job. Rather than divorce a wife whose husband wishes to remain married to her on the basis of comparative advantage, the *qadi* usually looks at the good of the community, that is, applies *'urf*, which makes it harder for a wife to divorce. If the wife sues and insists on separation, it becomes a case of "family dispute," and certain steps are taken that ultimately lead to financial disadvantages to the wife. In certain cases when a wife badly wants a divorce, she is even forced to forfeit child support, which the court finds acceptable, even though in denying a child financial support, the "good of the community" does not seem to figure.[32] One should also point out the fact that the "good of the community" is not even considered in reference to controlling husbands' abuse of their divorce rights or polygamy.

Another example of inconsistency in the laws is presented by Article 225 of the civil code: "What is traditionally known/accepted is like what is laid out as a condition in a contract." Article 226 involving trade contracts amplifies the meaning of Article 225: "What is known/acceptable between merchants is like/equal to conditions [to the contract] between them." At the same time, the civil code recognizes the power men have over women in actual life and that this power could be coercive and can cause enough fear to make women do what the husband wishes even against their will. Section 142 states: "The husband has authority over his wife and if he obliges her by beating or for example precludes her from her kin in order to have her forfeit any of her rights or grant him property and she does, her disposition shall not be effective."[33] Even though a husband's ability to coerce his wife is taken into consideration by law when it comes to property that could have been disposed of by the wife under duress from the husband, the same logic is not applied to situations in which the wife asks to be separated from her husband because of intimidation or fear of physical abuse without going to a *shiqaq wa niza'* court. Moreover, in *shiqaq wa niza'*, the onus of proof is on her shoulders, and fear of and intimidation by her husband are not cause enough to save the financial rights due her from her husband.

The recognition of Jordan's civil code that women could be coerced by husbands is a rather important point that can be used to support women in *shari'a* court, yet the opposite almost always happens. When a wife complains to the court of being abused or coerced into actions that she cannot approve of—for example, accepting that her husband's mother live with them—she has to present concrete evidence of her allegations or the court does not accept them. For example, it is well known that mothers-in-law are not exactly accommodating to wives and can make their lives miserable. In Jordan, quite often mothers live with their sons, the usual reason being financial need, which is acceptable under the law. But as everyone knows, mothers-in-law can become a source of friction. Although Jordanian laws recognize the right of a husband to house his impoverished mother and father with him regardless of whether his wife agrees, the understanding that a mother can live with her son is almost universally acceptable in Jordan, notwithstanding the social conditions of the mother and even if it contradicts the wife's *shari'a* rights recognized by Jordanian laws that guarantee her the right to a separate home. Court records from before and after the modernization of law throughout the Islamic world show that the wife's right to a separate home is not disputable and is based on the prophet Muhammad's tradition; he provided each of his wives with completely separate quarters that were considered hers. In Ottoman courts, when a wife sued for separation from her husband because he was not providing her with a proper home, the *qadi* either divorced her or asked her husband to prepare a separate legal home in which he was to live with his wife. Legal records of the Business and Professional Women's Club show that one of the most important reasons for family disputes involves the mother-in-law's presence in the family home as well as the interference of the mother- and the sister-in-law in a wife's affairs, even if they are not living with her. When the matter reaches court, notwithstanding the traditional and usual relations presented by this situation, the case becomes a *shiqaq wa niza'*, a solution not altogether to the advantage of the wife, as has been shown.

Here the problems are both bureaucratic and legal. On the bureaucratic side, a woman whom the courts have awarded financial settlements usually has to return to court many times before the paperwork is finalized and she can receive what is due her. Meanwhile, a divorced mother would have to find the means for transportation to and from the court, and money to feed her children, pay the rent, and support herself. At one time the wife's family could have helped, but from the BPWC's records I studied, it does not seem to be as feasible because of the death of her parents, or inability of her family to support her. The situation is therefore one in which a divorced woman faces real hardship, caught between financial needs, the court system, and often an abusive ex-husband. As the system stands, women are defined and dealt with as dependents. Financially, this denotation means that unless a woman has some wealth of her own, she is dependent on a father or husband for support. Because salary scales of most employed women in Jordan are low, even working women depend on a male to financially support them. Accordingly, one would imagine that in legal disputes the system would ensure that women would receive what support is due them in as expedient a way as possible. That assumption is not the case according to lawyers I interviewed, women who have had to deal with the system in regards to their *nafaqa*, and case records.

There are many situations in which court procedures delay payment of the wife's financial rights, according to cases from Jordanian courts. For example, a wife sues her husband for divorce. The court assigns two arbitrators to try to end the dispute. Arbitrators are chosen on the basis of closeness to the couple, one from her family and one from his. The judge could assign his own when family members are not available. If the arbitrators fail to reach a decision, the judge can assign a third. The arbitrators try to end the dispute, then they try to settle the matter out of court, and finally they bring their findings back to court. If they recommend divorce, they also recommend the amount of *nafaqa* that the husband should pay his wife based on his financial ability. The judge then makes his decision based on these findings. Very often, because of the relationship of the arbitrators to husband and wife, there is a great discrepancy between the suggested amounts. In a 1996 case, the Ibtida'i Court awarded the wife a *nafaqa* based on the findings of the arbitrators it assigned. The husband appealed the decision. The court of appeals concluded that there was a great discrepancy between the amount of *nafaqa* suggested by the arbitrators, two of whom suggested five hundred dinars as monthly alimony to cover the wife's expenses and estimated that the husband could easily afford this amount. A third arbitrator estimated that forty to fifty dinars would suffice to cover the wife's expenses and that the husband could not afford more. The appeals court decided that the two estimates were far apart and asked that the arbitrators present details supporting their conclusions. Meanwhile, the court's Ibtida'i Court decision awarding the wife *nafaqa* (decision 40971, dated July 27, 1996) was nullified until further deliberation (decision number 17743).[34]

From what I have been told by women lawyers who deal with these problems on a daily basis, this type of case is not unique but is exemplary of the frustrations women who sue for divorce face all the time. It is quite common for a judge to approve a husband's request to reduce his divorcée's *nafaqa* after she is awarded what the legal procedure has decided is due to her (see, for example, case 41006 dated July 31, 1996). The system is set and run in a fashion that discourages women from asking for financial rights, and very often after fighting a long battle, wives simply agree to accept whatever a husband wishes to give them and withdraw their cases. The records of the BPWC and the lawyers working there confirm this fact and indicate many cases in which a wife either chose to reconcile with the husband even after the court awarded her *nafaqa,* or accepted whatever settlement was offered rather than go without any support at all.

A further point that needs to be made is that most court decisions awarding *nafaqa* involve very small amounts that can hardly pay the rent, let alone cover the expenses of children. A rough figure would be forty to fifty dinars a month for a mother with two children. This contention is based on cases recorded by the club's hot line and legal files. As one wife after the other complained, the amount is not enough to cover a fraction of her expenses and the expenses of her children, and in many cases the husband must have been able to pay more because they often took another wife or bought a car or owned their own businesses. The ability to finance court cases is a heavy burden, particularly when one is destitute, as many of these women are. Ratib al-Zahir points to *shari'a* Courts as constituting a point of hardship and dilemma for women and suggests that they need to be made more efficient and their procedures homogenized and streamlined:

> These laws have now been in effect for 40 years, and there is a genuine need for change to insure a fast and fair judicial system especially in regards to the delivery of legal notifications which take too long by the time they pass through existing legal procedures. . . . [T]he law did not take into consideration time needed [for preparation] or for delay, which leads to big differences between procedures followed from one court to the other and one judge to the other. Therefore a maximum delay period must be established especially since a lot of the cases brought in front of *shari'a* courts need expedition because of the sensitivity of cases like *nafaqa,* child custody, and parental visitation. Family matters in particular need to be settled expeditiously so that the problems do not multiply and become more complicated thereby making it more difficult to solve.[35]

One last point that needs to be made is in regards to the prerogatives of the judges who sit on the bench in *shari'a* courts. Basically, a *qadi* is expected to apply the law as compiled according to personal status laws and according to defined procedures. Although doing so is meant to limit arbitrariness and allow for fairness in the judge's decision, this limitation of the judge's abilities is problematic because even though Jordanian laws stress the freedom of the judiciary, in fact the *qadi* does not use his own prerogatives and applies the law in its narrowest and most conservative sense. The philosophy applied therefore does not allow him to look at what he can see beyond the case being presented to him. For example, judges are aware of the general social belief that women could be under severe pressures from husbands, and even Jordanian laws allow her to get out of contracts that she may have signed under duress. A *qadi*, however, is not allowed to bring this type of logic into a marital dispute case because the codes and procedures have to be applied strictly, and this type of leeway is not included in personal status laws. Although most judges are quite conservative, the ones who could make a difference are constrained from doing so by the law.

To conclude, personal status laws constitute the most important hindrance to women owning their own businesses or being employed. They create a patriarchal order that places the burden of family and home on the shoulders of women. Women may work, but their primary function is seen as belonging in the home. She may be a lawyer or judge but is responsible for the marital home, cooking, cleaning, and raising the children, as if she did not work. Even though the husband helps, it is seen as voluntary on his part and not his duty. If marital disputes reach court (usually in cases of *shiqaq wa niza'*, which are very often relegated to arbitration), the wife's employment works against her because she is not paying sufficient attention to her home and children. Given the push factor in labor laws, the glass ceiling, low pay, and incentives to leave the job, working becomes less attractive except for some professional middle-class women or poorer women who cannot afford not to work.

The impact of personal status laws cannot be underestimated in regards to women, work, and participation in public life, the economy, or political system. As a totality, personal status laws confine women within predetermined patriarchal parameters, and give them only limited freedom of choice outside parental and husband approval. In short, with the exception of a few women, even the ones who enter the labor market or open their own businesses are in fact under the control of husbands.

There were significant differences in the treatment of *shari'a* courts of various periods. Even though the name "*shari'a* courts" applies to these types of court before and after Jordan's legal reforms, the differences are quite significant not only in regards to the type of cases brought before the courts, modern courts being specialized, but also in the specific areas of the law assigned to them. From the above we have seen differences in regards to marriage contracts and conditions acceptable to *shari'a* court judges from Ottoman courts as compared to modern courts. Differences in handling questions of divorce, *nafaqa, ta'a,* and so on are also documented. Perhaps the greatest difference concerns the agency of women in determining their own marriages, their relationships with their husbands, and the fates of the marriages. It was not up to the judge or the law applied in premodern *shari'a* courts to decide for the wife the conditions of her marriage, nor did he demand the approval of a male guardian in every action she took in regards to her personal life. Rather, she came to court alone or with a male family member or neighbor—it was up to her. No one asked where her guardian was unless she was a minor and had not been married before; otherwise she was a free agent who negotiated her divorce with her husband and determined her own future. The judge made sure that *shari'a* rules were observed in all these transactions; for example, he had to ensure that the *'idda* period was observed so there would be no confusion regarding paternity; that there was an *ijab wa qubul* statement so that the marriage would be legal with the exchange of vows; and that the marriage was witnessed, recorded, and thereby made public (*ishhar*), which is a requirement for Sunni marriages. But unlike *shari'a* judges in Jordanian courts today, there was no demand that a *waliy* be present to officiate in a marriage unless the bride or bridegroom was a minor; there was no need for a guardian to be present when a woman sued for a divorce, as is the case today if the woman is less than forty years old; nor did the judge insist on bringing in two arbitrators because the wife sued for divorce or demanded *khul'*, as is the case today in *shiqaq wa niza'* courts. In all these instances, it is the agency of women and the flexibility of the law that have been compromised.

The significance of this discussion is that it deconstructs what we have come to accept as *shari'a* law in most Islamic countries today. As explained earlier, the fact that personal status laws are understood to be *shari'a* laws has meant an inability to fight them. The above discussion of marriage shows that the definition of marriage and the philosophy behind marital laws in Jordan today are actually based on historical conditions earlier in the twentieth century. Such laws were greatly influenced by Europe's outlook toward gender during the nineteenth and early twentieth centuries. It is suggested here that given the changing conditions in Jordan and the world order, it is now time to begin to think seriously of changing outdated laws to fit with contemporary needs in a way that would hold on to fundamentals of the *shari'a* and traditions as they have evolved and changed, while at the same time taking into consideration the requirements of Jordan as it faces the need to develop and enter the twenty-first century.

7

Honor Crimes

ISLAM'S condemnation of pre-Islamic practices that allowed female genocide provides a glaring example of the contradictions that women face in their everyday lives today. Prohibiting *wa'd al-banat* is constantly used as the symbol of how Islam corrected cruelties against women that were practiced by primitive pre-Islamic idolaters. Unfortunately, the message Islam brought by prohibiting female genocide seems to have been forgotten with today's rising violence against women that is growing beyond any proportion witnessed before or after the coming of Islam.

Wa'd al-banat was a Bedouin tradition practiced by certain Arabian tribes, particularly during periods of hardship and food and water shortages. Tribes did not commit genocide on females alone, but like tribal communities in many other parts of the globe, newborn children were regarded as the most dispensable and replaceable, and therefore infants of both sexes suffered genocide during periods of deprivation and hardship. But that form of genocide was not the one that Islam abolished; it was a specific form of genocide that had to do with fears regarding honor: killing a newborn female child as a way of eliminating a potential source of dishonor. The message of the Qur'an therefore involves honor, and the complete and unquestioning prohibition of female genocide is in itself a prohibition of the attitudes toward women that regard them as a possible source of dishonor. The holy Qur'an reinforces this conclusion in its clear condemnation of the murder of the innocent. "When news is brought to one of them of the birth of a female child, his face darkens and he is filled with inward grief. With shame does he hide himself from his people because of the bad news he has had! Shall he retain her on contempt or bury her in the dust? Ah! what an evil they decide on?" (16:59).

But the Qur'an goes further to close the gap that ensnares and condemns women by prohibiting slander and protecting victims of gossip and hearsay. The

Qur'an does so by imposing punishment on the slanderer, he who passes judgment and tells stories without the required evidence set by the Qur'an and by the Prophet's example. Islam does not demand the punishment of the subject of gossip; rather, the stringent punishment due a slanderer was meant to stop such actions and protect potential victims of slander. Made into a *hadd* (offense against God), anyone who, without legitimate evidence, repeats suspicions against another about his or her morals and honor was to receive eighty lashes, which is the highest punishment prescribed by the Qur'an other than for adultery, one hundred lashes.

It is therefore a wonder that although all Muslims find great pride in these facts and repeat them to glorify Islam, "honor crimes" are still committed and justified, and their perpetrators are protected by the law and allowed to commit their crimes under the pretext of honor. These crimes take place despite the fact that one of the best-known Islamic stories is the one in which the prophet Muhammad himself stood in the position of a husband whose wife was the subject of gossip regarding her morals. What did he do? What did her father, Abu Bakr al-Siddiq, do? Did either of the two men take a knife and kill her so as to wipe his honor clean and stand tall in front of a community that had gossiped about her? No, the Prophet saw through it and set an example of how to act in such a situation, and it was on this occasion that God decreed the punishment for slanderers as a *hadd*. In other words, suspicions regarding the Prophet's own wife, 'Aisha, and gossip regarding her misconduct did not bring about a retaliation against her; rather, it brought about a Qur'an *aya* that made the suspicious person who repeated gossip without evidence not only a sinner in the eyes of God but also punishable by the authorities.

Where are the religious authorities today who should be the first to condemn honor crimes whose female victims fall to their fathers and brothers because of gossip and hearsay and without even receiving a hearing? How can people with religious knowledge and power not pay attention to what God has to say through his Qur'an about such matters but defer to the attitudes of their tribal traditions that Islam was sent to change in the first place? Where is the state with its modern laws that actually claims human rights and is signatory to many international agreements that demand enforcement of the law, especially that the main faith of the land gives clear evidence that supports the very principles of human rights that the state claims to uphold? The very fact that the Qur'an sets out conditions of evidence that require that at least four males must have in fact witnessed the actual act of *zina* (extralegal sexual intercourse) shows how far God was willing to go to stop these types of injustice.

But there is more to the question of honor and crime. Although a suspicious act of sexual misconduct on the part of a female brings about her murder and the murderer benefits from laws of leniency, when a male is proved to have raped a female, his act is not dealt with as a question of honor, even though what he has done is to commit the ultimate dishonor to both his family and hers. Ironically, rather than punishment to the full extent of the law, the payment of compensation is allowed to alleviate the antagonism between the clans: *diyya* becomes the way by which a tribe covers up the action of its male member. As for the victim of the rape, when it is a woman—quite often victims are young, helpless boys— she is considered lucky when her rapist offers to marry her or is forced to do so by the police so as to conclude the problem. She has little choice in the matter, being already despoiled and regarded with pity, and therefore she has to marry the same man who violated and raped her. In other words, girls are condemned and killed by their families for being suspected of having sexual relations, but men who commit the same act are left untouched and are actually supported by their clans when they commit the ultimate dishonorable crime of rape whose punishment in the Qur'an is prescribed as one hundred lashes. Once *diyya* is paid, no further punishment can be exacted, and once married to his victim, he then appears to be magnanimous and an ideal citizen.

Therefore, it is important to include rape as an honor crime and to emphasize the contradictory approach of both society and state to questions of honor. Besides, the number of regularly reported rape cases should raise serious concern. According to official Jordanian figures, 1995 witnessed 41 cases of rape (*ightisab*) and 192 of *hatk 'ird* (shame—differences with *ightisab* to be discussed later); 1996 witnessed 63 and 223 cases, respectively; and 1997 witnessed 57 and 215, respectively. These numbers are significant for a small country such as Jordan and are probably a fraction of what really occurs because a woman who accuses a man of raping her is actually also putting her own morals into question and could fear retaliation from her own family even if she is able to prove the accusation. Many, like their sisters all over the globe, simply prefer to keep quiet.

Why do such crimes take place? For one thing, they are not unique to Jordan but exist in almost all Arab and Islamic countries. They exist in Third World countries, Africa, Asia, and Latin America. In 2001 there were thirty honor crimes reported in Italy, and such crimes take place in other European countries such as Greece and Spain. So there is no monopoly over such crime for Jordan, even though the Western media have somehow pinned such crimes on Jordan alone. One should also emphasize that crimes tied to sexual conduct, or misconduct as the case may be, depending on how societies view them, exist and are on the rise throughout the globe. Certainly, daily news in the United States presents serial killers, pedophiles, and all sorts of other forms of sexual perversions that prey on women and children. So are wife beating, marital abuse, child abuse, and incest on the rise throughout the globe. Today, more women are coming forth to open the eyes of the world to their abuse not only by strangers but also by family members. Honor crimes are certainly not unique to Arab Muslims; Arab Christian women have been victims of such crimes for similar reasons. So there is nothing unique about Islamic or Arab societies as far as sexual crimes are concerned. What is serious in regards to honor crimes in Arab countries is that they are justified and given credibility on the basis that they are somehow condoned by Islam or the Islamic *shari'a*. No matter how much religious authorities correct such assumptions regarding Islam, the justifications continue. "Mr. Abu Abseh, the Jordanian who killed his sister with a paving stone, was doing more. He was administering God's law, he said. 'We are Muslims,' Mr. Abu Abseh's older brother said, 'and in our religion, she had to be executed.' " [1]

This attitude is serious and is quite widespread in Islamic countries. Yet it is quite baseless, as the following discussion will show. Rather, violence against women is a social phenomenon with multiple reasons that can actually be challenged by moral principles holding the family together and by religion rather than the other way around. As previous chapters have shown, women have been denied respect and equality and hence protection of the law in various aspects of their lives. Even when she is a mother fulfilling what the most conservative elements of society insist is her essential job, that is, taking care of her children, she does not receive fair rulings from court judges who deny her essential rights given to her by society, by law, and by the Islamic *shari'a* such as financial support, her delayed dowry, and even support for breast-feeding her infant son as is clearly established by Islamic law and schools of *fiqh*. Without going into more details about how a woman is raised and the peripheral role defined for her, it is enough that she is treated as an unequal and incomplete individual by the legal system for her to be the subject of abuse at the hands of a younger brother or an abusive husband. Weakness gives rise to contempt, and the weak are the usual victims of violence. As long as women are treated the way they are in the work space, in the home, and by the courts and government, they will continue to be victims of violence, will fear for their well-being, and will probably continue to act with fear in regards to angering male relatives. Sexual crimes against women may appear to be different from honor crimes against women, but in fact they all stem from a lack of respect toward women and recognition of their individual right to a decent, safe, and free life. Gender crimes are built on the concept of fear and control through shedding blood; a rape victim is as afraid of being hurt or killed as is a young girl afraid of being hurt or killed by a brother or a father. In the latter case it is more abhorrent because the very individuals in her life whom she has looked up to for protection are the ones who harm her.

This chapter will begin by discussing Jordan's criminal codes dealing with the issues of honor crimes and will emphasize the aspects of leniency that are the foundation of these laws. Rape will then be the focus of discussion with particular emphasis on the meaning of *zina*. Because Jordan's criminal code was adapted from Egypt's, a comparison with Egypt's criminal code helps explain the selectivity undertaken by Jordanian legists to fit with Jordan's particular needs; in this case, tribal needs regarding gender and honor seem to have played an important role in the construction of Jordan's criminal codes. Last, a discussion of the outlook of Islam regarding gender relations and morality should help draw the line between what is conceived as Islamic and what Islam actually prescribes in answer to the excuses used by men who commit honor crimes and the ones who allow them to get away with those crimes who insist that Islam sanctions their actions.

Honor Crimes and Laws of Leniency

Although Jordanian honor crimes have been exaggerated by women activists and the media when compared to similar crimes taking place in other countries, the fact still remains that Jordan has on its books a law that permits one person to kill another. This law is contrary to all legal traditions and puts into question the very idea on which legal systems are based. No one will dispute the fact that one of the fundamental reasons for the existence of law, why people accept to be ruled by laws and their enforcement, is protection of the weak from arbitrary actions by people with power over them. Jordanian labor laws recognize this fact, and state protection of the weak has always been their purpose. Yet Jordan's Penal Code actually allows a man to kill his wife, daughter, or sister if he discovers her with a strange man. The law may demand that the perpetrator must have "surprised" his victim while she was in the act of committing an extramarital sexual act, but Jordanian courts gloss over these specifics without anyone objecting. Justification of honor, morality, or Islamic sanctions not only are questionable, but also do not hide the fact that Jordan today has laws on its books that permit and hence encourage the killing of one person by another. Nothing in Islamic law gives such permission, nothing in tribal law gives such license, and certainly nothing in modern law permits the weak to suffer at the hands of the more powerful.

Although Criminal Law 340 is the culprit permitting murder, honor crimes are actually sanctioned by three specific laws in Jordan's criminal codes. These laws (340a, 340b, and 98) make it possible for someone, always a male, to get away with or to receive a reduced sentence for murdering a daughter, sister, wife, or cousin in the name of family honor. Violent crimes against women that could result in physical harm or death for alleged sexual misconduct have come to be known as "honor crimes" because they are justified as being crimes against the honor of a family or tribe. According to official statistics in 1995, a total of 181 honor crimes were reported, 35 of which were murders. The number rose in 1996 to a total of 201 honor crimes, 40 of which were murders, but fell in 1997 to 77 honor crimes, 16 of which were murders. Besides murder, the highest number of honor crimes fall under the description of attempted murder, reaching 117 in 1995, 137 in 1996, and 42 in 1997. Adding 7 crimes itemized under wrongful homicide in 1997 brings the number of actual honor crimes ending in death in 1997 to 23 rather than 16.[2] Observers have questioned these figures and consider them much lower than what actually takes place, especially because honor crimes are not always reported. In 1999 the reported number of homicides ending in death from honor crimes was estimated at 29–30, according to official figures.[3]

In honor crimes the victim is always a woman suspected of sexual misconduct, which is seen as the most serious offense to a family's honor and therefore necessitates redress if the family is to regain its respectability in the community. Given the fact that many of the victims are later found to be virgins, it is clear that there are other reasons behind such crimes, in particular competition over property and inheritance; getting rid of a sister (as is the case in many of these crimes) becomes a means of eliminating an obstacle to a brother's inheritance. Notwithstanding the wide belief among Jordanians that property and inheritance are at the heart of many honor crimes, it does not seem to be taken into any great consideration by the courts that almost always allow reduced sentences for brothers who kill their sisters, no matter how sexually innocent the sisters turned out to be once their bodies have been autopsied.

More important than the number of honor crimes committed is the fact that such crimes continue to take place and are growing in number. In honor crimes, the word of the victim is hardly considered, and Jordanian laws actually protect the perpetrator of the crime rather than the victim by treating honor crimes as lesser crimes and crimes of passion. Because of the growing number of honor crimes, the increased national and international publicity condemning them, and the deep anger of Jordanian women in regards to the way these crimes have been handled by the judicial system, Jordan's government has been particularly interested in changing the laws and taking a stiff stance against the continuation of such crimes. One of the first acts of King Abdullah II after coming to the throne was his letter of March 1999 in which he urged the amendment of any laws discriminating against women, which resulted in the Ministry of Justice's recommendation to the Jordanian Parliament that they eliminate Article 340 of the Penal Code. These efforts failed, notwithstanding the great efforts in that direction and the strong stand that had previously been taken by King Hussein and Queen Noor. Although the Upper House of the Jordanian Parliament approved the changes, it was the Lower House that diverted them and left them in limbo for later discussion, effectively ending the campaign to change them, at least at that time. Conservative elements brought about this rejection by deputies who refused any suggestion that honor crime laws be abolished or changed. They justified their stance on the basis of protecting the morals of Jordanian society. Perhaps because of the various political and economic problems faced by Jordan, the government chose not to pressure further; as is usual in such situations, sacrificing women's rights has always been an element of negotiation to achieve greater leverage and hegemony.

The attitude of the Jordanian Parliament is quite odd, especially because the excuse used has to do with maintaining morality and holding on to Islamic ideals and traditions that they insist are under attack by Western and American influences. Does that stance mean that Islam condones the killing of innocent women under mere suspicion? How could it be, when "throwing words" is a *hadd* punishable by eighty lashes? Actually, by its actions the Jordanian Parliament allows for leniency for the ones who not only "point the finger" but also commit the murder and thereby give the green light to others to follow suit. One wonders at what moral priorities are involved here. What makes the situation even more serious is the age of both killers and victims in honor crimes. Researchers have found that the killers were very young, ranging in age from nineteen to thirty. Furthermore, more than 58 percent of the killers were unmarried, 32.4 percent were illiterate, and 29.7 percent were enrolled in secondary schools and 23.1 percent in high schools. As for university students they constituted 3.7 percent. Therefore, there is a strong correlation between educational level and tendency toward honor and sexual crimes. Interestingly, whereas only 12.9 percent of the men were unemployed at the time they committed their crimes, the rest were mostly employed in seasonal or temporary jobs with little security. In other words, there is a clear correlation between social class and honor crimes. There is also a correlation between the locale and crimes, with 46.3 percent of the perpetrators of honor crimes living in popular urban quarters. One last important detail is the researchers' findings that this group was not stimulated by religious ethics: 69.4 percent did not perform their prayers, and 55.5 percent did not fast in a country that has punishments on its legal books against anyone who eats or drinks in public during Ramadan.[4]

Given the profile of honor crime perpetrators and the fact that 35.1 percent of the men in criminal rehabilitation centers have already served prison sentences for previous crimes, that they tend to act as bullies in their everyday lives, and that family conditions also played a role in these crimes (38.9 percent of the fathers of perpetrators were dead, 26.8 had a dead mother, 44.4 percent were children of polygamous marriages, and 24.1 percent were brought up in broken homes, the parents having divorced when the boy was five years old or younger in nearly 50 percent of the cases),[5] it is surprising that there is still a strong belief that honor crimes could be put in a special category involving family honor and that the state allows reduced sentencing as a form of leniency. Add the fact that medical examination of the victims of honor crimes found that 95 percent of them were quite innocent of the crimes that they were killed or assaulted for, and that these figures are well known and publicized, and the responsibility and actions of the people who control the laws and legal structures in Jordan should be a source of deep concern.

Perhaps some of the actual stories of violence may illustrate the seriousness of the contradictions between laws that do little to stop crimes against women—and thereby encourage crimes—and the claim by legislators and other elements of Jordanian society that it is a question of protecting Jordanian society and its moral fabric. A young girl called Khadija was killed by her father who claimed he was "cleansing the family honor." The medical examiner and investigation proved it to be absolutely false. When confronted with the evidence, the father admitted that he was motivated by suspicions of her misconduct and had no actual evidence of her committing any dishonorable act. A twenty-four-year-old man killed his wife because he suspected her of misconduct without bothering to ask her about his suspicions. In yet another case, a forty-year-old mother was killed by her much younger brother because he suspected her of misconduct.[6] A witness to an honor crime had the following story to relate. As she entered a hospital in Amman, a man came rushing toward an obviously pregnant woman leaving the hospital with her two children—a son and a daughter—followed by her husband carrying a third child. Brandishing a knife, the man attacked the pregnant woman, opened her abdomen, and then cut her throat in front of her husband and children. He then ran out of the hospital and took a cab to the police station to give himself up, as the witness later found out. The children were in shock, seeing their mother brutalized in front of their very eyes; so was the husband who proceeded to protect his wife's mutilated body with his jacket. It all took place within a few minutes and left the onlookers in shock. Presumably, as was later suggested by the media, the brother, as he turned out to be, suspected that the child the victim, his sister, was carrying was the result of an illicit affair. But how could it be if her husband was with her at the hospital for prenatal care and protected her body from onlookers while expressing immeasurable grief? These questions should have been asked by the court that later looked into this crime and allowed the brother a reduced sentence so that he spent no more than a few months in prison. The idea that a girl belongs to her male relatives beginning with the father, based on the principle of *wilaya* applied in Jordan (see chapter 5), is at the heart of this type of attitude by the courts.

The three particular laws of Jordan's Penal Code that provide a gap through which perpetrators of honor crimes get away with murder are:

- Law 340a exempts from punishment a perpetrator who discovers his wife, or one of his female relatives, committing adultery with another person, and kills, injures, or harms one or both of them: "A person who surprises (*yufagi'*) his wife or any of his *maharim* (those whose degree of relationship to him would not allow a marriage between them, for example sister or daughter or niece) while committing adultery (*zina*) with another person and he killed them or wounded them or harmed them both or one of them, benefits from this legitimising excuse (*'uthr muhallil*)."

- Law 340b actually exempts a perpetrator of an honor crime from punishment. Anyone—in every case a male—who commits a murder, physical injury, or another form of harm when he discovers his daughter, wife, sister, or other relative with another man in an illegitimate act can receive a reduced sentence. Law 340b "reduces the sentence of a person who murders, wounds, or harms . . . if he were to surprise his wife, or one of his *usul* [consanguine relatives] or *furu'* or his siblings with a man in an illegal situation."

- Law 98 allows for the reduction of the sentence received by an individual for a crime he committed in anger because of a wrongful act of great gravity committed by the victim.

A number of important issues need to be made regarding the titles and particular wording used for the laws.

- Legal code 340 is itemized under subtitle *"Al-'uthr fi al-qatl,"* a close translation of which is "Excuse for Murder." In other words, there is no question that the law recognizes that a murder has taken place, meaning that one individual has intentionally taken the life of another and such a murder is excused.

- Law 340a describes the person who benefits from the law as a "male" because it speaks of "he who surprises his wife," that is, there is no indication of a wife surprising a husband in such an act that would be considered *zina* under Islamic laws and is included as part of *hudud* crimes warranting punishment as prescribed by the Qur'an. The Qur'an talks about both men and women who indulge in extramarital sex as committing *zina*.

• The question of *"yufagi'"* needs to be addressed because there is no definition of the meaning of surprise. Does the law mean suspicion of adultery as "surprise," or does it indicate an actual act of adultery? *"Hal al-talabus"* (being caught in the act) are the words used in the law; it means that "surprise" by the husband involves his discovering his wife, sister, or daughter in the *actual* sexual act, as it is taking place. The rules of evidence are not included with the law, even though the rules of evidence are clearly stated in the Qur'an: four male witnesses or eight female witnesses of the *actual* act of fornication. The lack of rules of evidence opens the door to arbitrary interpretations of "surprise" and *"talabus."*

• The word *"maharim"* is defined as "being in a degree of consanguinity precluding marriage."[7] This definition would not include cousins because marriage is possible between them. Yet in practice courts have not differentiated between a brother and a cousin when they commit such a murder.

• Reduced sentencing for honor crimes committed by cousins and uncles and even further related members of a clan is allowed through 340b, which uses the same language as 340a but with significant differences. Although 340a speaks about *"uthr muhallil,"* that is, an excuse justifying murder, 340b concerns *"al-'uthr al-mukhaffif"* (an excuse allowing for reduced sentence) in case a man surprises his wife or one of his direct women blood relations while with a male "on a bed that is not legal" (*'ala firash ghayr mashru'*). So 340b covers any gaps in 340a by giving a reduced sentence to just about any member of a clan who kills or harms a female relative for what he considers to be sexual misconduct. Moreover, what is meant by "a bed" is not defined, yet the subtle differences between 340a and 340b would indicate a way by which the murder of a woman who is found with a man without any sexual act taking place between them would be excusable by law. This indication is confirmed by the way the law has been applied by the courts: even a chance meeting between a man and a woman could be interpreted as "a bed." So it is not only the law that is objectionable: even more so is the interpretation and application of said laws by the courts.

• Jordan's Penal Code recognizes other crimes that are excused by law that are included in the same section and under the same subheading of exemptions for honor crimes. These crimes include self-defense, killing or wounding trespassers who enter houses at night without permission with the intent to harm or steal, and involuntary manslaughter. In other words, honor crimes are equated with crimes committed in self-defense or defense of the home, both of which are internationally accepted causes for reduced sentencing or justifiable homicide. Strict rules of evidence are included and demanded by Jordanian laws for a self-defense plea. Unfortunately, stringent proofs are not expected in honor crimes for reduced sentencing, and all judges seem to require to apply leniency is evidence that the killer is an actual relation of the victim and had some provocation and suspicions about her morals.

• Law 98 closes the gap completely by making "passion" an excuse for crime. When an individual is under the influence of great anger, then his actions cannot be held against him. Here it is assumed that this anger would be proved and that premeditation was not part of the crime. Actually, extreme anger is taken for granted to exist because of the nature of the crime, and therefore no specific rules of evidence are detailed in the laws, nor are they expected by courts. This point does not mean that a trial does not take place, that the police do not investigate, or that witnesses are not brought in. It all takes place, except the intent seems to be to find a way out for the killer rather than prosecute him to the fullest extent of the law for having killed another human being. It is no wonder then that a young man who killed his teenage sister because she received an unsolicited love letter from a neighbor received a three-month prison sentence. What the evidence of her participation in such an act was, why such an act is one of dishonor, and how a judge could reach such a decision are explained by the willingness of the system to allow it and the continued acceptance of tribal *'urf* as part of the legal structure in Jordan.

From the above points we can conclude that as the laws themselves illustrate, the wording actually opens the door for a judge to let a murderer go free or with a sentence that amounts to less than smacking the hand of a child. The laws are loose and hedged enough to leave the definition of honor crime open to include just about any form of violence that could be undertaken against a woman by a male family member. Although 340a is specific about adultery, it does not indicate whether what is being discussed is proved adultery. What is the basis of the rules of evidence or of the rules regarding police investigation and the attitude of policemen in such crimes?

Are there methods to guarantee that a priori attitudes of the ones given the responsibility to investigate these crimes or who sit in judgment do not interfere with legal processes? Why is the involvement of the family in the criminal act not investigated by the police? Given the fact that too many contemporary honor crimes are enacted by juvenile boys, is it so difficult to conceive that they were put up to it by adult members of the family who would perhaps be treated more severely by the law?

Most significantly, why is premeditation not taken into consideration in honor crimes? Here Law 98 comes into play because it excuses what can be termed *crime of passion* because the person committing it is not acting rationally.

In this situation, premeditation is vital. The law itself is an import from French criminal codes and part of the modernization of laws throughout previous colonies of England and France. French laws of intent require that a crime of passion be committed on the spot, that is, under the influence of shock from discovery and influence of uncontrollable anger—hence the "surprise" in 340a. Crimes of passion, according to French laws, however, have particular rules of evidence. For example, if a person discovers his wife committing adultery and kills her immediately, he could go free; but if he leaves the room to find a weapon with which he proceeds to kill her, for example, then the "crime of passion" plea would not work. But "crime of passion" pleas are not treated this way in Jordan; a person could go a month before killing his victim and still be considered to be acting "out of his mind."

A comparison between Jordan's and Egypt's criminal codes may help explain the "tribal" nature of Jordan's laws, notwithstanding how modern they look or Islamic they are claimed to be. The absolute inequality of Jordanian laws and their patriarchal nature exemplified through the powers they give to a husband in regards to *zina* will be used as an example. Even though both Jordan's and Egypt's Penal Codes have great similarities—Egypt's having been taken as models for Syrian, Palestinian, Iraqi, and Jordanian laws—there are serious differences when it comes to honor crimes that should give us pause. Egyptian laws, like Jordanian laws, allow for reduced or commuted sentences for a crime committed under particular conditions and pressures. Article 62 of Egypt's Penal Code states: "[T]here is no punishment for a person who undertakes his action while out of his mind and lacking his own will due to madness or other mental incapacity."[8] Here there are no details given to explain the meaning of "crime of particular seriousness" or "crime of great injustice," as is the case in Law 98 of Jordan's Penal Code. Although "action" could be any crime in Egypt's Penal Code, the descriptions included in the Jordanian law are more of a reference to honor crimes than anything else. The most important difference, however, is that Egyptian laws do not allow for leniency or exemptions for honor crimes. In other words, Egyptian laws do not permit one person to murder under any pretext, as does Jordanian Law 340. The same goes for Syrian and Iraqi laws. Therefore, given the common origins of the criminal codes of these countries, one must look at Jordanian laws as being "cut to size" to fit with Jordanian priorities, in this case questions of tribal honor.

Furthermore, although leniency for crimes of passion does allow for an open door in Egyptian law, the rules of evidence required for a "passion crime" plea are very serious, and no exemptions are made in these rules for honor crimes. A killer of his daughter, wife, or sister is treated as he would be anywhere: as a murderer with the state prosecuting him to the fullest extent of the law, and when premeditation is proved, then he receives the death sentence or life in prison. The fact that an adulteress is caught in the act does not justify a crime against her or her partner except if the husband becomes immediately violent and commits his crime while not in his right mind. Nothing in the law justifies the killing of a sister or other female relative for committing a dishonorable act.

Here we are talking about laws regarding adultery and the treatment of adulterers. The shape, logic, heading, and subheadings of Jordanian and Egyptian Penal Codes are almost the same. The various issues included and covered by the codes are also the same, which is to be expected because they are modern codes modeled after European ones. The differences come in specifics according to acceptable traditions in each of the countries. However, it should be pointed out that in Egyptian society, killing a daughter for immoral acts is as common as it is in Jordan, the difference being that the law does not justify such a murder or allow a way out for its perpetrator. If caught, claims of family honor have no bearing on the decision of the judge because the law does not allow it. These discrepancies are important to point out because even though the codes of both countries are modern and are structured after European laws, the construction and interpretation of the law as well as the execution by the courts and law enforcement agencies of the two countries differ. Although in Jordan it is more important to cater to tribal traditions, in the Egyptian case, the law, at least in theory, is designed to punish perpetrators of capital crimes. Moreover, the usual and incorrect justification for laws condoning honor crimes in Jordan is said to be the Islamic *shari'a*. Yet both Egypt and Jordan have applied the Hanafi code since the nineteenth century as the basic source for *shari'a* laws, and one would therefore expect greater similarities in specifics regarding crimes, criminal behavior, and punishment, particularly given the discourse about the consistency with Islamic law.

As for adultery, Article 274 of Egypt's Penal Code reads: "The married woman whose adultery is proven will be sentenced to a prison term not exceeding two years but her husband can stop the execution of the court's decision by agreeing to live with her as before." That article corresponds to Jordan's Article 282a: "A consenting adulteress and her partner are to receive sentences of six months to two years." Article 284a-d eliminates any role for the state in regards to *zina* except if a husband asks the state to investigate his wife's adultery as long as they are still married or four months after a divorce takes place. Rules of evidence in regards to adultery are clearly spelled out in 282b of Jordan's Penal Code: "[T]he evidence that could be acceptable as criminal evidence to provide proof for this crime is [the adulterers'] arrest while they are in the actual act of committing the crime, or a legal confession, or the existence of letters or other written documents." The same rules of evidence are required in Egypt's Penal Code, Article 276, with two important differences. Although Jordan's law is directed toward a wife and her lover, that is, it privileges the husband who is seeking redress, Egypt's law is gender neutral by using the masculine word *"mutahim"* (defendant). In fact, Jordanian laws do not look at the husband as a possible subject of *zina* whose wife could have legal recourse against him; rather, it is the father in the case of a minor girl or unmarried daughter and the husband in the case of the wife who have the right to ask for the apprehension of the woman for committing *zina*. Thus, although Egypt's Penal Code, Article 275, in which the sentence for adultery was set at six months to two years, reads: "[A] male who commits *zina* is to receive the same sentence," there is no such law in Jordan's Penal Code. Furthermore, Egyptian Article 277 punishes the husband who commits adultery in the marital home: "Every husband who commits adultery in the marital home and this is proven according to a wife's complaint, receives a prison sentence of no more than six months." [9] Such a law does not exist in Jordan's Penal Code, and a wife has no recourse against her husband's *zina* because the law does not give her the right to bring forth a complaint in the first place but reserves such a privilege for the husband and father because the state cannot become involved in issues of adultery except if a complaint is brought by one of those two males.

Perhaps the only recourse against men and adultery in Jordan's legal codes comes in regards to what are considered acceptable public actions. Article 283a-b reads: "[A] husband will receive a prison sentence of one to two years if he takes a mistress in public in any place he could be. His partner receives the same punishment." [10] Here a husband who commits adultery in the marital home could ostensibly be prosecuted by Article 283, although because the home is not a public place, the case may be difficult to prosecute. Besides, the law may not indicate that the wife has the right to bring a complaint against him, but it does not exclude her. The law, however, is so vague that what is included or excluded is left up to the investigators and to the judge, and here because there are no indicated rules of evidence or definition of what a mistress constitutes, it becomes more of an arbitrary system left up to people in authority to determine. Perhaps Weber's idea of a *"qadi* justice" who rules arbitrarily without reference to legal codes has validity for legal systems dealing with gender today. In almost all cases, the *qadi*'s arbitrariness works against the woman, even though the ambiguity of the law could in fact be used to strengthen her rights vis-à-vis a husband's fidelity and her marital home.

In short, Jordanian laws dealing with adultery are directed against the wife as adulteress and not toward the husband as adulterer, and in fact other parts of Jordan's Penal Code make this fact quite clear. The modern period witnessed the establishment of gendered state-supported legal codes that placed women under the power of men. State laws and state police became instruments for ensuring these conditions. With growing gender struggles brought about by greater economic problems and social dislocations, the interpretation of law has proved to be an important method of increasing male control over women and children. As is usual in such situations, contradictions take place and usually work against the weaker party. For example, according to the penal code, the *waliy* has the sole right to ask the authorities and the court to intervene in *zina* cases involving minors. Otherwise, the state does not prosecute. A husband is given that same right regarding his wife, but the wife is denied any such right in case her husband is a proved adulterer. Thus, even though Jordanian laws provide procedures by which claims of adultery can be handled through the legal process, it depends solely on the wish of the male guardian of the female involved if unmarried and of her husband if married. She, however, does not have the same recourse in a situation where she catches her husband in the act of adultery; she cannot get the state to prosecute him and as corollary does not receive a reduced sentence for killing him.

Although it is usual to talk about honor crimes as constituting actions taken by women and dealt with by men of the same family whose concern is focused on their family's honor, actually any crime that is of a sexual or intimate nature that takes place outside of what is legally and traditionally acceptable constitutes an honor crime. At the same time, whereas *zina* is normally looked at as adultery in the sense of sexual intercourse between a male and a willing female, actually *zina* constitutes any sexual act outside of a legitimate relationship and involves coercion, at least in its Islamic definition. Therefore *zina* includes rape, an act in which a woman is coerced, male coercion being considered impossible, notwithstanding Qur'anic stories such as the one involving Zulaikha. The issue of rape will be covered in the next section of this chapter, but the modern laws of rape on Jordanian books today are important as a follow-up on the above thesis that Jordan's laws are purely patriarchal and intentionally misogynistic. Even when it comes to rape, the laws are not as "victim friendly" as the laws of other Arab and Islamic countries and can be considered encouraging to criminals.

Honor Crimes in Islamic and Tribal Laws

Theoretically, the first source of Muslim jurisprudence is the Qur'an, followed by traditions of the Prophet. The Qur'an is detailed in regards to gender relations and deals directly with *zina:* "Do not commit *zina,* for it is a shameful deed that leads to greater evil" (Qur'an 18:32).[11] *Zina* was proved by confession, and the prophet Muhammad required that a rapist confess four different times before being judged. The punishment for *zina* is clearly stated in the Qur'an as one hundred lashes, no difference being made between male and female. Using hadith as a reference, the *fuqaha'* have added stoning as a punishment and made a differentiation between married and unmarried men who commit *zina,* confining stoning to the married ones. However, there is no mention of stoning anywhere in the Qur'an, and the punishments mentioned for adultery are whipping and exile. There is also no evidence that stoning was resorted to as a punishment for *zina* until the modern period, at least not in the lands that previously belonged to the Ottoman Empire. There are court records showing the prosecution of acts of immorality, including conclusive or confessed prostitution, but even in these cases there is no stoning and the state in the shape of the judge and lieutenants of the court did not see any reason to take matters in their own hands, although it depended on the particular location.[12] When stoning is applied in Iran, Pakistan, and Afghanistan today, it is based on *fiqh* interpretations and not on the Qur'an, even though theoretically the Qur'an is the primary source of *shari'a* law and its dictates are not disputable by any other, including prophetic traditions. But that fact should not come as a surprise because most issues regarding gender are determined in the same way, with preference given to whatever source is most misogynistic.

Even though *zina* in modern law is applied exclusively to consensual intercourse outside of marriage, *zina* has the added meaning of nonconsensual sex in the Qur'an and *fiqh*. Thus, *zina* in the Qur'an is placed between a string of *ayas* dealing with social violence: forbidding the killing of one's children, forbidding murder because God made life sacred, and forbidding the robbing of a helpless orphan's property (Qur'an 17:30–34). Prophetic traditions also emphasize the dual meaning of *zina*. One tradition tells of a tribesman who asked the Prophet to punish him for having committed *zina*. The Prophet asked him several times if the woman acquiesced in any way. Because the man continued to deny her willingness, the Prophet ordered his punishment and not the woman's. In another tradition, however, when a woman confessed to consensual *zina,* she too was punished. In the first story the man's crime was extramarital sex in which the woman was not willing, which amounted to rape, so therefore only he was punished, but in the second story the woman participated and was therefore punished. According to the tradition, the punishment was by stoning.[13]

The prophetic traditions mentioned above show the meaning of *zina* in Islam as encompassing both rape and extramarital consensual sex. Punishment was meted out on whoever took an active part, and the punishment was equal regardless of whether it was a man or a woman who committed it. One must look for precedents from various periods of Islamic history to develop a picture of how the laws and attitudes of Islamic societies toward sexual crimes were formulated. During the early period of Islamic expansions when laws were being formulated to handle new situations, 'Umar b. al-Khattab (second caliph to the prophet Muhammad) is said to have offered a woman marriage to the man who had raped her. When she refused he had the man pay her the dowry of her peers as compensation. In another tradition 'Umar is said to have had a male slave whipped and then exiled for forcing a woman into *zina*. In both cases no stoning took place. The acts of the caliph 'Umar constituted an important source for the *madhahib* to follow, such as giving the victim of rape the choice of marrying her attacker or being paid compensation as a preferred method to corporal punishment.[14]

Following the precedent set by 'Umar b. al-Khattab, Muslim *fuqaha'* dealt with rape as a violation of "property" (*ightisab*) of what belonged to another. *Property* here is meant in the sense of "usage" and not in the absolute sense that the word connotes today. Thus, 'Asqalani includes *zina* in both *"kitab al-ikrah"* ("Book of Coercion") and under *"bab al-sariq hina yasraq"* ("chapter of the thief when he steals"), indicating that a "right" was stolen through coercion. The *fuqaha'* also used an important tradition of a promise given by the believers to the Prophet: "They *baya'u* [swore allegiance to] the Prophet that they would not steal nor [commit] *zina*." This statement is interpreted to mean that a man who committed *zina* was committing a *kabira* (major sin) and therefore a *hadd* crime whose punishment is prescribed by God and therefore cannot be reduced, increased, changed, or commuted by anyone.[15]

Although most *madhahib* agree with this tactic, Abu Hanifa, according to a tradition relayed by Abu Yusuf, is the only *faqih* who allowed commuting the *hadd* if one of the witnesses against a rapist died before the sentence was carried out or if the rapist married the woman he had violated because "the woman becomes the property of her husband through marriage in regards to his right to enjoy her."[16] In contradistinction, Malikis considered that once "a woman's claim of having been raped is proven, a legally competent (*mukalaf*) free Muslim had to be stoned, even if he was subsequently married [to his victim] by a binding marriage."[17] Shaf'is and Hanbalis agree with the Malikis on this point. It is interesting that the modern state found it preferable to apply the Hanafi code according to Abu Yusuf, even though there is no basis in either the Qur'an or hadith for doing so. Today in Jordan, when the rapist marries his victim and he is considered in "possession" of exclusive sexual rights to her, his crime is considered as never having taken place. This particular law has been changed in Egypt, and a rapist still has to undergo the punishment prescribed by the law and courts even if he marries his victim. Marriage was seen as a way of deterring rape, but Jordan has yet to change its laws to reflect the seriousness of the situation of rape today.

Notwithstanding the differences in the schools of law, they all agree that *zina* between a man and a woman constitutes illegal sexual intercourse punishable as a *hudud* crime and necessitating compensation and that *zina* means both extramarital consensual sex and rape. The following handling of rape by Shaf'i speaks for all the schools, regardless of particular differences among them:

> If a man forces a woman, the *hadd* must be applied to him but not to her because she was forced. She receives the dowry (*mahr*) of her equal whether she was a free woman or a slave. If she is a slave then her compensation is reduced in proportion to the reduction in her price [caused by the rape]. If she is a free woman then her injury is to be compensated over and above the marriage-dowry due to her: dowry is for sexual intercourse and compensation is for the crime.

Thus, redress was to be sought by the "property" owner; the rape of a person, or the "robbing" of virginity, was equated with a sense of personal proprietary right. Notwithstanding how dishonorable or psychologically harmful rape may have been, it is not that which was paramount in the mind of premodern *shari'a* courts as much as how the victim was to be compensated for the harm that had befallen her or him. A *diyya* had to be paid, same as the *diyya* for the *nafs* (life), loss of a limb—a nose or other parts of the body—or any other physical harm such as severe wife beating. Determination of *diyya* depended on a number of criteria pertaining to the particular case. Important criteria included the religion of the rapist and the age of the victim—whether she was a minor, a virgin, or an adult woman married, free, or a slave. The sex of the victim was also important because males were often victims of rape. The payment of *diyya* for rape in Jordan today is a continuation of tribal law and a concession to the continued tribal nature of Jordanian society.

Here we see another important contrast between Jordan's civil code and Egypt's civil code modeled after the French Penal Code of 1810. *Diyya* presents a good example of the serious differences between the penal codes of Jordan, Egypt, and France. *Diyya* places the law in private hands to determine the outcome rather than allow for the rule of law and its enforcement by the state, thereby limiting the state's ability to act as protector and enforcer of the laws. The Egyptian legal code, introduced in 1883, was acclaimed for its having moved away from payment of *diyya* and its enforcement of the state's role in establishing the rule of law. "[Egypt's Penal Code] clearly separated the civil side from the criminal which was previously confused with the blood-price and the right for remission of the crime or injuries by the injured party or his heirs. It secularized penal law. It softened the penalty. It instituted a simple penal law, clear and well regulated on the whole; a fixed law exempt from arbitrariness; a law [uniformly] equal for all, knowledge of which is accessible to all."[18] Jordan's laws followed the Egyptian or French model by separating the civil from the criminal, secularized penal law, and "softened the penalty" by eliminating corporal punishment and replacing it with prison sentences. However, Jordan continued to allow payment of the blood price and "the right for remission of the crime or injuries by the injured part or his heirs." The new laws did regularize and standardize the handling of crimes and corrected previous arbitrariness of courts and modernized the legal system to meet the needs of a centralized nation-state. However, Jordan's laws do not meet the changing needs of a fast-growing, business-oriented, urbanized society. The rationalization of the legal system did not act as an inhibitor and controller of crimes; rather, particularly when it comes to gender violence, the existence of a "way out" for perpetrators of these crimes through laws of honor and payment of *diyya* has only helped in the growth of gender crimes to "epidemic" proportions compared to what they were not even a decade ago.

It should be mentioned that Jordan's laws do not recognize wife rape. Even if the rape was to take place after divorce but within the *'idda* period and before a husband was to officially take his wife back, it is still considered a husband's right. The same approach to wife rape exists throughout the Islamic world as it does globally. According to Muslim jurists, by virtue of the marriage contract the wife has made herself sexually available to her husband and cannot withhold herself from him whenever he wants to have intercourse with her. The fact that the Qur'an admonishes men not to approach their wives unless they are willing does not seem to have had an impact on Muslim jurists or modern laws. Starting from these premises, discourses on women and sexuality have divided women into "good" and "bad." Good girls cause no trouble to families, and girls who did were bad and deserved what they got. Good wives submitted willingly and did not fight with husbands over their sexual rights or if he were to look elsewhere or marry other wives. As for women who asked for anything else, notwithstanding Qur'anic guarantees, they risked being looked at as "bad" and could suffer consequences. Victorianism, brought in as a middle-class ideology, only reinforced such sexual attitudes that blamed women for sexual misconduct.

Contemporary Jordanian laws and penal laws of other Muslim countries reflect this misogynistic attitude toward sexuality by devaluing sexual crimes in general, notwithstanding how personally injurious and humiliating such crimes are to women. This devaluation is exemplified by use of the concept of *hatk ʿird* as an alternative definition for sexual crimes that may or may not include rape. Although rape (*ightisab*) is clearly defined as sexual intercourse forced on an unwilling female, *hatk ʿird* is defined as a lesser offense involving an immodest action that could be physical, mental, or emotional and is within the realm of personal injury but does not include forced sex. *Hatk ʿird* includes touching a woman's body parts or using foul language that causes her embarrassment and challenges her modesty.

The concept of *hatk ʿird* was based on Egypt's Penal Code imported from French laws. Therefore, Jordanian and Egyptian penal laws are very similar in the words used to describe rape, but the Jordanian laws are superior in serious ways in comparison to Egypt's, even though the actual language of the law gives a different impression. Egypt's Article 267 of the penal code reads: "Whoever has sexual intercourse with a female against her will is to receive a permanent or limited life-sentence." [19] This article is reciprocated by Jordan's penal code with Article 292a: "Whoever has sexual intercourse with a female (other than his wife) without her willingness whether through the use of force or threat or deception or trickery, will receive a temporary prison life-sentence period of not less than ten years." [20] Although Jordan's law sets the punishment at a minimum of ten years, Egypt's code leaves the door open to the judge to reduce the number of years served, depending on the particular case. In fact, Egyptian courts have proved lenient in this particular situation, handing down sentences that are often quite offensive to the public and do little to stem the rising number of rapes faced by Egyptian women—and young boys—today. Furthermore, the Jordanian law covers every possible situation in which the rape could have taken place, by trickery or misconception. As for the Egyptian law (even though it too includes articles regarding rape of a victim while intoxicated or rape through trickery), it has left wide open the demeanor of the girl: did she encourage the rapist, and what does encouraging the rapist really mean, and what does it constitute? Here questions of intent are one way by which rapists get off easy.

Jordanian laws are also superior in the sense that they call for the death sentence for the rape of any girl who is less than fifteen years old, the recognized age of majority and marriage in Jordan. [21] Egypt's law until 1999 did not have a death sentence for rapists; rather, a rapist of a boy or girl who was less that sixteen years of age could have received a maximum sentence of temporary life imprisonment, fifteen years. In 1999 after the newspapers gave extensive publicity to the multiple rape of a two-year-old girl who was abducted from her home, the public outcry brought about government action to pass the death sentence on this rapist. However, Egypt's laws have always allowed for execution when rape was accompanied by abduction, the latter being a serious crime according to Egyptian laws. It remains to be seen whether the death sentence will stand in future rape cases and the type of rape case to which it could be extended. It should also be mentioned that one week before the rape of the two-year-old girl appeared in the news, a rapist was given a three-year prison sentence by a judge in Alexandria for having raped a three-year-old child. In other words, it took public anger and a serious campaign by the press to bring about the change in the laws.

But why establishing fifteen or sixteen as a cutoff age for capital punishment for a rapist at a time when the world is suffering from a rape epidemic is itself a matter open to question. After all, an eighteen- or twenty-eight-year-old woman is as much at the mercy of a violent rapist as a fifteen- or sixteen-year-old girl; the consequences to her life are even more severe given her older age and public gossip that often censures her even more than the rapist. Clearly, rape as a crime against women should be placed at the top of the agenda in regards to human rights issues in the Middle East and the world as a whole.

It should be added, however, that Jordanian laws are most significantly superior in comparison to Egyptian laws in defining the act of rape as *ightisab* in comparison to Egypt's inclusion of the act of rape under the description of *hatk 'ird*. As pointed out earlier, *"ightisab"* is a word that has the specific meaning of usurping something that belongs to another by force and against that person's will. It is an ugly word that is reprehensible and without any confusion in the mind of anyone who hears it. Although it is used mainly as sexual rape, it could also mean forced and illegal stealing of property, land, goods, money, and so on. Jordan's laws place the act of rape under the heading of *ightisab* with no ambiguity as to the nature of the crime, even though the meaning often gets confused with *hatk 'ird* in the wider discussion of sexual crimes including rape, which often allows for reduced sentencing in court. As for Egypt's laws, the word *"hatk 'ird"* is used to describe the very act of rape in preference to *"ightisab,"* which is used exclusively in the sense of legal usurpation of property such as checks or stocks and shares.[22] By describing the crime of rape as *hatk 'ird,* the impact of the crime itself becomes lost because *hatk 'ird* includes much lesser crimes such as touching a person's body or making sexual innuendos or advances that are very offensive to women but do not carry as stringent sentences as rape.

One area in which Jordanian laws fall short, however, involves the distinction made between "rape" and "incomplete rape." Although it is understandable that incomplete *zina* is not punishable because the crime never took place,[23] the idea of "incompleteness" is problematic when it comes to rape. Jordan's laws recognize rape only if actual intercourse has taken place. A Tamyiz Court decision concluded that rape could have occurred only if sexual intercourse had taken place "in the place intended for it," that is, a woman's vagina. If the rape involves any other part of her body or it is the rape of a boy, it is not considered rape.[24] Any such act would then be placed under the description of *hatk 'ird* and prosecuted accordingly. The attitude of the court opens the door to further leniency. In Tamyiz Court case 9/66 the court found that "simply holding the hand of the plaintiff and throwing her on the ground and trying to raise her clothing and touching any part of her that could be considered a *'awra* [genitals, usually hidden sexual areas of the body], does not constitute attempted rape but comes under the description of *hatk 'ird.*"[25] That conclusion was also reached by the court in a case in which the offender came to his victim's home late at night while her husband was absent and she was asleep. He approached her and began to kiss her, then raised the bedcover with the intention of raping. Such details were not enough for the Jordanian court to call it attempted rape, but they did consider it incomplete attempted rape. In yet another court case, a man asked a woman to have intercourse with him; when she refused he threw himself on her while his sexual organ was exposed and "ready." She fought him and managed to get away. The courts found the situation insufficient for a finding of rape and considered it incomplete rape, which warranted a minor sentence. Incomplete attempted rape is handled by Article 68 of Jordan's Penal Code and is seen as *hark 'ird* rather than rape. This type of definition can only constitute an encouragement, and sentencing for *hatk 'ird* is a far cry from sentences handed out for *ightisab*. Only when violence or threat is used in *hatk 'ird* is the sentence relatively significant, at least four years' hard labor (Article 297a). When a young boy is raped, as very often happens, the punishment is a minimum of seven years' prison sentence if the boy is less than fifteen years old (Article 296b), but if the victim of *hatk 'ird* is older than fifteen but younger than eighteen, the sentence is temporary labor (Article 299).

One last issue about rape needs to be discussed here: incest. Although it is normal for Jordanians to refuse to acknowledge the existence of incest in their society, today the facts show that it exists. Yet the subject of incest is a very sensitive one and not easily broached anywhere in the world, let alone a conservative society like Jordan. Still, today increasingly cases of incest are becoming more publicly known, and when talking with Jordanian women I realized that such cases are in fact existent although it is not clear to what extent. Society handles such cases differently depending on the place and situation. Although quite often a pregnant victim of incest is actually killed by her family rather than the family as a whole losing face, in other cases a victim of incest is married off to a relative or someone who is married, and so the shame is hidden. In one such case related to me by the actual family of the victim, a friend of her brother was paid one thousand dinars to marry her. The very fact that a man is willing to be paid to marry a woman in such a situation is in itself an indication that incest may be more widely known in Jordanian society than is admitted. This possibility is strengthened by the fact that the man who married the victim of incest in the above story was also a wife and child abuser. Evidence of such abuse was clear on his wife's face and hair; as for his children, three of them between the ages of four and six had received severe beatings with the man's belt that still showed clearly as long red and black lines days after the beatings had taken place. It seems that this father had punished his eight-year-old daughter through burnings in her vaginal area, an indication of the beginning of sexual abuse. The problem with such a picture witnessed by myself, neighbors, and social workers is that Jordanian laws do not really allow anyone other than the guardian to bring charges regarding child abuse to the attention of the authorities. Even doctors do not have that ability when confronted with possible abuse when examining children. When they do, the matter does not go far because the father's rights over his child are unquestioned in Jordan.

Discourses on Women, Violence, and Morality

Islamic perception of sexual and honor crimes will be discussed, and it will be shown that there is no law that places a clan's honor on the shoulders of women, nor is there a law that justifies the murder of innocents. Besides, if anything, Islamic law demands balance and presents an equal moral code and standards from both men and women. In other ways, it is not what the laws say as much as it is moral discourses that allow for the continuation of honor crimes and other forms of violence against women and make it possible for perpetrators of such crimes to get away with little punishment. At the heart of these discourses is the idea that women are a potential source of enticement and that they must be controlled so they do not seduce men into sin. In other words, men are ultimately seen as the victims of women's sexuality. Did not Zulaikha bring about the downfall of the prophet Yusuf? Was not Eve responsible for the Fall from Heaven? Neither woman could control her desires, and their actions brought about havoc and the fall of the men around them. Traditions have made women into the symbols of sirens, Jezebels who are out to lead men astray.

But this picture of a tempting siren is not acceptable in the Qur'an, notwithstanding how widely it is understood to be so. The story of Adam, Eve, the serpent, and the Fall is commonly repeated in Arabic literature and found in various books of *tafsir* (interpretation of the Qur'an). As in the case of the Old and New Testaments, Adam and Eve are tempted by the snake to eat from the forbidden fruit, and there is mention of that episode three times in the Qur'an in Surat al-Baqara 35–36, Surat al-A'raf 19–20, and Surat Taha 10–121. But nowhere in these *ayas* does the Qur'an condemn Eve for the temptation nor the eventual fall from grace. To the contrary, if anything the Qur'an can be read to question the very patriarchal order that puts man at the top of the pyramid of creation; after all, it is a fact that there is no mention of the story of Adam's rib in the Qur'an, a fact that is little known among Muslims who accept the biblical story that Eve was created from Arab's rib as Qur'anic. Actually, the Qur'an is rather ambiguous about who was created first, man or woman. Surat al-Nisa' 1 could actually be interpreted to mean women were created first, although a neutral *nafs* was most likely. It was really preexisting traditions and patriarchy that allowed for the propagation and confirmation of the patriarchal order, placing it within a "holy" religious absolutism that is hard to question. We do know the actual origins of these stories and the early Christian and Jewish converts who brought them into Islam.[26] The Judeo-Christian conception of the creation of Adam and Eve is narrated in detail in Gen. 2:4–3:24. God prohibited both of them from eating the fruits of the forbidden tree. The serpent seduced Eve to eat from it, and Eve, in turn, seduced Adam to eat with her. When God rebuked Adam for what he had done, he put all the blame on Eve, "The woman you put here with me—she gave me some fruit from the tree and I ate it." Accordingly, God said to Eve, "I will greatly increase your pains in childbearing; with pain you will give birth to children. Your desire will be for your husband and he will rule over you." This story has no bearing in the Qur'an or Islamic tradition, and yet it is an essential part of Islamic gender discourses.

The important thing is that even though historically we know the sources of stories that show women as a periphery of man or that she is the cause of original sin, it is almost universally accepted among Muslims and reinforces the image of a woman as either a Jezebel or a passive follower of an aggressive male. Only if the man is strong, physically and morally, are women kept in line. These beliefs are at the heart of crimes against women in the name of honor. Given the fact that the Qur'an has no concept of "original sin," this picture of the essential sinfulness of women can have no more than a spurious basis, especially given general rules set up by the Qur'an that do not see women as sinful by nature any more than men, nor is Eve blamed for the Fall, as she is in the Old and New Testaments. Actually, when the Qur'an discusses women and sin, it almost always discusses men and sin from within the same discourse and using a similar terminology. In Surat al-Nur (Qur'an 24:30–31) we are told, "Say to the believing men that they should lower their gaze and guard their modesty, that will make for greater purity for them, and God is well-acquainted with all that they do. And say to the believing women that they should lower their gaze and guard their modesty, that they should not display their beauty and ornaments except what (usually) appear thereof." [27] The Qur'an also lays out equal expectations of men and women and sees them as protectors and assistants of one another. "The believers, men and women, are protectors, one of another: they enjoin what is just, and forbid what is evil, they observe regular prayers, practice regular charity, and obey Allah and His Messenger. On them will Allah pour His Mercy: for Allah is Exalted in power, Wise" (Qur'an 9:71).

Unfortunately, even though the Qur'an recognizes both men and women as possible sinners, and, in fact, provides for equal punishment to both, we find that the issue of sin and shame has traditionally been put on the shoulders of women, who therefore must be secluded lest they cause evil. "Women are an *'awra*," meaning a weak spot or genitals; the implication is then sexual weakness. "When she leaves [her home], she is accompanied by the devil." [28] How can this image of woman as a walking *'awra* be reconciled with the above *ayas* from Surat al-Nur? And why are women and not men burdened with potential sinfulness when the Qur'an speaks with such equal terms about them?

Examples of the treatment of honor crimes by contemporary Islamic societies show that Jordan does not have a monopoly over such crimes, although it has become associated with such crimes by the international press to the point that when you mention "honor crime" there is an automatic reference to Jordan. Although not underestimating the seriousness of the situation in Jordan, it is important to illustrate how serious the problem is in other Islamic countries as well as to show how even though these societies claim to be Islamic and even though equal moral standards are expected of both men and women, a woman's actions are valued differently than the same actions of men by Muslim countries and receive only lip service by their governments. The following stories from Iran, Egypt, Kuwait, Pakistan, and Jordan should illustrate my meaning.

In the fall of 1986, Soraya, a thirty-five-year-old Iranian woman, was stoned to death by the men of her village after having been accused of infidelity by her husband. [29] The exact details of the story may be disputable, but certain facts are essentially true if for no other reason than their repetition in hundreds of similar cases in villages all over Iran since the success of the clerical revolution in Iran. Soraya had been accused by her husband and was stoned for fornication, even though the accusation was for flirtation and sexual enticement. The people who deliberated her crime were all men, and the new clerical leader in the village took the leading role in ensuring she received the maximum sentence. The determination of the crime and the sentence passed were based on the cleric's reading of "God's law" to assure God of vengeance for the crime and cleanse the village of the vile acts of one of its members. None of the women participated, and there was general mourning among them.

Were Soraya and the other hundreds of women stoned in Iran, Pakistan, and Afghanistan during the past two decades innocent, or had they committed the crime for which they lost their lives? It is a good question best answered through the very law that was being used to stone them. Although people who claim that stoning was ordained by Islam and demand its application, it is only women who have been stoned, whereas their presumed male partners have not. Can *zina* occur without a man's participation? If the Qur'an is to be taken as judge, there is no punishment of stoning anywhere in the Qur'an, and when *zina* is discussed, it is in reference to both male and female and is not used in reference to women alone. But this area is not the only one in which the law being applied was broken. There was no confession forthcoming from Soraya, nor from most of the other victims for that matter. There was no admission of guilt, nor was any proof presented of the act she was accused of. More important, fornication had not taken place, which is the reason that her "partner" was not stoned but was regarded as the victim of her efforts at seduction. Yet the legal basis for stoning fornicators is *hadith al-rajm* in which a male convert to Islam is said to have confessed to the Prophet that he had committed *zina* and demanded that he receive appropriate punishment. After repeating his confession four times on four consecutive days, the prophet Muhammad finally ordered that he be given what he was asking for.[30] In Soraya's case, she was judged and executed on the same day. The deployment of sexuality as an instrument of social and gender control was taking new twists and turns as the twentieth century moved to a close.

It was 1999 and the month of Ramadan, with hundreds of people waiting at the central overcrowded 'Ataba bus station in downtown Cairo. A young girl dressed conservatively in Islamic garb and accompanied by her mother was attacked and raped by perhaps four men, according to eyewitnesses. The four men were strangers, and the act was quite spontaneous. Hundreds witnessed the event, yet when it was finally brought to court, the decision was that no actual rape had taken place, that the girl was still a virgin, and the rapists went free without punishment. When the minister of the interior was asked on Egyptian television how such a crime could happen and in Ramadan, he answered that such events take place every day. His declaration brought about denials from the government and the outrage of a public already aware of the truth of his words.

Yet another case comes from Kuwait where a ten-year-old girl was kidnapped by four young men and kept for days, during which she suffered continuous rape from three of the four young men. According to Kuwaiti law, the rapists should have received the maximum Islamic penalty of death for kidnapping and rape. But the case was complicated. On the one hand, the girl was the daughter of an immigrant working in Kuwait, whereas the perpetrators belonged to Kuwait's elite families. Denial proved impossible because the fourth young man, who did not participate in raping the girl but only in her abduction, confessed all. Responsibility for enticing the rape could not convincingly be put at the door of a ten-year-old child who had been playing with other children in front of her home at the time of her abduction. As a solution, the Kuwaiti courts maneuvered to find a way out of Kuwaiti criminal laws by introducing concepts from tribal and Islamic laws that would allow for the payment of *diyya* and thereby reduce the perpetrators' punishment to financial compensation that their elite families could easily afford.

As for Pakistan, official statistics show more than one thousand honor crimes a year, but unofficial figures give much larger estimates. "On an average, regional newspapers in the country report almost five killings in the name of tribal 'honour' every day," reports Massoud Ansari, who relates the following story that exemplifies honor crimes as experienced in Pakistani tribal society:

> Last month, in the village of Sinjhoro in southern Pakistan, 18-year-old Bilkees was detained in a room for a night. The next morning, Bilkees saw her brother Ghulam Qadir enter the room with an old fashioned pickaxe in his hand. Bilkees tried to talk to her brother and the villager accompanying him but both of them did not listen to her. Instead, they dragged her towards the nearby fields, tied her to a tree and Qadir started hitting her with the pickaxe. . . . The reason for Bilkees being killed in such a brutal manner was that her brother had seen her talking to a boy. Qadir decided to kill Bilkees to save the "family honor." No relatives lodged a complaint against Qadir and Bilkees was buried without any funeral being observed. Bilkees' murder, performed in the name of "honor" is not an isolated case in Pakistan. In tribal societies, those suspected of "illicit" sexual relations are labelled Karo-Kari (Karo being the male and Kari the female) and killed. Anyone who kills a woman for being a Kari and the man she is involved with, is considered to be *gairatmand* (honourable) and is morally and legally supported by his kinsmen.[31]

Awareness of the peril under which many women live in fear for their lives, because of the intent of fathers or brothers to harm them because of suspicions of sexual misconduct, brought about the opening of detention centers where Jordanian women could be protected from possible harm. Lamis, one such "administrative detainee," as they are officially referred to, was being kept there for fear of being harmed by her father who was threatening to kill her. The father refused to accept the situation and complained to the authorities, asking that his daughter be released to him. Notwithstanding the girl's fears and her insistence that she not be turned over to her father, the father managed to get the authorities to release her because of his rights over her as her *waliy*. As soon as Lamis was delivered to him, the father killed her by slitting her throat. Put on trial, the courts found him guilty but sentenced him to nine months in prison. That this crime was premeditated with no chance of a reduced sentence on the basis of Article 98 of the penal code is unquestionable. That Law 340 also does not apply is also unquestionable because there was no element of "surprise." Still, the father got away with murder, and the legal system allowed him to walk.[32]

In July 2000 another honor crime was reported by the *Jordan Times*. A twelve-year-old girl from the town of Irbid was beaten to death by her father and thirteen-year-old brother. As the newspaper reported, the girl's father's justification for having committed this crime was that "she used to go out walking in the streets without permission." In other words, it was not that she committed an honor crime, but that her going out may mean she could potentially commit such a crime in the future. The connection with *wa'd al-banat* is significant. Pre-Islamic Arab men killed their daughters so as to stop any potential honor crime from even taking place; this modern Jordanian man killed his daughter for the same reason, and he expects to get away with it because what he did he regards as expected.

The above cases are but examples of the tens of others that remain unknown or are not publicized or even come to light and investigated. In all of them the victims were women and their assailants were men who got away with little more than a slap on the wrist. The diversity of the cases does not change the fact that they all had something to do with perceptions and discourses about sexual conduct. One should add another type of crime that intentionally manipulates moral discourses and the perception of a Muslim public to achieve political ends. Here I am referring to what can be termed the "deployment of rape" to coerce political interests, reported cases of which have come out of Pakistan, where the wives of candidates for the Pakistani Parliament were alleged to have been subjected to rape as a form of shaming and hence damaging their husbands and families, forcing their defeat or resignation.[33] In Iraq, rape was used as a systematic method of extracting evidence from enemies of the rule of Saddam Hussain, and according to one source, there are paid civil servants whose job is to undertake such rape.[34] The deployment of honor crimes as a way by which patriarchal power is kept in place seems to be forgotten in the wider discussion of laws handling honor crimes. A society in which half its citizens are "kept in line" through fear and intimidation can have little hope of democratic participation. Males and females all pay the cost of fear and intimidation, each group in its own way, notwithstanding that one group is held hostage by the other. To expect freedom of thinking and personal enterprise from such a situation is optimistic indeed.

8

Regarding Work and the
Modern Jordanian Woman

IF, as the saying goes, a civilization is measured by the lives of its women, then Jordan is a civilized country indeed. Given the patriarchal order under which women in Jordan continue to live, it is a wonder that life for Jordanian women, though filled with frustrations and problems, is still comfortable in comparison to Jordan's neighbors and other Muslim communities. Women's equality before the law and the right to vote, run for elections, and assume public office are guaranteed by constitutional law in Jordan. Jordan has also been a signatory of the United Nations Convention on the Elimination of Discrimination Against Women (CEDAW) since 1980 (ratified in 1992).

It is true that there are serious discrepancies between what the Constitution sets out and how the laws interpret and execute these rights, and it is also true that Jordan held specific reservations in regard to CEDAW; nevertheless, the fact still remains that equal rights are guaranteed by the Constitution unlike many other Arab countries such as Saudi Arabia, Kuwait, and other Gulf states, and that Jordan has made important strides in the implementation of CEDAW. Even though Jordanian women's participation in the political process has been disappointing, three women did sit in the seventy-five-member National Consultative Council from 1978 to 1984, four during 1980–1982; twelve women ran for elections, if unsuccessfully, in 1989. In 1993, the first woman to run for elective office did win and became a member of the Lower House, which was a cause for great excitement, notwithstanding the opposition and hardships that she herself was to face because of her success. Whereas the Upper House of Parliament has two appointed women members, the seventeen women who ran for public office in 1997 all failed in their bids for a seat to the Lower House. Women were more successful in their efforts to win elections to municipal councils. In 1995, nine women won such seats, and one was elected mayor. In 1999, eight women were

214

elected to municipal seats. The government admitted women to the cabinet, if not at an aggressive rate, and as is usual for other Arab countries, women were delegated to the more socially oriented top positions, particularly as minister of social development. However, the government of Jordan did depart from this pattern by assigning a woman to the position of minister of information in 1984, minister of trade and industry in 1993 and 1994, and minister of planning in 1996. The year 1999 witnessed the first woman deputy prime minister ever assigned anywhere in the Arab world. The most impressive accomplishment for Jordanian women when compared to their Arab sisters was in their assignments to the judiciary since May 1996. At present the numbers are growing, though we do not see any women judges in *shari'a* courts that are in great need of women to balance their patriarchal traditions.

According to the United Nations, women constituted 6 percent of the top government positions in Jordan in 1997, which is very impressive when compared to the 2 percent average for the Arab world and 7 percent for the world overall. The participation of women in the labor force has grown significantly during the past decade. Measured at 7.7 percent in 1979, women's participation has grown anywhere from 12 percent to 16 percent,[1] depending on the particular study. It should be noted that most studies do not take the "hidden" contribution of women in the workforce and the economy into consideration (see chapter 4). It is in fighting women's illiteracy that Jordan has shown a clear leadership position in regards to its neighbors. Illiteracy rates fell from more than 53 percent in 1972 to 14 percent in 1996.

Although, as this book has shown, there remains much to accomplish to provide women living in Jordan with equal job opportunities and the protection of a legal system that would also allow for equality before the law, important steps have been achieved to bring about transformations in women's lives vital for today's global structures. It is true that international agencies consider women of the Arab world, like their other "southern" non-Western sisters, as "invisible" as far as the economy is concerned, but in reality this "invisibility" is as much an expected result of the standards, methods of research, and priorities of international agencies as it is a reflection of the actual life of Arab women. For example, statistical evidence based on demographic representations of individuals through clan and family clusters whose property tenure patterns are communal—if registered under individual ownership—hides the actual contributions of women in large sectors such as agriculture, food production, and trade. This "invisibility" is a serious matter because not only does it deny the actual versus the perceived contribution of women in the economy, but by creating such an image it also lends credibility to social and legal constraints facing women in the workplace or business world. As various chapters of this book have illustrated, women have always contributed to the economy, whether formally or informally. Modern state structures and male-dominated modern economic configurations are what have kept women out as the state and modern companies and corporations have grown into the main job providers. Traditional methods of production have normally depended on women's participation and in fact still do. But as traditional sectors of the economy lost room to modern factories, offices, exchange, and retail, so did women also lose their importance as participants in the economy.

Today, efforts are being exerted to revive the productive and economic role of women and to open up the modern economy from which they were originally barred. Jordanian women activists are fighting for greater political representation and for serious participation in defining the future direction that Jordan should take. Here the battle has been waged in two directions that have the superficial appearance of conflicting. On the one hand, they have been working to achieve greater access for women to the public sphere in the shape of political appointments, administrative responsibilities, entering the professions, determining the country's laws, and gaining a more official and hence recognizable foothold among Jordan's working and labor forces. At the same time, women activists have been involved in an effort to change Jordan's labor laws and personal status laws so as to achieve greater gender equality in the workplace and within the marital home. The "rule of law" is central to these efforts; not only is protecting women victims of abuse in accordance with Jordanian laws demanded, but so is a change in the laws themselves to adjust the realities of Jordanian life to fit with the fundamental principles set out by the Jordanian Constitution.

The second direction of women's activism involves holding on to social and cultural traditions giving sanctity to the family, protection of children, and a woman's traditional role within her home and community. The woman's progressive movement that can be regarded as part of the general direction to modernize the structures of business, education, and government employment gives the perception of conflict with the simultaneous battle by Jordanian women to hold on to their traditions—whether Muslim or Christian—which they consider essential to the preservation of their families and society. Although fighting for a greater public role and greater gender equality, they at the same time hold on to the essentials of patriarchal society. To outsiders this move appears contradictory; to Jordanian women there is no contradiction. A more active life does not mean a freer social or sexual life. It also does not mean a more secular approach to their existence. Civil rights include greater equity within the marriage and family, but *civil* should not be confused with *secular*. That misunderstanding is perhaps the basic problem with international human rights and international organizations advocating greater rights for women. Women's rights have been closely connected with secular discourses. In such discourses, symbols such as Islamic garb, the veil, and even piety have been considered by outsiders to be indicators of gender discrimination and female passiveness. It has also meant that international organizations have put their financial and political weight on the side of discourses that privilege cultural Westernization, seeing it as a "must" preliminary step to achieving greater rights for women and greater participation by them in the economy. This approach is problematic because it has meant a rejection of Islamic discourses as possible venues for gaining greater awareness and participation by women in socioeconomic and political life.

As this book has stressed and contemporary women activists in Jordan confirm, without tackling issues from within discourses familiar to the very groups that are the subject of efforts of change, nothing much can be achieved that will have permanency. It therefore comes as no surprise that Jordanian women activists have in fact moved to using efforts that "bring the debate home," so to speak, by addressing women's issues from within paradigms familiar to Jordanian women. Using a discourse and language familiar and common to their societies, and in particular entering into and using traditional discourses, is increasingly resorted to as a method for advocating gender equality. In doing so, activists are slowly enhancing the gender debate that had once been unilaterally dominated by women with progressive agendas who saw civil rights through secular terms. Although the achievements and influence of feminists with secular Westernized agendas such as Nawal Sa'dawi cannot be overemphasized, the new revivalist atmosphere and large-scale continuous movement of people and the traditions by which they live, from countryside to town, require that the feminist discourse, and the knowledge and language of that discourse, be inclusive if it is to have any relevance.

This chapter is enriched by interviews with women in various professions as well as a number of male lawyers and judges. A number of questions guide the argument presented here, such as where does the Jordanian woman stand today? What is her future? What are the major concerns facing Jordanian women, and what solutions can be proposed for major problems and constraints standing in the way of women's participation in Jordan's economy, workforce, and political and public life? The results of the inquiry make clear the point above: although women are interested in greater participation in public life, they are not willing to compromise their families and traditions to achieve it. At the same time, the general perception is that there is no contradiction between being pious and being dynamic in performing a job or acting as a public advocate. Veiled women in particular do not see their choice of dress as contradicting their professional, business, or social achievements. In fact, an opposite conclusion could be drawn from the connection between wearing the veil, Islamic feminist activism, and fighting for a greater public and professional role for women. Advocating gender segregation by certain conservative women can be looked at from within a feminist paradigm calling for greater access of women to work and greater opportunities based on gender differences.

At the center of Islamic or conservative discourses on women and work are issues such as "gender mixing," "woman's nature," or "the role of women." Although it is generally assumed that Islamic discourses stand against the work of women, and that Muslim clergymen, Islamic thinkers, and veiled women stand for a patriarchal structure in which women play a repressed role, the reality of these discourses is that there is great consistency between the Islamic discourses on women's work and the general attitude of Jordanian society toward the work of women. Islamic discourses on women and work will therefore form the first part of the chapter to define basic concepts and general social attitudes controlling a public role for women. The discussion will then move toward three specific topics that appear to be the focus of feminist activism today. These themes are women's political and legal activism, women and business opportunities, and education (*taw'iyya*), meaning the dissemination of knowledge and awareness. Here the discussion will involve the work of Jordanian women as feminist activists and political activists who work toward greater public participation by women in the country's politics. Because women in the legal, educational, medical, and journalistic professions have their own outlook on the situation of women in Jordan and the future they can look forward to, their approaches toward their jobs, families, and perceptions of the problems facing women are particularly insightful. Jordanian women are today showing a greater interest in opening their own businesses, in finding jobs, and in improving their lives through education. The success experienced by businesswomen, already established or trying to carve out a place for themselves in the Jordanian market, will also be discussed as well as women engaged in microfinancial projects to round up the discussion regarding the future of Jordanian women and the most severe obstacles that they face today.

Discourses on Women and Work

Women in the Islamic world, like their sisters elsewhere, have constituted an active part of the historical process not only in day-to-day matters, but also in areas that are usually considered to be a male's exclusive domain. Proving that a woman can do a job as well as a man, however, does not seem to have put an end to misogynistic attitudes that judge a woman's contribution against a "male" gauge that considers jobs as "male," then judge a woman's abilities on how "male" she may or may not be. This argument dominates among people who consider women to be inferior to men, regard jobs as a male's domain, and demand that women be kept out of jobs that should be made available to men. According to such minds, men have the duty of supporting women, an important principle among people who oppose the work of women in Jordan and the rest of the Arab and Islamic world.

The famous misogynist thinker 'Abbas Mahmud al-'Aqqad is representative of this attitude. In the 1960s, 'Aqqad mocked proponents of women's equality for blaming the inequality between modern women and men on long-term handicaps caused by historical conditions that denied women equal training and opportunity. If it was economic and political conditions that kept women behind, 'Aqqad asks, why have they continued to be so backward and unequal to men in so many areas and for so very long? If they were not inherently unequal, why were they not able to achieve equality? His answer speaks for wide audiences inside and outside the Islamic world who find women's continued weakness to be natural, given biological differences between men and women. As evidence of inherent gender inequality, 'Aqqad, like other enemies of women's rights, quotes the Qur'an, *"wa lil-rijal 'alayhima daraja"* ("and men have a degree over them") (Baqara 228), as evidence of God's plan for male superiority. He sums up the gender conflict around which the social discourse on women revolves in three points: "1. Her nature, which includes her [physical] capabilities, and her [inherent] ability to serve her sex (*naw'uha*) and her people. 2. Her rights and duties within the family and society. 3. Social relations [*al-Mu'amalat*] that are required by custom and public morality most of which are matters of traditions and manners."[2]

These three points seem to form the center of the debate regarding women and work. Modern laws pertaining to women and work, the type of work women are said to be capable of performing and the type they are incapable of, their need for protection because of their fragile nature, and society's responsibility for protecting its moral standards are directly related to women in the public space. These issues are all based on principles that take the "nature" of woman as limiting her right to full equality, and, though ensuring her legal competence as an adult, actually limit and frame this legal competence to make her legally dependent on male relatives. Laws discriminating against women in the working place in Jordan today are largely based on this idea of "woman's nature" that, for example, forbids or limits women from working in mines, at night jobs, or overtime. A woman's physical or biological ability, her need for protection, and her primary job as "mother" define these limitations. But these issues are subject to hot contention because the new world order is bringing about deep structural change, and societies will have to adjust if they are to survive.

The Jordanian Islamic thinker Ibrahim al-Qisi begins his study about the role of women in the Islamic world, *al-Mar'a al-muslima bayn ijtihadat al-fuqaha' wa mumarasat al-muslimin,* by decrying the condition under which Muslim women live. He attributes the situation to a lack of proper understanding of the words of the Qur'an and Sunna and the wrongful execution of the rules they set out. He also criticizes wrongful interpretations by *fuqaha',* their dependence on weak traditions that are popular among the public, the wrongful treatment of women by men against God's laws, and the wrong that women do unto themselves by not abiding by God's laws and by imitating Western women.[3] Only if women recognize their nature and abide by Islamic teachings will they live honorable, productive lives. Quoting al-Ahzab:33, *"waqarin fi buyutakun,"* al-Qisi reaches the following conclusions on women's work:

1. The husband has the right to stop his wife from leaving the home after having paid her advanced dowry. However, this right like any other right should not be misused by the man.

2. A Muslim woman should not go out too much, leaving her home must be for an important reason.

3. A Muslim woman should prefer to bear children and raise them, and watch out for her family's needs rather than work outside the home. However, there is nothing against her going out to work if there is a need as when there is no one to support her, but on condition that her work be according to conditions laid down by Islam (i.e. allowable by the *shari'a*), that said work does not take her away from her husband or children and that it not be in circumstances where she would work with men.[4]

Al-Qisi completes the picture by allowing women to visit a doctor, preferably a woman doctor; if not, then a decent male doctor and only in her husband's presence and without removing any unnecessary clothes.[5]

The conservative outlook toward women is therefore centrally concerned with morality, which seems to be completely focused on sexuality. Women, different from men by nature, should not in any way entice men to act indecently. In other words, both men and women are reduced to their essential nature as potential sinners, an idea that is actually quite alien to Islam, which does not believe in original sin or blame Eve for the Fall. Standards of morality are defined by local *'urf* that are actually highly dependent on socioeconomic conditions.

This assertion is supported by a Shi'a clergyman's attitude to women's work. He approached the same issues, used the same discourse, but came up with a different picture. In his book *Huquq al-zawjiyya: Haqq al-mar'a fil-'amal*, Sheikh Muhammad Mahdi Shams al-Din, the Lebanese Shi'i ayattollah, presents a dual argument that often divides discourses on women and work today. Confirming that Islam does not take a stand against women's work in public and in the professions, he confirms the belief in an unchanging *shari'a*:

> There are those who want to push [women] into the professions and the economy without any *shari'a* controls or rules by . . . claiming that such rules were not set up by the *shari'a*, or that these rules were suited for a society that no longer exists, and so we must change the *shari'a* to fit with the needs of our age, its knowledge and its needs. To those who make such claims, the *shari'a* is like a costume whose size and style changes according to its wearer's appearance.[6]

Having placed jurisdiction over women's work under the auspices of the *shari'a*, the sheikh then attacks people who interpret the *shari'a* as forbidding women from working outside the home and consider women's sole role as serving their husbands, children, and families. "They claim that . . . allowing a woman to work is a transgression of the *shari'a*, and a transgression against God's laws that jeopardizes her by [leading her] to dangers that threaten her chastity and family role."[7] In answer to these "false" claims, the sheikh presents his interpretation of the *shari'a* toward women's work:

> The legality of woman's employment, her right to earn a living and enjoy the income of her work, and her right therefore to earn a salary equal to her contribution is the same as a man's right. Being a woman does not deny her that right. The legality of this has been proven by Islam, it is a God-given right that a woman need not struggle to achieve to save herself from the control of men and their power over her, nor [does a woman have] to prove her humanity and individuality as was the case in Western societies that did not recognize a woman's [inherent] right to work except after the social changes brought about by the Industrial Revolution and the need for working labor. . . . The economic independence of women is legally proven through the Islamic *shari'a* which grants her full economic competency. The husband, father or brother has no custody over her from that aspect.[8]

Are you asking why a woman would want to work? The answers include so-cially accepted reasons such as the need to supplement her family's income, tak-ing up jobs more suited to women, replacing men when there is a labor shortage such as during war, and voluntary work to serve national causes. But it is the first reason given by the shaikh that calls attention to the changed outlook of even conservative clergymen toward gender and family. "[A woman should work] so as to utilize her energies and her time to enrich her community with her produc-tive capacities rather than squandering energy and wasting time in indolence and laziness (*tarakhi wa kasal*)."[9] Because women have a responsibility toward their society and nation, it becomes the responsibility of the nation to train and prepare them to become partners in building it.

However, and here is where concerns regarding women's work are explained and the two takeoffs of the sheikh come together, women's work has to be guided by *shari'a* rules that are meant to protect her and prevent any possibility of im-morality. Like most of the Muslim clergy, Shaikh Shams al-Din does not con-done mixing in the workplace and demands that women wear the garb that he believes Islam prescribes. He does, however, differentiate between normal mod-est wear and what is required by extremists, which includes covering the face and making it almost impossible for women to function in the workplace. In other words, it is not the work of women that is in question, but the moral issues that could arise from women's work in a public and mixed-gender environment. Contrary to what is usually imagined as the stance of the Islamic clergy vis-à-vis the work of women, most renowned sheikhs of Islam, at least in the Arab world, encourage women to be educated and work; their main concern is really with so-cial morality and the protection of women who could be helpless or harassed in the workplace. Forbidding women from working, forbidding them from partic-ipation in public life, or prescribing a strict dress that almost hides their identity has little to do with Arab women and certainly much less so in Jordan. For such strict censure of a public domain for women one needs to look east beyond Iraq, particularly to Iran and Afghanistan. The situation is quite different in the Arab world.

Islamic Discourses and Women's Activism

Feminist activism seems to confirm the points made above but goes further. Pushing for an Islamic agenda that calls for the separation of sexes takes a dis-tinctive form of class and gender struggle. By advocating separation of the sexes, Islamic activists are at the same time giving women an edge in the struggle for any profession or business catering to women. In a professional and business world where men have the upper hand as "natural" holders of professional positions or owners of businesses with greater access to markets, having a "captive" clientele becomes a great advantage to women professionals and business owners, giving them a better chance of making it as doctors, nurses, chiropractors, dentists, lawyers, beauticians, hairdressers, and so on. Women even gain an edge as preachers and *shaikhas* catering exclusively to women. *Shaikhas* are not new; as chapter 3 detailed, they were included in religious endowments of mosques that provided them with schooling and housing. Today, women's religious circles are a feature of Islamic societies, and in such circles only women *shaikhas* are usually allowed, with the rare appearance of a male *faqih* to answer some particular questions that the ladies of a group may wish to have answered by a *faqih* or *mufti* of the law.

This type of advocacy for a "captive" clientele for women professionals is not unique to the Islamic world. One has only to look at the larger NGO movement worldwide and see its interconnection with international businesswomen, a relationship that has been sponsored and advocated by women activists, female politicians, and businesswomen looking for an edge in their struggle to compete in a male-dominated business world: in other words, women as better partners to women in business. That lesson is one of the most important learned in Beijing by women who realized that catering to the needs of other women and doing business with other women are important venues for women today, at least in this stage of their history.

Perhaps the best example of this type of Islamic feminist advocacy comes in the push to have women be treated only by women doctors. As al-Qisi pointed out and as is today practiced among many classes in the Islamic world, women are advised that Islam demands that they should be examined only by female doctors. If we were to look back at premodern medical practice, we would find that women were normally treated by women practitioners. When there was a need for an expert opinion that could be provided only by a male doctor, it was a woman who undertook the examination and described the condition to the male physician who attended the examination but did not touch the patient. Women acted as heads of guilds, including medical guilds; hospitals were divided into male and female sections; and only women provided service in the female sections. Most important, however, what in the modern world are known as gynecology and obstetrics were the domain of midwives whom the modern state all but disenfranchised by forbidding them from using medical instruments and disallowing their practice in hospitals. With modernization, medical schools were opened that admitted only men for a long time, and women began to lose their hold on women's bodies and the medical trade catering to them. In Egypt, where a woman's hospital has graduated *hakimas* (women doctors) since 1839, women did succeed as doctors and provided service to women, particularly in outlying areas, which helped bring epidemics such as smallpox under control. By the last quarter of the nineteenth century, however, as the nation-state became more centralized and patriarchal, the school was demoted into a school of nursing and the word *"hakima,"* once reciprocal to the male *"hakim,"* or male doctor, changed to connote a chief nurse. Meanwhile, with the modernization of gender relations, obstetrics had become one of the most lucrative businesses as women turned in greater numbers to modern medicine. Interestingly, all sorts of male specialists turned toward practicing obstetrics. The market for bringing children into the world was vast, as would be expected with the simultaneous growth in populations that the modern period has witnessed. The same patterns were repeated throughout the Arab world. Today, the growth of Islamic revivalism is bringing about a marked increase in the practice of women doctors who specialize in all areas of medicine, especially obstetrics and gynecology with the exception of surgery, which was not an area for women's practice in traditional Islamic societies.

In her book *Wazifat al-mar'a al-muslima fi 'alam al-yawm* (The job of the Muslim woman in today's world), Khawla 'Abdal-Latif al-'Itiqi discusses jobs that Islamic feminists consider to be suitable to women today. She begins by discussing woman's work as "mother and nurturer" (*mu'alima was murabiyya*) the way Islam meant her to be and ideally what society needs her to be. "How can societies that wreck the home grow? How can a society be built by women who leave their work at home to ignorant servants who originate from the lowest and most backward of social classes?"[10] The elitism of such a statement cannot be discounted and illustrates the ambitious level at which Islamic intellectual feminists talk. They do not present a populist discourse because of their choice of dress and social attitudes; rather, they are quite exclusive in the way they look at themselves and the role that many of them earmark for themselves. Although quoting the Qur'an's Surat al-Ahzab 33, as do male Islamists, calling for women to stay at home, al-'Itiqi proceeds to present a clear referendum on women and work:

> We believe in women's work and that [a woman] has an important role to play in today's world that she must not give up so as to complement the role played by the male whom God has designated together with her over this universe. We believe in all this but we do not wish to loosen the reigns to that role and leave the woman stumbling through the uncharted areas of this crazy bitter world, and we

do not wish for a mixing of roles between women and men, but we want scientific and useful work within limits and measures that befit the nature of the Islamic religion and suitable to the nature of the Muslim woman which God has shown us in the rules of His Book and what He inspired to His Prophet.[11]

Here the key word continues to be woman's *nature,* and the emphasis is on difference and the necessity of working from within Islamic parameters. The methodology then followed by the author is typical of the general conservative discourse regarding women and work. By referring to Islamic precedents, Qur'an *ayas,* and traditions of the prophet Muhammad, the discourse aims at two things. On the one hand, there must not be mixing between the roles of women and of men, and on the other, women can undertake most work performed by men and are even better at some jobs. "Women are more competent and patient than men in the field of education, which is one of the most honorable and lofty professions." Here the "nature" of woman is defined as that of an "educator by nature" because of abilities with which God endowed her. The discussion then moves to a woman's work as a doctor and nurse, "especially in the field of women's and children's medicine." Here we are told that this field is vital for a society in which women can play an important role because "many women do not like to expose themselves to men and are embarrassed to do so, therefore the right person and location must be provided for them." The reasoning is then sharpened further, making becoming a doctor or nurse a duty and suggests that women are better in providing medical care for women and children because "a woman doctor is better able to sympathize with a woman's feelings than a male [doctor]; she shares with her the same difficulties and the same psychological characteristics that makes her better equipped to understand her, bond with her and treat her."[12] This bond becomes even more essential in Islamic societies today experiencing revivalism where women refuse to have male strangers touch them because of God's injunction that there should be no mixing between men and women.

What other jobs are indicated for women? The selection is quite wide: "There are women whom God has endowed with artistic talent such as excellence in sewing, embroidery, cooking and putting a house in shape which is what is known today as decorating. These talents should not be neglected by women, for these are jobs that women could actually perform without having to leave the home or mix with men." The truth of this statement is reflected in the large number of women in Jordan who are involved in handicrafts, embroidering national costumes and other items for sale to tourists or to overseas designers. Interestingly, embroidery is a very popular project among women entrepreneurs, NGOs, and even such women's organizations as the Jordan River Foundation that owns showrooms in which are sold the handicraft products of women from workshops run by the foundation. Al-'Itiqi makes a very interesting statement recalling the importance of artistic work as an area of women's employment before modernization by which she also delineates this area as a "woman's" area. "It is the West that put in our minds the idea that male cooks, clothes designers, and decorators are better qualified and have a more refined taste than that of women."[13]

Two other jobs, one advocated for women and one censured by Muslim feminists, need to be pointed out. First is the full-time job of a *da'iyya* (missionary for Islam). Here women are to call upon their sisters to follow God's word. They are best suited to do so because Islam forbids gender mixing, and so a woman missionary is best equipped to discuss religious matters and give answers to questions asked by other women. Of course, to be a *da'iyya* requires particular characteristics and training, not the least of which is setting a good example by observing Islam's dictates regarding dress code, modesty, and gender mixing. The second is women's work in politics, and here again the influence of the West is blamed for women's wish to work in the political field. According to Islamic feminists, women are not suited for political work because Islam "is very cautious and even rejects the work of women in politics, not because women do not have the abilities because there are highly educated women of strong character who can perform such work, but because of the social harm that could rise from it and the patent violation of Islamic norms and morals and the injury that woman causes to the family and its cohesion if she works in this field."[14] The experience of Tujan Faisal, to be discussed in the following section, comes to mind. Islamic discourses are not used exclusively by Islamic feminists to promote the rights of women. Activists resort to Islamic sources such as the Qur'an, hadith, and historical precedence and traditional language to be able to communicate with Muslim women from conservative sectors of society. For example, rather than speak of human rights, feminists are today resorting to rights as established by Islam to benefit and improve the situation of women. What is promoted by the latter is little different from discourses of "human rights," but it is placed within a language and context familiar to the culture and everyday lives of the women and men of Jordan. A further reason for using Islamic discourses has to do with the fact that many women activists are actually attacked through the use of religious symbols, knowledge, and language. Activists had in fact to rethink their methods and speech to be able to counter these attacks and have consequently become more knowledgeable about *shari'a* and *fiqh*, as well as traditional social attitudes toward women and work.

The lawyer In'am 'Asha, well known for her magazine articles and TV programs that introduce sensitive gender issues to the public, tells the story of the oral attack she faced while giving a lecture on women and law. Her attacker did not bother to discuss the substance of her presentation or enter into any of the debates she presented; instead, he simply dismissed all she had to say by pointing out that she had forgotten to use the word *"sayyidna"* ("honorable" or "our master") as a title to the caliph 'Umar b. al-Khattab when she referred to him during her presentation. Her experience was not unique because it has become a "classic" method by which fundamentalists attack speakers for not being "Islamically correct," which is then turned into a conclusion that they are not good Muslims to begin with and that their knowledge is defective. Other forms of attack on women activists involve the use of language and Arabic grammar. Pointing out a mistake in syntax or tense and even *tashkil* (diatribes) become methods of putting down the speaker. Women activists have therefore been forced to mind their p's and q's, so to speak, sharpen their knowledge of Islamic history, and become more familiar with *shari'a* debates on women's issues. As Rihab al-Qaddumi explains, she too has had to change strategy, especially when speaking to conservative audiences or when talking in public in the presence of journalists or groups clearly in the opposition. She has also integrated Islamic discourses in her writings so as to widen her audience and better illustrate her meanings. This strategy is followed elsewhere by women activists who integrate principles of human rights into an Islamic traditional language, realizing that they have to give relevance to their cause from within the parameters of the society that they are addressing. Zaynab Radwan, dean of the School of Arab and Islamic Studies of Cairo University, Fayum Branch, plays a prominent role in this area. As a professor of Islamic philosophy she is well placed to enter into this wider Islamic discourse in the battle for greater rights for women. In her book *Al-Mar'a fi al-manzur al-islami: Ba'd al-qadaya* (Women from an Islamic perspective: Some issues), she gives an almost comprehensive list of the various areas in which women and men are equal according to the Islamic *shari'a*. The language she uses is simple and easy to understand, and her usage of Qur'an *ayas* where needed is effective at delivering the message. Beginning with a discussion about the "Principle of Equality in Islam," which she bases on *aya* 4:1, "People, fear God who created you from one soul and created from it its mate and dispersed from them many men and women." The generic *soul* here is obvious and important to discussions of equality. "Islam came to underline the unity of all humanity since creation . . . in life and death, rights and duties in front of the law and . . . God, in the here now and hereafter. No credit except for the good deed, and no honor except for the more pure. It destroys the artificial basis of difference, and returns mankind to their larger truth and their single origin."[15]

The categories of gender equality in which she frames her discussion are somewhat unusual and illustrate the discipline of philosophy to which she belongs. Thus, she talks about "equality between man and woman in human value" and points out that the Qur'an never discusses "wives" but rather uses the masculine "spouse" and its plural when referring to either husband or wife. On this basis, she then proceeds to talk about "the equality of man and woman in public life":

> One of the major realities of the Qur'an is that it determined complete legal competency (*ahliyya kamila*) and full rights—without conditions except what all Muslims have been forbidden by God and His Prophet—in all civil transactions, and economic and personal ones, so that He gave her full right and ability to own money no matter how large the amount, to inherit, to will [her property], to take out loans and own real estate, to undertake transactions, to earn and profit, to negotiate, to sue, and to deal in whatever she holds or owns.[16]

These are strong words that cannot be contested in Islamic terms, yet Jordanian laws fall short of what they signify. Most interestingly and in contradistinction to al-'Itiqi's Islamic discourse, Radwan gives an Islamic basis for the "right of women to political participation" by using the *bay'a* statement in the Qur'an in which God calls on the Prophet to give and accept the *bay'a* from the women who accept Islam and wish to give him their oath of allegiance.[17] For Radwan, political participation becomes a duty dictated by Islam and not just a right. She uses the same methodology to prove Islam's demands of "equality before the law" and "equal rights to work." Here Radwan echoes the call of feminists all over the Islamic world who are studying the Qur'an from a novel perspective. Islamic discourses on gender should be considered vital for opening up the woman question and fighting against conservative forces holding women back. Such a conclusion does not come as a surprise to Jordanian women in public service. Dr. Sireen Musmar is a specialist in surgery and community medicine, and heads the section of Umuma wa Tufula (Motherhood and Childhood) Reproductive Health program of Jordan's Ministry of Health. According to Dr. Musmar, forty-four health centers in six Jordanian provinces were chosen for the four-year project on reproductive health. The centers were reconstructed, refurbished, and provided with counseling rooms, medical equipment such as ultrasound machines and computers, and fully equipped clinics. The main reason for the project is family planning to teach Jordanian women various methods of birth control and help them choose the one most appropriate. Significantly, male-oriented birth control methods do not have much chance of success in Jordan except for the use of condoms, which seems to be acceptable in certain areas, though in other areas the very idea of men undertaking birth control all but closes the subject. The centers have also been effective in other ways, such as screening for cervical cancer and breast cancer and teaching women breast self-examination. The centers are also active in teaching young people about sexually transmitted diseases (STDs), particularly AIDS, and hold workshops to provide information and answer questions. The results of the program are undoubtedly successful, even though budget allocations hardly meet the need.

As part of her work, Dr. Musmar and other members of her staff deliver lectures on various aspects of their work to people in and outside the forty-four centers of their program. The lectures are focused on STDs, child health care, early detection of breast cancer and cervical cancer, adolescent health, and, most important, methods and reasons for birth control. These subjects are all sensitive, and speaking about them to groups of women who are usually accompanied by their husbands is no easy matter. Because the subject deals with medical issues, Musmar has no choice but to go into scientific descriptions of what is involved, and she has found doing so to be quite acceptable and that it helps bring about positive results among her audience. But scientific jargon cannot be taken out of a cultural context, particularly when it comes to birth control, especially when a large family is a basic ambition for most Jordanians. Supplementing her lectures with religious stories, prophetic traditions, and Qur'anic quotations has helped ease the tensions, give relevance to the sensitive subjects under discussion, and promote the success of the programs. Dr. Musmar believes that efforts should be intensified and strategies changed in existing health programs serving schools throughout Jordan. A new culture and awareness can be created through TV programs on adolescent health and cancer awareness, especially among women. Altogether, better health leads to better thinking and a greater workforce. As an example of success of the approach and methods, Musmar points to the difficulty the program first had with training doctors to become involved in adolescent health. Today, more doctors deal with such diseases as part of their work and do not question their appropriateness. But it was no easy matter. Doctors were invited to attend lectures, and here too the influence of tradition was brought to bear. In fact, to be able to get a hearing in many of the areas served by the health centers, the tribal chiefs of the areas were approached and their support sought. Dr. Musmar mentioned the name of one such tribal leader, Barjas al-Hariri, who facilitated matters greatly by lending his support to her program's efforts, thereby giving it legitimacy in and outside of his area. Here Musmar pointed to the possible importance of the traditional midwife who has been forbidden by law from putting in a contraceptive loop (*lawlab*), although their close connection with the general public makes them ideal for the job.

Musmar and 'Asha are not unique in the methodology they are using to achieve greater success in their efforts for a better life for women. The same approach is taken by lawyers such as Hanan al-Qinna and Manal Shamut of the Business and Professional Women's Club as they lecture to women's groups and students about gender and labor laws. Traditional discourses framing issues of women's rights come naturally to the speakers and to the listeners. Refining such discussions can push for only wider participation of women in public and economic life and, at minimum, present a different outlook toward the role of Islam and its support for women's work.

Fighting for Gender Equality and Human Rights

The past few years have seen an intensification of efforts to improve the legal and professional situation of Jordanian women. The results have been somewhat contradictory and show a general willingness to make it more possible for women to enter the job market but a strong unwillingness to see them play an effective role in decision making. Looking positively at the accomplishments made by women in Jordan, Princess Basma, head of the Jordanian National Committee for Women (JNCW), established in 1992, sees this success as the result of "a strong political will and a wave of interest and commitment across Jordan from state level to civil society." [18]

During the past decade, Jordan has recognized the need for implementing economic reforms to bring about structural adjustments crucial for its future developmental efforts. Women were to play an important role in these projects, as they have in similar programs in other parts of the world. Today with globalization, the imperative for development is greater than ever, and it is becoming clear that changes in the economy cannot take place without the implementation of change in other sectors, notwithstanding traditional resistance to any form of change that threatens the patriarchal order. However, this resistance cannot be underestimated. It may be true that today Jordan has women in the army and policewomen to direct traffic in Amman, that Jordan's deputy prime minister and planning minister were both women in a previous government, or that a woman was appointed as head of the state-owned radio. These examples should not lead to conclusions that "Society is beginning to accept as a fact women's ever-growing role in the daily affairs of public life." [19] Rana Husseini's assessment that these examples may be "brilliant but not enough" is correct, given the severe constraints women face in their struggle for greater human and legal rights. Although the efforts of Queen Rania, Queen Noor, Princess Basma, and other members of the royal family have been powerful and sustained, there remain crucial areas where achievements are yet to make headway. Women may be allowed to provide leadership in areas involving special education, orphan children, and handicrafts, but the political system is all but closed to them, as are positions that involve decision making of particular significance to Jordanian society, politics, or the economy. In other words, women are kept away from serious forms of empowerment.

Conversations with women activists interviewed for this book illustrate their conviction that economic dependence constitutes a fundamental reason for the persistent weakness and peripheralization of women from public life, whether we are talking about the home front or the public front. As long as women are economically dependent, it would be senseless to expect them to become empowered within their families, let alone have a say in the political system. Rather, just as they passively accept the power of a male provider, they will also accept political decisions without question, except perhaps if they involve family or tribe. As the lawyer-activist Reem Abu Hassan explains, women will vote with the nominee of the tribe, and that nominee will always be a male. Samiha al-Tal, who made a bid for a parliamentary seat in Irbid, was boycotted by her own tribe and therefore had no chance of winning.[20] In the Tafila area, a woman who contemplated entering the 1997 elections was actually threatened by members of the tribe because they saw her actions as an insult to the tribe's pride. Abu Hassan explains that a woman's entry into an election gives the impression that there are no men in that tribe who could run for election.

Moral issues pertinent to women's work are very much part of the discourse that keeps women confined politically. The outlook toward gender mixing and morality, discussed earlier, is widely accepted by Jordan's political society and is undoubtedly an important consideration in attitudes regarding confining women's political role. It is, after all, in politics and power that Jordan's patriarchal order is most resistant toward women's participation. It is also here that moral discourses are the most vocal, as in the experience of Tujan Faisal, the first woman, and so far the only woman, elected as deputy to Jordan's Parliament to the great acclaim of Arab women everywhere. Soon after entering the Lower House in 1993, Faisal found herself in trouble for being an outspoken "maverick" unwilling to play the usual token role outlined for women in governments and legislatures of Arab countries. Although Faisal ran on a platform advocating greater rights for women, she soon made enemies of conservatives and the governmental elite. In her earlier career as a television personality, Faisal had made a name for herself as a woman activist, and the feminist platform on which she won the 1993 election called for an end to polygamy and discrimination against women. The Islamic Right was particularly offensive toward Faisal from the beginning of her entry into the Lower House. Not only did she receive death threats, but a parliamentary colleague became so incensed that he threw an ashtray at her. Her insistence to dress as she always had and not cater to Muslim fundamentalists by dressing closer to their concept of Islamic garb angered fundamentalist and conservative members of Parliament. "An orthodox leader offered her a free wardrobe if she would wear a veil, which she refused," and "a fellow deputy, Islamist Abdul Munem Abu Zant, greeted her style of dress with an offer of Islamic garb and sweets if she would agree to stop wearing makeup and change her fashion preferences." [21] The condescension and patriarchal attitude are more than obvious in the offer of sweets by Abu Zant. This clash was not the first between Faisal and Islamists: they had tried to block her effort to run for election by accusing her of apostasy and actually sued in *shari'a* Court, which accepted the case even though it had no jurisdiction; by doing so the court made sure that Faisal was delayed until it became impossible for her to run effectively for office. [22] Like the Nasr Hamid Abu Zayd case in Egypt, Islamic fundamentalists asked the *shari'a* courts to divorce Faisal from her husband on the basis that she had become an apostate for advocating anti-Islamic ideas. The similarities in both cases cannot be coincidental and show the extent to which fundamentalists are willing to go to intimidate and manipulate law to achieve their ends. In both cases, the governments simply stood by and let things happen, perhaps because both Abu Zayd and Faisal also happened to be critics of the government and social inequalities. Faisal herself blames Jordan's government for losing her bid for reelection to the Lower House in 1997. Both fundamentalists and the government "worked hard to prevent her from winning in the elections." [23]

Perhaps governmental opposition existed because Faisal did not stick to women's issues that seem to be acceptable for women politicians in Jordan. It is when women step outside of "women's issues" that they are resented and face insurmountable opposition. "Women's issues do concern me, but there are priorities, because I believe a nation is lost. There are problems such as corruption, poverty and unemployment, which I feel I must fight for. . . . Corruption and the abuse of power have created a huge gap between society's sectors. . . . [T]his will not end unless we have a true democracy which allows the public to question officials." [24]

Faisal's treatment by Jordan's government and judiciary is an important reason for women's reluctance to run for election and for the loss of credibility in women's electability to public office. The Faisal episode must be seen as a major setback for Jordanian and Arab women, even though the animosity was regarding her personally. Even though sixteen women besides Faisal were encouraged and supported by women's groups and by Princess Basma bint Talal, sister of King Hussein and the acknowledged leader of women's issues in Jordan, none of the women candidates had enough credibility to win in the 1997 elections. Today, not a single woman sits in Jordan's Parliament. Kuwait has been severely criticized for refusing to pass a law by which women could run for election, whereas Jordan has been acclaimed for declaring political reforms and vocally encouraging women to participate in public life. Yet, the results have been the same: the Parliaments of both countries have no women representatives.

Many advocates consider a quota system that would assign a number of seats in the Lower House to women as a must for the political system to be opened to women's participation. Opponents see quota systems as an insufficient way to achieve ultimate equality. But the mechanism for quotas already exists; Jordan's National Assembly (Majlis al-Umma) embraces quotas, with twelve seats reserved for Christians and Circassians out of a total of eighty. Allowing women a voice in legislatures is imperative if there is any hope of open, constructive discussions of laws. Quota systems can be temporary, if that method is the only one for allowing women any form of effective political participation. Otherwise, talk of democracy or democratization is just rhetoric. Given the shape of political society in Jordan, however, practical attempts to bring women into decision making are perhaps fallacious. One has but to look at the 1997 elections to understand why. These elections were boycotted by opposition Islamic parties (only five out of nineteen parties ran) such as the Islamic Action Front Party and parties referred to as left wing (members of both groups did run as independents). The justifications for the boycott are the same reasons that greater political participation of women should not be expected unless critical structural steps are undertaken to ensure their involvement. After all, the main reason for boycotting elections was the continued favoritism of Bedouin tribes and families that remain the bulwark of political and military hegemony in Jordan. This situation is normal of tribal-ethnic states, as is the suppression of the freedom of the press through restrictive laws such as the ones passed in 1997. It is important to note that out of the eighty seats in the National Assembly, sixty-eight are held by tribal chiefs. So we are really talking about what I would call the "legislaturization" of tribalism that permeates Jordan's laws. What is ironic and serious about this situation is that to support the existing hegemony, Jordan's political class is representative of tribalism at a time when tribalism itself is a dying way of life and hardly representative of Jordan's population. It is certainly the main reason that change of the conditions of women and Jordan's efforts to expand its economy face insurmountable difficulties. There is sincere interest in development and greater participation of all sectors of Jordan's society, but hegemony and the holding of power stand in the way of these transformations to the ultimate detriment of the very hegemonic sectors that refuse to allow change.

When one considers that King Abdullah's instructions to the Jordanian government regarding abolishing Law 340 allowing for honor crimes were ignored by Jordan's deputies, after having been passed by the Senate (Majlis al-A'yan), several things become clear. The Senate is composed of forty members, all chosen by the king and representing important persons and groups in Jordan. Three women were chosen as members, and their presence and sponsorship without doubt played an important role in seeing that this effort passed successfully to the deputies for consideration. After its defeat by the deputies, the Senate was still able to have the matter shelved for future consideration. Here is an example of a situation where women are included and their opinions heard and where the majority of a council represent liberal and business elements of Jordan's society whose experiences and interests go beyond the existing hegemonic order. In the Lower House, however, the initiative failed drastically, notwithstanding royal patronage, government efforts, and social activism. Hamza Haddad, the highly respected minister of justice at the time of the vote, explained the difficulties the government faced in trying to change this law against the opposition's claim that these tamperings with social traditions were being forced on Jordan by the West and Zionism, rhetoric that always seems to be unleashed to face serious demands for change. A proposal by Haddad to tighten laws dealing with honor crimes by the addition of a line to Law 340 of Jordan's criminal code stating that "law 98 does not apply in situations involving law 340" was also opposed in Parliament. Law 98 opens the door to reduced sentencing of perpetrators of honor crimes by allowing for a looser interpretation of "crimes of passion," as discussed in chapter 7. The change seemed simple and fitting with the actual intent of Law 340, but the proposal failed to pass. One can say that such failure is partially owing to the form that the battle to change the laws took, the language used, and the proposals made that were more attuned to human rights debates and not framed through cultural constructs familiar to the Jordanian general public.

Perhaps a different approach such as is used by women activists 'Asha and Qaddumi, or government executives such as Musmar, would achieve different results. Although the door is not open to women to participate in the political process, it is wide open for them when it comes to women's organizations and activities that concern women and children. The earliest women's organization with the aim of working for improving the status of women in Jordan was the Jordanian Hashemite Women's Society formed in 1949, followed in 1950 by the Young Women's Christian Association whose goals included promoting women's socioeconomic role and training them in leadership skills. The agenda set out by these early organizations continues to be at the heart of programs advocated by various women's groups in Jordan today. Later associations, such as the League to Defend Women's Rights formed in 1952, were to add political activism to the agenda. Since 1953, the Jordanian Women's Union, with nearly five thousand members, has acted as the leading women's organization, supporting a strong feminist agenda calling for equal rights for women and ending gender discrimination. The union's program is quite ambitious and multidirectional, providing free legal counseling to women who cannot afford to pay for it, spreading literacy among women, as well as pushing for legal reforms to provide women with greater work opportunities and leverage in personal status laws. Among important women's organizations is the Business and Professional Women's Club established in Amman in 1976 that is very active in providing legal counseling and has a hot line that any woman can call to have legal questions about personal status laws or business answered by lawyers who specialize in these fields. The BPWC also holds important seminars and provides the wider community with legal and business information through lectures delivered by its lawyers and members in schools and civil centers. Besides an impressive legal and business library, the club provides a unique service in the form of what they refer to as a business incubator. There, women entrepreneurs can start their businesses without having to shoulder overhead costs when starting out. The incubator leases them office space, and provides secretarial help and business hardware such as computers, telephones, and Internet access.

In 1977, the Queen Alia Fund for Social Development was established under the leadership of Princess Basma bint Talal. The goals of the fund reflect the continued concerns of Jordanian women regarding the need to spread educational awareness, raise literacy and health standards, and struggle for greater rights for women. With chapters in various parts of Jordan, it is important to coordinate such activities among various communities. The Princess Basma Women's Resource Centre, established in 1996, was a further effort to support and coordinate the women's committees and other organizations around the country. In 1992 the Jordanian government asked Princess Basma to establish and head the Jordanian National Committee for Women, which was designed as the highest policy-making body for women in Jordan. The committee was intended to push for greater women's rights, to coordinate different women's organizations, and to submit laws to the Jordanian Parliament that pertain to women's issues.

The committee has been the center through which most efforts to change Jordan's labor and personal status laws have taken place. In this aspect, the JNCW can be said to have played a dual role. According to the lawyer-advocate Nur al-Imam, the committee has been a force in organizing and coordinating efforts to change laws and political activism. In the last elections held in Jordan, the committee sponsored thirteen candidates, helping pay for their campaigns and giving them greater access to the media. However, none of them succeeded, which in itself illustrates the problems with such government-sponsored national committees that have little contact with and hence impact on the constituencies they are supposed to represent, in this case Jordanian women who showed no tendency to support the committee's nominees. But the JNCW has succeeded in fighting for and passing laws that provide women with greater rights in regards to child care on the job for working mothers in industries that hire ten or more women, to free movement at night for women without being stopped on suspicion of prostitution, to maternity leave, and to better working conditions and pay (see chapter 4). But according to al-Imam and Qaddumi, the committee has also acted as a buffer controlling the activities of women and molding women's demands to the "temper" and intents of the state. Projects and demands for legal changes are filtered through the committee so that by the time they are submitted to the Parliament they are what can be described as "politically correct." Here, little that would disturb the hegemony is allowed to pass through. A good example has to do with the minimum age for marriage, a subject that unifies all activists as an essential step for gaining greater rights for women. At present the minimum age of marriage for girls is fifteen. At such an age a girl has not even finished school. By the time she is eighteen and reaches legal majority, she would be a mother of one or two children with little chance of continuing her schooling, taking a job, or opening her own business. Her peripheralization is ensured before she has left her childhood. Raising the minimum age of marriage for girls to eighteen would allow her to finish school, reach legal majority, and play an actual role in defining her future. Furthermore, marrying and having children at an early age have health repercussions that cannot be discounted. The opposition to raising the minimum marital age comes mainly from tribal areas where the predominant belief is that marrying a daughter early controls possible promiscuity and hence protects family honor. Feminist efforts to have two minimum ages for marriage by which tribal women could be married at fifteen but not the rest of Jordan have failed. The biggest problem in this battle, according to activists, is that the committee has stalled in fighting for it in the Parliament. A new effort to change the minimum age for marriage is at present being undertaken by the Jordanian government. The law is intended to satisfy all parties by setting the minimum age at eighteen while at the same time allowing the judge to permit the marriage of a girl at fifteen if the situation is appropriate and with the agreement of the parents and the bride and bridegroom (similar to laws governing marriage in many Western countries). Although the law keeps the door open for earlier marriage, establishing eighteen as the minimum age and controlling the judicial process by which earlier marriage would be allowed should prove to be a step in the right direction. In fact, if Jordan does pass this minimum-age law, then it would be at the forefront in regards to this issue because other Islamic countries recognize the age of sixteen as the minimum age for marriage.

At the heart of the battle for women's rights stand the clear and admitted contradictions between intentions represented by the Constitution and the royal and administrative leadership's vocalized ambitions to improve the life of women in Jordan. Any changes involve jockeying among various interests and reducing the intent and impact of the laws, as exemplified by the efforts to reduce the minimum age for the marriage of girls. In other words, changing laws is proving extremely difficult; in fact, a proposed amended personal status law that incorporates very modest changes has been stalled in the Parliament for years. A new effort to change gender laws was launched by King Abdullah soon after being seated on Jordan's throne. A new human rights committee was formed and assigned the job of supervising Jordan's laws and courts to ensure compliance with international human rights agreements to which Jordan is a signatory. The committee was also given a mandate to come up with suggestions regarding personal status laws through which greater protection for women and children could be ensured. Given structural transformations caused by a changing economy and social conditions, there is a recognized need to develop the political system so as to expand democracy and greater participation in Jordan's political institutions. Therefore, the mandate given by the king to the Jordanian government and hence to the Committee on Human Rights is to look at standing laws and suggest changes that promote human rights and general freedoms, to study the realities of human rights in Jordan, and to give specific suggestions regarding the relations of citizens with the various administrative structures of the government so that there would be greater equal opportunity for political participation and to ensure the rule of law and greater justice in the legal system for all Jordanian citizens equally. The mandate is wide and has the full support of the king who chose the former prime minister of Jordan, Ahmad 'Ubaidat, one of the most highly respected public figures in Jordan's political and civil societies today, to head the committee.

Meeting with 'Ubaidat was very informative regarding Jordan's outlook toward gender questions, the priorities that Jordan's elders place on the various constraints facing women, and the possible solutions to these problems. The structure of the committee and its executive organization, which includes a subcommittee interested in complaints and grievances (*shakawa* and *Mazalim*) that listens to the public to ascertain the most pressing problems and try to come up with solutions. A second subcommittee focuses totally on penal and personal status laws with special emphasis on how *shari'a* courts handle cases concerning women and children. The third subcommittee discusses methods of education and instruction (*taw'iyya*) that are necessary, according to 'Ubaidat, because "the problem is not only the lack of action but also the lack of communications and cooperation between people and the various institutions of government. There is need to educate and inform the public so there would be some acceptance to be able to advance human rights. Here important roles are to be played through ministries of education, culture and *awqaf* all of which are represented in the Committee."

The selection of the penal code (*qanun al-'uqubat*), followed by personal status laws (*qanun al-ahwal al-shakhsiyya*) dealing with marriage, divorce, and child custody, was intended to make the law more equitable for women from within Islamic parameters as well as human rights principles. The Egyptian experiment in passing *khul'* divorce laws in January 2000, which opened the door to women to receive a divorce within three months after submitting a request to the judge, is an important precedent. As in Egypt, where Islamic principles and legal traditions were used to change personal status laws, the committee, like most Jordanians, agrees that it is only through Islamic parameters that the laws of Jordan can be changed. Open dialogue and discussions of gender issues in the Egyptian media and among different civil groups are particularly impressive, and 'Ubaidat is hoping that the same openness will be applied to the committee's legal suggestions. It is only by involving the wider public in the debate that solutions can be hammered out and the laws refined. It would also make the new laws more acceptable to the public, who would gain greater knowledge and participate in the debates. This fact would be particularly true because the language used would stem from what is familiar to the general public (*khususiyat*) and would not be in conflict with traditions or obfuscated by an unfamiliar language more suited to international women's movements. Here 'Ubaidat voices his concern with the overemphasis that has been given to women's groups that worked hard and put forth important proposals but with little success. 'Ubaidat makes an important point here. Having women's groups and large numbers of "closed-in" women activities that include very few Jordanian women from within particular social classes are of little use, no matter how important the suggestions being made by these groups. The debate has to become public, widely discussed by women groups and all other groups, and then we can hope for a greater understanding of what it is that is being tried.

Religious schools (*kuliyat al-shari'a*) and *shari'a* court judges (*al-qada' al-shar'i*) also have a serious break from the public that 'Ubaidat hopes to remedy. As he informed me during our meeting:

There is a lack of understanding of Islam in schools and the type of teaching that goes on in *kulliyat al-shari'a* has little to do with what Jordan and its people need today. This is particularly so in the education and training of preachers. Such training is very important because they are the ones who determine the relations and fate of society particularly as judges. Their standard today is quite poor. The question of leadership is of the essence here, the right person must be chosen for the minister of *awqaf,* he must be highly educated and open-minded giving greater attentions to Jordan's laws and courts rather than focusing primarily on the yearly pilgrimage (*hajj*), fasting and other matters. This position must be one characterized by continuity.

What are the priorities set out by the committee to give greater human rights to women? Although recognizing the need to stop honor crimes, the committee concluded that this fight would have to take a secondary position when compared to the most severe problem facing Jordanian women today: divorce and destitution of not only women but also children from broken marriages. Court records and legal complaints to the BPWC's legal advice division and their hot line confirm the committee's finding. Without doubt, the greatest hindrances facing Jordanian women are the ease with which husbands can divorce them and their lack of effective legal recourse to receive financial support or entitlements due to both the divorced wife and her children (see chapters 4 and 6). "The husband leaves, no *nafaqa* is available, the decision from court has little effective meaning, her pride is in tatters and all the money is gone." As an answer, 'Ubaidat proposes that a *sunduq al-zakat* (religious tax box) be used to pay a woman her alimony until her husband can be found and made to repay it. "The *sunduq* has a lot of money in it and can be put to good use." As for divorce, which occurs at alarming rates, the committee is suggesting that all divorces be referred to committees of conciliation (*lijan islah);* before a man can divorce his wife he has to allow the committee to reconcile him with his wife and vice versa. This suggestion follows with Islamic rules stated by the Qur'an and should be widely acceptable to the public. A married man would also have to go in front of such committees if he wants to take another wife. Here, principles of the general good, need (*darura*), and financial ability (*qudra 'ala al-infaq*) would apply. The husband would have to prove that having a second wife promotes the general good of his family and society, that there is an imperative need for a second wife, and that he has the ability to support both. If the *qadi* accepts his proof and permits him to take another wife, both his existing wife and the new bride he intends to marry would have to be informed about each other before the marriage can take place. Without doubt, such steps, in keeping with Islam, would reduce the number of second marriages, which constitute a major cause for divorce today.

Changing gender laws is no easy matter, according to 'Ubaidat. Gender struggle causes only greater confusion and mistrust between men and women that cannot bring about positive results because no side is willing to compromise in such conflicts.

> Twisting arms are counter-productive when they are in conflict with social traditions that are very difficult to change and that often have very little to do with religion. The real differences between those who want to change the life of women and act not only locally but internationally is that they leave most women confused about what it is that they are talking about. The problem with feminism in Arab world is not question of roles, but personal gains. But possibilities are there for positive changes regarding women; education in particular is very important to change these conditions. All activities seem to be isolated in the salons of Amman and quite isolated from the real problems that Jordanian women face. They need to look at the real problems without big slogans (*manshitat*) that are not understood. For example, feminists talk "Peking," but this has very little to do with what people understand. There is no focus on priorities that take the realities in consideration, so many groups and committees. This fragmentation (*tashatut*) needs to be looked at. It has become more of gaining positions, funding, titles, rather than a real cohesive populist movement among women meaning to address the real problems facing Jordanian women today.[25]

The Committee on Human Rights's findings and suggestions have been completed and presented to the Jordanian Parliament for integration into the legal system. Will the Parliament accept its suggestions? Will they be adopted and applied? It remains to be seen, but already King Abdullah has moved to pass the committee's suggestions, which were approved by Jordan's government in November 2001, into temporary law, which would continue in effect until and unless the Jordanian Parliament votes against it. It has been almost two years since the completion of this book manuscript, and the present changes in the law are going into effect in Jordan as the book goes to press. The suggested legal changes are important enough to warrant discussing them, even though they are clearly much less than needs to be done or what the Committee on Human Rights proposed, and it is too early to know whether they will stand the Parliament's scrutiny or prove as effective as their potential indicates. The watering down of legal proposals to fit with political realities in Jordan is itself illustrative of the incredible difficulties involved in changing these laws. A good example is the question of minimum age for marriage discussed earlier and the suggestion that two minimum ages for marriage be allowed to satisfy tribal concerns. Previous efforts in that direction failed because the philosophical outlook toward parental control is not confined to the existing tribal areas but is in fact part of the Jordanian social fabric, as this manuscript has pointed out. The new temporary laws for 2001 came in the form of a compromise to satisfy these patriarchal concerns, while at the same time giving civil rights and women's groups what they have long fought for by setting the minimum age for the marriage of both male and female at eighteen, though leaving the door open for marrying girls at the age of fifteen if the situation fits criteria to be set by the chief *qadi* of the *shari'a* courts of Jordan. In other words, fifteen years of age would not be confined to tribal areas but would apply to all women in Jordan. Given social practices and traditions of marriage based largely on culture and class, even if this law is not reversed by Parliament, it does not achieve much except to give the appearance that the minimum age for the marriage of girls has been raised when in fact it will depend on criteria set by the chief *qadi*. Given precedence and the traditions followed in Jordan's *shari'a* courts, the criteria established by the chief *qadi* are bound to fit with patriarchal authority.

The same observations apply to Law 340 of Jordan's criminal code, which permits reduced sentencing for perpetrators of honor crimes. As explained in this book, Law 340 is one of the most serious laws in regards to limiting the effectiveness of the rule of law. This fact has been recognized by Jordan's government, women activists, and the legal system at large. The previous minister of justice, Hamza Haddad, tried to change the law by limiting its applicability, but his efforts failed to pass because of resistance by Jordan's Parliament. Two dramatic results appear in the proposed changes to Law 340. The first is the inclusion of the words *"fil hal,"* which roughly means "immediately," "instantly," or "without delay." The new temporary law would require that to be able to benefit from reduced sentencing, "a man is surprised (*fugi'*) by [finding] his wife or any of his first degree or second degree female relatives [*usul* or *furu'*, meaning direct blood relations such as first cousins, or secondary relations] or his sisters committing adultery (*zina*) or in an illegal bed and killed her on the spot (*fil hal*)."[26] Here the fulfillment of "intent," pointed out in chapter 7 of this book, is met. This law, which still has to stand the scrutiny of Parliament, could prove to be of great significance in limiting leniency toward perpetrators of honor crimes because most of these crimes are committed long after discovery of a "dishonorable" act and mostly on the basis of hearsay. However, success of this law will depend on the full cooperation of the police, particularly in regards to evidence and findings, and on the judiciary and its willingness to apply *fil hal* as intended by the meaning of the word *"fugi'"* (shocked by surprise and hence acting irrationally, which is the requirement for reduced sentences in case of honor crimes). If this rule of law is not followed strictly—that is, if courts choose to interpret and apply the obvious and clear meaning of the intended law differently—then little will have been achieved.

Another change to the criminal code extends the benefits of reduced sentencing to a woman who kills or harms her husband, his female companion, or both if she catches them committing *zina* in the marital home. This law corrects the gender inequality in regards to the penal codes involving *zina* discussed earlier in this book. This step, which brings Jordanian laws closer to their counterparts in France from which the idea of "intent" originates, is in the right direction. The inequality, however, continues because the law confines the woman's discovery of her husband's cheating to the marital home and applies only to cheating with other women, thereby restricting the meaning of *zina* to heterosexual relationships. Nonetheless, the proposed laws are clear steps forward.

Perhaps the greatest achievement of the new temporary laws concerns the wife's right to *khul'* divorce. Following the success of the Egyptian precedent in *khul'* divorce that recognized *khul'* as a woman's divorce and allowed her to sue for a divorce that she would receive within three months without the approval of the husband or agreement of the *qadi,* Jordan is pursuing the same line in its newly suggested laws but went one step further by reducing the waiting period between suing for divorce and receiving that divorce to one month. The woman would have to give up the dowry paid to her by her husband and other financial benefits following her divorce. Without doubt, this achievement is the most important of the new laws and will, one hopes, withstand the scrutiny of Parliament once it is back in session.

It is important to point out that the committee followed a line of thinking of changes in personal status laws from within Islamic traditions and with concepts of *maslaha, istihsan,* and *istihbab* in mind. This basis should be important for the success and permanency of these laws.

Given the discussion presented earlier in this chapter illustrating the importance of the Islamic and traditional discourse, whether we are talking about the advocates of women's rights or conservatives who refuse to grant much leeway to women, particularly in regards to political activism, the suggestions of 'Ubaidat's Committee on Human Rights bridge an important gap between various groups. If the committee's suggestions meet with success and become in fact a mandate for the government to enforce as Jordan's king seems to want, Jordan will have set an important precedent for Arab and Islamic countries that are facing the same issues and problems in trying to implement greater rights for their citizens.

Economic Empowerment: Women in Business

How are discourses on women and work reflected in the actual, practical lives of women? Does the "nature" of woman make her incapable of being a successful business- and professional woman who is confined in her abilities to perform only particular jobs suited to that nature? Or are personality, experience, training, and personal abilities more important factors in the making of a woman's career? Interviews with women in various types of business give answers to these important questions. Here we find important contradictions between the experience of businesswomen and the rhetoric regarding women's work. Although women have proved quite successful in Jordan, finding no difficulty in being accepted by male counterparts with whom they do business, there is still significant appreciation of dominant moral discourses, if perhaps without the same slant. Women entrepreneurs I interviewed did not seem to find any difficulty working with men and in being respected by them. They attributed that fact to their seriousness and professionalism and because they "deliver," which is essential in the business world. In private enterprise, therefore, women have found themselves not as confronted with efforts to push them out of the market as have their sisters who are employed in white-collar jobs and who Islamic fundamentalists insist are taking jobs that should be given to men. Three types of entrepreneurs are interviewed here, ranging from large-scale businesswomen, small-scale women who do business at the microfinancial level, and women who are in the process of building their own businesses and who describe the frustrations and severe difficulties in trying to achieve such a dream. All are women who live in Jordan, representing different sectors of society, and all are believers in the ability of women to achieve as much as men, if given the opportunity.

"Readiness and a sense of adventure are the necessary elements for any woman to succeed in private enterprise." This statement was Sanaa Burqan's answer to my question "What does it take for a woman to succeed in developing her own business?" Burqan is a pharmacist trying to build her business of marketing for pharmaceutical companies whose representation she was able to win. Like her other four colleagues who run their business from the BPWC business incubator in Amman, she was frank and open in her discussion of the many difficulties that women who are trying to build their businesses face. These difficulties range from opposition of family, discouragement of friends, lack of capital, requirements of the BPWC in regards to use of the club's incubator, and the business community at large. All who attended the meeting agreed with Burqan that a woman, like a man, must have the will and ambition to go into business and that she must also be willing to take a chance and have a sense of adventure. Established businesswomen such as Hind 'Abdel-Jaber and Sobhiyya al-Ma'ni voiced the same opinion when asked the same question. In 'Abdel-Jaber's case, she felt that her family had an important role in giving her a business sense that she would otherwise have lacked. It was this business sense that made her understanding of the market easier, gave her the courage to enter into the business world, and gave her credibility among her business colleagues. Readiness and training are vital for a woman to succeed, according to 'Abdel-Jaber.

A sense of adventure, the wish to do something productive, the need to support the family or supplement its income, and the will to succeed were central answers given in microfinancial projects started by women with whom I met. It is this will that helps the individual overcome the severe difficulties, particularly when the enterprise fails, as quite often happens, especially because of lack of marketing experience, understanding of the market, support, and capital. "If you fail, try again," said one lady who borrowed money to open a women's clothing shop. She lives in a nice house with her husband and two children, and had time on her hands and a need to supplement her income to meet the rise in the cost of living. Even though there are no clothing stores in that area, it soon became clear that the hilly area outside Amman did not attract customers because they preferred to go to shop where there is a greater variety. Faced with failure, she decided to try again and came up with the idea of opening a hairdressing shop that had a better chance of success for numerous reasons. The most important overhead cost was the shop itself, for which she opened access from the street to the first floor of her house and made it into the salon. A microfinancial loan allowed her to buy the equipment needed for the shop, and the running expenses were manageable. This solution is important because the tradition in such small businesses is to sell clothes on credit. Doing so facilitates sales, but it also means that there is no money to pay off loans or to buy new products. The risk factor is not the problem, because this system of buying on credit from small retailers is widespread and well accepted in Jordan. Almost all such sales are paid for. It is the timing and the nature of the business that are problematic, especially if the owner wants to increase the size of the business.

Selling on credit seems to be in the background of problems with microfinancial projects. The various women involved in selling to the public from their homes, which constitutes an important sector of customers, all seemed to face the same problem. Because loans have to be paid on time and interest is calculated from the time the loan is contracted, business owners seem to hesitate to renew such loans for fear of reneging on payments, not because they are unsuccessful in marketing their products but particularly because they sell on credit and have to wait for their customers to receive their salaries or, in many cases, for their husbands to provide them with the funds. Buying on credit was a method used not only in clothes retailing but also in buying home furnishings (pots, pans, blankets, and so on) and groceries. Umm Khalid and Umm Muhammad's groceries both sell on credit. Although the latter's grocery also has a brisk cash business, she too has difficulty in meeting financial obligations, although she admits she would not have been able to keep her shop or furnish it with the extensive selection of goods if it had not been for such loans. It is the interest on the loans that is the same as regular banking loans with no breaks for these projects as well as the conditions according to which the loans have to be repaid that are of particular concern to these women. Some resort to seasonal business to be able to raise capital to pay for the loans and keep their businesses going. In one such case, the microfinancial loan was taken out to help establish a dairy business, to produce cream and cheese for customers in Amman. But the borrower resorted to growing a nursery of houseplants to supplement her income. She also buys sheep from the countryside, growing them in her garden until the time of the big feast when she sells them for slaughter. She had stopped doing so after taking out her loan with the hope of expanding her dairy business, but the weight of the repayments made it difficult for her business to increase, and she had to turn back to old methods for raising capital. In this particular case, she encourages both her son and her daughter to take jobs outside the home, even though they too are involved in the business. The mother has no problem with her daughter working, but she permits her to do so only in an all-women workplace. Questions of morality are of particular importance here, even though she herself travels, buys the sheep, and undertakes sales.

Shortage of capital seems to be the most important problem facing women entrepreneurs who are involved with the business incubator of the BPWC.

When Maha al-Misri made up her mind to go into business for herself, it was not an easy decision. Mother of four, including twins, she had little capital to start her business. Having graduated with a degree in computer programming, she was hoping to find stable employment in one of the many companies opening in Jordan with large computing needs. Things did not work out that way: women were the last employed and the first to be let go, jobs were insecure, and in small businesses it was hard for a pregnant woman or mother to keep her job. Her last resort was to open her own business. She had the ideas and the will and believed that a woman could be as successful as a man. Her project was to produce CDs for children that would teach them through pictures and sound not only how to read but also the various subjects they take in school as well as introduce literature suited to their age. Her husband was willing to go along, even though it meant that his salary would have to pay for all household expenses as well as her project until it began to pay for itself. Interestingly, his only stipulation was that she not let anyone know that she was starting her own business until she succeeded. This way they would not be open to social criticism. She learned about the incubator when she called the BPWC asking for business consultation. Seeing a good opportunity, she applied to the club and was approved to receive the facilities provided by the incubator. As she began to develop her product, however, a number of matters became evident. For one thing, the promises made to her and her colleagues had been exaggerated. There was no money to help them start their businesses, which had been their primary attraction to the club. Moreover, the expenses for office space, office equipment, computer usage, photocopying, and business training were too heavy for a business that had yet to start, let alone take off. Most important for al-Misri was access to the Internet. The club charged for using the telephone, and therefore the cost of getting on the Internet was all but prohibitive, even though it was essential for al-Misri's software development. Why had they accepted her project in the first place if they knew that they could not provide her the facilities that her project required? That good question is one that al-Misri asks as she faces the possibility of having to close down after all the money and effort spent. The actual assistance she has been given by the club was paltry in her estimation, a sentiment voiced by most of her colleagues.

Mona Mundhir Malhas added another dimension to the financial problems facing businesswomen who are struggling to become established. An architect by profession, Malhas worked in a design office for many years before deciding to venture out on her own. Her reasons for doing so were not only that she had the will and the ambition, but also that employment in small businesses in Jordan appeared to be a dead end for employees like herself. Advancement and raises were slow and rare. Realizing that she would face a financial crunch were she to quit her job without having established her business and started earning an income, she faced two problems. First, the BPWC, whose facilities she needed if she were to be able to begin her business, required that she have no other employment before they would agree to sign any contracts with her. Second, her license could not be registered in two working places at the same time. To be able to license her business, she had to remove her license from the office where she was employed. For a business such as hers to take off she needed time, but such time was not granted her by the club, whose new regulations require termination if a monthly payment is missed. To pay her bills while establishing her business, Malhas has had to take in partial jobs that are throwbacks to the type of work she performed when she first graduated from college. Nevertheless, she is enthusiastic, is beginning to design houses for customers, and believes that the hardship has been worth it. Like her colleagues, however, she too saw the club as short-changing her when it came to expectations and the heavy financial burden that she did not anticipate when she first started her business with the incubator.

Notwithstanding the criticism addressed to the club, there was general agreement that without the incubator these entrepreneurs would not have been able to open their own businesses. It not only facilitated matters, provided them with office space, and saved them crippling overhead costs, but also provided business and legal advice that they could not have afforded elsewhere. The disappointment voiced was not regarding what the club has been able to give them so far, but pertained to the obvious deterioration and lack of fulfillment of promises that seem to have grown significantly during the past year. Infighting and a lack of funds seem to have been the main reasons for this deterioration, according to the entrepreneurs. The fact that a man was hired as the head of the incubator seemed to stick in their throats; a woman would have presented a much better front for a business built on women's enterprise. The club itself is an important center that opened in 1976 and is a member of the International Federation of Professional and Business Women whose membership extends throughout 130 countries and includes three-quarters of a million women who own businesses or are members of professions. Jordan was one of the first Arab countries to create such a club, founded by the important feminist In'am al-Mufti, who was counselor to Queen Noor and a former minister of social development. Hind 'Abdel-Jaber was vice president for the National Federation when al-Mufti was its president; later 'Abdel-Jaber became the president of the BPWC until last year when Buthaina Jarana was elected to that position. With a strong belief in helping women start their own businesses, 'Abdel-Jaber ran for election to the National Federation, and as its new president she is today expanding the idea of a business and professional club outside of Amman, with three more clubs in Irbid, Aqaba, and Zarqa'. The National Federation for Professional and Business Women today has a membership of five hundred women, and it is spreading its activity throughout Jordan, which is particularly necessary with the increase in women's education (especially at university and higher education levels), job opportunities, and interest among women who want to open their own businesses.

There is a serious demand for the business training and legal knowledge that these clubs can provide in areas outside of Amman. 'Abdel-Jaber is a strong believer in the need to disseminate information about potential businesses and possibilities to women throughout Jordan. "Being focused on Amman alone serves little purpose, not only because there is a need to involve larger strata of Jordan's women in business, but also the potential for business expansion is much larger." Here 'Abdel-Jaber outlines what she believes are business methods that would bring large numbers of women into the productive process but would also be very suitable to the nature of Jordanian society. "Women want to work, they ask for help to find jobs. Their husbands are not opposed to their work. The problem is the working-environment and conditions where they are employed." To 'Abdel-Jaber, discourses that call upon women to stay at home are really in the past and have no place today. What she sees is a new dynamism and a wish to live a better life among both women and men throughout Jordan. In her efforts to educate and disseminate knowledge of business opportunities for women outside of Amman, 'Abdel-Jaber was not surprised that she was approached by women who came to listen to lectures, attended meetings, or simply heard of her organization's efforts. Not only did they want to know about job opportunities and ways in which they could earn money to help supplement their families' income, but they were also asking for help in finding jobs or ways to bring work home so as to earn a living and help cover the financial needs of their families. Pointing to the silk-growing experience of Philippine women who are organized in a cottage industry that farms out the business at its various stages—from silkworm to weaving—allowing women in various areas of the Philippines to participate and make an income, each within the area fitting her capabilities, the Philippine silk industry has provided large numbers of women with jobs all over the country. She points to the same type of approach taken by other Asian countries in such industries as bicycles and clothing, and believes that such a model is well suited for Jordanian women. Her reasons are interesting and worthwhile pursuing. First, Jordanian women are used to working from the home; it is part of their traditions, and they are more than willing to be involved in cottage industries. Second, cottage industries are nothing new to them but have traditionally been part of their social history. Third, tribal women are central to production and sale of goods at home such as spinning and weaving wool or embroidery that they sell individually or as part of NGO efforts. What is needed is an organized effort in particular towns that could be involved in particular trades and would provide employment to wider sectors of society. Such an experiment has yet to be attempted in Jordan.

Most important, such an approach does not conflict with the traditions of Jordanian families, but instead supplements and reinsures them. So, women who are looking for work can do so but from within traditional methods of production. Another important finding of 'Abdel-Jaber is that contrary to presumptions, husbands are usually supportive of their wives' efforts, and want their wives to work and find jobs that would bring supplemental income to the family at a time of increased financial difficulties. So the question to be asked is not "Should women work?" but rather "What work can they do?" or "How can they be helped in finding work?" and "What industries are best suited for women?" Without industries to provide employment, there should be little expectation that more women will strive to be educated or enter the workforce.

Because most women who live outside of urban centers dress conservatively and are often veiled, the connection between wearing what is considered to be a symbol of oppression and women's willingness and ability to work should be treated as rhetoric rather than as representative of reality. I have found it to be true among women involved in microfinancial projects, all of whom are small-scale, if aspiring, entrepreneurs. They are mostly veiled and live conservative lives, which does not stop them from pursuing their businesses and interests. Of course, the key here, as 'Abdel-Jaber emphasizes, has to do with background, training, and knowledge of the job market and business opportunities. It is through wider programs that will provide women with business knowledge, not necessarily advanced but at a very basic level, especially in regards to how to open and run a business and the advantages of being in the market, that greater participation can be achieved. Most efforts of this type have been concentrated in or around Amman, yet the needs are far greater outside Amman where women are interested in work but have little opportunity or business knowledge. That these areas are conservative should not mean that they have no business viability. To the contrary, the lack of blue- or white-color work means that the potential for women to become interested in private enterprises and cottage industry is much greater. The conservative and Islamic discourses may talk about a moral framework involving no gender mixing, but they encourage women to work and be productive.

The picture in Jordan is positive for women. There is movement at every level and a willingness to fight back when faced with failure and opposition. The will is there, and, perhaps more important, so is awareness that the millennium is bringing about transformations and opportunities for women, and Jordan's women are ready to get involved. New ideas and methods are clearly required to push forward, and, even more important, more financial allocations are necessary if entrepreneurial and microfinancial projects are to be expanded. Rules regarding allocation of capital and loans also need to be reviewed with activism in mind. Women want to be involved, but simply do not have the capital to do so, and the interest rates charged to small businesses are oriented toward profit making rather than allowing small and microbusinesses to grow. Without growth there will be little enthusiasm for more Jordanian women to join the experiment. But the interest is there, and the new Jordanian woman is clearly ambitious in education, work, political activism, and business. She simply needs a boost from the government through more equitable laws that protect her, a different discourse that recognizes her as both a working woman and a traditional mother with strong religious beliefs, and an economic system that would give her a wider berth.

Conclusion

What Next?

JORDANIAN women run state radio stations and satellite channels, sit on municipal councils, advise the king on economic affairs and direct traffic in Amman's unruly streets. . . . But despite the encouragement they are getting, many complain that the male-dominated traditionally conservative society in Jordan continues to deny them some of their basic rights." [1] These words seem to sum up the dilemma in which Jordanian women find themselves today. On the one hand, sincere and extensive efforts are exerted to open up the economy to women, but on the other hand, basic rights and freedoms are closed to them and without these freedoms ambitions are curtailed. A few years ago, women's meetings held in Irbid, Mafraq, Aqaba, and Zarqa' made a list of the most serious challenges faced by Jordanian women today. A national agenda was set and demands made for legal changes that they viewed as imperative for the future of women if Jordan was to enter the new millennium with any hope of parity with other countries of the world. This 1997 agenda attempted to answer legal, political, and social contradictions complicating the lives of women expressed in Princess Basma's words quoted above and analyzed in this book. [2] The agenda also supports the conclusions reached by the Committee on Human Rights, headed by 'Ubaidat, that the number-one problem faced by Jordanian women today is polygamy and a man's right to divorce his wife at will and without controls. Not only does it cause psychological fear and hence increase male patriarchy and power, but it also increases the numbers of destitute women and children who are left without any financial support. Making things even harder, the legal system is inadequate in meeting the challenge of enforcing its own laws and is itself characterized by patriarchy from the judiciary down to the very safekeeping forces whose job is to execute the law. Interestingly, the women's agenda parallels the Committee on Human Rights in demanding redress by the govern-

251

ment of unilateral divorce through a change of the laws to ensure that there are justifiable reasons for divorce, that alimony support for wife and children be sufficient, that payment of alimony be enforced, and that women be protected against polygamy. Of the other nine priorities on the agenda, four deal with personal status issues, ranging from the need for a law to protect women and children from emotional and physical abuse to a law to protect them against homelessness. Here too there is agreement with the Committee on Human Rights.

In this book, I have tried to explain the problems facing Jordanian women today, particularly the obstructions in the job market or opening their own businesses. Labor laws figure strongly in this argument because many of them not only contradict each other, but also discriminate against women and often act as a push factor encouraging them to leave their jobs. Significantly, the study emphasizes the connection between women's work and personal status laws that determine gender relations and place women under the legal authority of male relatives. As the NGO leader and Peking veteran Sahar Naseer articulated to me, "If a woman has no power at home, we cannot expect her to have a leadership role in business. Empowerment must begin in the home." Naseer's argument is an important one and is vocalized not only by Jordanian women, as the women's agenda and Princess Basma's words illustrate, but by women who live under similar conditions the world over as well. Jordanian laws make no mystery of this fact by making it a requirement for any married woman to receive her husband's permission before she can take a job. Legal constraints that inhibit women from entering the market as employees or employers are therefore to be looked for in various legal codes, such as penal codes that permit violence against women, inhibit them from taking leadership positions, allow them to work only to serve their families, and promote fear of retaliation if they "don't tow the line" set for them by fathers, husbands, brothers, uncles, and male cousins. Protection of the law becomes constrained in a situation where the honor of the family is placed exclusively on the shoulders of women, whereas any dishonorable action by a man is dismissed through the payment of *diyya* compensation to the (usually female) victim's family.

Marrying girls early leads to the same results. Early marriage and motherhood mean less of a chance for education and potential for involvement in the country's economy. The possibilities are nipped in the bud. As Maha al-Misri stressed during our meeting at the Business and Professional Women's Club, the literacy rate may be high among women in Jordan, but that fact does not mean that education is widespread. Jordan is not a "reading culture and there is little education to be learned outside of school." This situation is an important reason behind efforts to raise the minimum age of marriage for girls. Besides the physical and psychological health repercussions caused by early marriage and motherhood, women activists who are fighting for a greater economic and political role for women recognize the difficulty of bringing substantial change if early marriage continues. Training later in life becomes harder for women and cannot be as widely inclusive. Many associations in Jordan have directed their efforts toward training women in leadership and business skills, but much more is needed, as Hind 'Abdel-Jaber has pointed out and is working for. But as noted by Jordanian educators, much more can be accomplished if girls get a chance to mature, achieve some level of self-confidence, and realize some of their potential before being hustled into marriage.

Patriarchy extends throughout the life of a Jordanian woman. Early marriage is a part of this cycle, but it extends throughout her life so that even when she is asking for a divorce, court judges will not even hear the case if her father is not present with her in court and accepting of her actions. It remains to be seen how the new *khul'* laws will be applied. The sum total of personal status laws is to deny women full legal competence. The Jordanian Constitution may declare all citizens equal before the eyes of the law, but in actual fact Jordan's laws contradict that statement, and the execution of the law deteriorates women's rights further. The penal code and other laws regarding election, citizenship, national health insurance, and social security all work to undermine women's rights further, giving them second-class status within their communities and extending a sense of helplessness and constant worry about each action that they take that may have repercussions for their future welfare. It is therefore imperative that in trying to encourage women to enter the job market or to open their own businesses that the close connection between the various legal codes in Jordan be understood. Women have always worked in Islamic societies, but it is the environment and questions pertaining to family and honor that determine if they will or will not leave the home for any type of activity, commercial or otherwise. In Jordan, we are talking about certain traditions that guide these social relations, and these traditions happen to be primarily tribal. Jordanian activists realize that fact, and most women I spoke to indicate that the society is tribal and unwilling to move too far from its traditions. What makes it problematic, however, is that *tribal* is confused with *Islamic,* so it is not tribalism that gives gender relations validity, but the "Islamicness" of this tribalism that gives legitimacy to discriminatory laws and ensures the continuing patriarchal order.

Keeping these points in mind, the methodology applied in this book was to first study the genesis of Jordan's existing legal codes with the purpose of deconstructing them to illustrate their origins so there would be no confusion as to what is Islamic and what can be traced to other origins. My takeoff here is that law is in process, changing with time and context. Even *shari'a* law is in process, even though the perception is that it is the unchanged law of God given through the Qur'an and the teachings of the prophet Muhammad. Yet the main schools of Islamic law were not formulated until centuries after the death of the Prophet and continued to branch out and change throughout Islamic history. The modern period witnessed a major overhauling of the legal system the world over, diffusion of law from one part of the globe to the other, together with technological change that included urbanization, industrialization, commercial globalization, transportation, media, and so on. To continue to believe that a country's legal system has not changed since the tenth century defies logic. Besides, there is a close connection between culture and hegemony: a hegemonic order dependent on particular sectors of society will endorse a discourse friendly to these sectors. Discourse goes beyond rhetoric: it focuses all thoughts, ideas, laws, politics, and ultimately the economy to support and promote the beneficiaries from a hegemony. That eventuality is the case in Jordan as it is elsewhere, no matter how liberal or conservative the discourse may appear to be. An example used here involves the usage of fundamentalism and veiling as a means by which women can promote jobs for women. This usage is very clear in the discourse presented by women Islamic thinkers, even though it is missing in Islamic discourses presented by their male counterparts. It is therefore normal for a hegemonic order formed of Jordanian political and commercial elites and their tribal allies who constitute an important bloc of the security forces to espouse a discourse that supports mobilizing their power over Jordanian politics and wealth. Tribalism, patriarchy, peripheralization of women, payment of *diyya,* reduced sentencing in lieu of effective criminal procedures against perpetrators of honor crimes, and ultimately the lack of rule of law are manageable and absorbable as long as they do not destabilize the hegemony. Therefore, one must begin by questioning the culture and the cultural discourse that supports it, in this case the discourse that presumes to give Islamic legitimacy to the system. Jordanian women are mindful of the type of hegemony that defines their life; they realize that wider political participation by women is a must if any change is to take place. Therein lies the serious interest in trying to get women elected to Jordan's Parliament and the incredible opposition faced by women running for election, as well as women who won elections, from both conservative and government forces, as the treatment of Tujan Faisal by the Jordanian courts, in which the courts were able to obstruct her ability to run and win election, illustrates.

Deconstructing law is no simple matter, especially because of the sensitivity of the issue. To undertake this effort, it was imperative that Jordanian laws be scrutinized against Islamic laws of the various schools of jurisprudence, tribal laws as presented by tribal judges and scholars, European laws that are an important part of the Jordanian legal system even though that fact is little recognized, and most important the various types of traditional law that are an integral part of the Jordanian legal system. My findings on this matter (see chapter 2) were discussed with a number of Jordanian lawyers and four court judges. Ratib al-Zahir, a previous judge in Jordan's *shari'a* courts, gave comprehensive answers to ten questions I set out for him about Islamic law, illustrating the validity of the need for deconstruction of these laws to differentiate what can legitimately be called Islamic and what is questionable. His methodology came close to my own, and his contribution to this study cannot be underestimated. Hamza Haddad was particularly instructive about the history of modern Jordanian laws. Confirming that Jordan's Civil Code was based on Egypt's, which in turn was based largely on European laws, Haddad agreed that what is considered Islamic law in Jordan actually has different origins. He also agreed that as long as the public accepts unquestioningly the presumption that Jordan's laws are based on the *shari'a* it will be very hard to change them. His own experience in trying to change Law 340 in the Jordanian Parliament was illustrative: tribal traditions were at play, and representatives would not budge. Yet there is a general belief that Law 340 and others allowing for reduced sentencing for honor crimes are Islamic laws, even though they are a combination of tribal and French laws. Muhammad Abu-Hassan, a judge in Jordan's High Court, explained the important connections between social traditions and the laws. Protection of women and the social fabric constitutes the basis upon which courts execute the law, according to Abu-Hassan. Farouk al-Kilani added an important twist to this discussion by pointing to the fact that there is no constitutional court in Jordan that is the final arbiter of conflicts between the Jordanian Constitution and laws. As Reem Abu-Hassan emphasizes, without such a court there is no way to correct contradictions that limit the rights of women granted to them by the Constitution. Al-Kilani believes that there is a mechanism of redress that is not utilized in Jordan: the Jordanian High Court, which can take up questions of legal conflict and set precedents that could be made obligatory for other courts to follow. Although a constitutional court would be the ideal institution to solve such matters, there is no reason the High Court could not be used. The big problems in the legal system, according to al-Kilani, are inefficiency and corruption, particularly among court judges who seem not to respect the rule of law and instead follow other inclinations, guided quite often by tradition in preference to legal precedent and the specifics of the law. Without the rule of law there can be no justice, and women in particular cannot be protected by the legal process, according to Abu-Hassan.

In other words, there is a great need to understand how the legal system in Jordan works, and how laws are interpreted and executed. Changing the laws alone would not be enough as long as the legal process itself does not observe the very purpose for the existence of law, which is ultimately directed toward establishing rules by which the state interacts with its citizenship, people interact, and the weak are ultimately protected from the aggression of people in power over them. These givens are recognized in Jordan, but they are more words than actual reality. It is here that justifications and excuses, almost always in the form of protection of the family and honor, are used to deny the weaker, in this case women and often children, protection of the law and legal process. This fact is what 'Ubaidat, Abu-Hassan, Haddad, al-Kilani, and other members of the legal profession recognize and try to redress.

Women's work is at the center of the gender debate today, not only in Jordan but also in most Islamic countries, except for oil-rich states that do not have the same type of economic problems faced elsewhere, at least not for the time being. Islamic discourses define the gender debate, and it is therefore toward such discourses that deconstruction must be addressed. The myth is that women did not work but were kept secluded at home until the coming of the West and foreign influence that caused them to begin demanding rights that they never had before, including the rights to leave the home and to work. This belief is supported by most histories written inside and outside of the Islamic world that take the modernization paradigm as a given. According to the modernization or coming-of-the-West paradigm, the Islamic world slumbered along in backwardness until the arrival of Napoléon Bonaparte, followed by other Western armies that caused a shock that awakened these countries from their slumber and began to introduce modernity and civilization to them. Women, once secluded and enslaved, began to be educated and informed of the new world with its capabilities. Islam is presented as the major force in trying to hold these societies back from people calling for greater Westernization and as the bulwark against the destruction of family and traditions among the people who oppose social modernity. To both, Islam has been confused with tradition, and in the case of Jordan these traditions are largely Bedouinism and peasant culture. This picture needs to be deconstructed and the history of women recovered in order to rethink the concept of women and work to illustrate the important contribution that women have always played in their communities' economies, that this role was not questioned by their spouses or families, and that the courts dealt with women, work, and business no differently than they did with men, work, and business. Chapter 2 of this study first deconstructed the legal system to show how laws were made and to illustrate the important distinctions that existed between actual legal practices in courts dating from before the modernization of law and what religious discourses that represented opinions of scholars on social and moral issues of the day had to say about different aspects of the law. In other words, to retrieve the history of women one must look at legal practice and not what theologians and legists have to say about how they interpret gender laws. Chapter 3 then discussed the evidence pointing to the important activities of women since the time of the Prophet. Not only were the Qur'an and Prophetic traditions utilized, but also literature and most significantly *awqaf* and court records that give us specifics and minute details about people's lives and the various transactions they were involved in. We find evidence of the concrete contributions of women to economic life. It is my hope that these two chapters will give direction to further deconstruction of Jordanian laws and that through the method presented here new laws could be passed that are more fitting with Jordan's needs today. One hopes that new methodologies will be attempted to make us understand the genesis of law even more and in terms that will make the Jordanian public as well as the legal community take note and make contributions to the Islamic world at large. Women's history is an old science in the Western world, but it is still taking its first true steps in Jordan and the rest of the Islamic world. It is my hope that by introducing methods by which religious sources and archival records can be used to write legal history, this task will be undertaken by students and scholars to further our understanding of that history. Perhaps the media will also take note of the existence of thousands of records in Jordan's archives that speak of a deep and lasting civilization in which women and men played such dynamic roles on a day-to-day basis—it would certainly put a curve in modernization paradigms. Media efforts to show the lives of women as lived rather than as they were supposed to have been lived according to medieval scholars would go a long way toward changing the image of women among Jordan's public, particularly among young girls, who would learn that women have always played a much more important role than as mothers and wives.

The importance of media cannot be discounted in efforts to educate. Jordanian women groups such as the BPWC have resorted to *taw'iyya* as a concrete method of educating the public, particularly women, about personal laws as well as laws pertaining to work and opening businesses. Having attended many such lectures, I believe that this effort should be expanded, more lawyers trained, and activities spread throughout Jordan. Jordan is ahead in this area of indoctrination and education; its experience should be spread and implemented in other countries. The number of seminars held in Jordan to discuss such topics may seem to be too large for the country's needs, but actually the intensity of participation and exposure by the media of what they are trying to do have been of particular help in making the problems better known and advancing possible solutions for public discussion. Without opening legal questions to public discussion, there is little hope of success if new laws are to be promulgated and accepted by the general public. When discussing media possibilities, however, it is always pointed out that the most important medium in Jordan is the television and that it is prohibitively expensive to advertise. However, the television belongs to the government of Jordan, and there should be no reason that the programs are not redirected to offer a more positive image of women in both the past and the present. Rather than religious programs that emphasize a dual good-evil or mother-prostitute image of women that seems to dominate Arab television and literature, real stories from Jordanian and Arab history that show complexity and industriousness could be featured. The historical record is on the side of the latter: the contemporary life of Arab women also illustrates complexity and productivity, but why is there such an insistence on imagery that has little to do with reality? Here is an important job for women's groups: to criticize and advocate a new media approach to women. As this book has tried to illustrate, there is also important work to be done in screening and rewriting school textbooks so that engendering would not take place in either obvious or subtle ways. It is during a child's early years that culture takes root; at present, textbooks throughout the Islamic world reinforce patriarchal attitudes and the submissiveness of women.

The most important form of media, however, has yet to be utilized in any way in the struggle for equality and economic growth in Jordan, let alone for women's rights. Here I am referring to mosques and churches. The speech from the pulpit is without a doubt the best way to get any message across to the general public. Placed from within a religious discourse and backed by religious arguments, a sheikh or a priest could prove extremely effective in swaying the public or at least opening up debates about important issues. As it is, the clergy is already used in most Arab countries. The subject of the speech to be presented in mosques following the Friday prayers is always approved by the Ministry of Awqaf, and quite often specific sensitive or political subjects are chosen by the ministry for these prayers, written out, and distributed to the various mosques. When there are specific holidays or feasts, the Friday speech from the pulpit is coordinated, and all mosques in any particular country will have more or less the same subject and approach to be presented to their members. When there are politically sensitive issues or economic problems about which the government wishes to present a particular point of view, the speech from the pulpit is the most effective way. There is a general realization that not only will it be listened to but it will also be discussed after prayer and among colleagues and family members. In other words, the pulpit can become a major media resource to get a message across, as long as the government supports that message because all clergymen who work in government mosques are government employees. Take, for example, the issue of honor crimes. Learned Muslims, including the clergy, are quick to emphasize that such crimes are not sanctioned by Islam, so why should the Friday sermon then not be about that subject? Using the Qur'an and Prophetic traditions to back up their arguments, the parallelism between female infanticide (*wa'd al-banat*) and the pre-Islamic period of Jahiliyya (abhorrent to all Muslims as a period of ignorance that Islam directly addressed and came to redress) could be made and driven home. No Muslim could condone what Islam has come directly to forbid. As it is, people are confused about what Islam says about such matters.

In the final analysis, history has illustrated that for laws to change and cultures to be transformed, existing conditions must first bring about new historical blocs with new concrete realities. This fact has been particularly so in the experience of women and minorities. Although conditions have allowed more women to work, the fact that women become participants in their countries' economies brings about greater empowerment of women and more acceptable public and political roles. It is therefore imperative that methods be found to bring about a greater participation of women in Jordan's economy. Although efforts are being exerted to change the laws, to grant women greater human rights and more protection by law, it is just as important to train women, educate them, teach them leadership roles, and make sure that the door is open to them to share in both the burdens and the advantages of economic productivity. How to accomplish that task has occupied the minds of women leaders in Jordan who have worked hard on the national and international fronts to open up various venues for women's participation. This study has pointed to the most important laws and traditions obstructing women when it comes to work. They include constraints found in labor laws, social security laws, and other legal codes such as the penal code and personal status laws. In regards to specific constraints in labor laws, the first problem pointed out was the very philosophy behind labor laws that reflects the patriarchy of other Jordanian legal codes and sets the tone of discrimination against women when it comes to work. Even though labor laws are supposed to be civic in nature, in fact they are overtly based on Jordanian *a'raf*. "Work is the right of all citizens" may be the wording in the Constitution, but a woman's inability to work without her husband's permission is in clear violation because it is no longer a "right" as such. A woman may be assigned as judge in Jordanian courts, but even then her husband must approve her work. This situation is no different philosophically from a father's permission being needed for a girl who has reached legal majority to be married; otherwise, she would have to get a judge to agree that her father acted unjustly. In both cases, there is no "right" for women to determine their own fates. This patriarchal philosophy means that direct differentiation between genders is included in labor laws that view women as having by "nature" the need for protection and special treatment. Here I am referring in particular to not allowing women to undertake particular "dangerous" jobs or to work at night. Furthermore, the law allows women to receive their contributions to their social security when they leave a job as a lump sum. This law was meant to make things easier for them in case they have family problems or are getting married. Ironically, if a woman is not married this law does not apply. Thus, if an employee wants to open her own business and wants to take advantage of the law that would allow her to take out her social security, thereby giving her the capital by which she could venture into that business, she is denied, whereas a woman who wants to use the money to furnish a home can have access to it. How logical is such a law? It may not be logical, but it is patriarchal and fits with the philosophy underlying labor laws that considers women as temporary workers, as replaceable by men, or as working because they have no male support and are in financial need. But the concept of permanency for women is not emphasized. This fact works against women in many ways but most important in allowing for the existence of a glass ceiling beyond which women do not move. Denial of equal access to work opportunities and advancement dissuades women from seeking employment and encourages them to leave work when they marry or become pregnant.

Another push factor out of the workplace has to do with sexual harassment on the job. The myth is that such harassment does not take place, and some women actually blame each other for it. According to Mona Haddad, a computer entrepreneur at the BPWC incubator, "women who are harassed deserve what they get because they dress in clothes that are too tight or show their legs." She was contradicted by the other five entrepreneurs attending the interview who derided this type of conservative justification. The point is that both Haddad and her colleagues agreed that sexual harassment is a constant on the job and that women face it on a day-to-day basis with little recourse if they want to stay on the job. Jordan has no laws against sexual harassment, and complaints to the court have fallen on deaf ears. Even when the case is proved as *hatk 'ird*, the guilty party gets a sentence equal to a slap on the wrist, whereas his victim may suffer dire consequences from her family, who may ultimately view her as responsible. There is clearly a need for labor laws that define sexual harassment and ensure against them. In a way it is ironic that Jordan's labor laws that purport to "protect" women from dangerous jobs do not offer them protection when it comes to questions of honor that are clearly violated by sexual harassment.

Without going into all the details of discrimination in labor laws, retirement benefits, and social security benefits (covered in chapter 4), it is important to speak about the market for the employment of women. As pointed out in the study, without a market for women there would be no expectation for them to work. If anything, there seems to be a shortage of jobs for women, even though there is significant potential for women in particular sectors of the economy in other countries. Here in particular one needs to point to the tourist industry that offers employment for women worldwide as tourist guides, airline personnel, executives, designers, advertisers, and so on. Tourism remains a poorly developed area of the Jordanian economy, a fact made obvious when visiting Jordan's incredible heritage in places such as Jarash or Petra. Hardly any hotels, restaurants, shops, or touring offices exist at these locations. There also seems to be misallocation of financial aid that comes through international organizations that seem to favor big banks, businesses, and foundations, according to women entrepreneurs who are unable to find financial resources to help them make a start in the business world. Even in microfinancial enterprises, the interest rates are very high, and as in all loans, women must find someone to ensure them. With entrepreneurs like the ones at the BPWC, they must produce guarantors (*kafils*) who hold government jobs so that their salaries can be garnished in case of default in repaying the loans. Microfinanciers have other methods of ensuring repayment, and here they depend on methods dating back centuries, as discussed in chapter 3. By keeping women in groups of four or five, they are all held responsible for each other, and if one defaults the rest have to cover for her. If they are unable to cover for each other, then they can no longer depend on microfinancial loans.

The projects supported also seem to favor handicrafts, which is problematic in many ways, particularly when it comes to production and marketing. Randa Qibti, who is successfully building a business reminiscent of old farming-out methods by which she involves large numbers of women who produce tourist items such as national costumes, explains that the problem with these ventures is that they do not always produce high-quality products and therefore do not find a market for them. Although the same is true of other countries that depend on selling national items to tourists, Sobhiyya al-Maʿni is right in pointing out that there is no international market for local products and that Jordan has to work toward producing for an international market if it is to have a viable economy. In short, other types of industries and production need to be pursued, not only for women's employment but also for the Jordanian economy as a whole.

The final conclusion to be drawn from this book is that legal changes are essential but cannot stand on their own. There has to be a concerted effort to enlarge the economy, to open up new venues for women's economic contributions, and to find new approaches to educating the public and future generations.

Notes
Glossary
Bibliography
Index

Notes

1.Introduction: Women in Jordan Today

1. Samih 'Ali Khalid al-'Azm (al-Shaikh), *Samma: Qariya min biladi,* 11–14, 45–49.

2. The book names 175 men who graduated with a B.A. from university and 87 who received a diploma from a higher educational institution. Of 42 men who received degrees in Qur'anic and *shari'a* studies, 14 received an M.A. and 5 a Ph.D. Ten became doctors, and 18 became engineers. Sixty-three were teachers, and 3 were university professors. Fifteen graduates lived in the United States, 19 in Germany, 6 in Romania, 3 in Bahrain, 1 in Canada, 5 in Austria, 2 in Belgium, 13 in Saudi Arabia, 12 in the Emirates, and so on. Again, none were women. Ibid., 50–64, 206–14.

3. Ibid., 90–91.

4. *Arab Women and Education,* 13.

5. See http://www.ameinfo.com/1/g/5/.

2. Background: *Qadis, 'Asha'ir,* and Modern Law

1. Selim Rustum Baz al-Libnani, *Sharh al-majala,* 7.

2. Bernard Botiveau, *Al-Shari'a al-islamiyya wal-qanun fil-mujtama'at al-'arabiyya,* 59.

3. 'Ali al-Tantawi, *Al-Qada' fil-islam,* 6–8.

4. Susan A. Spectorsky, trans., *Chapters on Marriage and Divorce: Responses of Ibn Hanbal and Ibn Rahwayh.*

5. Amira Sonbol, "Adults and Minors in Ottoman Shari'a Courts and Modern Law."

6. Haifaa Khalafallah, "Rethinking Islamic Law: Genesis and Evolution in the Islamic Legal Method and Structures. The Case of a 20th Century 'Alim's Journey into His Legal Traditions, Muahmmad al-Ghazali (1917–1996)."

7. Haifaa Kahlafallah, "Reclaiming the Islamic Legal Method in the Twentieth Century: Public Leadership," ms. p. 63.

8. Denise Spellberg, "History Then, History Now: The Role of Medieval Islamic Religio-Political Sources in Shaping Modern Debate on Gender," ms. p. 6.

9. Botiveau, *Al-Shari'a al-islamiyya wal-qanun,* 32.

10. Mohammad Fadel, "Two Women, One Man: Knowledge, Power, and Gender in Medieval Suni Legal Thought."

11. Al-Quds Shari'a Court, A.H. 1057 (A.D. 1647), 28–140:53–2 (film number, sijill number, page number, case number), Amman.

12. Christian churches found such practices unacceptable, but *shari'a* courts functioned more as civil courts than they did as religious courts and provided services to anyone who came there.

13. Al-Quds Shari'a Court, A.H. 1054 (A.D. 1604), 27–134:324–1, Amman.

14. Law 41 for 1951, "Qanun tashkil al-mahakim al-shar'iyya."

15. Law 19 for 1972.

16. Laila Sabbagh, *Al-Mar'a fi'l-tarikh al-'arabi qabl al-islam,* 43–46, 136.

17. Ahmad ibn Muhammad ibn 'Abd Rabbih, *Al-'Iqd al-farid,* 61.

18. Abu 'Uthman al-Jahiz, *The Epistle on Singing-Girls of Jahiz,* 16.

19. Sabbagh, *Al-Mar'a fi'l-tarikh al-'arabi qabl al-islam,* 150.

20. Ibid.

21. Zafer al-Qasimi, *Al-Hayat al-ijtima'iya 'ind al-'arab,* 24–25.

22. Sabbagh, *Al-Mar'a fi'l-tarikh al-'arabi qabl al-islam,* 151.

23. Ibid., 139.

24. Diana Richmond, *'Antar and 'Abla: A Bedouin Romance;* and Muhammad Farid Abu Hadid, *Abu'l Fawaris 'Antara b. Shadad.*

25. Richmond, *'Antar and 'Abla: A Bedouin Romance,* 6.

26. Al-Qasimi, *Al-Hayat al-ijtima'iya 'ind al-'arab,* 26.

27. Kamal Abdallah al-Hilw and Said Mumtaz Darwish, *Customary Law in Northern Sinai,* xxi.

28. Laurie Brand, "Women and the State in Jordan: Inclusion or Exclusion?" 101.

29. Ibid., 93–96.

30. The examples here are too many to mention. But an interesting title that appeared in both Arabic and English, that is, it was an address to an international Muslim audience, is by Muhammad Abdel Ghany Abdel Rahman, *Wives of Muhammad: The Prophet and Wisdom of Polygamy.*

3. Women's History and Work

1. Ahmad b. Hajar al-'Asqalani, *Fath al-bari bi-sharh sahih al-Bukhari,* 9:210–11.

2. Ahmad Suwayyid, *Nisa' shahirat min tarikhina,* 7, 13.

3. 'Abdullah Yusuf 'Ali, *The Meaning of the Holy Qur'an,* 1065.

4. Al-Qasimi, *Al-Hayat al-ijtima'iya 'ind al-'arab,* 12.

5. 'Isam al-Sioufi, *Al-Mar'a fi'l-adab al-jahili,* 22–23.

6. Ibid., 19.

7. Suwayyid, *Nisa' shahirat min tarikhina,* 28–33.

8. Ibid., 60–66.

9. Ibn Battuta, *Travels in Asia and Africa, 1325–1354,* 340.

10. See, for example, Ottaviano Bon, *The Sultan's Seraglio: An Intimate Portrait of Life at the Ottoman Court,* which was originally published in the seventeenth century and painted an exotic picture of Ottoman courts, with harems and women.

11. Leslie Peirce, *The Imperial Harem: Women and Sovereignty in the Ottoman Empire;* Farhad Daftary, "Sayyida Hurra: The Isma'ili Sulayhid Queen of Yemen."

12. Peter Jackson, "Sultan Radiyya 'Bint Iltutmish."

13. Mary Ann Fay, "The Ties That Bound: Women and Households in Eighteenth-Century Egypt," 155.

14. Hambly, "Becoming Visible: Medieval Islamic Women in Historiography and History," 18, 19; Stephen P. Blake, "Contributions to the Urban Landscape: Women Builders in Safavid Isfahan and Mughal Shahjananabad," 409.

15. Ibid.

16. See Fatima Mernissi, *The Veil and the Male Elite: A Feminist Interpretation of Women's Rights in Islam.*

17. Bukhari and Muslim quoted in *Tahrir al-mar'a fi 'asr al-risala,* by 'Abdal-Halim Abu Shaqra, 14.

18. See Barbara Freyer Stowasser, *Women in the Qur'an, Traditions, and Interpretations,* for a discussion of the women's *bay'a.*

19. Abu Shaqra, *Tahrir al-mar'a fi 'asr al-risala,* 22.

20. Al-Quds Shari'a Court, A.H. 1054 (A.D. 1644), 27–135:181–3, Amman. In this dispute a woman complained of another who, together with her daughter, hit her on the head.

21. Ibid., 27–135:325–4, 136:3–3.

22. Ruth Roded, *Women in Islamic Biographical Collections: From Ibn Sa'd to Who's Who,* 45–46.

23. Jonathan Berkey, *The Transmission of Knowledge in Medieval Cairo: A Social History of Islamic Education,* 165.

24. Roded, *Women in Biographical Collections,* 68.

25. Berkey, *Transmission of Knowledge,* 167.

26. Ibid., 170.

27. Ibid., 171.

28. Ibid.

29. Nablus Shari'a Court, A.H. 1276–1277 (A.D. 1861–1862), 2–13:95–96.

30. Dumyat Shari'a Court, Ishhadat, 176:252–240, Cairo.

31. Nablus Shari'a Court A.H. 1276–1277 (A.D. 1860–1861], 2–13:183.

32. Ibid., A.H. 1263–1266 (A.D. 1847–1850], 2–11:105, 113.

33. Margaret L. Meriwether, *The Kin Who Count: Family and Society in Ottoman Aleppo, 1770–1840,* 183.

34. Al-Quds Shari'a Court, A.H. 952 (A.D. 1545), 17:4–2, in *Nahiyat al-quds al-sharif fil-qarn al-'ashir al-hijri,* by Muhammad Ahmed al-Ya'qubi, 246.

35. Meriwether, *Kin Who Count,* 188, 189.

36. Amman Shari'a Court, A.H. 1316 (A.D. 1898), 5:71–72, in *'Amman wa-jiwariha: 1864–1921,* by Nufan al-Sawariyya, 197; and al-Salt Shari'a Court, A.H. 1316 (A.D. 1898), 3:65–90, Amman.

37. Al-Quds Shari'a Court, A.H. 1229 (A.D. 1814), 297:94; A.H. 1229 (A.D. 1813), 297:61; A.H. 1228 (A.D. 1812), 296:26, in *Al-Qanun al-madani al-urduni,* 112, 114, 115.

38. Mahmoud Yazbak, *Haifa in the Late Ottoman Period, 1864–1914,* 185; Haifa Shari'a Court, A.D. 1903–1904, 1321:274–42, quoted in ibid.

39. Nablus Shari'a Court, A.H. 1284–1285 (A.D. 1866–1867), 2–15:183, Amman.

40. Amman Shari'a Court, A.H. 1320 (A.D. 1902), 2:39–37, in *'Amman wa-jiwariha,* by al-Sawariyya, 197.

41. Al-Salt Shari'a Court, A.H. 1328 (A.D. 1912), 16:179–104, Amman.

42. Hambly, *Women in the Medieval Islamic World: Power, Patronage, and Piety,* 20.

43. Nablus Shari'a Court, A.H. 1284–1285 (A.D. 1866–1867) 2–15:166, Amman. Also see

Jerusalem Shariʻa Court, 12 Shawwal, A.H. 793 (A.D. 1394), in *Wathaʼiq muqadissiya tarikhiyya: muqaddima hawla baʼd al-masadir al-awwaliyya li-tarikh al-Quds,* by Kamil Jamil al-ʻAssali, 2:46–47.

44. Jerusalem Shariʻa Court, 15 Jamadi al-Akhira, A.H. 796 (A.D. 1397), in *Wathaʼiq muqadissiyya tarikhiya,* by al-ʻAssali, 2:44–45.

45. Ibid., 14 Muharram, A.H. 797 (A.D. 1398), in *Wathaʼiq muqadissiya tarikhiyya,* by al-ʻAssali, 2:37–39.

46. Nablus Shariʻa Court, A.H. 1266–1276 (A.D. 1850–1860), 2–12:173, Amman.

47. Ballas Shariʻa Court, A.H. 1279 (A.D. 1862), 24:8–12, Cairo.

48. Nablus Shariʻa Court, A.H. 1282–1284 (A.D. 1864–1866), 2–14:157, 78, Amman.

49. Yazbak, *Late Ottoman Period,* 183.

50. Al-Quds Shariʻa Court, A.H. 1231 (A.D. 1816), 290:195, in *Al-Qanun al-madani al-urduni,* 118.

51. Ibid., A.H. 1033 (A.D. 1622), 20–107:98–2, Amman. In this case the woman was present in court to register the deed for buying a house with an orchard containing fruit trees, namely, grapes, figs, and quince.

52. Ibid., A.H. 1230 (A.D. 1815), 290:169, in *Al-Qanun al-madani al-urduni,* 118.

53. Ibid., A.H. 1222 (A.D. 1807), 290:43, in *Al-Qanun al-madani al-urduni,* 117.

54. Nablus Shariʻa Court, A.H. 1282–1284 (A.D. 1866), 2–14:166, 317, Amman.

55. Ibid., 2–14:314.

56. Ibid., A.H. 1284–1285 (A.D. 1866–1867), 2–15:183, 31.

57. Al-Quds Shariʻa Court, A.H. 972 (A.D. 1564), 46:12–2; A.H. 939 (A.D. 1532), 3:95–3; A.H. 1010 (A.D. 1601), 83:156–6, 235–5; A.H. 937 (A.D. 1530), 1:267–2; A.H. 939 (A.D. 1532), 3:12–1; A.H. 957 (A.D. 1550), 23:585–12, in *Nahiyat al-quds,* by al-Yaʻqubi, 1:127.

58. Document published in al-ʻAssali, *Wathaʼiq muqadissiyya tarikhiyya,* 1:108–21.

59. Muhammad ʻIsa Salahiyya, *Sijil aradi alwiya (Safad, Nablus, Ghaza, and Qadaʼ al-Ramlah, 974H–1556,* 15.

60. Ibid., 43–45.

61. Al-Salt Shariʻa Court, A.H. 1320 (A.D. 1902), 7:97–206, Amman.

62. Nablus Shariʻa Court, A.H. 1266–1276 (A.D. 1850–1860), 2–12:199, Amman.

63. Al-Quds Shariʻa Court, A.H. 1238 (A.D. 1822), 303:73, in *Al-Qanun al-madani al-urduni,* 152.

64. Ibid., A.H. 1228 (A.D. 1813), 296:64, in *Al-Qanun al-madani al-urduni,* 152.

65. Ibid., A.H. 1245 (A.D. 1829), 313:135, in *Al-Qanun al-madani al-urduni,* 155.

66. Ibid., A.H. 1229 (A.D. 1831), 297:148, in *Al-Qanun al-madani al-urduni,* 158.

67. Salahiyya, *Sijil aradi alwiya,* 58.

68. Al-Quds Shariʻa Court, A.H. 1225 (A.D. 1810), 293:112, in *Al-Qanun al-madani al-urduni,* 172.

69. Salahiyya, *Sijil aradi alwiya,* 55.

70. Al-Quds Shariʻa Court, A.H. 1221 (A.D. 1806), 288:78, in *Al-Qanun al-madani al-urduni,* 92.

71. Ibid., A.H. 1227 (A.D. 1812), 290:93, in *Al-Qanun al-madani al-urduni,* 93.

72. Al-Yaʻqubi, *Nahiyat al-quds,* vol. 1, referring to records of al-Quds Shariʻa Court, A.H. 974 (A.D. 1566), 47:86–1; A.H. 976 (A.D. 1568), 47:181–1; and A.H. 978 (A.D. 1570), 53:667–2.

73. Al-Quds Shari'a Court, A.H. 1223 (A.D. 1808), 295:53, in *Al-Qanun al-madani al-urduni*, 167.

74. Alexandria Shari'a Court, A.H.1705 (A.D. 1130), 65:141–247, Cairo.

75. Ze'evi Dror, *An Ottoman Century: The District of Jerusalem in the 1600s,* 185; Huda Lutfi, *A History of Mamlûk Jerusalem Based on the Haram Documents,* 305.

76. Al-Quds Shari'a Court, A.H. 1058 (A.D. 1648), 28–140:332–5, Amman.

77. Mahmud 'Ali 'Atallah, *Watha'iq al-tawa'if al-hirafiyya fil-Quds fil-qarn al-sabi' 'ashar al-miladi,* 1:9.

78. Al-Quds Shari'a Court, A.H. 972 (A.D. 1564), 46:12–2; A.H. 939 (A.D. 1532), 3:95–3; A.H. 1010 (A.D. 1601), 83:156–6, 235–5; A.H. 937 (A.D. 1530), 1:267–2; A.H. 939 (A.D. 1532), 3:12–1; A.H. 957 (A.D. 1550), 23:585–12, in *Nahiyat al-quds,* by al-Ya'qubi, 1:127.

79. Nablus Shari'a Court, A.H. 1280–1282 (A.D. 1864–1866), 2–13:60, Amman.

80. Al-Quds Shari'a Court, A.H. 1230 (A.D. 1815), 299:88, in *Madinat al-Quds wa-jiwariha: 1800–1830,* by Ziyad 'Abdal-'Aziz al-Madani, 81.

81. Lutfi, *History of Mamlûk Jerusalem,* 294, 300.

82. Al-Quds Shari'a Court, A.H. 1320 (A.D. 1902), 2:39–49, in *'Amman wa-jiwariha,* by al-Sawariyya, 350.

83. Amman Shari'a Court, A.H. 1230 (A.D. 1814), 291:322, in *Al-Qanun al-madani al-urduni,* 90.

84. Ahmad al-'Alami, *Waqfiyat al-maghariba,* 60–61.

85. Al-Salt Shari'a Court, A.H. 1328 (A.D. 1912), 16:17–16, Amman.

86. Al-Quds Shari'a Court, A.H. 1040 (A.D. 1631), 117:282–4, 7, in *Watha'iq al-tawa'if,* by 'Atallah, 1:172.

87. Ibid., A.H. 1041 (A.D. 1632), 119:121–2, in *Watha'iq al-tawa'if,* by 'Atallah, 175.

88. Ibid., A.H. 1054 (A.D. 1644) 27–134:131–6, Amman.

89. Ibid., 27–134:131–5.

90. Ibid., A.H. 1071 (A.D. 1661), 151:603–1.

91. Ibid., A.H. 973 (A.D. 1555), 31:606–3; A.H. 978 (A.D. 1570), 53:520–3; A.H. 1010 (A.D. 1601), 83:209–3.

92. Sami Khalaf Hamarneh, *Health Sciences in Early Islam: Collected Papers,* 42.

93. Bab al-'Ali Shari'a Court, A.H. 1152 (A.D. 1736), 221:283–429, Cairo.

94. Brand, "Women and the State in Jordan," 102.

95. Ibid., 100; Afaf Lutfi al-Sayyid Marsot, *Women and Men in Late-Eighteenth-Century Egypt,* 6, 7.

96. Afaf Lutfi al-Sayyid Marsot, "Women and Modernization," 46–47.

4. Women and Work in Jordan Today

1. *Jordanian Women's Guide to Participation in Public and Political Life,* 23.

2. Donna K. Flynn and Linda Oldham, "Women's Economic Activities in Jordan: Research Findings on Women's Participation in Microenterprise, Agriculture, and the Formal Sector."

3. *Jordanian Women's Guide,* 23.

4. Ghalib 'Ali al-Dawudi, *Sharh qanun al-'amal al-urduni,* 5–6.

5. Ratib Al-Zahir, "Lamha tarikhiyya 'an tashkil al-qada' al-shar'i wa tatawuruhu fi al-urdun," 57.

6. 'Abbas Mahmud al-'Aqqad, *Al-Mar'a fil-Qur'an,* 6, 3.

7. Al-Din Muhammad Mahdi al-Sheikh Shams, *Huquq al-zawjiyya: Haqq al-mar'a fil-'amal,* 179.

8. Ibid., 180.

9. Ibid., 183.

10. Ibid., 184.

11. Marwan Ibrahim al-Qisi, *Al-Mar'a al-muslima bayn ijtihadat al-fuqaha' wa mumarasat al-muslimin,* 9–25.

12. Ibid., 56.

13. Ibid., 57.

14. Mary Lyndon Shanley, *Feminism, Marriage, and the Law in Victorian England,* 8–9.

15. Tamyiz Court, case 21332, Amman.

16. Tamyiz Court, case 41157, Amman, Sept. 3, 1996.

17. Tamyiz Court, case 20876, Amman, June 1979.

18. Tamyiz Court, case 248/92, Amman.

19. Tamyiz Court, case 21332, Amman.

20. Hilary M. Lips, "Women, Education, and Economic Participation."

21. Ibid.

22. *Majmu'at al-tashri'at al-'umaliyya,* 97.

23. Ibid., 122.

24. Ibid., 124.

25. Ibid., 152.

26. Ibid., 6. Item G of Article 12, as amended, was first published in the *Official Gazzette* number 4192, issued Apr. 4, 1977.

27. *Jordanian Women's Guide,* 23.

28. Tamyiz Jaza'i, 593/95, published in *Majallat niqabat al-muhammin,* 4:1607–10.

29. At present, Egyptian courts have been delaying a case brought to court by a woman who has been denied the position of judge. Another case also delayed by the courts involves a woman who was not allowed to take the job of prosecutor.

5. Laws of Guardianship and the Construction of Gender

1. Mustafa Ibrahim al-Zalmi and 'Ali Ahmad Salih al-Mahdawi, *Usul al-fiqh fi nasijuh al-jadid wa tatbiqatuh fi al-tashri'at al-qanuniyya wa khassa al-qanun al-madani al-urduni raqam 43 li sanat 1976,* 31, 82.

2. Ibid., 82–84.

3. Kamel S. Abu Jaber, Fawzi A. Gharaibeh, and Allen Hill, *The Badia of Jordan: The Process of Change,* v.

4. Nayif al-Nawayisah, *Al-Tifl fi al-haya al-sha'biyya al-urduniyya,* 28–29.

5. Ibid., 139.

6. Fatima Barbari 'Abdallah, "Lament for Her Dead Daughter," 223.

7. Meeting in high school with Manal Shamut, July 1999.

8. Abdulla M. Lutfiyya, *Baytin, a Jordanian Village: A Study of Social Institutions and Social Change in a Folk Community,* 143.

9. Ibid., 158.

10. Abu Farwa al-Rajbi, "Saya'ti," 19–29.

11. Elizabeth Warnock Fernea, "Childhood in the Muslim Middle East," 5.

12. Al-'Asqalani, *Fath al-bari bi sharh sahih al-Bukhari,* 12:334.

13. Al-Nawayisah, *Al-Tifl fi al-haya al-sha'biyya al-urduniyya,* 29.

14. Lutfiyya, *Baytin, a Jordanian Village,* 158.

15. Emile Butaye and Gaston de Leval, *A Digest of the Laws of Belgium and of the French Code Napoléon,* 64.

16. *The Jordan Civil Code,* 7.

17. Shari'a Court, case 24624 (during the 1990s), in Abdel-Fattah 'Ayish 'Umar, *Al-Qararat al-qada'iyya fi'l-ahwal al-shakhsiyya hata 'am 1990,* 5.

18. Jerusalem Shari'a Court, 2 Ramadan, A.H. 789 (A.D. 1390), in *Watha'iq muqadissiyya tarikhiyya,* by al-'Assali, 2:109.

19. Nablus Shari'a Court, A.H. 1276–1277 (A.D. 1861), 2–13:27, Amman.

20. Al-Salt Shari'a Court, A.H. 1328 (A.D. 1912), 16:180–105, Amman.

21. Al-Quds Shari'a Court, A.H. 1058 (A.D. 1648), 28–140:317–2, Amman.

22. See chapter 3.

23. Al-Salt Shari'a Court, A.H. 1352 (A.D. 1933), 34:5–3, Amman.

24. Ibid., A.H. 1350 (A.D. 1932), 34:66–18, 82–49, 95–69, 102–82.

25. Ibid., A.H. 1342 (A.D. 1925), 27:98–4.

26. "Distribution of Secondary Education Students According to Sex and Type of Education for the School Years, 1995/1996, 1996/1997, 1997/1998," table 11.

27. Discussion at the Business and Professional Women's Club, Aug. 2000, Amman.

28. "Basic Education Curriculum and Study Plan (1997–1998)," educational statistics of the MOE for the years 1995–1996, table 9, Amman.

29. *Al-Tarbiyya al-ijtima'iyya wal-wataniyya,* year 3, pt. 2, Amman.

30. Ibid., year 4, pt. 2: 43–45.

31. Ibid., year 4, pt. 2: 37.

32. Ibid., year 5, pt. 2: 111.

33. Ibid., year 3, pt. 2: 51.

34. Al-Salt Shari'a Court, A.H. 1344 (A.D. 1925), 35:241–194, Amman. This case involves two minors married through the power of their respective fathers who were then being divorced in court by them.

35. "Turkish First-Grade Text from Jinn Ali Starts School, Cin Ali Publications, Ankara," 295.

6. Marriage, Obedience, and Work

1. Personal Status Law, no. 66a.

2. Personal Status Law, no. 68.

3. Court decision quoted in Ahmad Salim Milhim, *Al-Sharh al-tatbiqi li-qanun al-ahwal al-shakhsiyya al-urduni,* 101.

4. Tamyiz Court, case 41157, Sept. 3, 1996, Amman.

5. Tamyiz Court, case 20876, June 1979, Amman.

6. Tamyiz Court, case 248/92, Amman.

7. Personal Status Law for 1976.

8. Personal Status Law for Syria.

9. Personal Status Law for Iraq.

10. Personal Status Law for Algeria.

11. Nablus Shari'a Court, A.H. 1266–1276 (A.D. 1850–1860), 2–12:37, Amman.

12. *The Jordan Civil Code,* 5–6.

13. Ibid., 11.

14. Al-Zahir, "Lamha tarikhiyya 'an tashkil al-qada' al-shar'i wa tatawuruhu fi al-urdun," 10.

15. Ma'an Shari'a Court, *Sijil hisr irth,* 1932, 2:26–27, Amman.

16. Al-Quds Shari'a Court, A.H. 1043 (A.D. 1634), 24–122:137–1, Amman.

17. Muhammad Sayf al-Nasr abul'Futuh, "Al-Ahwal al-ijtima'iyya fi madinat Isna," 232.

18. Isna Shari'a Court, Sigilat, A.H. 1193 (A.D. 1777), 31:cases 43–46, 53, 61, Cairo.

19. Manfalut Shari'a Court, Ishhadat, A.H. 1238–1239 (A.D. 1819–1820), 5–50, 51, Cairo.

20. See, for example, Ma'an Shari'a Court, A.H. 1316 (A.D. 1899), 34–43, Amman, in which the wife compensated her husband with fifty riyals and she relinquished her rights to a *nafaqa* for the *'idda.*

21. Nablus Shari'a Court, A.H. 1276–1277 (A.D. 1861–1862), 2–13:76, Amman.

22. Ibid., 2–13:37.

23. Al-Quds Shari'a Court, A.H. 1043 (A.D. 1634), 24–122:287–1, Amman.

24. Ibid., 22 Jamadi al-Akhira, A.H. 785 (A.D. 1385), in *Watha'iq muqadissiya tarikhiyya,* by al-'Assali, 51.

25. Jami' al-Hakim Shari'a Court, Sijillat, A.H. 966 (A.D. 1559), 540:200–898, Cairo.

26. Amended by Law 18 for 1973, Law 7 for 1978, Law 25 for 1979, and Law 25 for 1983.

27. Ma'an Shari'a Court, A.H. 1317 (A.D. 1899), 34–44, Amman.

28. Al-Quds Shari'a Court, 2 Rabi' al-Akhar, A.H. 792 (A.D. 1392), in *Watha'iq muqadissiya tarikhiyya,* by al-'Assali, 2:118.

29. Ibid., 15 Dhul-Hijja, A.H. 795 (A.D. 1396), 19:653, in *Watha'iq muqadissiya tarikhiyya,* by al-'Assali, 2:19.

30. *The Jordan Civil Code,* 2, 9; *Al-Qanun al-madani al-urduni,* 19.

31. A good example of how comparative advantage is applied is in regards to the right to construct a window in a wall of a house that overlooks the house of another. Such a window would allow fresh air and sunshine to the home owner but would deny the neighbor his privacy and could expose his womenfolk to the eyes of strangers. Here the judge would have to decide if the benefits of the home owner outweigh the disadvantages to the neighbor and reach his decision accordingly.

32. See Shari'a Court, case 10902, in *Al-Qararat al-qada'iyya fil ahwal al-shakhsiyya hata 'am 1990,* by 'Umar, 4.

33. *The Jordan Civil Code,* 21.

34. Published in 1183.

35. Al-Zahir, "Lamha tarikhiyya 'an tashkil al-qada' al-shar'i wa tatawuruhu fi al-urdun," 9.

7. Honor Crimes

1. Douglas Jehl, *New York Times,* June 20, 1999, p. 4.

2. Lamis al-Nasser, Bashir al-Bilbisi, and Diana 'Atiyyat, *Al-'Unf did al-mar'a fil-mujtama' al-urduni: Al-khasa'is al-dimoghrafiyya lil-dahaya wal-junat,* 14.

3. A 1998 U.S. State Department report found that there were four times as much crimes as are mentioned by Jordanian government reports *(Washington Post,* Feb. 2, 2000, C15).

4. Al-Nasser, al-Bilbisi, and 'Atiyyat, *Al-'Unf did al-mar'a fil-mujtama' al-urduni,* 14.

5. Ibid., 16.

6. Cases reported by Lima Nabil in *Al-Ra'yy,* Nov. 24, 1998.

7. J. M. Cowan, ed., *Arabic-English Dictionary: The Hans Wehr Dictionary of Modern Written Arabic,* 172.

8. Ibrahim Saleh, *Qanun al-'uqubat al-mu'adal bil-qanun raqam 97 li-sanat 1992,* 37.

9. Ibid., 192.

10. Ramzi Ahmad Madi, *Qanun al-'uqubat raqam (16) lisanat 1960,* 136.

11. Also see Qur'an 24:2–3, 4:15.

12. For example, consider the case of a prostitute who was caught and brought to court with her two male accomplices. She confessed to her activity and to her being forced into immoral acts with men, her attendance at parties where they drank and sang and had sexual orgies. The court, however, was rather interested in the activities of a particular sheikh and wanted to know if he had ever had sex with her; she denied any knowledge of him, and the case ended. There is no mention of further prosecution or of the application of any particular punishment that would be *ta'zir* in this type of case. See al-Quds Shari'a Court, A.H. 1043 (A.D. 1634), 24–122:277–1, Amman.

13. Al-'Asqalani, *Fath al-bari bi-sharh sahih al-Bukhari,* 12:118–19.

14. Ibid., 336–37.

15. Ibid., 326, 82, 61, 63. Besides *zina, hudud* crimes include slander, drinking alcohol, theft, armed robbery, apostasy, and prostitution ('Abd al-Qadir 'Awda, *Al-tashri' al-gina'i al-islami,* 1:78–83.

16. 'Awda, *Al-tashri' al-gina'i al-islami,* 2:367.

17. Anas b. Malik. *Al-Muwatta' al-Imam,* n.d., p. 327.

18. J. Grandmoulin, *Le Droit penal Egyptian indigène,* 1:42.

19. Saleh, *Qanun al-'uqubat,* 190.

20. Madi, *Qanun al-'uqubat,* 140.

21. Ibid., 140.

22. See Article 325 of Egypt's Penal Code; Saleh, *Qanun al-'uqubat,* 216.

23. See a good discussion about this subject in Kamil al-Sa'id, *Sharh qanun al-'uqubat: Al-jara'im al-waqi'a 'ala al-akhlaq wal-adab al-'ama wal-usra,* 248.

24. Mentioned in ibid., 8.

25. *Majallat niqabat al-muhamiyyin,* p. 711 for 1966, in ibid., 14.

26. For example, Wahb ibn Minabih began telling these stories from the Bible soon after his conversion to Islam (al-'Aqqad, *Al-Mar'a fil-Qur'an,* 17–18).

27. Translation of the Qur'an by Yusuf Ali, in his *Meaning of the Holy Quran,* 873.

28. 'Abd al-Mit'al M. al-Jabri, *Al-Mara fi'l-tasawwur al-islami* (Woman in Islamic Perception), 92–93.

29. Freidoune Sahebjam, *The Stoning of Sorya M.*

30. Al-'Asqalani, *Fath al-bari bi sharh sahih al-Bukhari,* 12:119.

31. *Hindu,* June 25, 2000.

32. Letter to Jordanian Prime Minister, His Excellency Abdul-Ra'uf Rawabdeh, Aug. 9, 1999, Human Rights Watch and *Jordan Times,* Oct. 19, 1997, Amman.

33. Shahla Haeri, "The Politics of Dishonor: Rape and Power in Pakistan," 161–74.

34. See Kanan Makiya, *Power and Patriarchy in Iraq.*

8. Regarding Work and the Modern Jordanian Woman

1. The 1994 Population Census estimated women were 16 percent of the workforce.

2. Al-'Aqqad, *Al-Mar'a fil-Qur'an,* 6, 3.

3. Al-Qisi, *Al-Mar'a al-muslima bayn ijtihadat al-fuqaha' wa mumarasat al-muslimin,* 9–25.

4. Ibid., 56.

5. Ibid., 57.

6. Shams, *Huquq al-zawjiyya,* 179.

7. Ibid., 180.

8. Ibid., 182–83.

9. Ibid., 184.

10. Khawla 'Abdal-Latif al-'Itiqi, *Wazifat al-mar'a al-muslima fi 'alam al-yawm,* 25.

11. Ibid., 24.

12. Ibid., 28, 30.

13. Ibid., 32.

14. Ibid., 45.

15. Zaynab Radwan, *Al-Mar'a fi al-manzur al-islami: ba'd al-qadaya,* 9.

16. Ibid., 15.

17. Ibid., 21.

18. "Working Women Supported by Strong Political Will—Princess Basma."

19. "Women Make Big Strides in Conservative Jordan."

20. Raed al-Abed, "Lack of Awareness and Dull Campaign Tactics Behind Women Failure to Reach the Dome."

21. "Woman Parliamentarian Call for More Women in Office."

22. Rana Husseini, "Former Deputy Faisal Aims to Blaze Trail for Women in 2001 Elections."

23. *Jordan Times,* Apr. 18, 1998.

24. Ibid.

25. Ahmad 'Ubaidat, interview at his home, Amman, Aug. 2000.

26. Article 9 of the temporary amendment to original criminal law number 16 for 1960 issued in 2001 by Abdullah bin Hussain, king of the Hashemite Kingdom of Jordan, in accordance with Article 94, clause 1, of the Constitution, and by approval of the decision of the Council of Ministers dated Nov. 12, 2001.

Conclusion: What Next?

1. "Women Making Big Strides."

2. Rami Khouri, "A Kick in the Pants: Women Call for Democracy."

Glossary

'adab: literature
adila naqliyya: textual evidence
adila tab'iyya: derivative evidence
'afifa: chaste
ahliyya qanuniyya, ahliyya kamila: complete legal competence
akhmas: fifths
'ala al-barr: "on the shore," not yet embarked
'alim: clergyman
'allaq: conditioned
'amil: worker
amir: prince
ansab: posterity
'aqa'id: central beliefs, faith
'aql: rational behavior
a'raf: traditional laws; plural form of *"'urf"*
'asha'ir: clans, tribes
'attar: herbalist
awqaf: religious endowments; same as *"waqfs"*
'awra: genitals, usually hidden sexual areas of the body
aya: Qur'an verse
bay'a: oath of allegiance
baya'a: woman seller
baya'u: swore allegiance to
bi'a: environment
bikr: virgin
bulugh: puberty
da'iyya: missionary for Islam
dalala: mobile or door-to-door salesperson, vendor
daman al-zaitun: olive oil trade
darura: need
daya: midwife

275

diwan: council, office

diyya: blood price

dukan hiyaka: a shop for sewing clothes

dukhla: consummation of a marriage

faqih: theologian; plural form is *"fuqaha'"*

faqihat: women theologians

faskh: annulment

fatawi: theological opinions

fida'iyyin: freedom fighters

fil hal: immediately, instantly, without delay

fiqh: Islamic theological

fuqaha': legists, Islamic thinkers; plural form of *"faqih"*

furu': branches

ghayr ma'mun: not to be trusted

ghazwas: raids

hadana: custody of infants

hadd: crime against God

hakimas: women doctors

hal: dowry that is due before the consummation of the marriage

halal: allowed

hal al-talabus: being caught in the act

hamams: baths

haram: forbidden

hatk 'ird: to disgrace, rape; offending modesty

haykal 'asha'iri: tribal makeup

hurma: married woman

hijab: veil

'ibadat: creed or rituals guiding man's relationship with God

ibra': act by which a wife absolves her husband of all financial obligations in return for divorce

'idda: three-month period following divorce or a husband's death during which the wife cannot be married to another

ightisab: rape

ihtibas: confine a wife in her home

ijab wa qubul: exchange of vows

ijazas: certificates of competence in a particular science

ijtihad: speculative thinking, rational thought

'ilmi: scientific

imam: religious leader

ishhar: public

'isma: marital knot

istihbab: applying what is commendable, desirable, popular *istihsan:* discretion; application of discretion in a legal decision

jarima: crime

jins: race or sex

jumud: rigidity

kabira: major sin

kafa'a: social parity

kafil: sponsor

kahala: pseudo-oculist who uses *kuhl* as cure

katb al-kitab: marriage signing

khalila: mistress

khul': divorce in which wife compensates husband in return for divorce

khurj: covering placed under the saddles of horses and donkeys

al-kimaj: type of bread

kiswa: wardrobe

kufr: religious apostasy

kuhl: antimony; eye-liner

kuttab: mosque school for children

lawlab: contraceptive loop

lijan islah: committees of conciliation

madhahib: schools of law

madhhab: school of law

ma'dhun: cleric who officiates in a marriage or a divorce

madrasas: mosque schools

maghazi: campaigns

maghribis: North Africans

mahakim diniyya: religious courts

mahakim khassa: special courts held for specific reasons

mahakim nizamiyya: national courts

maharim: unmarriageable relation: sister, daughter, or niece

mahr: dowry

majlis: council

mar'a: woman

maristans: hospitals

masafat al-qisr: distance that can be traveled in one day

ma'sara: olive oil juicers

masatib: sale spots

mashata: hairdresser, beautician

maslaha: promoting advantage or the common good

mawlana al-hakim: the judge, head of judiciary council

mi'ad: Day of Judgment

mihna: crisis, revolt

mu'ajjal: advanced dowry

mu'akhkhar: delayed dowry

mu'alima: female master of trade

mu'amalat: relation of man to man, or laws pertaining to human relations

muftis: Muslim scholars, jurisconsuls

muhajirun: migrants who went on hegira from Mecca to Medina with the Prophet

muhtassibs: marketplace supervisors

mukalaf: free, legally competent individual

mukhayyam: Palestinian refugee camp

multazims: tax farmers

muqaddam: advanced dowry

muruwa: chivalrous

mut'a: compensation of supplies or enjoyment

mutabiqa: corresponding, exactly like

mutahim: defendant

nafaqa: financial support

nafs: life

nashaz: disobedient

nazir, nazira: male, female supervisor or guardian

nubuwwa: prophethood

Odabashi: head of an Ottoman army unit

qabila: midwife

qadi: shari'a court judge

qadi al-quda: chief justice of Shari'a Courts

qirat: $^1/_{24}$ of one acre

qiwama: guardianship or support

qudra 'ala al-infaq: financial ability

rashida: adult

ratls: approximately $2^1/_2$ kilos

ribat al-nisa': circle of women in mosque school

rushd: majority

sabils: buildings that house water wells and areas for ablution and prayer

sadaq: dowry

sahabi: male companion; plural form is *"sahaba"*

sahabiyyat: women companions

sanad: credit bill

saqqas: water carriers

shaikhas: female sheikhs

shaikhs: Muslim clergymen

shiqaq wa niza': "discord and conflict," family dispute court or irreconcilable-differences court

simsara: agent who earns a commission on sales

sira: Prophet's history and traditions

sufis: mystics

sunduq al-zakat: religious tax box

ta'a: obedience

tabaqat: biographical dictionaries

tabib: doctor

tabi'un: followers

tafsir: interpretation of the Qur'an

tahil lahu shar'an: a woman who is legal to him

tahmish: peripheralize

talabus: being caught in the act

talaq: husband's unlimited right to divorce his wife

talfiq: patching, patchwork

taqlid: imitation

tasari: taking a slave concubine

tatliq: divorce through a *qadi*

tawabi' mahr: furniture and furnishings expected from the husband according to traditions and agreement

ta'warikh: chronicles

tawhid: oneness of God

taw'iyya: education

thawbs: long shirts worn by men

thayib: previously married woman

turath: heritage

'ulama': Islamic clergy

umma: Islamic nation

umm al-walad: mother of the boy

'urf: customary or traditional law; plural form is *"a'raf"*

'urfi: common law; for example, common law wife

'usul: consanguine relatives

al-'uthr al-mukhafaf: an excuse allowing for a reduced sentence or for justifying murder

al-'uthr fi al-qatl: excuse for murder

'uthri: platonic

'uthr muhallil: legitimating excuse or absolution

wa'd al-banat: female genocide

wakil: agent, proxy, person with power of attorney

waliy: legal guardian

waqf dhurri: endowment to benefit heirs

waqf khayri: philanthropic endowment to benefit the community through a particular service such as a mosque, water fountain, or school

waqfs: religious endowments; same as *"awqaf"*

wasi: guardian with power over property of minor orphan

wilaya: guardianship

wilayat al-ijbar: the right to force
wisaya: child custody
yufagi': surprise
zakat: charity
zawaj: marriage
zawiyas: hospices for mystics
zina: adultery

Bibliography

Archival Sources

Egypt

Cairo. National Archives. Shari'a Court Records: Alexandria, Bab al-'Ali, Ballas, Dumyat, Isna, Jami' al-Hakim, Mafalut.

Jordan

Amman. University of Jordan Library. National Archives. Ottoman Shari'a Court Records: Irbid, Ma'an, Nablus, al-Quds (Jerusalem), al-Salt.
Tamyiz Court, cases 20876, 21332, 248/92, 41157.

Government Documents

Article 69 of Labor Law.
Educational statistics of the MOE for the years 1995–1996.
The Jordan Civil Code. Translated by Hisham R. Hesham. Amman: al-Tawfiq Printing Press, 1990.
Jordanian Constitution of 1952.
Law 19 for 1972.
Law 41 for 1951, "Qanun tashkil al-mahakim al-shar'iyya."
Personal Status Law, nos. 66a, 68.
Personal Status Law for Iraq, Law 188 for 1959.
Personal Status Law for 1976, published in the *Official Gazette,* no. 2668, Dec. 1, 1976.
Personal Status Law for Syria, Law 59 for 1953 amended by Law 34 for 1975.
Al-Tarbiyya al-ijtima'iyya wal-wataniyya. Year 3, pt. 2. Amman: Ministry of Education, 1998.
Al-Tarbiyya al-ijtima'iyya wal-wataniyya. Year 4, pt. 2. Amman: Ministry of Education, 1998.

Al-Tarbiyya al-ijtima'iyya wal-wataniyya. Year 5, pt. 2. Amman: Ministry of Education, 1998.

Other Sources

'Abdallah, Fatima Barbari. "Lament for Her Dead Daughter." Translated and collected by Jamal Zaki ad-Din al-Hajjaji, Susan Slymovics, and Suzanne Qualls. *Children in the Muslim Middle East,* edited by Elizabeth Fernea. Austin: University of Texas Press, 1995.

Abdel Rahman, Muhammad Abdel Ghany. *Wives of Muhammad: The Prophet and Wisdom of Polygamy.* Beirut: Dar al-Massira, 1991.

Al-Abed, Raed. "Lack of Awareness and Dull Campaign Tactics Behind Women Failure to Reach the Dome." *Star: Jordan's Political, Economic, and Cultural Weekly On-Line* (Nov. 13, 1997): http://star.arabia.com/971113/JO3.html.

Abu Hadid, Muhammad Farid. *Abu'l fawaris 'Antara b. Shadad.* Cairo: Ministry of Education, 1979.

Abu Jaber, Kamel S., Fawzi A. Gharaibeh, and Allen Hill. *The Badia of Jordan: The Process of Change.* Amman: Publications of the Univ. of Jordan, 1987.

Abul'Futuh, Muhammad Sayf al-Nasr. "Al-Ahwal al-ijtima'iyya fi madinat Isna." In *Abhath nadwat tarikh misr al-iqtisadi wal'ijtima'i fil' 'asr al-'uthmani, 1517–1798,* edited by Raouf Abbas and Daniel Crecelius. Vol. 57 of *Majallat Kuliyyat al-Adab.* Cairo: Cairo Univ. Center of Publication, 1992.

Abu Shaqra,'Abdal-Halim. *Tahrir al-mar'a fi 'asr al-risala.* Vol. 3. Kuwait: Dar al-Qalam lil-Nashr wal-Tawzi', 1990.

Al-'Alami, Ahmad. *Waqfiyat al-maghariba.* Amman: Markaz al-Watha'iq wal-Makhtutat, 1981.

Al-'Aqqad,'Abbas Mahmud. *Al-Mar'a fil-Qur'an.* Cairo: Nahdat Misr, 1977.

Arab Women and Education. Beirut: Monographs of the Institute for Women's Studies in the Arab World, Beirut Univ. College, 1980.

Al-'Asqalani, Ahmad b. Hajar. *Fath al-bari bi-sharh sahih al-Bukhari.* Cairo: Dar al-Rayyan lil-Turath, 1987.

Al-'Assali, Kamil Jamil. *Watha'iq maqdissiya tarikhiyya: Muqaddima hawla ba'd al-masadir al-awwaliyya li-tarikh al-Quds.* Vols. 1–2. Amman: Matba'at al-Tawfiq, 1983.

'Atallah, Mahmud 'Ali. *Watha'iq al-tawa'if al-hirafiyya fil-Quds fil-qarn al-sabi' 'ashar al-miladi.* Vol. 1. Nablus: Jami'at al-Najah al-Wataniya, Markaz al-Tawthiq wal-Makhtutat wal-Nashr, 1991.

'Awda, 'Abd al-Qadir. *Al-Tashri' al-gina'i al-islami.* Cairo: Mu'asasat al-Risala, 1992.

Al-'Azm (al-Shaikh), Samih 'Ali Khalid. *Samma: Qariya min biladi.* Amman: Matba'at al-'Azm, 1997.

Berkey, Jonathan. *The Transmission of Knowledge in Medieval Cairo: A Social History of Islamic Education.* Princeton: Princeton Univ. Press, 1992.

Blake, Stephen P. "Contributions to the Urban Landscape: Women Builders in Safavid Isfahan and Mughal Shahjananabad." In *Women in the Medieval Islamic World: Power, Patronage, and Piety,* edited by Gavin G. Hambly. New York: St. Martin's Press, 1998.

Bon, Ottaviano. *The Sultan's Seraglio: An Intimate Portrait of Life at the Ottoman Court.* London: Saqi Books, 1996.

Botiveau, Bernard. *Al-Shari'a al-islamiyya wal-qanun fil-mujtama'at al-'arabiyya.* Translated by Fuad al-Dahhan. Cairo: Sina lil-Nashr, 1997.

Brand, Laurie. "Women and the State in Jordan: Inclusion or Exclusion?" In *Islam, Gender, and Social Change,* edited by Yvonne Haddad and John Esposito. New York: Oxford Univ. Press, 1998.

Butaye, Emile, and Gaston de Leval. *A Digest of the Laws of Belgium and of the French Code Napoléon.* London: Stevens and Sons, 1918.

Cowan, J. M., ed. *Arabic-English Dictionary: The Hans Wehr Dictionary of Modern Written Arabic.* 3d ed. Ithaca: Spoken Language Services, 1976.

Daftary, Farhad. "Sayyida Hurra: The Isma'ili Sulayhid Queen of Yemen." In *Women in the Medieval Islamic World: Power, Patronage, and Piety,* edited by Gavin G. Hambly. New York: St. Martin's Press, 1999.

Al-Dawudi, Ghalib 'Ali. *Sharh qanun al-'amal al-urduni.* Jarash, Jordan: n.p., 1999.

Dror, Ze'evi. *An Ottoman Century: The District of Jerusalem in the 1600s.* Albany: State Univ. of New York Press, 1996.

Fadel, Mohammad. "Two Women, One Man: Knowledge, Power, and Gender in Medieval Sunni Legal Thought." *International Journal of Middle East Studies* 29 (1997): 185–204.

Fay, Mary Ann. "The Ties That Bound: Women and Households in Eighteenth-Century Egypt." In *Women, the Family, and Divorce Laws in Islamic History,* edited by Amira Sonbol. Syracuse: Syracuse Univ. Press, 1996.

Fernea, Elizabeth Warnock. "Childhood in the Muslim Middle East." In *Children in the Muslim Middle East,* edited by Elizabeth Warnock Fernea. Austin: Univ. of Texas Press, 1995.

Flynn, Donna K., and Linda Oldham. "Women's Economic Activities in Jordan: Research Findings on Women's Participation in Microenterprise, Agriculture, and the Formal Sector." Washington, D.C.: WIDTech, 1999.

Grandmoulin, J. *Le Droit penal Egyptien indigène.* Le Caire: Ministère de l'Instruction Publique, Imprimerie National, 1908.

Haeri, Shahla. "The Politics of Dishonor: Rape and Power in Pakistan." In *Faith and Freedom,* edited by Mahnaz Afkhami. Syracuse: Syracuse Univ. Press, 1995.

Hamarneh, Sami Khalaf. *Health Sciences in Early Islam: Collected Papers.* San Antonio: Zahra Publications, 1984.

Hambly, Gavin. "Becoming Visible: Medieval Islamic Women in Historiography and History." In *Women in the Medieval Islamic World: Power, Patronage, and Piety,* edited by Gavin G. Hambly. New York: St. Martin's Press, 1998.

Al-Hilw, Kamal Abdallah, and Said Mumtaz Darwish. *Customary Law in Northern Sinai.* Cairo: Printshop of the American Univ. in Cairo, 1989.

Husseini, Rana. "Former Deputy Faisal Aims to Blaze Trail for Women in 2001 Elections." *Jordan Times.*

Ibn 'Abd Rabbih, Ahmad ibn Muhammad. *Al-'Iqd al-farid.* Beirut: Al-Matba'a al-Kathulikiya, 1961.

Ibn Battuta. *Travels in Asia and Africa, 1325–1354.* Translated by H. A. R. Gibb. Vol. 2 of *The Travels of Ibn Battuta.* N.p.: South Asia Books, 1986.

Al-'Itiqi, Khawla 'Abdal-Latif. *Wazifat al-mar'a al-muslima fi 'alam al-yawm.* Rabat, Morocco: Al-Munazama al-islamiyya lil-Tarbiyya wal-'Ulum wal-Thaqafa, 1991.

Al-Jabri, 'Abd al-Mit'al M. *Al-Mara fi'l-tasawwur al-islami* (Woman in Islamic perception). 6th ed. Cairo: Maktabat Wahba, 1983.

Jackson, Peter. "Sultan Radiyya 'Bint Iltutmish." In *Women in the Medieval Islamic World: Power, Patronage, and Piety,* edited by Gavin G. Hambly. New York: St. Martin's Press, 1999.

Al-Jahiz, Abu 'Uthman. *The Epistle on Singing-Girls of Jahiz.* Translated by A. F. L. Beeston. Warmister, England: Aris and Phillips, 1980.

Jordanian Women's Guide to Participation in Public and Political Life. Amman: Al Kutba Institute for Human Development and the Konrad Adenauer Foundation, 1999.

Khalafallah, Haifaa. "Reclaiming the Islamic Legal Method in the Twentieth Century: Public Leadership." In *A History of Her Own: Muslim Women and the Deconstruction of Patriarchy,* edited by Amira Sonbol. Syracuse: Syracuse Univ. Press, forthcoming.

———. "Rethinking Islamic Law: Genesis and Evolution in the Islamic Legal Method and Structures. The Case of a 20th Century 'Alim's Journey into His Legal Traditions, Muahmmad al-Ghazali (1917–1996)." Ph.D. diss., Georgetown Univ., 1999.

Khouri, Rami. "A Kick in the Pants: Women Call for Democracy." Reprinted from the *Jordan Times:* http://www.geocities.com:0080/Wellesley/3321/.

Al-Libnani, Selim Rustum Baz. *Sharh al-majala.* Beirut: Dar al-Kutub al-'Ilmiyya, 1904.

Lips, Hilary M. "Women, Education, and Economic Participation." Keynote address presented at the Northern Regional Seminar, National Council of Women of New Zealand, on Women and Economic Development, Auckland, Mar. 1999. Reprinted at: http://www.runet.edu/~gstudies/sources/nz/key.

Lutfi, Huda. *A History of Mamlûk Jerusalem Based on the Haram Documents.* Berlin: Klaus Schwarz Verlag, 1985.

Lutfiyya, Abdulla M. *Baytin, a Jordanian Village: A Study of Social Institutions and Social Change in a Folk Community.* London: Mouton, 1966.

Al-Madani, Ziyad 'Abdal-'Aziz. *Madinat al-quds wa-jiwariha: 1800–1830.* Amman: n.p., 1996.

Madi, Ramzi Ahmad. *Qanun al-'uqubat raqam (16) lisanat 1960.* Amman: Maktabat al-Thaqafa wal-Nashr wal-Tawzi', 1998.

Majallat niqabat al-muhamiyyin. Amman: Niqabat al-Muhamiyyin.

Majmu'at al-tashri'at al-'umaliya. Amman: Niqabat al-Muhamiyyin, 1997.

Makiya, Kanan. *Power and Patriarchy in Iraq.* New York: W. W. Norton, 1993.

Malik, Anas b. *Al-Muwatta'.* Beirut: Dar al-Nafa'is, 1977.

Marsot, Afaf Lutfi al-Sayyid. *Women and Men in Late-Eighteenth-Century Egypt.* Austin: Univ. of Texas Press, 1995.

———. "Women and Modernization." In *Women, the Family, and Divorce Laws in Islamic History,* edited by Amira Sonbol. Syracuse: Syracuse Univ. Press, 1996.

Meriwether, Margaret L. *The Kin Who Count: Family and Society in Ottoman Aleppo, 1770–1840.* Austin: Univ. of Texas Press, 1999.

Mernissi, Fatima. *The Forgotten Queens of Islam.* Translated by Mary Jo Lakeland. Minneapolis: Univ. of Minnesota Press, 1993.

———. *The Veil and the Male Elite: A Feminist Interpretation of Women's Rights in Islam.* Translated by Mary Jo Lakeland. Cambridge, Mass.: Perseus Publishing, 1992.

Milhim, Ahmad Salim. *Al-Sharh al-tatbiqi li-qanun al-ahwal al-shakhsiyya al-urduni.* Amman: Maktabat al-Risala al-Haditha, 1998.

Al-Nasser, Lamis, Bashir al-Bilbisi, and Diana 'Atiyyat. *Al-'Unf did al-mar'a fil-mujtama' al-urduni: Al-khasa'is al-dimoghrafiyya lil-dahaya wal-junat.* Amman: Al-Multaqa al-Insni li Huquq al-Mar'a, 1998.

Al-Nawayisah, Nayif. *Al-Tifl fi al-haya al-sha'biyya al-urduniyya.* Amman: Ministry of Culture, 1997.

Peirce, Leslie. *The Imperial Harem: Women and Sovereignty in the Ottoman Empire.* Studies in Middle Eastern History. Princeton: Princeton Univ. Press, 1993.

Al-Qanun al-madani al-urduni. Amman: Niqabat al-Muhamin, 1994.

Al-Qasimi, Zafer. *Al-Hayat al-ijtima'iya 'ind al-'arab.* Beirut: Dar al-Nafa'is, 1981.

Al-Qisi, Marwan Ibrahim. *Al-Mar'a al-muslima bayn ijtihadat al-fuqaha' wa mumarasat al-muslimin.* Rabat, Morocco: Al-Munazama al-islamiyya lil-Tarbiyya wal-'Ulum wal-Thaqafa, 1991.

Radwan, Zaynab. *Al-Mar'a fi al-manzur al-islami: Ba'd al-qadaya.* Cairo: Wizarat al-Shu'un al-Ijtima'iyya, 1999.

Al-Rajbi, Abu Farwa. "Saya'ti." In *Ibda'at qisassiyya: Min ibda'at qasasi nadi usrat al-qalam al-thaqafi, al-Zarqa'.* Amman: Ministry of Culture, 1997.

Richmond, Diana. *'Antar and 'Abla: A Bedouin Romance.* London: Quartet Books, 1978.

Roded, Ruth. *Women in Islamic Biographical Collections: From Ibn Sa'd to Who's Who.* Boulder: Lynne Reinner Publishers, 1994.

Sabbagh, Laila. *Al-Mar'a fi'l-tarikh al-'arabi qabl al-islam.* Damascus: Manshurat Wizarat al-Thaqafa wa'l-Irshad, 1975.

Sahebjam, Freidoune. *The Stoning of Sorya M.* New York: Arcade Publishing, 1990.

Al-Sa'id, Kamil. *Sharh qanun al-'uqubat: Al-jara'im al-waqi'a 'ala al-akhlaq wal-adab al-'ama wal-usra.* Amman: Maktabat Dar al-Thaqafa lil-Nashr wal-Tawzi', 1994.

Salahiyya, Muhammad 'Isa. *Sijil aradi alwiya (Safad, Nablus, Ghaza, and Qada' al-Ramlah): 974H–1556.* Amman: Jami'at Amman al-Ahliya, 1999.

Saleh, Ibrahim. *Qanun al-'uqubat al-mu'adal bil-qanun raqam 97 li-sanat 1992.* Cairo: n.p., 1995.

Al-Sawariyya, Nufan. *'Amman wa-jiwariha: 1864–1921.* Amman: n.p., 1996.

Shams, al-Din Muhammad Mahdi al-Sheikh. *Huquq al-zawjiyya: Haqq al-mar'a fil-'amal.* Beirut: Al-Mu'assasa al-Dawliyya lil-Dirasat wal-Nashr, 1996.

Shanley, Mary Lyndon. *Feminism, Marriage, and the Law in Victorian England.* Princeton: Princeton Univ. Press, 1989.

Al-Sioufi, 'Isam. *Al-Mar'a fi'l-adab al-jahili.* Beirut: Dar al-Fikr al-Libnani, 1991.

Sonbol, Amira. "Adults and Minors in Ottoman Shari'a Courts and Modern Law." In *Women, the Family, and Divorce Law in Islamic History,* edited by Amira Sonbol. Syracuse: Syracuse Univ. Press, 1996.

Spectorsky, Susan A., trans. *Chapters on Marriage and Divorce: Responses of Ibn Hanbal and Ibn Rahwayh.* Austin: Univ. of Texas Press, 1993.

Spellberg, Denise. "History Then, History Now: The Role of Medieval Islamic Religio-Political Sources in Shaping Modern Debate on Gender." In *A History of Her Own: Deconstructing Women in Islamic Societies,* edited by Amira Sonbol. Syracuse: Syracuse Univ. Press, forthcoming.

Stowasser, Barbara Freyer. *Women in the Qur'an, Traditions, and Interpretations.* New York: Oxford Univ. Press, 1996.

Suwayyid, Ahmad. *Nisa' shahirat min tarikhina.* Beirut: Mu'assasat al-Ma'arif, 1990.

Al-Tantawi,'Ali. *Al-Qada' fil-islam.* Jeddah, Saudi Arabia: Dar al-Manara, 1988.

"Turkish First-Grade Text from Jinn Ali Starts School, Cin Ali Publications, Ankara." In *Children in the Muslim Middle East,* edited by Elizabeth Fernea. Austin: Univ. of Texas Press, 1995.

'Umar, Abdel-Fattah 'Ayish. *Al-Qararat al-qada'iyya fi'l-ahwal al-shakhsiyya hata 'am 1990.* Amman: Dar Yamman, 1990.

"Woman Parliamentarian Calls for More Women in Office." *Feminist News* (Nov. 4, 1997) and Associated Press (Nov. 3, 1997): http://www.feminist.org/news/newsbyte/november97/1104.html.

"Women Make Big Strides in Conservative Jordan." *Arabia On-Line* (Mar. 8, 2000).

"Working Women Supported by Strong Political Will—Princess Basma." *Jordan Times* (July 26, 2000).

Al-Ya'qubi, Muhammad Ahmed Seiir. *Nahiyat al-quds al-sharif fil-qarn al-'ashir al-hijri,* Vol. 1. N.p.

Yazbak, Mahmoud. *Haifa in the Late Ottoman Period, 1864–1914.* Leiden: E. J. Brill, 1998.

Yusuf 'Ali,'Abdullah. *The Meaning of the Holy Qur'an.* Brentwood, Md.: Amana, 1993.

Al-Zahir, Ratib. "Lamha tarikhiyya 'an tashkil al-qada' al-shar'i wa tatawuruhu fi al-urdun." Unpublished report.

Al-Zalmi, Mustafa Ibrahim, and 'Ali Ahmad Salih al-Mahdawi. *Usul al-fiqh fi nasijuh al-jadid wa tatbiqatuh fi al-tashri'at al-qanuniyya wa khassa al-qanun al-madani al-urduni raqam 43 li sanat 1976.* Al-Irbid, Jordan: Al-Markaz al-Qawmi lil-Nashr, 1999.

Index